EDUCATIONAL THEORIES AND PRACTICES FROM THE MAJORITY WORLD

EDUCATIONAL THEORIES AND PRACTICES FROM THE MAJORITY WORLD

Edited by
Pierre R. Dasen
Abdeljalil Akkari

$\mathbf{S}$ SAGE Los Angeles • London • New Delhi • Singapore
www.sagepublications.com

First published in 2008 by

 SAGE Publications India Pvt Ltd
B 1/I-1 Mohan Cooperative Industrial Area
Mathura Road, New Delhi 110 044, India
www.sagepub.in

SAGE Publications Inc
2455 Teller Road
Thousand Oaks, California 91320, USA

SAGE Publications Ltd
1 Oliver's Yard, 55 City Road
London EC1Y 1SP, United Kingdom

SAGE Publications Asia-Pacific Pte Ltd
33 Pekin Street
#02-01 Far East Square
Singapore 048763

Published by Vivek Mehra for SAGE Publications India Pvt Ltd, typeset in 10/12pt Century Schoolbook by Star Compugraphics Private Limited, Delhi and printed at Rajkamal Electric Press, New Delhi.

Library of Congress Cataloging-in-Publication Data

Educational theories and practices from the majority world/Edited by Pierre R. Dasen and Abdeljalil Akkari.
     p. cm.
Includes bibliographical references and index.
     1. Educational sociology—Developing countries—Cross-cultural studies. 2. Educational anthropology—Developing countries—-Cross-cultural studies. 3. Indigenous peoples—Education—Cross-cultural studies. 4. Critical pedagogy. 5. Ethnology. I. Dasen, P.R. II. Akkari, Abdeljalil.

LC191.8.D44E385   306.43—dc22   2008   2008037756

ISBN: 978-81-7829-877-1 (HB)

The SAGE Team: Rekha Natarajan, Anupam Choudhury, Mathew P.J., and Trinankur Banerjee

CONTENTS

Section III: Education and Religion

Section IV: Global Political Issues

INTRODUCTION

ETHNOCENTRISM IN EDUCATION AND HOW TO OVERCOME IT

PIERRE R. DASEN AND ABDELJALIL AKKARI

The primary purpose of this book is to draw attention to ethnocentrism in educational research and practice, and to suggest some means to fight it wherever it manifests itself. Ethnocentrism is a universal psychological process: everyone, everywhere, tends to believe that there is only one best way to do things and to view the world—his or her own. This tendency is particularly strong in the social sciences, because they have been developed mainly in a single cultural context, the Western world. Psychology, for example, is very much enculturated in the middle class, industrial societies of North America and Europe (Dasen, 1993), and therefore, strongly reflects their individualist, competitive values. Cross-cultural psychology in its various forms (including cultural psychology and indigenous psychology) represents an attempt to counteract this ethnocentrism (Berry et al., 2002; Segall et al., 1999). Its impact on general or mainstream psychology is, however, minimal.

The field of education is no exception in the prevalence of ethnocentrism. Whether we consider it from the point of view of educational theory and research ('educational sciences', as they are called in some languages, such as, French) or in terms of pedagogy, that is, educational policies and practices, most of the discourse is strongly marked by one single model, Western schooling, or what Serpell and Hatano (1997: 362) have called the 'hegemonic imposition of

Institutionalized Public Basic Schooling (IPBS)'. This model has become so widely accepted throughout the world that it is, in fact, very often no longer seen as Western.

Yet, educational sciences and pedagogy, as part of human and social sciences, have historically been marked by an elitist, inegalitarian perspective on the non-Western world. Scientific knowledge about education is typically seen as Western and, if anything, non-Western contexts are only the objects of study upon which Western paradigms of inquiry are imposed. This intellectual posture is reinforced by the persistent European belief of bearing a civilizing mission, which consists in replacing supposed archaisms by modernity.

In many scholarly fields, this cultural imperialism is usurpatory in two ways. On the one hand, the non-Western cultural heritage is plundered (for example, the knowledge of traditional medicine is used by pharmaceutical multinational companies), and on the other hand, the right to produce scientific knowledge of a universal nature is denied to non-Western people. The French Observatory of Science and Technology (OST, 2002) recently showed that sub-Saharan Africa, which contains 10 per cent of the world's population, produces only 0.4 per cent of the world's research and development. In the same vein, the trend for museums to separate 'primary' art (not to say 'primitive') from 'contemporary' art (exclusively Western!) shows such pernicious reasoning. The objective of this book is to breach this double usurpation.

Contemporary pedagogy and educational sciences have mainly been developed in the industrialized societies of Europe and North America, which has given them a specific cultural character. In this book we will examine the conceptual contribution of formal and informal educational methods of the 'majority world' (to be defined subsequently). These methods existed before the importation of Western educational formats during the colonial period. They continue to provide original solutions to educational problems in many parts of the world. Thus the goal of this book is to carry out a cultural decentration, on the one hand, by exposing the ethnocentrism of educational sciences (Akkari, 2000), and on the other hand, by showing what advantages could be derived from taking into account the contributions of educational methods in other cultural contexts.

In disciplinary terms, the role of the king's fool, pointing out the weaknesses of the dominant paradigms and the attractiveness of alternatives, belongs to anthropology of education insofar as it deals with education as all forms of cultural transmission, including the various social institutions invented in different cultures for this purpose. Comparative education sometimes partakes of this endeavour, as long as it is not confined to government statistics about IPBS systems. Most of the authors in this volume share an interest in anthropology and the comparative method, within a more general multidisciplinary outlook.

WHAT DO WE MEAN BY 'MAJORITY WORLD'?

Kagitçibasi (1996) rightly remarked that rich, industrialized nations, geographically of the West and North, are in fact in the minority when one looks at population; hence the term 'majority world'. Of course, it is in fact practically a synonym of 'non-Western' that we have used so far in this text, but its facetiousness has the advantage of challenging, in itself, Western ethnocentrism. In French, 'North and South' are the current way to demarcate the dichotomy, since it has become politically incorrect to speak of 'the Third World' or of 'developing countries'. Even though the latter are indeed located mainly in the inter-tropical regions, that is, in the 'South' of Europe, the term does not have so much a geographical as a metaphorical meaning; it is in fact an euphemism used to refer to poorer countries (the designation chosen by Herzog, this volume), and is easily applied also to underprivileged segments of the population in rich countries.

There is no easy solution to this conundrum in terminology, each word being likely to be misinterpreted. In fact, we believe that any dichotomy that produces a 'great divide' (Segall et al., 1999: 132) is an oversimplification, and should be avoided. Yet we do need a term to designate our field of interest.

The notion of the 'majority world' in this book dealing with education designates educational ideas, theories, and methods considered to be outside of 'mainstream' formal schooling mentioned above as IPBS. Thus we will discuss informal or traditional education, and also formal institutions of instruction often linked to various religions throughout the world, as well as innovations that attempt to make formal schooling culturally more appropriate. In many countries, be they rich or poor, the term 'majority world' may refer to indigenous populations that have been pushed, through socio-economic and cultural pressure, into becoming minorities (whatever their number), and now have specific educational needs.

Educational methods of the majority world

If we wish to speak of educational methods from the 'majority world', then which educators should we hear from? Who do we have in place of Rousseau, Pestalozzi, Ferrière, Montessori or even Piaget or Vygotsky? In fact, there are not many famous educators from the 'majority world'. Why is this? Is it due to the culture of oral transmission, which does not formalize theory? Or, in cultures with written traditions, is it due to the fact that such educators write in Chinese, Hindi or Arabic and may never have been translated into European languages or whose translations are little known? This might explain things partially. The main explanation, however, certainly comes from elsewhere. Unlike educational ideas from the North, which generally come from theorists who work as individuals, ideas of the 'majority world' are often advocated by a community or by larger social institutions:

> Perhaps the closest one can get to describing unity in Indigenous Knowledge is that knowledge is the expression of the vibrant relationships between the people, their ecosystems, and the other living beings and spirits that share their lands. These multi-layered relationships are the basis for maintaining social, economic and diplomatic relationships—through sharing—with other peoples. (Battiste and Henderson, 2000: 42)

Thus, in informal education, it is the entire community that becomes educator. This undoubtedly corresponds with a collectivistic orientation of the society rather than an individualistic one (Kagitçibasi, 1997), even if this dichotomy is certainly over-interpreted as a cultural explanation (Berry et al., 2002), just like any great divide theory. In the format of traditional religious schools (covered in several chapters of this volume), education is entrusted to specialists, but these specialists do not attempt to create educational theory with the goal of changing the system. Traditional pedagogy of the majority world is more related to socio-cultural reproduction rather than social change.

Certain educational theorists of the 'majority world', Freire (Akkari, this volume) and Boal (Hemma Devries, 2004) in particular, were heavily influenced by theorists of the North (Mesquida, 2004). The same could be said for Mariategui (1970), a Peruvian educational theorist, whose critical orientation came from Marxism. As for Krishnamurti, who wrote several books on education (Krishnamurti, 1966, 1974, 1985), it is through studies in England that he developed his original hybridization between Indian philosophy and social revolutionary criticism. Also, it was to schools in the North that he sent letters and it was mainly these northern schools that applied his ideas. Drawing thus from Indian philosophy, he envisaged a global education that would integrate the cognitive and the spiritual:

> The function of education is to create human beings who are integrated and therefore intelligent. We may take degrees and be mechanically efficient without being intelligent. Intelligence is not mere information; it is not derived from books.... Education should help us to discover lasting values so that we do not merely cling to formulas or repeat slogans. (Krishnamurti, 1966: 14)

But, at the same time, he was against all state institutions and all religious dogma, and this would have been hard to imagine if he had never left his homeland. Here are some excerpts that illustrate this revolutionary position:

> Government control of education is a calamity. There is no hope of peace and order in the world as long as education is the handmaid of the State or of organized religion.... This conditioning of the child's mind to fit a particular ideology, whether political or religious, breeds enmity between man and man (p. 77).... Education throughout the world has failed, it has produced mounting destruction and misery. Governments are training the young to be the efficient soldiers and technicians they need (p. 80).... All sovereign governments must prepare for war, and one's own government is no exception. To make its citizens efficient for war, to prepare them to perform their duties effectively, the government must obviously control and dominate them. They must be educated to act as machines, to be ruthlessly efficient (p. 81).... The sovereign State does not want its citizens to be free, to think for themselves, and it controls them through propaganda, through distorted historical interpretations, and so on. That is why education is becoming more and more a means of teaching *what* to think and not *how* to think.

If we were to think independently of the prevailing political system, we would be dangerous; free institutions might turn out pacifists or people who think contrary to the régime. (Krishnamurti, 1966: 80–81)

This quotation from Krishnamurti could easily have come from the pen of Illich (1972, 1973) or of Freire (1970), even if, overall, his educational philosophy is more spiritual than political. Taking into account the whole student means reflecting on life's fundamental questions and on what unites us as human beings beyond our personal and cultural differences (Ferrer and Allard, 2002).

Other educational theorists of the 'majority world' combine their local traditional knowledge with outside influences connected with development and international cooperation in education. This is an encouraging educational syncretism that assumes that education is neither completely alienating nor completely liberating. The potential effects of education always depend upon its local cultural rootedness.

In northern societies, mass educated for over a century, knowledge acquisition naturally refers to the IPBS model: 'Since the school's mission is to instruct, from the most elementary to the highest level, the definition of what we mean by "knowledge" goes hand in hand with today's universally shared experience of schooling' (Chartier and Jacquet-Francillon, 1998: 6).

If anthropologists have long described the existence of knowledge collectively transmitted from generation to generation in societies without schools or even without a written culture, IPBS has always looked on out-of-school knowledge with great suspicion:

Knowledge derived from traditional practices, transmitted by 'seeing and doing' as well as 'hearing and telling', can only be questionable or condemnable, mixing up indistinguishably rites and myths, beliefs and superstitions, magic formulas and everyday routines. Against this archaic form of knowledge, imposed by an arbitrary, authoritarian tradition, knowledge from the republican school was set up to be the knowledge of liberating modernity: Enlightenment knowledge against obscurantist beliefs, scientific knowledge against empirical practices, secular knowledge versus religious dogma, urban knowledge versus rural folklore, knowledge from reason and progress versus irrational and backward-looking traditions. (Chartier and Jacquet-Francillon, 1998: 6)

Contrary to this Manichean view of knowledge, the synthesis attempted by educational theorists of the 'majority world' aims to weaken the belief that equates knowledge exclusively with schooling. Furthermore, an analysis of educational processes in contexts where the hegemony of the school format is not complete allows one to see that this institution, from its very inception, has had serious problems with cultural differences. By ignoring differences and at the same time practising discrimination, formal schooling has not necessarily carried the ideals of enlightenment.

A CRITIQUE OF SCHOOLING

It is inevitable for us to take a critical position towards the Western school model that was exported during the colonial period, and that became on a planetary scale the hegemonic institution of IPBS. (Serpell and Hatano, 1997). This school has played, and continues to play, a very ambiguous role, and for this reason can be presented either as a panacea that will bring development and peace throughout the world or as an unprecedented catastrophe. Long considered the ideal solution for the integration of cultural minorities, for social mobility, and for development, the IPBS format can no longer refuse to critically examine itself and to dissect its own ethnocentrism.

Perhaps the first person to have voiced a critical analysis was Nyerere (1967), president of Tanzania and himself a teacher. Nyerere realized that in his newly independent country, a school system keeping the colonial model, established to provide mainly local administrative personnel, continued to create a privileged 'elite' for the 'modern' sector, to the exclusion of the majority of the rural population. Most students would quit school with a feeling of failure, as the system was entirely oriented towards higher-level studies, being highly selective at the same time. The students, after only two or three years of primary school, felt themselves superior to their non-educated peers, and would refuse agricultural work, preferring to wait for an illusory job in the city. Thus the school system was the primary cause of rural exodus and widening generation gap.

Throughout the last decades of the 20th century, these criticisms were restated and elaborated by different theorists (Carnoy, 1974; Carnoy and Samoff, 1990; Erny, 1977; Hallak, 1974; Malassis, 1975; Mukene, 1988), who raised the suspicion that school education does not automatically bring about economic development, contrary to what was predicted by human capital theory. On the other hand, historically, it was this colonial school that allowed the emergence of an organized opposition to colonial control. This would eventually lead to independence under the direction of Western educated leaders such as Habib Bourguiba in Tunisia or Jomo Kenyatta in Kenya.

On the positive side, it is often mentioned—and this is certainly the majority view defended by organizations such as United Nations Children's Fund (UNICEF) and United Nations Educational Scientific and Cultural Organization (UNESCO)—that schooling allows for the promotion of hygiene and public health, lowering of birth rate (Cochrane, 1979), improvement of the status of women (Kagitçibasi, 1996, 1998), and respect for democracy and human rights.

Further, as Dasen (this volume) shows in his chapter, research in cross-cultural psychology has found that schooling, more than literacy itself, has an effect on cognitive functioning. This comes about not through the production of new cognitive processes, but through the emphasis on a 'theoretic' cognitive style: schooling trains students to accept working on content that is distanced from everyday life. However, there are different types of schools: Mishra and Dasen (2004), reviewing research on the cognitive effects of schooling in India, mention the importance of considering factors such as school quality.

This raises the question of the cultural appropriateness of schools as they currently exist throughout the world. The detour through studying differences in educational practices should allow us, wherever we are, to look closely at our own educational institutions and their degree of sensitivity to the cultural diversity of their students. Innovations in devising culturally appropriate education for indigenous populations, such as reported by Gasché (1998, 2004) and in some chapters of this volume (Battiste, Gajardo et al., Mishra, Teasdale), may exist at the heart of pedagogical alternatives in the face of the world education crisis.

Nevertheless, this book intends to go beyond a simple criticism of school. There is only Herzog (this volume) to suggest that we would be better off, at least for certain adolescents in certain contexts, by completely getting rid of this institution. Most of the proposed approaches consist in adapting and transforming schools so that they better respond to the needs and aspirations of local populations.

A FEW INNOVATIVE CONCEPTS

In recent reflections on the cultural adaptation of schooling, new concepts have emerged such as 'appropriation', 'empowerment', 'community of practice' 'ethnotheories', and 'conscientization', all of which may contribute to a pedagogical alternative to the hegemony of IPBS. Concepts of 'ownership' and 'appropriation' are used by Teasdale (this volume) in a way that goes beyond simple material possession: educational actions need to be conceived in a way that the people concerned can appropriate and use them actively. These concepts then are strongly linked to those of participation and identification, that can be illustrated by Teasdale's injunction to give control over the curriculum to the local community, or what Serpell (1993) referred to as 'local accountability', the fact that the school needs to be accountable to the local population rather than to central institutions like ministries of education.

An important concept in anthropology of education is the 'hidden curriculum', alongside the formal curriculum (content, teaching methods and goals, measures for initial and continuing teacher training); schools transmit unwillingly and unconsciously a series of attitudes and values. Students learn, for example, which questions are legitimate and which are not. This hidden curriculum includes implicit rules of educational communication and school life, which are imposed by dominant social groups (Apple, 1990). The school conveys implicit values through the selection of subject matters and the organization of streaming, teacher recruitment and training policies, and the conceptualization of learning. The hidden curriculum represents what is actually being done, rather than what is stated in policy documents (Gatto, 1991; Roegiers, 1997).

The concept of a 'community of practice' refers to the process of social learning that occurs when people who have a common interest collaborate over an extended period to share ideas, find solutions, and build up knowledge. In Lave and Wenger's work (1990), the learner's position within a social setting is conceptualized as a movement from 'peripheral participation' to the 'centre' of a community of shared meanings. Also, the development of the concept of 'situated learning' has led to a new look at informal learning and traditional knowledge, in the 'majority world' (Akkari, this volume) as well as in the North (Herzog, this volume). Effective learning processes are not unique to schools, but can also take place in real-life contexts, through social interaction and collaboration (Lave and Wenger, 1991; Segall et al., 1999).

The concept of 'ethnotheory' comes from anthropology and refers to what the members of a community, in particular parents and teachers, feel, think, and know about educational processes (Akkari, 2000; Dasen, this volume). It may represent an alternative to Eurocentric objectivism, which is based on logic and rationalism and reflects how a minority of the world's population perceives the world and gives it a partial and biased view (Battiste and Henderson, 2000).

The Brazilian educational theorist Paulo Freire widely disseminated the concept of 'conscientization' in the fields of education and training (Akkari, this volume). To explain his educational theory, Freire (1970) presented the pedagogy of the oppressors as a 'banking' conception, where the teacher controls knowledge and the truth and the student is a simple recipient. This common conception, overwhelmingly shared by IPBS, is oppressive in the sense that students are considered to be empty vessels that need to be filled, without ever being given the tools necessary for a critical understanding of the world. Freire's alternative model is based on a real exchange between students and teachers, to the point where these roles become interchangeable. The students are considered to be individuals endowed with a conscience, and the task of education is to give them the means to appropriate knowledge. Freire's pedagogy of conscientization does not take place in a vacuum, but occurs through action, aimed at developing the students' ability to raise issues related to their surroundings and to the oppression under which they suffer. The trend of critical pedagogy, inspired by the writings of Freire, is currently at the centre of educational debates in North America, especially about multicultural education (Akkari, 2001; Freire, 1997).

Freire's conscientization comes close to the concept of 'empowerment' (Akkari and Perez, 2000). In the framework of an educational project, empowerment consists of increasing the capabilities and the means of underprivileged persons to act upon the context in which they are living. The development of empowerment in such a project requires that the people involved understand the context of their life and the disparities to which they are subjected, in terms of the distribution of knowledge, power, and resources.

Conscientization and empowerment necessarily lead to control by local communities of the educational institutions that serve them.

But the task is not an easy one because of the social evolutionary conceptions that have long prevailed concerning the development of countries in the 'majority world'. Today it is the concept of 'globalization', the present version of so-called modernization, which ensures the economic and cultural domination of one part of the world over another (Marín, this volume), and scholars from both the North and the 'majority world' must work together to decide on new educational objectives as alternatives to neo-liberal globalization (Hickling-Hudson, 2006; Marín and Dasen, 2007).

The military, political, and economic domination of the nations and people of the 'majority world' has been widely exposed in the social science literature. No force has possibly been as efficient as IPBS in the oppression of the 'majority world' and in the marginalization of local educational knowledge. Through its subtle influence, this cognitive imperialism has effectively destroyed and deformed non-Western educational methods. This book is also an attempt to approach the essence of the complex educational knowledge of the people of the 'majority world'.

Indigenous ways of knowing share the following structure: (a) knowledge of and belief in unseen powers in the ecosystem, (b) knowledge that all things in the ecosystem are dependent on each other, (c) knowledge that reality is structured according to most of the linguistic concepts by which indigenous people describe it, (d) knowledge that personal relationships reinforce the bond between persons, communities and ecosystems, (e) knowledge that sacred traditions and persons who know these traditions are responsible for teaching 'morals' and 'ethics' to practitioners who are then given responsibility for this specialized knowledge and its dissemination, and (f) knowledge that an extended kinship passes on teachings and social practices from generation to generation (Battiste and Henderson, 2000: 42).

PRESENTATION OF THE BOOK

The volume is structured into four sections. The first section, informal and indigenous education, starts with a chapter by Dasen on informal education and learning processes, in which the author presents an integrated theoretical framework for the cross-cultural study of human development and education defined as cultural transmission. This is followed by a critique of Western ethnocentrism in developmental psychology and educational sciences by one of the leading African advocates of an 'indigenous' perspective, Nsamenang, who illustrates the teachings of an 'Afrocentric' perspective on the example of current research in Cameroon. A similar African voice comes from Zambia, with Serpell's concept of 'participatory appropriation'. He shows how an African approach to education for social responsibility has taken shape within the context of public primary and secondary schools in Zambia. We leave the African continent for France with the chapter by Herzog, an American anthropologist who studies a particularly successful system of apprenticeship called 'compagnonnage'.

The second section of the book deals with the search for a culturally appropriate schooling for aboriginal people in various parts of the world. While Teasdale reports several innovative examples from Australia and the Pacific, Mishra deals with tribal education in India, and Battiste with what she calls 'decolonizing' aboriginal education in Canada. Gajardo, Carrarini, Marín, and Dasen provide an overview of so-called intercultural and bilingual education programmes in Latin America. What all of these chapters have in common is a search for culturally appropriate forms of schooling for local, indigenous populations. Whether these are demographically a minority or not, they have been culturally and socio-economically dispossessed over a long period of time, and are now trying to regain their autonomy and cultural identity. Gaining control over the education system is an important part of this process.

The third section presents several examples of formal educational institutions that are not based on the Western model, but are linked to various religions. Akkari deals with Islamic or Quranic schooling, Mishra and Vajpayee as well as Broyon with Sanskrit schooling in India, and Changkakoti and Broyon, also mainly in the Indian subcontinent, with Buddhist schooling. While all of these examples are linked to the so-called major religions, those based on written scriptures, Hounkpe reveals the little known existence of boarding schools linked to the animistic voodoo religion in Benin. The purpose of studying these various forms of schooling is obviously not to suggest that these could be exported beyond their respective sphere of influence, but to show that in various parts of the world, there have been and still are very influential formal systems of education, beyond IPBS, that have the advantage of being locally rooted and hence culturally more appropriate, and which use interesting pedagogical methods.

The fourth and last section of the book raises some global political issues, such as the educational crisis produced by globalization. Akkari shows how one of the foremost pedagogical theorists, Paolo Freire, is still very influential in suggesting innovative educational alternatives from and for the majority world. Marín deals with the historical roots of Western cultural domination through schooling, and the current problems created by the unchecked expansion of economic capitalism. In the concluding chapter of the volume, Akkari and Dasen follow up by examining some of the current challenges facing schooling in a global perspective.

Some of the chapters in this book were prepared for a post-graduate course organized by the co-editors in 2002 under the auspices of the Conférence Universitaire de Suisse Occidentale (CUSO), a granting commission of the francophone universities in Switzerland, and were initially published in French (Akkari and Dasen, 2004). Others have been solicited specifically for this book.

The goal of this book is to start a new debate on a long-term educational construction: to build schools that are open to all and which hold the values and worldviews of the majority world. This is a salutary undertaking to reconstruct the schools of tomorrow, which questions the very foundations of the IPBS format. With its mass attendance, the current school model is becoming less and less adequate in terms of the needs of an ever-changing world. It produces more and more students who are maladjusted, and disgusted for life with learning. At the same time, an active and cooperative continuing education system is more and more a necessity. Far from being backward-looking, educational methods from the 'majority world' respect the needs and rhythms of learners, and allow them to establish an active relationship with knowledge. By contributing to build a new educational project, this volume hopes to represent an alternative to Western educational 'modernity' in fostering an inclusive pedagogy.

REFERENCES

Akkari, A. 2000. 'Au-delà de l'ethnocentrisme en sciences de l'éducation', in P.R. Dasen and C. Perregaux (eds), *Pourquoi des approches interculturelles en sciences de l'éducation?* (pp. 31–48). Bruxelles: DeBoeck Université (Collection«Raisons éducatives»vol. 3).

Akkari, A. 2001. 'Pedagogy of the Oppressed and the Challenge of Multicultural Education', *Interchange*, 32(3): 271–93.

Akkari, A. and P. R. Dasen (eds). 2004. *Pédagogies et pédagogues du Sud.* Paris: L'Harmattan.

Akkari, A. and S. Perez. 2000. 'Education and Empowerment', in D. Matheson (ed.), *Educational Issues in the Learning Age*, pp. 144–56. London: Cassell Professional Publishing.

Apple, M. W. 1990. *Ideology and Curriculum.* New York: Routledge, Chapman and Hall.

Battiste, M. and J. Henderson. 2000. *Protecting Indigenous Knowledge and Heritage: A Global Challenge.* Saskatoon (Canada): Purich Publishing.

Berry, J. W., Y. H. Poortinga, M. H. Segall, and P. R. Dasen. 2002. *Cross-Cultural Psychology. Research and Applications* (Second, Revised Edition). Cambridge: Cambridge University Press.

Carnoy, M. 1974. *Education as Cultural Imperialism.* New York: David McKay.

Carnoy, M. and J. Samoff. 1990. *Education and Social Transition in the Third World.* Princeton, NJ: Princeton University Press.

Chartier, A.M. and F. Jacquet-Francillon. 1998. 'Éditorial, Les savoirs de la pratique. Un enjeu pour la recherche et pour la formation', *Recherche et Formation*, 27: 5–14.

Cochrane, S. 1979. *Fertility and Education: What Do We Really Know?* Baltimore, MD: Johns Hopkins University Press.

Dasen, P. R. 1993. 'L'ethnocentrisme de la psychologie', in M. Rey (ed.), *Psychologie clinique et interrogations culturelles*, pp. 155–74. Paris: L'Harmattan.

Erny, P. 1977. *L'enseignement dans les pays pauvres: modèles et propositions.* Paris: L'Harmattan.

Ferrer, C. and R. Allard. 2002. La pédagogie de la conscientisation et de l'engagement: pour une éducation à la citoyenneté démocratique dans une perspective planétaire. *Éducation et francophonie*, XXX (2), Available at http://www.acelf.ca/revue/30-2/articles/04-ferrer-2.html.

Freire, P. 1970. *Pedagogy of the Oppressed.* New York: Herder and Herder.

———. 1997. 'A Response', in P. Freire, J. W. Fraser, D. Macedo, T. McKinnon, and W. T. Stokes (eds), *Mentoring the Mentor: a Critical Dialogue with Paulo Freire*, pp. 175–99. New York: Peter Lang.

Gasché, J. 1998. 'Revalorization culturelle et structure du Programme de formation d'instituteurs interculturels et bilingues de la confédération indienne amazonienne AIDESEP et de l'Institut supérieur pédagogique 'LORETO' au Pérou', in *DiversCité Langues : En ligne*, Volume III, Available at http://www.uquebec.ca/diverscite.

———. 2004. 'La motivation politique de l'éducation interculturelle indigène et ses exigences pédagogiques. Jusqu'où va l'interculturalité?', in A. Akkari and P. R. Dasen (eds), *Pédagogies et pédagogues du Sud*, pp. 107–38. Paris: L'Harmattan.

Gatto, J. T. 1991. *Dumbing Us Down: The Hidden Curriculum of Compulsory Schooling*. New York: New Society Publishers.

Hallak, J. 1974. *A qui profite l'école?* Paris: PUF.

Hemma Devries, A. 2004. 'Augusto Boal et le théâtre de l'opprimé: vers une éducation sans frontière nord-sud', in A. Akkari and P. R. Dasen (eds), *Pédagogies et pédagogues du Sud*, pp. 295–308. Paris: L'Harmattan.

Hickling-Hudson, A. 2006. 'Cultural Complexity, Post-Colonialism and Education Change: Challenges for Comparative Educators', *International Review of Education*, 52: 201–18.

Illich, I. 1972. *Deschooling Society*. New York: Harper & Row.

———. 1973. *Celebration of Awareness: Call for Institutional Revolution*. Harmondsworth: Penguin Books.

Kagitçibasi, C. 1996. *Family and Human Development Across Countries: A View from the Other Side*. Hillsdale, NJ: Erlbaum.

———. 1997. 'Individualism and Collectivism', in J. W. Berry, M. H. Segall and C. Kagitçibasi (eds), *Handbook of Cross-Cultural Psychology, Social Psychology*, Second Edition. Vol. 3, pp. 1–50. Boston: Allyn & Bacon.

———. 1998. 'Human Development: Cross-Cultural Perspectives', in J. Adair, D. Bélanger and K. L. Dion (eds), *Advances in Psychological Science: Vol. 2. Developmental, Personal, and Social Aspects*, pp. 475–94. London: Psychology Press.

Krishnamurti, J. 1966. *Education and the Significance of Life*. London: V. Gollancz.

———. 1974. *Krishnamurti on Education*. New Delhi: Orient Longman.

———. 1985. *Letters to Schools*, Vols I and II. Ojai, CA: Mirananda.

Lave, J. and E. Wenger. 1991. *Situated Learning: Legitimate Peripheral Participation*. Cambridge, UK: Cambridge University Press.

Malassis, L. 1975. *Ruralité, éducation et développement*. Paris: Masson.

Mariategui, J. C. 1970. *Temas de educacion*. Lima: Ed. Amauto.

Marín, J. and P. R. Dasen. 2007. 'L'éducation face à la mondialisation, aux migrations et aux droits de l'homme', in M. C. Caloz-Tschopp, V. Chétail, and P. R. Dasen (eds), *Mondialisation, migrations et droits de l'homme: Un nouveau paradigme pour la recherche et la citoyenneté* (Vol. 1), pp. 285–320. Bruxelles: Bruylant.

Mesquida, P. 2004. 'Philosophie et éducation: les influences européennes sur la pensée de Paulo Freire', in A. Akkari and P. R. Dasen (eds), *Pédagogies et pédagogues du Sud*, pp. 275–94. Paris: L'Harmattan.

Mishra, R. C. and P. R. Dasen. 2004. 'The Influence of Schooling on Cognitive Development: A Review of Research in India', in B. N. Setiadi, A. Supratiknya, W. J. Lonner, and Y. H. Poortinga (eds), *Ongoing Themes in Psychology and Culture. Selected Papers from the Sixteenth International Congress of the International Association for Cross-Cultural Psychology*, pp. 207–22. Yogyakarta: Kanisius.

Mukene, P. 1988. *L'ouverture entre l'école et le milieu en Afrique noire.* Fribourg: Editions Universitaires.

Nyerere, J. M. 1967. *Education for Self-Reliance.* Dar es Salaam: Government Printer.

Observatoire des Sciences et des Techniques. 2002. *Science et technologie. Indicateurs 2002.* Paris: Economica.

Roegiers, X. 1997. *Analyser une action d'éducation ou de formation.* Bruxelles: De Boeck Université.

Segall, M. H., P. R. Dasen, J. W. Berry, and Y. H. Poortinga. 1999. *Human Behavior in Global Perspective: An Introduction to Cross-Cultural Psychology* (Second, revised edition). Boston: Allyn & Bacon.

Serpell, R. 1993. *The Significance of Schooling. Life-Journeys in an African Society.* Cambridge: Cambridge University Press.

Serpell, R. and G. Hatano. 1997. 'Education, Schooling, and Literacy', in J. W. Berry, P. R. Dasen, and T. S. Saraswathi (eds), *Handbook of Cross-Cultural Psychology, Basic Processes and Human Development,* Second Edition. Vol. 2, pp. 339–76. Boston: Allyn & Bacon.

Section I   Informal and 'Indigenous'
Education

1

INFORMAL EDUCATION AND LEARNING PROCESSES[1]

PIERRE R. DASEN

The term 'education' often refers only to schooling, both in common parlance and in the documents of international organizations and NGOs, as well as in the academic world of educational sciences. In this chapter, however, we will deal with education in a much wider acceptation, namely all aspects of cultural transmission. Schooling is of course part of that, but education also includes informal learning, resulting from enculturation and socialization, that is, it proceeds informally in everyday situations, either through observation and imitation or active inculcation. As Bruner (1996: ix) remarks: '... schooling is only one small part of how a culture inducts the young into its canonical ways. Indeed, schooling may even be at odds with a culture's other ways of inducting the young into the requirements of communal living'.

On the dimension of formal to informal, Ahmed (1983) distinguished the following categories of education:

1. Formal education or schooling.
2. Non-formal, or out-of-school education, which includes all educational programmes aimed at those left out of formal education (very young children, the discards of the school system, young people in post-primary education, non-literates, and so on).
3. Informal education, which may also be called 'traditional' education. In contrast with the first two, it is neither provided nor directed by governmental or non-governmental institutions.

This chapter deals with the third category, referring to the other two only as a contrast. Note that we first have to dispose of a problem of vocabulary: 'traditional' education may wrongly suggest that this type of education is linked to the past, that it is no longer being practiced, or then only in traditional, for example, rural, sectors of society. This is not at all what is intended, and hence I prefer to speak of 'informal' education. But that label may also be misunderstood: it may wrongly suggest that this education does not have any form, that it is unstructured and haphazard. As we will shortly see, that is not at all the case: there is distinctly an informal pedagogy, although it often remains implicit and even those who practice it are not conscious of it. To describe this informal pedagogy, detailed ethnographic (observational) research is needed.

These problems of definitions have led Montandon (2005) to suggest that the distinction formal/non-formal/informal should be abandoned, if only because it implies that schooling is the norm with which the other forms are compared. She proposes much more complex theoretical schemes, such as a profile of each type of education on a list of 28 variables, which is not all that different from the schemes of Désalmand (1983) or Greenfield and Lave (1982) presented later, or a typology derived from the cross-table of contexts and contents. While acknowledging the complexity of the issue, I will nevertheless continue to use the term 'informal' for the remainder of this chapter.

There is an abundant literature on traditional education in numerous societies, often dating back to the middle of the 20th century, as part of ethnographic monographs, and in particular in the 'culture and personality' school of American cultural anthropology. It would be beyond the reach of this chapter to review this extensive literature. As good examples, I think of Jomo Kenyatta (1965) who studied anthropology with Malinowski long before becoming the first president of Kenya, or Myer Fortes (1938) in Nigeria, and, among more recent publications, Lancy (1996) about the Kpelle of Liberia, Chamoux (1981, 1986) among the Nahua of Mexico, or Delbos and Jorion (1984) in France[2]. Traditional education also includes institutions that are quite formalized, such as initiation ceremonies, and instruction provided in age-grade societies and secret societies. Erny (1981) has provided an excellent overview of the various strands of ethnography dealing with traditional education. One way to summarize this material might be to conclude that traditional education, in contrast to schooling, is in essence adapted to the local cultural system, which it tends to perpetuate.

Désalmand (1983) pointed out the major characteristics of traditional African education as compared to schooling. Traditional education is provided everywhere, all the time, and by everyone (in contrast to occurring in a specialized place, at a specific time, with specialized personnel), it is closely tied to the environment, integrated with productive work, and addresses the needs of the society. It emphasizes cooperation rather than individual competition, and everyone is allowed to be successful at it (as opposed to the elitism of schools, with their selection and streaming roles). In traditional education, parents and elders play an important role; relations among participants are personalized and occur in the local language. Traditional education has a broad character, and includes moral and spiritual aspects as well as physical education and manual labour.

A similar typology was elaborated by Greenfield and Lave (1982): Informal education is embedded in daily life, with teachers being relatives, but the responsibility for learning lies with the learners, their motivation stemming from the social contribution they are able to make and their participation in the adult community of practice. Observation and imitation are the main learning processes, and demonstration (without verbal exchange or questioning) the predominant teaching procedure. The maintenance of continuity and traditions is the primary goal of informal education.

Greenfield and Lave point out that in instances where informal education transmits specific, economically-useful knowledge, particularly knowledge tied to crafts and occupations, it can include a very structured, albeit implicit, pedagogy. This was demonstrated in a study of weaving apprenticeship among Zinacanteco girls in Mexico (Greenfield and Childs, 1977; Childs and Greenfield, 1980). The mothers, although claiming in interviews that they did not do anything to teach their daughters, employed mainly scaffolding, which implies quite a sophisticated even if unconscious pedagogy: the mother has to constantly assess the learner's level of skills, so as to adapt her intervention.

Greenfield and Lave (1982) distinguish three types of processes: (*a*) trial and error, (*b*) shaping, and (*c*) scaffolding. In the trial and error process, learners are confronted by a new situation constituting a conflict with what they already know. They have to try different approaches, and usually succeed only after making successive adjustments.

According to Piaget, this process should lead to conceptual knowledge. In this type of learning, motivation is seen as internal to the learner. Conflict and making errors are seen as positive features, leading to progress.

Shaping is a process where the learner's responses are controlled by a teacher, who organizes problems according to a sequence of small steps designed, as much as possible, to avoid errors. Correct responses are reinforced by external rewards. Much of schooling, and particularly programmed learning is of this type.

Learning by scaffolding also involves an adult, and also tries to avoid errors, but the whole task (too difficult to be managed by the novice alone) is presented immediately in its entirety. The expert provides support to the novice, intervening, even taking the apprentice's place, when some step appears to be too difficult. Scaffolding therefore involves continuously assessing the ability level of the learner. The expert's intervention diminishes in the course of the apprenticeship until it is no longer needed. Scaffolding allows the novice eventually to do alone what at the beginning could be done only with help from the expert. Thus, scaffolding is an instructional process which always involves social interaction. It illustrates Vygotsky's concept of a 'zone of proximal development'.

Greenfield (1984) proposed that the concept of learning by scaffolding characterizes especially those situations where the economic stakes are high. By contrast, where cost doesn't matter, as in many school-based situations, trial-and-error learning is more common. Shaping can be combined with either of the other learning processes. Learning by observation and imitation, and especially through scaffolding is congruent with a value system oriented towards the maintenance of traditional ways. In contrast, trial-and-error learning is found where innovation is valued more.

These predictions were confirmed in a long-term longitudinal study when Greenfield (2004) returned to the same Zinacantec Maya community in Mexico twenty-one years after her initial study of weaving apprenticeship. The girls had become mothers, who in turn had daughters who were learning to weave. But the learning processes, Greenfield found, had changed substantially in many families: girls were often learning much more by themselves, by trial and error, only calling for help when they deemed it necessary. Mothers were often busy with their own work, and were not providing any direct scaffolding. In other words, the Zinacantec teaching/learning style has changed from Vygotskian to Piagetian!

This change in learning processes went along with extensive social change. In the intervening years, the community had started transport companies and developed much more frequent contacts with the town of San Cristobal, and even contacts with Mexico City. Woven artefacts produced in the village were being sold there, both to foreign and Mexican tourists. Although still based on the traditional patterns, they were now made of commercially produced thread of many different colours, and the women were competing in inventing new styles of decorations, or copying them from books. Errorless learning had become less essential, since thread had become cheaper. The changes in weaving apprenticeship from more scaffolded to more independent trial-and-error learning was concentrated in families where mothers and daughters were more involved in textile-related commerce (Greenfield et al., 2003).

Would this change in the learning styles also produce changes in cognitive processes? Greenfield's longitudinal study also dealt with this question.

COGNITIVE EFFECTS OF INFORMAL EDUCATION: THE PROBLEM OF TRANSFER

As a cross-cultural psychologist, specializing in cognitive development, I have been concerned with the topic of 'culture and cognition' (Dasen, 1993; Mishra, 1997; Segall et al., 1999). Within that vast topic, the question of cognitive variations produced by literacy and schooling, as opposed to informal education, has been a main concern (Mishra and Dasen, 2004). Summarized in a nutshell, the conclusions of empirical cross-cultural research are that literacy *per se* has only a limited impact (Berry and Bennett, 1992; Scribner and Cole, 1981), while Western type schooling produces a 'theoretic' cognitive style, by which schooled individuals are willing to reason on purely hypothetical contents, as opposed to the 'empirical' style, where the premises have to correspond to social reality (Scribner, 1979; Tapé, 1994). In other words, schooling does not produce new or different cognitive processes, but allows their application to a wider range of contexts.

The theoretic cognitive style comes close to what psychologists call 'transfer', namely the ease with which a skill learned in one context can be generalized, that is, used in other, novel situations. There has been much controversy about 'transfer', the general conclusion being that informal education tends to produce contextualized knowledge, or in Hatano's (1982) terminology, procedural rather than conceptual knowledge.

In their first study of learning to weave among Zinacanteco girls, Greenfield and Childs (1977) explored the cognitive effects of weaving on the representation of patterns. The lack of generalization from weaving to these test situations demonstrated the specificity of this kind of know-how, at least in cultural contexts in which innovation is not valued. In the follow-up study, Greenfield (2004) repeated the experiment in which weavers and non-weavers were asked to represent designs with sticks, both copying existing traditional patterns and expanding novel designs. The results showed that the stages of cognitive development had remained the same over the generations, but that girls now tended to use more abstract representations. This could have been due to the change in teaching/learning processes from scaffolding to trial and error, and/or to the effects of schooling.

Among many other studies of weaving in traditional settings (for example, Chamoux, 1981; Rogoff, 1990), Rogoff and Gauvin (1984) examined the transfer of this skill among adult Navajo women. Weaving skill was the best predictor of performance on a task resembling weaving (continuing a woven pattern) but not for other tasks (continuing a pattern with pipe cleaners, or in a multiple choice format). Schooling contributed little. The overall conclusion was that transfer was rather limited both for everyday skills and for schooling.

Different conclusions come from a study of the generalization of schooling and weaving skills among Dioula young men in Côte d'Ivoire (Tanon, 1994). The study included weavers and non-weavers, both schooled and unschooled. The training of young boys as weavers starts at ten to twelve years. Scaffolding is used for the beginning of the practice, the setup of the warp, and the production of the first large cloths, where mistakes would be difficult to correct and hence have financial consequences. Trial and error is used in the weaving of more complex patterns or innovative designs that can be easily corrected if noticed immediately. At the beginning, boys slide into the father's loom during his absence, and try to weave. When the father returns and notices it, he asks around 'Who sat to weave on my loom?', and he corrects the mistakes. This little game goes on until the father no longer notices any difference in the weaving. At that time, the boy receives his own loom, and the apprenticeship continues. Among the Dioula, the invention of new patterns is highly valued, the weavers are organized in a cooperative, and are active in selling their products, especially to tourists.

Tanon devised two tasks of planning skills, one involving pattern matching based on either traditional or commercial cloths, and one involving the loading and unloading of passengers and luggage in a small bus (taxi van). Loading had to be done taking into consideration the order in which the passengers would disembark at various stops. Both weaving and schooling had significant effects on planning skills in both tasks and the schooled weavers had the best performance overall. On the taxi van task, the weavers did better than the non-weavers, in particular in carrying the planning task to the end. In this case, the control procedures that allow planning, stressed in strip weaving, transferred to a new task, unrelated to weaving.

A series of studies carried out in Recife, Brazil (Nunes et al., 1993) demonstrated transfer in proportional reasoning among minimally-schooled adults, who use it in the practice of their craft. For example, Brazilian foremen with little or no schooling, observed on building sites, are capable of calculating proportions by using unfamiliar scales (for example, 1/40 while they normally use 1/100). A similar result was found with fishermen, who were accustomed to using proportional reasoning for price calculation and for estimating the proportions of processed to unprocessed fish and shellfish. The problems given to them required that they invert the normal procedures: they had to calculate the unit price from the price of a large amount or calculate the amount of fish that had to be caught in order to obtain a given weight of filets. Again, performance was not correlated with amount of prior schooling (which varied from one to nine years). Nunes, Schliemann, and Carraher (1993) concluded from this whole set of studies that everyday activities foster the development of transferable, flexible knowledge, which is conceptual and not merely procedural.

On the other hand, Schliemann and Acioly (1989) found that illiterate lottery bookies could not transfer their experience of permutations to other structurally similar problems, such as working out the permutations of colours or of letters, while those who had nine or more years of schooling could do so. The illiterate ones justified their refusal in ways very similar to the unschooled Vai in Scribner's (1979) study of syllogistic reasoning, namely that they could not deal with letters because they had not learned to read. This 'empiric' cognitive style hence is a serious limitation to the transfer of existing cognitive processes to new situations.

What may we conclude from the various studies of transfer in informal education? We seem to have a contradiction between a series of studies showing that everyday cognitions are most often tied to the context in which they are usually applied, and other research that show evidence of transfer. Schliemann, Carraher, and Ceci (1997: 202) conclude that:

> [E]veryday activities do promote the development of conceptual knowledge rather than only procedural knowledge for specific problems. As such, knowledge acquired in specific everyday activities does transfer to other activities, but this is more likely to occur for those subjects who also benefited from school instruction.

For those studies that did not find transfer, the test situations were often artificial (for example, 'weaving' with wood sticks or pipe cleaners, choosing designs in a multiple-choice format) and were therefore inherently strange. Might not transfer be more easily demonstrated in situations that are new, but, at the same time, not so foreign, such as those used in some of the Recife studies? As regards knowledge acquired in formal schooling, even if it is more open to generalization than everyday cognition, it, too, has limits and is, in a certain sense, contextualized. Increasingly, school (and the laboratory) is seen as simply another context for learning, with its own specific cognitive outcomes. School knowledge can also be more procedural than conceptual, that is, it is closely linked to the conditions in which it was acquired (Delbos and Jorion, 1984).

GUIDED PARTICIPATION IN CULTURAL ACTIVITY

Rogoff, Mistry, Göncü, and Mosier (1993) observed caregivers, usually mothers, and their toddlers in four different settings: Mayan Indians in a small town in Guatemala, a tribal village in India, and two middle class urban neighbourhoods in Turkey and United States. They found both similarities across communities in the process of guided participation, the way caretakers structure children's participation in activities, and differences in how this occurs. In the first two communities, children were non-verbally encouraged to observe ongoing adult activities, but they were basically responsible for their own learning. In the two middle class settings, mothers tended to structure explicitly their children's learning, used verbal interactions and provided 'lessons' removed from the context of ongoing activities. These mothers also tended to organize their schedule so as to separate adult activities from time devoted to interacting with children. In the other two communities, adults shared their attention among a variety of activities, managing several tasks at the same time, including socializing with other adults and facilitating the children's involvement and learning.

The learning style of the middle class mothers can be seen as a preparation for schooling. Rogoff et al. (1993) however suggest that many school reforms move in the direction of group work in which the children become more responsible for their own learning. The teacher's role changes 'from the inculcation of skills out of the context in which they are actually used to communicate or to solve problems to the practice of literate activities in the context of communicating and solving problems' (p. 160). This is close to Stevenson's (1994) portrait of the teacher in many Asian schools:

> The East-Asian teacher acts as a knowledgeable guide. Indeed, the two characters in the Japanese term for teacher (sensei) mean 'living or being before'—one who has had the experience and now can guide others through it. The teacher is not a lecturer but nevertheless knows what should be learned and the types of techniques that will lead children to learn. The teacher does not act as an authoritarian dispenser of knowledge and judge of what is correct but leads children to construct knowledge and evaluate the reliability of their own and other solutions. (Stevenson, 1994: 320)

A SUMMARY OF TEACHING AND LEARNING PROCESSES

Figure 1.1 depicts the different learning and teaching processes that we have discussed, combining elements from Chamoux (1981), Greenfield (1984) and Strauss (1984). On the left side of the figure are the mechanisms that tend to predominate in informal education (observation, imitation) and on the right side those of formal education (trial and error). But the processes do not divide cleanly across the informal/formal dichotomy. Chanting, a technique in which memorization is helped by rhythmic body movements, is characteristic

Figure 1.1 Learning/teaching processes in formal and informal education

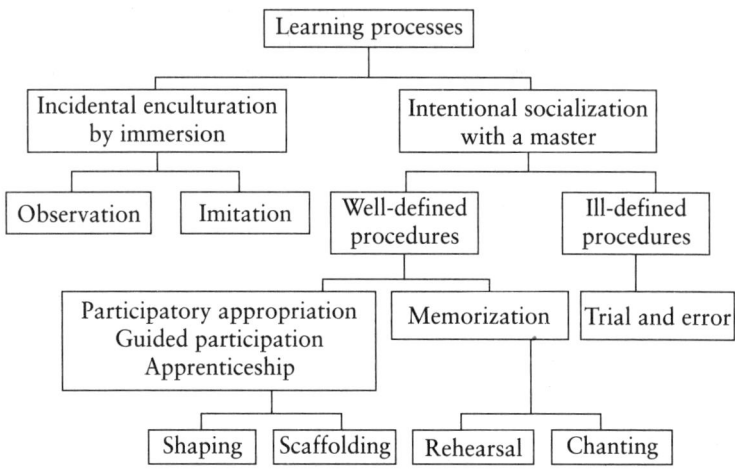

Source: Modified from Segall et al., 1999.

of formal, traditional education, such as religious schooling (see in this volume the chapters by Akkari; Changkakoti and Broyon; Mishra and Vajpayee). The distinction between well-defined and ill-defined procedures (Strauss, 1984) does not imply a value judgement, but derives from studies on artificial intelligence and problem solving. Well-defined procedures are those in which the necessary information is fully laid out, and the steps to be taken and goals to be attained are completely specified, while in ill-defined procedures, the learner is confronted with uncertainty, which requires proceeding by trial and error.

Cultural differences with respect to these learning processes consist primarily of the degree to which they predominate in any particular setting, and not in the presence or absence of any one process. The differential frequency of settings itself characterizes different societies.

AN INTEGRATED THEORETICAL FRAMEWORK FOR INFORMAL EDUCATION AND HUMAN DEVELOPMENT

Education defined as the process of cultural transmission can be placed within a larger theoretical framework of human development, presented in Figure 1.2.

Figure 1.2 An integrated theoretical framework for the cross-cultural study of human development

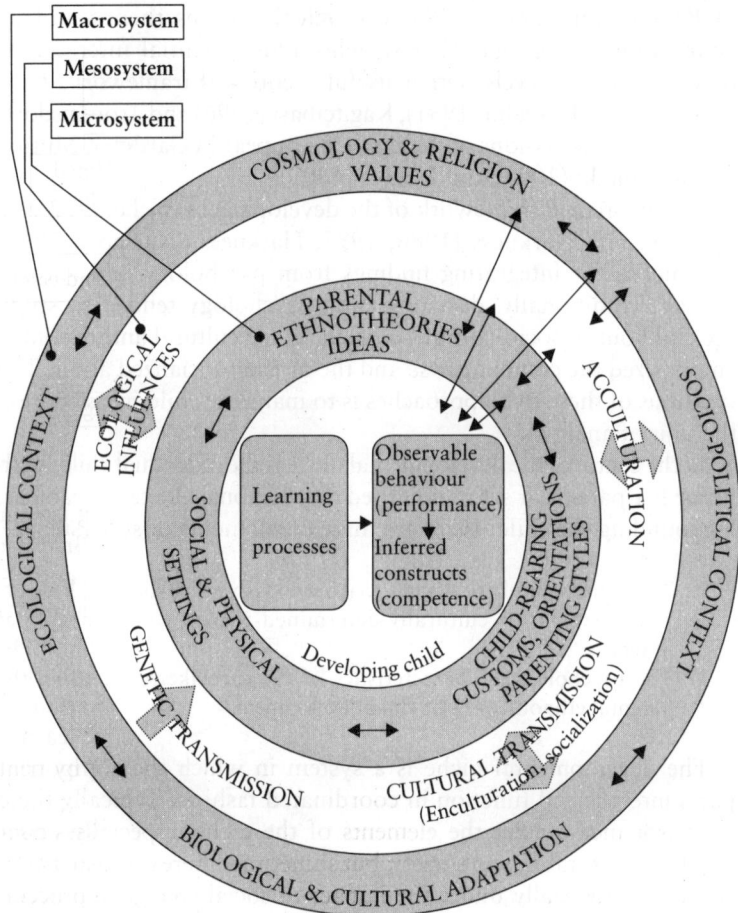

Source: Slightly modified from Dasen, 2003.

This integrated theoretical framework (Dasen, 2003) is in fact a composite of several more specific frameworks that I have found useful over the years, starting with Berry's eco-cultural framework that has been the backbone of our textbooks of cross-cultural psychology (Berry et al., 2002; Segall et al., 1999). Especially relevant to informal education is the 'developmental niche' of Super and

Harkness (1997; see also Bril, 1999), that will be detailed sub-sequently. The integrated framework uses the concentric circles of Bronnfenbrenner's (1989) ecological systems theory and its adaptation by Georgas (1988), who adds potential interactions between various levels. Other useful theoretical frameworks have been provided by Ogbu (1981), Kagitçibasi (1996) and Trommsdorff (1999), and discussions of these models appear in Gardiner, Mutter, and Kosmitzki (2005) and Rogoff (2003).

The theoretical framework of the developmental niche, proposed by Super and Harkness (1986, 1997; Harkness and Super, 1996) is a means for integrating findings from psychology and anthropology. Traditionally, developmental psychology tended to study the child out of socio-cultural context, while cultural anthropology emphasized the context *per se* and the already socialized adult. The synthesis of these two approaches is to make the child in its context the unit of analysis.

At the centre of the developmental niche is the individual child, with his or her particular set of inherited dispositions, like temperament. Surrounding the child, there are three components or subsystems:

1. The settings, or physical and social contexts in which the child lives;
2. The customs, or culturally-determined rearing and educational practices;
3. The psychological characteristics of the caretakers, including the parental ethnotheories of child development.

The developmental niche is a system in which the component parts interact and function in coordinated fashion. Typically there is consonance among the elements of the niche, especially under conditions of stability in society, but sometimes there are also inconsistencies, especially under the impact of social change and acculturation. Moreover, it is an open system where each component is linked with other aspects of the more general environment. Super and Harkness (1986, 1997) explain that the organism and the developmental niche adapt to one another. Thus, as the individual adapts to its surroundings, the niche also adapts to the individual. Certain maturational changes in cognition and personality determine the expectations that adults have with respect to children of different ages. The developmental niche thus changes itself in the course of ontogenesis.

Physical and social settings

Concerning the first component, B. Whiting (1980) noted that culture influences child development primarily by serving as a 'provider of settings', that is, by furnishing the diverse contexts of daily life. For example, in some parts of Africa, babies participate fully in the daily activities of the extended family, a setting where several different people are continuously involved with them. This is a very different setting from that of a baby who spends much of its first few months in a crib or a playpen. The social context formed by the persons with whom the child interacts shapes social behaviour, norms, and values. By the same token, certain characteristics of the social context are also strongly influenced by institutions (for example, the school).

Bril and Zack (1987) have used video recording to compare the physical and social settings of French infants brought up in the home with those who spend most time in a day-care centre (with dozens of playmates and several adult caretakers), and infants in a village in Mali. The home-based infants spend much of their time in a room filled with toys, alone or in the sole company of their mother, and possibly one other sibling. In contrast, the babies in Mali partake of the daily life, full of noise and movement, of their mothers and sibling caretakers.

Much research on the importance of various social settings comes from the research coordinated at the Harvard Graduate School of Education by B. Whiting and J. Whiting, in particular their 'Six Cultures study' (1975; see also Minturn and Lambert, 1964; Whiting and Edwards, 1988). Although this research is now fairly old, it is worth recalling. For example, Munroe and Munroe (1971) studied the effects of household density on infant socialization among the Logoli of Kenya. Infants in high-density households were held more often and attended to more quickly when they cried. On the other hand, the mother was less accessible to them: she was less often the baby's main caretaker, and was less often in close range, due to the greater economic responsibilities she bears in a large household. Weisner and Gallimore (1977) reviewed the role of child caretakers in socialization. Child care is one of the most important tasks delegated to children by mothers with many offspring and a heavy workload. Sex differences in social behaviour may well result from differential assignment to social settings (Whiting and Edwards, 1988).

The presence and role of grandparents change the child-rearing setting to a large extent. Grandparents often have more time for focused interaction with the child, since they are less pressed by subsistence tasks. The respective salience of the mother and of the father and in particular the father's (real or symbolic) absence, seem to be influential aspects in the development of personality and in particular of sex role identity.

The size and composition of peer groups is another feature that shows important cultural diversity. The custom of placing the child in a large same-age peer group, with most of the socialization done by an adult who is not part of the family, produces a very special setting, and it may not be an optimal one for learning. In informal education, most of the enculturation and socialization occurs through 'horizontal transmission' (Berry et al., 2002: 20), that is, through peers. When peer groups comprise children of various ages, the younger ones learn a lot from the older ones. This process has been, of course, one of the distinguishing features of youth groups such as scouts and in schools too small to have same-age classes, as in many rural areas.

Language acquisition can be analyzed in terms of enculturation, that is, the selection of a particular context, since there is usually no conscious choice of which language(s) are spoken around the baby. While infants are potentially able to learn any language, they become attuned early to pay attention to a particular set of sounds and acoustic distinctions. When they start speaking themselves, they practice only the relevant distinctions, to the point where the pronunciation of some unusual syllables may become impossible (or at least very hard to learn) after the early teens. Children who grow up in a plurilingual environment rapidly discriminate between the specific sounds of the languages they hear.

CUSTOMS: CHILD REARING PRACTICES

Cross-cultural research on child-rearing practices, both archival and field studies (such as the Six Cultures study), show how socialization practices are adaptive and linked to eco-cultural dimensions such as food accumulation. Within these constraints, child-rearing practices vary enormously. For example, different baby-carrying techniques determine the type and amount of bodily contact with the mother, and thus the habitual posture, both of which can influence motor development and perhaps even the personality of the child (cf. Berry et al., 2002; Bril and Lehalle, 1988). In some societies people believe that infants will be hurt if lifted by an arm, or if the head is not constantly supported; in contrast, a typical West African grandmother gives the baby a rather robust massage, during which she does not fear to lift it by pulling on an arm, hold it up by the head, or stretch it by pulling on the hands and feet.

Bril and Sabatier (1986) and Bril, Zack, and Nkounkou-Hombessa (1989) analyzed the link between the diversity of settings and child-rearing practices. Regarding the postures infants find themselves in, for example, French babies spend more than half of the day time in a horizontal position in contrast to Bambara babies in Mali who were more often in a semi-vertical or upright sitting position. These different postures provide different types and amounts of stimulation. The Bambara babies learn early to adjust to frequent changes in posture, and the caretakers monitor their manipulations as a function of the infant's developing motor abilities. Child-rearing practices also lead to different types of mother-infant communication, on the proximal/distal dimension. When the baby is in constant body contact, communication can be non-verbal, while the baby who is put away in a crib has to broadcast its needs.

Research on sleeping routines shows diversity not only in where and with whom the child sleeps, but when and how long a child sleeps, as well as the bedtime routines. For example, Spanish children stay up late in the evening, children in Africa have no bedtime and they go to sleep whenever they choose (and sometimes in the middle of a noisy, dancing crowd). In Japan, China, and Taiwan, they go to bed late and get up early because of homework for school. Harkness and Super (2006) have organized a large-scale cross-national study to better document some of these routines in various European countries. Co-sleeping (that is, the practice for the baby to sleep near her mother), although strongly discouraged by Western pediatricians, is in fact very common, including in industrial nations such as Japan (Gardiner et al., 2005).

PARENTAL ETHNOTHEORIES

The third component includes the beliefs and values about the development of children, that is, parental ethnotheories (Goodnow and Collins, 1990; Harkness and Super, 1996). These are not always fully developed and conscious theories in the sense of a set of scientific laws, but are commonly shared in a social group, and hence might also be called social representations (Jodelet, 1989). These ethnotheories influence child development, in particular by determining contexts and training practices, but it also happens that parents do not always act according to the normative rules they convey verbally (Bril, 1999).

As part of cognitive anthropology, ethnoscience studies the way in which different societies conceptualize aspects of the environment that correspond to different branches of science. Thus there is ethnomathematics, ethnobotany, ethnomedicine, ethnoastronomy, and so on. Similarly, in what Bruner (1996) calls folk psychology and folk pedagogy, each society develops ideas about why people behave the way they do, and how children grow up and become adults. Most often, these ideas have not been formalized, nor written down; sometimes they seem to emerge only as a researcher asks about them.

Research on parental ethnotheories was presaged in the studies of child rearing of the 'culture and personality' school, epitomized by the work of Margaret Mead and Ruth Benedict. They, too, were interested in the way child development is conceptualized as part of a cultural system. The difference between earlier and contemporary research is mainly one of methodology. Researchers now use interviews and questionnaires as well as systematic observations with fairly large samples, and take into account intra-cultural variations in parental beliefs. They also try to assess the extent to which the verbally expressed beliefs are actually reflected in cultural practices. The consistency of the belief/practices system has become a matter of empirical enquiry rather than a postulate.

Erny (1981), summarized much ethno-psychological work on the African child, explaining how an African world-view and philosophy influences the way the child is perceived by society. Similar information about West Africa in general, and the Nso of Cameroon in particular, is available in Nsamenang (1992, 2004). From the time of her pregnancy, the mother and the (future) child are the most highly valued assets of an extended family, understood as a 'lineage' (Rabain, 1979), that includes not only the living family members but also the deceased ancestors. The child, then, does not belong to the biological parents only, but to the whole community. This is reflected, for example, by the fact that anyone is allowed to ask a child for help in a chore, or to punish a child for a misbehaviour, like not showing due respect to an elder. Indeed, social aspects of intelligence (such as being helpful, respectful and obedient) are more valued than cognitive aspects (Dasen, 1984). Similarly, in India (Saraswathi and Ganapathy, 2002), parents value 'a *sanskari* child, one who is obedient, respectful of elders and socially conforming' (p. 84).

Hamilton (1981), who studied child rearing among Australian Aborigines, also showed the influence of parental ethnotheories on child-rearing practices. Aborigines believe in a form of reincarnation where the souls of the deceased stay in some sacred and secret location for some time, until one of them jumps into the womb of a woman passing nearby. Sometime after birth, the father, or a shaman, tries to determine who the child really is, and names it accordingly. A baby, being a respected ancestor, hence comes with a full-fledged personality that has to be respected. This ethnotheory is the opposite of one in which a neonate comes as an empty vessel that has to be filled up, shaped to conform to parents' wishes. Aboriginal child rearing is, correspondingly, exceedingly 'laissez faire'. Children are not taught to obey, and they are always immediately given whatever they ask for, but they always have to share it with others.

Parental ethnotheories derive partly from the adults' observations of child development, just as their practices influence the latter. It is a circular system, in which it is difficult to detect cause and effect (Sabatier, 1994). For example, the physical and social settings of the Bambara babies in Mali, as well as the postures they find themselves in, and the stimulations they receive because of child care practices, form such a system. Bambara mothers say that babies should be able to sit alone between three and four months, and this is indeed the age at which their babies can do so, as against the age of seven months given by Western scales of psychomotor development and the age of six months predicted by French mothers (Zack and Bril, 1989). This precocious sitting is not linked, as was previously believed, to an overall African infant precocity, but is a motor skill specifically trained for in many African societies in which it is believed to be an important marker of child development (Super, 1981).

CULTURAL TRANSMISSION IN THE ECOCULTURAL FRAMEWORK

The developmental niche as a microsystem is in interaction with the wider macro-system of the ecological and socio-political contexts, and the biological and cultural adaptation to these. This interaction occurs through processes in the meso-system, among which cultural transmission is of course of special interest for our purpose. This consists of enculturation and socialization.

Enculturation happens largely through the selection of contexts. Children learn what there is around them to be learned. But this selection of contexts is usually simply part of the cultural setup; it is not under the conscious control of parents. Consider the number of books available in a home; this is usually a function of the level of literacy and socio-economic status of the parents. In more educated households, there are more books around. Some parents purposefully buy 'educational' children's books, or even an encyclopaedia to help with schoolwork (more often, now, as a CD-ROM). In such a case we would speak of socialization rather than enculturation. Some customs and child-rearing practices are illustrative of enculturation, because they are mainly unconscious, while others are closer to socialization, because they are willingly chosen.

Child-care practices are usually very homogeneous within a society: There is one, and only one, proper way of handling a baby, the one way that has been practiced over the generations, without any questions asked (or the one advocated by the currently fashionable paediatrician, be it Spock or Brazelton). These practices, however, vary greatly between societies; a cross-cultural comparison is needed to become aware of the diversity.

The third subsystem of the developmental niche is typical of socialization, because cultural belief systems represent conscious explanations or rationalizations for customs of child rearing. Hence, the developmental niche represents the whole spectrum between enculturation and socialization, and in the eco-cultural framework, these processes are linked to culture, and ecological and socio-political contexts, on the one hand, and determine the child's behavioural development on the other. Acculturation and social change are processes that strongly influence the system, and genetic transmission is also recognized, particularly in terms of the child's temperament.

CONCLUSION

This very short summary of some of the research dealing with informal education demonstrates its interdisciplinary character: it draws on anthropology, (cross-)cultural psychology, life-span developmental psychology and family studies, and produces a complex picture of cultural transmission with both universal processes and culturally specific implementations. Formal education, particularly schooling, should be seen as one specific form of cultural transmission, often lacking in cultural appropriateness; this problem could no doubt be lessened by searching for ways to bring schooling more in line with informal education, while maintaining its specific advantages, for example in its possibility to foster flexible knowledge suited to dealing with ever increasing social change.

NOTES

1. This chapter is largely based on my previous writings on the topics of informal education and everyday cognition, notably in one of our textbooks of cross-cultural psychology (Segall et al., 1999). See also Dasen (2000, 2004; Trommsdorff and Dasen, 2002).
2. The research by Chamoux and by Delbos and Jorion is reported in some detail in Segall et al. (1999).

REFERENCES

Ahmed, M. 1983. 'Le non-formel et les questions critiques de l'éducation', *Perspectives*, 13(1): 37–47.

Berry, J. W. and A. Bennett. 1992. 'Cree Conceptions of Cognitive Competence', *International Journal of Psychology*, 27: 73–88.

Berry, J. W., Y. H. Poortinga, M. H. Segall and P. R. Dasen. 2002. *Cross-Cultural Psychology Research and Applications* (Second Revised Edition). Cambridge: Cambridge University Press.

Bril, B. 1999. 'Dires sur l'enfant selon les cultures: état des lieux et perspectives', in B. Bril, P. R. Dasen, C. Sabatier and B. Krewer (eds), *Propos sur l'enfant et l'adolescent. Quels enfants, pour quelles cultures?*, pp. 5–42. Paris: L'Harmattan.

Bril, B. and H. Lehalle. 1988. *Le développement psychologique est-il universel?: Approches interculturelles*. Paris: PUF.

Bril, B. and C. Sabatier. 1986. 'The Cultural Context of Motor Development: Postural Manipulations in the Daily Life of Bambara Babies (Mali)', *International Journal of Behavioural Development*, 9: 439–53.

Bril, B. and M. Zack. 1987. *Motricité au quotidien: de la naissance à la marche-Paris-Dugurakoro* [Video film, 53 min.]. Paris: Centre d'Etudes des Processus cognitifs et du Langage, EHESS.

Bril, B., M. Zack and E. Nkounkou-Hombessa. 1989. 'Ethnotheories of Development and Education: A View from Different Cultures', *European Journal of Psychology of Education*, 4: 307–18.

Bronnfenbrenner, U. 1989. 'Ecological Systems Theory', *Annals of Child Development*, 6: 185–246.

Bruner, J. 1996. *The Culture of Education*. Cambridge, MA: Harvard University Press.

Chamoux, M. N. 1981. 'Les savoir-faire techniques et leur appropriation: le cas des Nahuas du Mexique', *L'Homme*, 21(3): 71–94.

———. 1986. 'Apprendre autrement: aspects des pédagogies dites informelles chez les Indiens du Mexique', in P. Rossel (ed.), *Demain l'artisanat?* Paris, *PUF*, 16: 211–335. Genève: Cahiers de l'I. U. E. D.

Childs, C. P. and P. M. Greenfield. 1980. 'Informal Modes of Learning and Teaching: the Case of Zinacanteco Weaving', in N. Warren (ed.), *Studies In Cross-Cultural Psychology* (Vol. 2), pp. 269–316. London: Academic Press.

Dasen, P. R. 1984. 'The Cross-Cultural Study of Intelligence: Piaget and the Baoule', *International Journal of Psychology*, 19: 407–34.

———. 1993. 'Schlusswort. Les Sciences Cognitives: Do They Shake Hands In the Middle?', in J. Wassmann and P. R. Dasen (eds), *Savoirs quotidiens. Les sciences cognitives dans le dialogue interdisciplinaire*, pp. 331–49. Fribourg: Presses de l'Université de Fribourg.

———. 2000. 'Développement humain et éducation informelle', in P. R. Dasen and C. Perregaux (eds), *Pourquoi des approches interculturelles en sciences de l'éducation?*, pp. 107–23. Bruxelles: DeBoeck Université (Collection: *Raisons Educatives* vol. 3).

———. 2003. 'Theoretical Frameworks In Cross-Cultural Developmental Psychology: An Attempt at Integration', in T. S. Saraswathi (ed.), *Cross-Cultural Perspectives In Human Development: Theory, Research, and Applications*, pp. 128–65. New Delhi: Sage Publications.

———. 2004. 'Education informelle et processus d'apprentissage', in A. Akkari and P. R. Dasen (eds), *Pédagogies et pédagogues du Sud*, pp. 19–47. Paris: L'Harmattan.

Delbos, G. and P. Jorion. 1984. *La transmission des savoirs*. Paris: Maison des Sciences de l'Homme.

Désalmand, P. 1983. *Histoire de l'éducation en Côte d'Ivoire, vol. 1*. Abidjan: CEDA (Hatier/Harmattan).

Erny, P. 1981. *The Child and His Environment in Black Africa: An Essay on Traditional Education*. New York: Oxford University Press. (First published in French, 1972).

Fortes, M. 1938. 'Social and Psychological Aspects of Education in Taleland', *Africa*, Supplement to Volume XI: 1–64.

Gardiner, H. W., J. D. Mutter and C. Kosmitzki. 2005. *Lives Across Cultures: Cross-Cultural Human Development* (3rd edition). Boston: Allyn & Bacon.

Georgas, J. 1988. 'An Ecological and Social Cross-Cultural Model: the Case of Greece', in J. W. Berry, S. H. Irvine and E. B. Hunt (eds), *Indigenous Cognition: Functioning in Cultural Context*, pp. 105–23. Dordrecht, The Netherlands: Nijhoff.

Goodnow, J. J. and W. A. Collins. 1990. *Development According to Parents. The Nature, Sources and Consequences of Parents' Ideas.* East Sussex: LEA.

Greenfield, P. M. 1984. 'A Theory of the Teacher in the Learning Activities of Everyday Life', in B. Rogoff and J. Lave (eds), *Everyday Cognition*, pp. 117–38. Cambridge, MA: Harvard University Press.

———. 2004. *Weaving Generations Together.* Santa Fe, NM: SAR Press.

Greenfield, P. M. and C. P. Childs. 1977. 'Weaving Skill, Color Terms and Pattern Representation: Cultural Influences and Cognitive Development among the Zinacantecos of Southern Mexico', *Interamerican Journal of Psychology*, 2: 23–48.

Greenfield, P. M. and J. Lave. 1982. 'Cognitive Aspects of Informal Education', in D. A. Wagner and H. W. Stevenson (eds), *Cultural Perspectives on Child Development*, pp. 181–207. San Francisco: W. Freeman.

Greenfield, P. M., A. E. Maynard and C. P. Childs. 2003. 'Historical Change, Cultural Learning, and Cognitive Representation in Zinacantec Maya Children', *Cognitive Development*, 18: 455–87.

Hamilton, A. 1981. *Nature and Nurture: Aboriginal Child-Rearing in North-Central Arnhem Land.* Canberra: A.I.A.S.

Harkness, S. and C. M. Super. 2006. 'Themes and Variations: Parental Ethnotheories in Western Cultures', in K. H. Rubin and O. B. Chung (eds), *Parenting Beliefs, Behaviors, and Parent-Child Relations. A Cross-Cultural Perspective*, pp. 61–80. New York: Psychology Press.

———(eds). 1996. *Parent's Cultural Belief System. Their Origins, Expressions, and Consequences.* New York: Guilford.

Hatano, G. 1982. 'Cognitive Consequences of Practice in Culture-Specific Procedural Skills', *Quarterly Newsletter of the Laboratory of Comparative Human Cognition*, 4(1): 15–18.

Jodelet, D. (ed.). 1989. *Les représentations sociales.* Paris: Presses universitaires de France.

Kagitçibasi, C. 1996. *Family and Human Development Across Cultures: A View from the Other Side.* Hillsdale, NJ: Lawrence Erlbaum.

Kenyatta, J. 1965. *Facing Mount Kenya: The Tribal Life of the Gikuyu.* New York: Vintage Books, Random House.

Lancy, D. F. 1996. *Playing on the Mother-Ground. Cultural Routines for Children's Development.* New York: Guilford Press.

Minturn, L. and W. W. Lambert. 1964. *Mothers of Six Cultures: Antecedents of Child Rearing.* New York: John Wiley.

Mishra, R. 1997. 'Cognition and Cognitive Development', in J. W. Berry, P. R. Dasen and T. S. Saraswathi (eds), *Handbook of Cross-Cultural Psychology, Basic Processes and Human Development*, Second Edition. Vol. 2, pp. 143–76. Boston: Allyn and Bacon.

Mishra, R. C. and P. R. Dasen. 2004. 'The Influence of Schooling on Cognitive Development: A Review of Research In India', in B. N. Setiadi, A. Supratiknya, W. J. Lonner and Y. H. Poortinga (eds), *Ongoing Themes in Psychology and Culture. Selected Papers from the Sixteenth International Congress of the International Association for Cross-Cultural Psychology*, pp. 207–22. Yogyakarta: Kanisius.

Montandon, C. 2005. 'Formes sociales, formes d'éducation et figures théoriques', in C. Montandon and O. Maulini (eds), *Formel? Informel? Les formes de l'éducation*, pp. 223–43. Bruxelles: DeBoeck Université.

Munroe, R. H. and R. L. Munroe. 1971. 'Household Density and Infant Care in an East African Society', *Journal of Social Psychology*, 83: 3–13.

Nsamenang, A. B. 1992. *Human Development in Cultural Context: A Third World Perspective*. Newbury Park, CA: Sage Publications.

———. 2004. *Cultures of Human Development and Education: Challenge to Growing Up African*. New York: Nova Science Publishers.

Nunes, T., A. S. Schliemann and D. W. Carraher. 1993. *Street Mathematics and School Mathematics*. Cambridge: Cambridge University Press.

Ogbu, J. 1981. 'Origins of Human Competence: A Cultural-Ecological Perspective', *Child Development*, 52: 413–29.

Rabain, J. 1979. *L'enfant du lignage*. Paris: Payot.

Rogoff, B. 1990. *Apprenticeship in Thinking. Cognitive Development in Social Context*. New York: Oxford University Press.

———. 2003. *The Cultural Nature of Human Development*. Oxford: Oxford University Press.

Rogoff, B. and M. Gauvain. 1984. 'The Cognitive Consequences of Specific Experiences: Weaving Versus Schooling Among the Navajo', *Journal of Cross-Cultural Psychology*, 15: 453–75.

Rogoff, B., J. Mistry, A. Göncü and C. Mosier. 1993. 'Guided Participation in Cultural Activity by Toddlers and Caregivers', *Monographs of the Society for Research in Child Development*, 58(8): 236.

Sabatier, C. 1994. 'Parental Conceptions of Early Development and Developmental Stimulation', in H. Bloch and M. H. Bornstein (eds), *Francophone Perspectives on Early Development*, pp. 299–314. Hillsdale, NJ: Erlbaum.

Saraswathi, T. S. and H. Ganapathy. 2002. 'Indian Parents' Ethnotheories as Reflections of the Hindu Scheme of Child and Human Development', in H. Keller, Y. H. Poortinga and A. Schoelmerich (eds), *Between Biology and Culture: Perspectives on Ontogenetic Development*, pp. 79–88. Cambridge: Cambridge University Press.

Schliemann, A.D., D. Carraher and S. Ceci. 1997. 'Everyday Cognition', in J. W. Berry, P. R. Dasen and T. S. Saraswathi (eds), *Handbook of Cross-Cultural Psychology, Second Edition. Vol. 2: Basic Processes and Human Development*, pp. 177–216. Boston: Allyn & Bacon.

Schliemann, A. D. and N. M. Acioly. 1989. 'Mathematical Knowledge Developed at Work: The Contribution of Practice Versus the Contribution of Schooling', *Cognition and Instruction*, 6(5): 185–221.

Scribner, S. 1979. 'Modes of Thinking and Ways of Speaking: Culture and Logic Reconsidered', in R. O. Freedle (ed.), *New Directions in Discourse Processing*, pp. 223–43. Norwood, NJ: Ablex.

Scribner, S. and M. Cole. 1981. *The Psychology of Literacy*. Cambridge, MA: Harvard University Press.

Segall, M. H., P. R. Dasen, J. W. Berry and Y. H. Poortinga. 1999. *Human Behavior in Global Perspective: An Introduction to Cross-Cultural Psychology*, Revised Second Edition. Boston: Allyn & Bacon.

Stevenson, H. 1994. 'Moving away from Stereotypes and Preconceptions: Students and Their Education in East Asia and the United States', in P. Greenfield and R. Cocking (eds), *Cross-Cultural Roots of Minority Child Development*, pp. 315–22. Hillsdale, NJ: Lawrence Erlbaum.

Strauss, C. 1984. 'Beyond "Formal" Versus "Informal" Education: Uses of Psychological Theory in Anthropological Research', *Ethos*, 12: 195–222.

Super, C. M. 1981. 'Cross-Cultural Research on Infancy', in H. C. Triandis and A. Heron (eds), *Handbook of Cross-Cultural Psychology. Vol. 4. Developmental Psychology*, pp. 17–54. Boston: Allyn & Bacon.

Super, C. M. and S. Harkness. 1986. 'The Developmental Niche: A Conceptualization at the Interface of Child and Culture', *International Journal of Behavioral Development*, 9(4): 545–70.

———. 1997. 'The Cultural Structuring of Child Development', in J. W. Berry, P. R. Dasen and T. S. Saraswathi (eds), *Handbook of Cross-Cultural Psychology: Basic Processes and Human Development*, Second Edition. Vol. 2, pp. 1–39. Boston: Allyn & Bacon.

Tanon, F. 1994. *A Cultural View on Planning: the Case of Weaving in Ivory Coast*. Tilburg: Tilburg University Press.

Tapé, G. 1994. *L'intelligence en Afrique. Une étude du raisonnement expérimental*. Paris: L'Harmattan.

Trommsdorff, G. 1999. 'Autonomie und Verbundenheit im kulturellen Vergleich von Sozialisationsbedingungen', in H. R. Leu and L. Krappmann (eds), *Zwischen Autonomie und Verbundenheit*, pp. 392–419. Frankfurt/Main: Suhrkamp.

Trommsdorff, G. and P. R. Dasen. 2002. 'Cross-Cultural Study of Education', in N. J. Smelser and P. B. Baltes (eds), *International Encyclopedia of the Social and Behavioral Sciences*, pp. 3003–3007. Oxford: Elsevier Science.

Weisner, T. S. and R. Gallimore. 1977. 'My Brother's Keeper: Child and Sibling Caretaking', *Current Anthropology*, 18: 169–90.

Whiting, B. and C. Edwards. 1988. *Children of Different Worlds. The Formation of Social Behavior*. Cambridge, MA: Harvard University Press.

Whiting, B. B. 1980. 'Culture and Social Behavior: A Model for the Development of Social Behavior', *Ethos*, 8: 95–116.

Whiting, B. B. and J. W. M. Whiting. 1975. *Children of Six Cultures: A Psycho-Cultural Analysis*. Cambridge, MA: Harvard University Press.

Zack, M. and B. Bril. 1989. 'Comment les mères françaises et bambara du Mali se représentent-elles le développement de leur enfant?', in J. Retschitzki, M. Bossel-Lagos and P. R. Dasen (eds), *La recherche interculturelle*, Volume 2, pp. 7–17. Paris: L'Harmattan.

2
ETHNOTHEORIES OF DEVELOPMENTAL LEARNING IN THE WESTERN GRASSFIELDS OF CAMEROON

A. BAME NSAMENANG, PASCALINE J. FAI, GLADYS N. NGORAN, MAIRAMA Y. NGEH, FEDELIS W. FORSUH, EUNICE W. ADZEMYE, AND GLORY N. LUM[1]

INTRODUCTION

In all societies throughout human history, people have educated their children (Reagan, 1996). Indeed, a universal characteristic of human civilizations is a concern for preparing the next generation. Such preparation, along with undergoing the processes of psycho-social differentiation, predates the emergence and exportation of academic disciplines, including educational science. For Fafunwa (1974), the history of education in Africa is incomplete without adequate knowledge of the indigenous education systems that existed in the distant past before the arrival of Arabic-Islamic and Western-Christian versions of education (Nsamenang, 2005b), to confer on Africa its contemporary triple education heritage (Mazrui, 1986). Indigenous education has survived in Africa till today. Inspite of its hybridization through cultural contact, acculturation and cultural impositions, Africa's indigenous education shows no signs of disappearing from the education scene. It has survived in spite of the overwhelming weight of institutional education and pressure of scientific disciplines (Nsamenang, 2005b).

The institutionalization of education and scientific disciplines are a product of specific historical and cultural circumstances. Centuries prior to the rise of institutional education and the evolution of disciplinary psychology and other scientific disciplines, human cultures shared folk modus vivendi (Nsamenang, 2001). However, in the course of history a 'slippage' occurred and the centre of the world was displaced from Asia to Europe (Dussel, 1998). Thereafter, an intrusive ideology sprouted from an 'Enlightened Europe', was cultivated, and has increasingly been embellished into a progressive positivism and instrumental theory of the universe, to overwhelm all others (Nsamenang, 2007). That is, disciplinary psychology, like institutional education, is erected and edified on the narrative conventions of Western cultures which are saturated with Anglo-American ideologies, epistemologies and cultural values (Gergen, 1992), though they are not in themselves homogeneous. 'Scientific knowledge is regarded as the only legitimate kind of knowledge in a disciplinary context, though in other life contexts individual psychologists may well appreciate the value of other kinds of knowledge' (Danziger, 2006: 271).

The social Darwinian project to universalize 'Enlightenment' psychology and institutional education or schooling tends to disregard the fact of it being 'an article of export from one part of the world to another' (Danziger, 2006: 271). In fact, Europe has since the Enlightenment actively exported its conception of 'modernism' in education and other disciplines and life domains to the rest of the world (see Allwood and Berry, 2006; Danziger, 2006). The foundational presumption of the modernization motif in Africa is that development and progress will continue to elude the Dark Continent until it is infused with at least a threshold dose of Western 'civilization' (Nsamenang, 2005b). This deficit model fails to draw strength from the fountain of Africa's uncharted rich ethnotheories and the wisdom of her timeless traditions (Callaghan, 1998).

It is in recognition of these uncultivated knowledge systems that this chapter focuses on introducing the ethnotheories and indigenous practices that undergird developmental learning in one part of Cameroon—the Western Grassfields (Nkwi and Warnier, 1982). A history of the Cameroon Grassfields reveals population movements, the adjustments of cultural patterns and adaptations to the ecology to evolve 'common political and social institutions with only slight variations' (Nkwi, 1983: 102). The political and social organization of the Western Grassfields is structured into ethnic kingdoms, commonly referred to as Fondoms, which are shaped by kinship ties. The clans or ethnic communities are distinct for their specialized patterns of governance. The clan ruler, traditionally titled *Fon*, is the custodian of the people's cultural heritage. These Fondoms or 'native-states' and the visible grip of their Fons on ethnic members exist together with the local governing structures of the nation-state.

By developmental learning we are referring to learning, without the idea of schools, which is vital to children's survival and development. The indispensability of schooling today is not being questioned here. What is questionable is the insinuation that without schools or academic channels children cannot learn. There are unexplored but viable non-academic pipelines outside the school in most African societies. Our grand hypothesis is that the most profound and most utilizable cultural learnings for most Africans, including the erudite, occur outside school, within African family traditions and peer cultures.

THEORETICAL MOORINGS AND CONCEPTUAL ISSUES

Although ethnotheories of education do not conventionally belong to educational science, they are integral to ethnocultural precepts and representations. As such, they are part and parcel of a people's social reality. They oblige an ethnocultural vision of the universe. Every cultural community possesses a worldview or theory of the universe that includes an image of the child and his or her preparation for adult life.

Worldviews regard the child as a cultural agent to whom the future hopes of society and survival of its culture is entrusted (Reagan, 1996). Bruner (1996) coined notions of ethnopsychology and ethnopedagogy to make the point that each society develops its own ethnotheories of why people behave the way they do and how children grow up to become the adults they turn out to be. The understanding of 'Africa's remarkable adaptability and resilience' (Nsamenang, 2004a: 93) in the face of daunting adversity lies in an objective exploration of Bruner's (1996) indigenous concepts, the primary task of this chapter.

The social world in which children live and grow influences the way they develop (Bronfenbrenner, 1979; Cochran and Brassard, 1979). Because 'social context is, at a variety of levels, intrinsic to the developmental process itself' (Richards, 1986: 7), an understanding of children's social worlds constitutes a prerequisite condition for understanding their development, particularly in traditional Africa, where context, cosmology and the human being are conceptually inseparable (Bongmba, 2001). More specifically, in African family traditions, children are an intricate part of social relationships (for example, La Fontaine, 1986). In fact, in the Western Grassfields children's social ecologies are 'a multitude of male and female adults and children who vary in age, status, background, kinship bonds and commitment' to their care and wellbeing (Nsamenang, 1987a: 5).

Basically, the personalities and futures of youngsters are instantiated by their life circumstances. They vary by their actual lived experiences and imagined futures (Nsamenang, 2006a). The child is a *situated* organism, who sometimes moves or is moved across different contexts at different stages of development (Nsamenang, 2004a). Children evoke different reactions from their social environments in response to a variety of factors, including the physical conditions and the attitudes and behaviours of peers and moral authorities. This last point implies that social and moral standards strongly regulate children's behaviour.

WHAT IS DEVELOPMENTAL LEARNING: IS IT OBTAINABLE ONLY THROUGH ACADEMIC PIPELINES?

Children are not born with the knowledge with which to cope with life and make sense of the world, but they are born ready to learn. They acquire culture and competencies in the process of development. Key elements of such learning can be achieved without 'the usual sense of classrooms and schools' (Bruner, 1996: ix). Every human culture makes the learning of survival knowledge and self-actualization skills possible by conceiving of human nature in its own terms and organizing development and learning according to that cultural image (Nsamenang, 1995). Institutional education or schooling is a Euro-American tool, which ignores the many ways that other societies have educated and have made their young responsible, to ascertain the survival of their people and culture (Reagan, 1996).

Our inclusive view of education is as a process that seeks to orient children to the world and into learning the tasks of life or the responsibilities liaised to a specific duty. Such learning is embedded in the language, culture, institutions, social history, and so on, of cultural communities. Although all cultures throughout history, including those of the Western Grassfields, have educated their offspring into culturally competent members of their next generation, Western forms of institutional education are the centrepiece of the modernization motif and intervention or social Darwinian packages that are applied throughout Africa in disregard of the huge diversity in children's learning circumstances and strategies. Euro-American versions of education do not build on an African worldview 'that constitutes a very different *psychological frame of reference* from that which informs' Western psychology and schooling (Serpell, 1994: 18).

An often ignored dimension of *The Significance of Schooling* (Serpell, 1993) in Africa is that experts and teachers attempt to move children and their families forward without accepting their ecocultural background and life circumstances. Callaghan's (1998) record of the South African situation is similar to that of the Western Grassfields, characterized by 'a blindness and inability to see and value Africans in the African context' (Callaghan, 1998: 31). Current conceptualization and best practices are as if educators and education experts and policy planners have been 'educated' to discount the stark realities and contexts of Africa's life-journeys and livelihoods (Serpell, 1993).

Education is a basic necessity because, to survive and thrive, every human being requires vital knowledge of self, the environment, and the universe (Nsamenang, 2004a). Core elements of this knowledge and skills can be acquired at home or in society, especially through participatory learning. The theory of cultural learning (Tomasello et al., 1993) was postulated to connect children's development to their increasing participation in cultural activities (Maynard, 2002; Rogoff, 2003). Children are born ignorant of, but grow into, the knowledge of their cultural curriculum because of a genetic disposition to learn and use culture. To better understand the force of culture on developmental learning, which the Eurocentric ethnotheory abbreviates as institutional education or schooling and African ethnotheory posits as the 'school of life' (Moumouni, 1968: 29), it makes sense to adopt Rogoff's (2003) stance 'that people develop as participants in cultural communities'.

Thus, developmental learning in African children *can be understood only in the light of the cultural practices and circumstances of their communities* (Rogoff, 2003: 2). It is more so in the Western

Grassfields of Cameroon, where educational precepts and practices are embedded in family traditions, daily routines and social and communal activities. The curriculum is arranged to progressively connect children from an early age into the culture's heritage, especially the social values and accumulated knowledge and skills repertoire that exist already in agrarian cultures, which need them (Ogbu, 1994). The curriculum and learning are sequenced systematically across the stages of life.

With the foregoing as the backdrop, it is not at all bizarre to ask for research-based comparison of the genre of businesspeople that are thriving in Cameroon, whether they are more equipped with ethnotheories as hinted above or are more imbued with schooled knowledge or Harvard and London School of Economics MBAs. This challenge is more compelling in the face of Diawara's (1998) observation that 'In West Africa today, traditional markets still pose the strongest obstacle to the nation-states' and 'the World Bank and other global institutions that consider the nation-states the only legitimate structure with which to conduct business in Africa' (Diawara, 1998: 116).

ETHNOCULTURAL EDUCATION IN THE WESTERN GRASSFIELDS OF CAMEROON

The bulk of the rest of this chapter is devoted to exposing ethnotheories of developmental learning and teaching in the Western Grassfields of Cameroon, but without much emphasis on the dynamics of their coexistence and acculturative or adaptive shifts and reciprocity of influence. The framing principle of the chapter is an African precept that does not endorse the compartmentalization of human knowledge into this or that discipline (Nsamenang, 2004b).

Our task is to attempt to weave together into a coherent picture apparently disparate ethnotheories that are subtly interconnected domains of human life, such as cosmology, family life, agricultural practices, communitarian processes and language acquisition.

Developing and learning within the cosmology of the Western Grassfields

The German philosopher Johann Gottfried von Herder perceived human understanding and meaning of life as organized 'in the light of particular goals, values, and pictures of the world' (Berlin, 1976: 195). These and other facets of human cognition accrue and blend into a cosmology or collective outlook to the universe, which we referred to earlier as worldview, which is an operative theory of the universe. Intentionality structures cosmologies in general and in particular the nature of developmental learning a given culture organizes for its children. That is, theories of the universe engender how cultures and individuals constitute themselves (Rogoff, 1990). As a broad concept that encapsulates various facets of visualizing, relating to and dealing with the world, worldview can be interpreted as 'a theorist's view of development [that] is closely tied to his or her view of human nature, a view intimately tied to his or her conception of how the universe works' (Nsamenang, 1992: 210).

Ngeh (1996) sees children of the Western Grassfields of Cameroon, as children everywhere, born into a pre-existing social world not only of knowledge, attitudes, practices and skills but more so of a language environment and community. These are elements of a cultural curriculum that children eventually learn and with which they increasingly make sense of life and the world throughout their ontogeny.

The Wimbum are one of the ethnic kingdoms of the Western Grassfields, whose worldview, like that of every ethnic group in Cameroon, 'is the interplay of social, religious, and political roles, working together to ensure the well-being of the people' (Bongmba, 2001: 7). Holism is intrinsic in this worldview; it does not imagine any neat distinction between the sacred and the secular. An intermeshing of religion, culture, and social life makes it difficult to isolate purely secular from religious activity or role. Religious ideas such as the theocentric origin of the child (Nsamenang, 1992) are explicit or implicit in every aspect of life, especially the extended family and other cultural institutions. These institutions structure and give content to the cultural curriculum, which is sequenced according to culturally perceived stages for children's developmental learning.

An individual's understanding of oneself is embedded contextually in a sense of community in which ancestors participate. As guardians of traditional values, ancestors spur behavioural social norms that control their living progeny (Brannen, 2005). Within Grassfield's traditions, individuals generate their personhood from socio-affective premises. Kinship is the nucleus from which social networks ramify, moral behaviour is initiated and prosocial values, productive skills and the mother tongue are learned. The family is central to all this, because it ensures the supply and maintenance of new members without whom the society would fail in its generative role.

The family as a sphere of developmental influence and foundation of learning

Whiting and Whiting (1975) proffered culture as a *provider of settings* for child care and development. On her part, Rabain (1979) characterized child socialization as the process by which children acquire the social ways of being human by learning the cultural code of their people. This implies that every human culture possesses its own folk curriculum of how children can become competent members of the cultural community, for example, becoming an American (Harkness et al., 1992).

African cultures express the value of the family through the manner in which procreation and child-rearing are inserted into family life. For most children, the family environment is the most intimate and encapsulating source of experiences and exposures (Siddiqi et al., 2006). This is particularly applicable in the Western Grassfields where reproductive ideologies and childcare norms are integrated into kinship networks as ramifications of the institution of the family. For this reason the family is best regarded as the first formal 'environment' for initiating children's learning. In fact, the foundation of child development is laid in the family prior to child birth (Nsamenang, 1996).

Whereas Ngoran (2005) examined Grassfields family traditions through the coping strategies marital couples brought into the family, Forsuh (2005) explored them through providing counseling services to needy family members in a community-based centre. Both studies identified some underlying traditions and practices that ordain family life and children's school and out-of-school learning. One pervasive feature of the Grassfields family is the high value placed on fertility and the desire for many children.

The legitimate way to procreate and have socially integrated children in the Western Grassfields is through marriage. The conjugal pair is the acceptable procreative unit; the foundation of the family. After marriage, a young man or woman is regarded as a proto-adult until the birth of his or her child. As in Kenya, 'the social position of a married man and woman who have children is of greater importance and dignity than that of a bachelor or spinster' (Kenyatta, 1965: 158). Thus, the *full-person status* of parenthood is signified by calling the individual by the name of his or her child: 'father-of-...' or 'mother-of-...' (Brannen, 2005). As such, growing up in the ethnic kingdoms of the Western Grassfields, to borrow from Goodnow (1988), involves gaining 'a sense of group membership that carries with it some obligation to acquire the kinds of ideas and knowledge appropriate to being a mother or father' (Goodnow, 1988: 289). Accordingly, it is inconceivable that a Grassfields person would be childless by choice (Nsamenang, 1992).

Marriage interconnects spousal kin into networks of extended or joint families. The main principles for allocating time, attention and resources to children within these networks are sex of child, generation or age cohort, and laterality or the side of the lineage to which a child belongs (Nsamenang, 1987a). In polygamous families, a wife's uxorial rank is used as another resource-allocating principle.

The syntax in the terms used to express the values and expectations of kinship is not merely rhetorical but morally binding. For example, brothers are not expected to discriminate against one another's children and cousins may take full charge to pay for the education of an impoverished nephew's children. Thus, kinship syntaxes 'instruct' kin to behave true to the cultural scripts of the terms used (Ayisi, 1979). Accordingly, kin are expected to offer support and assistance, whether it is solicited or not, to uphold the tacit principle of being each other's keeper. Such values are so deeply ingrained that it is difficult not to accept help from kin or not to offer it to a disadvantaged or needier kin. Kin feel a particularly strong obligation to help out and share responsibility in childcare, sometimes by 'placing' children in the homes of non-biological parents. There is dismay when kin fail to live up to these expectations, as recent clinical evidence from a Bamenda counseling centre has revealed (Forsuh, 2005).

Given that children do not belong to their parents, *per se*, but they belong to the lineage, almost every kin retains some responsibility for raising them—a role that may mean that grandparents, uncles, cousins and other relatives, even significant friends, may have, and indeed have exercised, authority over sensitive decisions regarding the futures of relatives' children (Nsamenang, 1987a). In fact, kinsmen and kinswomen are subject to pressures and sanctions, or at least a loss of face, if they depart widely from normative expectations of cooperation, sharing and mutual support in childcare and family welfare. This romantic system has somehow been bartered, but in poverty-stricken communities like our discourse region, support of a needier family member, for example, by paying school fees for his or her child, merits preservation. The salience of the African proverb 'It takes a village to raise a child' (Swadener et al., 2000) becomes self-evident within the logic of this vigorous sense of community, and nostalgic in the face of an accentuating poverty index.

The structure and function of the family is a critical factor in family dynamics, particularly in the care and education of children. For instance, in polygamous families, wives have unequal access to resources. The typical polygamous scenario is one in which each wife takes charge of her children, a social situation which obviously places some wives and their offspring in serious disadvantage (Ssennyonga, 1997). Such family structures and resource-allocation systems now tend to stir up various degrees of acrimony and hardship, therein causing stress and constituting conflictual learning contexts for many children, both at home and in school (Forsuh, 2005). A good example is matrilineal inheritance and succession which can be really upsetting to children who worked hard to help their fathers accumulate wealth, whereas, they inherit from a maternal uncle who had barely scratched a living. As a result, many children are no longer motivated to feel committed to working hard in their father's farm or enterprise if the results would go to others, who did not join in accumulating the wealth (Nsamenang, 1987b).

Learning and role-taking are organized to conform to the stages of life. A garden metaphor that conveys this process as graduated development is that of a *seed*, nursed to maturity in a dense socio-logical field (Nsamenang, 2002). The extended family, along with neighbours and peers, is the primary sociological garden in which cultural knowledge and responsibility training, sprout and flourish or is stifled. From the anchor of the family, children's exploratory search for meaningful understanding and 'the right ways' of the world begins with parents, as well as with siblings, long before they encounter and learn from non-familial members and peers in the neighbourhood and at school. As the first educators and cognitive stimulators of children, parents are the source of primary knowledge and cognitive skills for children's start on life and school. The inter-actional networks within the family set the pace and quality of children's learning of culture and expansive skills. The family determines development and learning because it is a major source of nurturance, emotional bonding, socialization and children's window of opportunity to the world (Nsamenang, 1996).

Participative learning is integral to cultural and economic life in the Western Grassfields. 'Liberal' parental values and expectations encourage and enhance co-participation of children in the routine work of the family and community and their anticipatory priming into the adult roles they will take in future (Nsamenang and Lamb, 1995). In this way, children's cognitive development is fostered by apprenticeship and contextual learning through guided participation (Rogoff, 1990) in culturally structured familial, social and economic sectors with parents, other adults and peers. The gradation of such education is meant to progressively connect children to their cultural heritage and follows from the principle that everything cannot be taught or learned at once (Nsamenang, 2005c). Accordingly, the tasks and skills to be taught and learned are sequenced within an unwritten curriculum as well as across culturally perceived stages of social development.

At each successive stage of life, the child faces, and must achieve, developmental tasks, each of which is defined by the culture according to important markers in growing up through participative learning of family and community roles commensurate to the child's perceived developmental stage. In a certain sense, during ontogeny, children are 'cultivated' into the 'pivot' roles which correspond to their various 'stations' of life. Through such participation, children systematically master their language, rule systems, and the competencies which their culture requires. Concretely, they perform family duties, are silent listeners to adult discourse and conversations and practise with proverbs, mental arithmetic, dilemma tales, legends, and so on, sometimes with adults, but often by themselves in the peer culture. By the end of adolescence, normally developing girls and boys are expected to have completed their social, intellectual, moral, practical, and responsibility training (Ministère de l'Information et de la Culture, Cameroun, 1981).

Participatory spheres for children's developmental maturation

Gauvain (1995) reminded us of a largely ignored but obvious fact: children progressively grow and mature into the competencies of their cultures. Ogbu (1994) reinforced this reality with the clarification that children do not learn a universal curriculum, but they learn the social values and accumulated knowledge and skills that exist already in their culture, which needs them. African social ontogeny recognizes and addresses the transformation of the human newborn en route to the most cherished human status–adulthood–from a biological imperative into a viable cultural agent of a particular cultural community. During ontogeny, children slowly but surely grow into and assume different levels of being, identity, and maturity (Nsamenang, 2005a).

In the Western Grassfields of Cameroon, familial, agrarian, and communitarian spheres are the main participatory sectors within which children instantiate their developmental learnings. It is in 'helping' parents and other adults or in farming activities and communal projects that most children of the Western Grassfields progressively gain in identity formation, social competence and responsible intelligence (Nsamenang, 2006b). Examples of the duties children perform include domestic chores, communal work, street hawking as well as in urban market-gardening (Adzemye, 2005).

In the Grassfields, as elsewhere, a normal family unit sets the pace and sustains children's learning of their cultural curriculum (Rogoff, 1990; Tomasello et al., 1993). The family also prepares children for school entry, societal participation and other expansive roles, albeit with clearly different levels of adeptness dependent on the literacy level in the family or the family's kin network. The orienting value to learning is participatory, not instructional. It is based on a belief that children are competent and capable of taking on responsible roles from an early age, even in their own development and learning. Parents use evidence that a child has the ability to give and receive social support, and notice and attend to the needs of others as markers of graduated development and responsible or 'intelligent' behaviour (Nsamenang, 2005a). Responsibility training is by allocating to children household duties like cleaning tasks, fetching water or firewood, and so on, or sending them on neighbourhood errands to give or bring articles, deliver messages, purchase items, and so on.

Children's 'work' socializes prosocial and responsible values, socio-cognitive and productive skills and eases life transitions and social integration. The moral lessons and skills children learn from such work are extracted from social interactions, cultural life, and economic activities. In general, children are seldom instructed, but by themselves they extract livelihood lessons from the knowledge, skills, and intelligences 'situated' in the familial and communal life of which they are recognized participants. When their contributions are accepted they see themselves as significant social partners. Like Rogoff (2003), we are interpreting this type of learning and social integration as transformation in the child brought about by participation in familial and societal life.

Children's learning in the early years is also factored into the peer culture, agrarian, and commercial activities. For instance, from the toddler age children are not conventionally 'raised' by adults, except through the imported system of early childhood services and schooling but they spend more time with peers than with parents or other adults. Elder peers or siblings rather than adults readily supervise, correct, and mentor them (Nsamenang, 2006b). From their interaction within the peer culture, the environment and with one another, children generate, acquire and control knowledge and competencies unlike with schooling where the instruction of 'posited' knowledge is a primary value. The free spirit of the peer culture challenges children to address and resolve conflicts, take perspective and notice and attend to the needs of others. They also learn how to plan and organize activities and collaborate. In so doing, children progressively cognize, internalize, and integrate adult models into their own personalities and worlds.

In the Western Grassfields of Cameroon, as elsewhere in sub-Saharan Africa, children can be seen in various places and spaces, typically unaccompanied by adults but engaged in a variety of survival activities, responsible roles or sometimes in destructive and self-defeating activities. As they mature through socially recognized life stations, they are assigned gender-appropriate roles and tasks. For example, while boys of six to seven years of age are sent on errands in the community, to the fields or neighbouring villages (Dasen et al., 1978) and may tether goats, girls assist in food preparation and tend chicken. Some male and female city children participate in street-vending a variety of wares, while some are major participants in urban agriculture of gardening marketable vegetables (Adzemye, 2005), usually as a part-time or after-school activity.

While the thrust of this chapter is on how to profit from taking indigenous knowledge into account, we have introduced, in the next section, one line of research which hypes Africa's growing but unaddressed dilemma with 'emancipatory' efforts to pull it into modernity, out of its obscurity in underdevelopment. Most of such interventions starkly, albeit imperceptibly, discount Africa's ethnocultural realities and strengths. Our focus on second language learning in an African ethnic community—the Nso of western Cameroon—exemplifies how the focus of most interventions on the Dark Continent is not on enhancing indigenous African skills and knowledge systems, but instead accentuates bypassing and/or replacing them.

THE INTERSECTION OF PROFICIENCIES IN THE MOTHER TONGUE AND THE SECOND LANGUAGE

Language, according to the *Webster's Ninth New Collegiate Dictionary*, is 'the words, their pronunciation, and the methods of combining them used and understood by a considerable community'. This definition identifies four core components of language, namely, sounds, words, methods of combining words, and the communal uses that language serves (Cole and Cole, 1996). These components confer on every child at birth a specific language environment and community, which becomes part and parcel of 'an ethnocultural reality ... or crucial fact' of that child's existence and developmental learning (Soyinka, 1990: 17). The ethnocultural language reality in the Western Grassfields of Cameroon today confuses everyone concerned in the sense that children are now exposed not solely to their ethnic languages but also to second languages—English, French, or Arabic.

This language landscape is problematic to teaching and learning both the first and second languages. Foreign or second languages rather than first languages are the medium of school instruction. The ethnic languages have thus been unwittingly relegated to inferior status as *receiving* languages because foreign languages—English and French—have been elevated to superior status as official languages and the medium of school instruction in both rural and urban settings throughout Cameroon.

It is from this backdrop that Fai (1996) took an otherwise deficit point of view, which goes against current theorizing on bilingualism, to examine a major but often ignored African predicament of how *received* knowledge—the English language—portrays traditional or local knowledge (of the first language) as a problem for schooling in particular and modernization in general. This was because the most common method of expanding ethnic lexicons is to borrow from English language concepts and words. Given a national devaluation of ethnic languages, they are obliged to adjust their linguistic systems by resorting to loaning new lexical items and expressions from the dominant or 'received' language. Fai (1996) specifically examined how Lamnso', the first language (mother tongue) of the Nso, one of the largest Grassfields kingdoms, has been influenced or has influenced the learning of a received (second) European language—English. A notable conclusion of her research is that proficiency in Lamnso' did not 'help' English language acquisition but instead hindered it.

Accordingly, Fai (1996) revealed how, at points of intersection of Lamnso' and English, an imposed-etic mindset judged Lamnso' as 'inadequate' or lacking in the corresponding vocabulary items to match or reflect the English language lexicons. In fact, acculturative circumstances compel Lamnso' to expand its lexicons with concepts and ideas from the English language. In almost all domains of life, imported images and received knowledge clash or coexist with indigenous African versions. As such, African communities today must cope not only with many lexical inadequacies, but also with many other shortcomings that are perceived with social Darwinian lenses.

Language acquisition does not occur in a vacuum; it begins in an ethnocultural niche—the family—prior to the introduction of formal language learning at school. Most Nso pupils in the Western Grassfields, as do other ethnic children elsewhere in sub-Saharan Africa, start schooling, especially in rural communities, proficient in their mother tongues. This implies that at the age they begin learning formal English or other second languages at school, they were already thinking in their mother tongues first, prior to learning how to translate and express their thoughts in English (Fai, 1996). Instead of studying or fostering how mother tongue proficiency can facilitate second language acquisition, research and interventions have instead focused on the converse: how proficiency in the mother tongue distorts the learning of European languages. The deficit view can be detected in different doses in all interventions throughout Africa.

CONCLUDING REFLECTIONS

Undoubtedly, Africa's situation is despicably undesirable. Africa does not deserve it and should get out of it soon. However, current studies or interventions of Africa's sorry state, like Fai's (1996), only deepen its misunderstanding and worsen an already bad condition. The good often interns in the bad, however. For instance, in attempting to understand proficiency in Lamnso' as distortional of the acquisition of 'Oxford English', Fai (1996) unconscionably, but cogently, brought into sharp relief the havoc putative knowledge has wrought on Africa. This point adds force to the message of this chapter: the future progress of Africa hinges on enhancing and promoting indigenous Africa and not on importing whatever 'civilized' or advanced models are available to replace it.

Without denying that African and Western civilizations have mutually influenced each other, we have to reiterate forcefully that imposing foreign language acquisition undermines the knowledge of African first languages (mother tongues). Even more importantly, it distracts Africans from their logic systems and truncates their cognitive repertoires. Kishani (2001) expresses similar sentiment with respect to African languages and philosophy. He wondered whether Africans can only philosophize in European languages and 'accordingly to European models of philosophy as if African languages cannot provide and play the same roles' (Kishani, 2001: 27).

Historical truncations of Africa's social thought and cognitive abilities constitute the continent's most crippling factor that has brazenly been ignored by both the development community and native-born African governing and elite classes, including some of Africa's splendid scholars and experts, who have acquiesced to the conceited claims that indigenous African realities are inimical to progress. Some remain silent even when they notice strategies they know will permanently emasculate or further enfeeble Africa. Accordingly, there has been spirited search for illusive modernity and 'development' without a strand of the African soul or roots in the African soil. An unexamined effect of these extraverted strategies has been the alarming failure rate or unrequited development in the Black Continent. Underlying this are highly perfected but very sneaky tactics that operate to bypass Africa's distinctive ethnocultural realities and social capital, which are 'little appreciated' (Ellis, 1978: 1), even with the so-called participatory approaches. Kishani (2001), like many before him, detects 'both the lettered and "oraural" traditions of Africa' as inviting 'Africans to practice self-reliance' in these sensitive matters about which change is long overdue (Kishani, 2001: 27).

Emerging efforts to retrace research footsteps is a promissory sign for Africa, which has suffered unimaginable harm from the misjudgement and misinterpretation of its ethnotheories and whose tremendous resources are a high risk or predatory factor. LeVine (2004), for one, revisited decades-old child development research in Africa to reverse previous condemnation of sibling caretaking, which is 'deviant' by Euro-American norms, but 'research to date has shown no sign of increased risks to child survival or psychological development from sibling care in Africa' (LeVine, 2004: 163). Can such rethinking, backed by 'following footsteps', multiply to cast a liberatory light on Africa's non-western ethnotheories and 'sets of standards'? (Nsamenang, 2008).

The essence of this chapter is to take indigenous African knowledge in research, policy and programmatic development and practice seriously. But the ideological and theoretical positioning, the relevant conceptual systems and appropriate procedural modalities that are sensitively tuned to Africa and will usefully serve Africa's multiple needs are not yet in place. Elsewhere (Nsamenang, 2008), we ponder in what image these critical matters will take shape and whether they will emerge from within Africa, or from outside it? Or, does where they come from not matter? To what extent do efforts to evolve a dignifying educational science for Africa engage indigenous voices? Has the African Union (2006) engaged all shades of discourse to open up to the insights and novelty of Africa's timeless educational traditions within which for centuries Africans have successfully practiced child-rearing to produce an incomparable icon like Nelson Mandela? Can the African Union inspire education systems premised on Mandela's humanism and forgiving heart, without bitterness?

It is perhaps unimaginable but compelling to point out that Western-type of education initiates Africa's children into an educationalization process by which they, from the lowest developmental stage to the next, increasingly gain in unfamiliar knowledge and skills but disturbingly dip into alienation (Kishani, 2001) and ignorance of their cultural circumstances and agrarian livelihoods by education curricula and service programmes that are deficient on local content and insensible of national skill demands (Nsamenang, 2005b). Thus, in general, 'modern' educationalization, beginning with early childhood development services, in spite of its emancipatory potential, systematically transforms Africans into citizens who are ignorant of their resources, and worst of all, inept to act on their own felt needs. What kind of education is that?

Africa's greatest priority then is 'to listen to and learn from, the African worldview, seeing a holistic and integrated way of looking at the family and the universe' in order to 'see things in a new way' (Callaghan, 1998: 31). It is only in this way that Africans would be able to relevantly conceptualize, develop and bequeath to their progeny a future and an education system that begins from deep within the African soul and family and that retains indigenous Africa's participative spirit and processes. It must reflect Africa's rich cultural heritage and the timeless wisdom of the long ignored accomplishments of her agrarian livelihoods.

NOTE

1. All the co-authors are affiliated to the Human Development Resource Centre (HDRC). Address all correspondences to Prof. A. Bame Nsamenang, HDRC, P.O. Box 270, Bamenda–NWP, Cameroon.Email: bame51@yahoo.com.

REFERENCES

Adzemye, E.W. 2005. *A Study of the Contribution of Urban Agriculture to the Economic Development of the Bamenda Sub-Division*. Research Project for a Bachelor of Science Degree in Agriculture, Faculty of Agriculture and Rural Development, Bamenda University of Science and Technology. Bamenda, Cameroon.

African Union 2006. *Second Decade of Education for Africa (2006–2015): Draft Plan of Action*. Addis Ababa, Ethiopia: Department of Human Resources, Science and Technology.

Allwood, C.M. and J.W. Berry. 2006. 'Preface: Special Issue on Indigenous Psychologies', *International Journal of Psychology*, 41(4): 241–42.

Ayisi, E.O. 1979. *An Introduction to the Study of African Culture*. Ibadan: Heinemann.

Berlin, I. 1976. *Vico and Herder*. London: Hogarth.

Bongmba, E.K. 2001. *African Witchcraft and Otherness: A Philosophical and Theological Critique of Intersubjective Relations*. New York: New York University Press.

Brannen, G.E. 2005. *Tikari Traditions of Cameroon Grassfields: Explanatory Models of Illness*. Bamenda, Cameroon: Anoh's Printing Service.

Bronfenbrenner, U. 1979. *The Ecology of Human Development*. Cambridge, MA: Cambridge University Press.

Bruner, J. 1996. *The Culture of Education*. Cambridge, MA: Harvard University Press.

Callaghan, L. 1998. 'Building on an African Worldview', *Early Childhood Matters*, 89: 30–33.

Cochran, M.M. and J.A. Brassard. 1979. 'Child Development and Personal Networks', *Child Development*, 50: 601–16.

Cole, M. and S.R. Cole. 1996. *The Development of Children*. New York: Freeman.

Danziger, K. 2006. 'Comment. Special Issue on Indigenous Psychologies', *International Journal of Psychology*, 41(4): 269–75.

Dasen, P.R., B. Inhelder, M. Lavallée and J. Retschitzki. 1978. *Naissance de l'intelligence chez l'enfant Baoulé de Côte d'Ivoire*. Berne: Hans Huber.

Diawara, M. 1998. 'Toward a Regional Imagery in Africa', in F. Jameson and M. Miyoshi (eds), *The Cultures of Globalization*, pp. 103–24. Durham: Duke University Press.

Dussel, E. 1998. 'Beyond Eurocentrism: The World-System and the Limits of Modernity', in F. Jameson and M. Miyoshi (eds), *The Cultures of Globalization*, pp. 3–31. Durham: Duke University Press.

Ellis, J. 1978. *West African Families in Great Britain*. London: Routledge.

Fafunwa, B. 1974. *A History of Education in Nigeria* London: Allen & Unwin.

Fai, P.J. 1996. *Loan Adaptations in Lamnso' and Effects on the Teaching of English*. Yaounde, Cameroon: DISPES II Memoir of Ecole Normale Superieure, University of Yaounde.

Forsuh, F.W. 2005. *Establishing a Community-Based Counselling Service Centre in Bamenda, Cameroon: Process and Prospects*. Master of Education Dissertation. Bamenda University of Science and Technology, Bamenda, Cameroon.

Gauvain, M. 1995. 'Thinking in Niches: Sociocultural Influences on Cognitive Development', *Human Development*, 38: 25–45.

Gergen, K.J. 1992. 'Toward a Postmodern Psychology', in S. Kvale (ed), *Psychology and Postmodernism*, pp. 17–30. London: Sage Publications.

Goodnow, J.J. 1988. 'Parents, Ideas, Actions, and Feelings: Models and Methods from Developmental and Social Psychology', *Child Development*, 59(2): 286–320.

Harkness, S., C.M. Super and C.H. Keefer. 1992. 'Learning to be an American Parent: How Cultural Models Gain Directive Force', in R.G.

D'Andrade and C. Strauss (eds), *Human Motives and Cultural Models*, pp. 163–78. New York: Cambridge University Press.

Kenyatta, J. 1965. *Facing Mount Kenya*. London: Heinemann.

La Fontaine, J. 1986. 'An Anthropological Perspective on Children in Social Worlds', in M. Richards and P. Light (eds), *Children's Social Worlds*, pp. 27–41. Cambridge: Harvard University Press.

Kishani, B.T. 2001. 'On the Interface of Philosophy and Language in Africa: Some Practical and Theoretical Considerations', *African Studies Review*, 44(3): 27–45.

LeVine, R.A. 2004. 'Challenging Expert Knowledge: Findings from an African Study of Infant Care and Development', in U.P. Gielen and J. Roopnarine (eds), *Childhood and Adolescence: Cross-Cultural Perspectives and Applications*, pp. 149–65. Westport, CT: Praeger.

Maynard, A.E. 2002. 'Cultural Teaching: The Development of Teaching Skills in Maya Sibling Interactions', *Child Development*, 73(3): 969–82.

Mazrui, A.A. 1986. *The Africans*. New York: Praeger.

Ministère de l'Information et de la Culture, Cameroun. 1981. *Encyclopédie de la République Unie du Cameroun*. Douala, Cameroon: Eddy Ness.

Moumouni, A. 1968. *Education in Africa*. New York: Praeger.

Ngeh, M.Y. 1996. *Songs and Social Regulations in the Wimbum Land*. Master of Arts Thesis. Yaounde, Cameroon: Faculty of Arts, University of Yaounde.

Ngoran, G.N. 2005. *An Exploration of Coping Strategies of Marital Relationships in Bamenda, Cameroon*. Master of Education Dissertation. Bamenda, Cameroon: Bamenda University of Science and Technology.

Nkwi, P.N. 1983. 'Traditional Diplomacy, Trade and Warfare in the 19th Century Western Grassfields', *Science and Technology Review*, 1(3–4): 101–16.

Nkwi, P.N. and J. P. Warnier. 1982. *A History of the Western Grassfields*. Yaounde, Cameroon: University of Yaounde Press.

Nsamenang, A.B. 1987a. 'A West African Perspective', in M.E. Lamb (ed), *The Father's Role: Cross-Cultural Perspectives*, pp. 273–93. Hillsdale, NJ: Erlbaum.

———. 1987b. *Kinship Networks and the Socialization of Children: A Bamenda Grassfields Profile*. Bamenda, Cameroon: Institute of Human Sciences.

———. 1992. *Human Development in Cultural Context: A Third World Perspective*. Newbury Park, CA: Sage Publications.

———. 1995. 'Theories of Developmental Psychology for a Cultural Perspective: A Viewpoint from Africa', *Psychology and Developing Societies*, 7(1): 1–19.

———. 1996. 'Cultural Organization of Human Development within the Family Context', in S. Carr and J. Schumaker (eds), *Psychology and Developing Societies*, pp. 60–70. Westport, CT: Greenwood.

Nsamenang, A.B. 2001. 'Indigenous View on Human Development: A West African Perspective', in N.J. Smelser and P.B. Baltes (eds), *International Encyclopedia of the Social and Behavioral Sciences*, pp. 7297–299. London: Elsevier.

————. 2002. 'Adolescence in Sub-Saharan Africa: An Image Constructed from Africa's Triple Inheritance', in B.B. Brown, R.W. Larson and T.S. Saraswathi (eds), *The World's Youth: Adolescence in Eight Regions of the Globe*, pp. 61–104. Cambridge: Cambridge University Press.

————. 2004a. *Cultures of Human Development and Education: Challenge to Growing Up African.* New York: Nova.

————. 2004b. *The Teaching-Learning Transaction: An Africentric Approach to Educational Psychology.* Bamenda, Cameroon: HDRC Publication.

————. 2005a. 'African Family Traditions, Education', in C. Fisher and R. Lerner (eds), *Encyclopedia of Applied Developmental Science*, pp. 61–62. Thousand Oaks, CA: Sage Publications.

————. 2005b. 'Educational Development and Knowledge Flow: Local and Global Forces in Human Development in Africa', *Higher Education Policy*, 18: 275–88.

————. 2005c. 'The Intersection of Traditional African Education with School Learning', in L. Swartz, C. de la Rey and N. Duncan (eds), *Psychology: An Introduction*, pp. 327–37. Cape Town: Oxford University Press.

————. 2006a. 'HIV/AIDS Intervention with Youth in Cameroon: Theoretical Insights and Methodological Challenges', Paper presented at the 19th Biennial Meetings of ISSBD, Melbourne, Australia, 2–9 July.

————. 2006b. 'Human Ontogenesis: An Indigenous African View on Development and Intelligence', *International Journal of Psychology*, 41(4): 293–97.

————. 2008. '(Mis)Understanding Early Childhood Development in Africa: The Force of Local and Global Motives', in M. Garcia, A. Pence and J. Evans (eds), *Africa's Future–Africa's Challenge: Early Childhood Care and Development in Sub-Saharan Africa*, pp. 135–49. Washington, DC: The World Bank.

————. 2007. 'Origins and Development of Scientific Psychology in Afrique Noire', in D. Wedding and M. J. Stevens (eds), *Psychology: IUPsyS Global Resource (Edition 2007)* [CD-ROM], *International Journal of Psychology*, 42 (Suppl. 1).

Nsamenang, A.B. and M.E. Lamb. 1994. 'Socialization of Nso Children in the Bamenda Grassfields of Northwest Cameroon', in P.M. Greenfield and R.R. Cocking (eds), *Cross-Cultural Roots of Minority Child Development*, pp. 133–46. Hillsdale, NJ: Erlbaum.

————. 1995. 'The Force of Beliefs: How the Parental Values of the Nso of Northwest Cameroon Shape Children's Progress Towards Adult Models', *Journal of Applied Developmental Psychology*, 16(4): 613–27.

Ogbu, J.U. 1994. 'From Cultural Differences to Differences in Cultural Frames of Reference', in P.M. Greenfield and R.R. Cocking (eds), *Cross-Cultural Roots of Minority Child Development*, pp. 365–91. Hillsdale, NJ: Erlbaum.

Rabain, J. 1979. *L'enfant du lignage*. Paris: Payot.

Reagan, T. 1996. *Non-Western Educational Traditions: Alternative Approaches to Educational Thought and Practice*. Mahwah, NJ: Erlbaum.

Richards, M. 1986. 'Introduction', in M. Richards and P. Light (eds), *Children's Social Worlds*, pp. 1–25. Cambridge: Harvard University Press.

Rogoff, B. 1990. *Apprenticeship in Thinking: Cognitive Development in Social Context*. New York: Oxford University Press.

———. 2003. *The Cultural Nature of Human Development*. Oxford: Oxford University Press.

Serpell, R. 1993. *The Significance of Schooling: Life-Journeys into an African Society*. Cambridge: Cambridge University Press.

———. 1994. 'An African Social Ontogeny: Review of A. Bame Nsamenang (1992): Human Development in Cultural Context', *Cross-Cultural Psychology Bulletin*, 28(1): 17–21.

Siddiqi, A., E. Hertzman, I. Poureslami, G.L. Irwin and C. Hertzman (eds). 2006. *Total Environment Assessment Model for Early Childhood Development*. Draft Paper prepared on behalf of the Organizational Hub for Early Child Development, a Knowledge Network for ECD World Health Organization, Commission on the Social Indicators of Health. Vancouver: HELP.

Soyinka, W. 1990. 'The African World and the Ethnocultural Debate', in M.K. Asante and K.W. Asante (eds), *African Culture: The Rhythms of Unity*, pp. 13–38. Trenton, NJ: Africa World Press.

Ssennyonga, J.W. 1997. 'Polygyny and Resource Allocation in the Lake Victoria Basin', in T.S. Weisner, C. Bradley and C.P. Kilbride (eds), *African Families in the Crisis of Social Change*, pp. 268–82. Westport, CT: Bergin & Garvey.

Swadener, B.B., M. Kabiru and A. Njenga. 2000. *Does the Village Still Raise the Child? A Collaborative Study of Changing Childrearing and Early Childhood Education in Kenya*. Albany, NY: State University of New York Press.

Tomasello, M., A.C. Kruger and H.H. Ratner. 1993. 'Cultural Learning', *Behavioral and Brain Sciences*, 16: 405–552.

Whiting, B.B. and J.W.M. Whiting. 1975. *Children of Six Cultures: A Psycho-Cultural Analysis*. Cambridge, MA: Harvard University Press.

3

PARTICIPATORY APPROPRIATION AND THE CULTIVATION OF NURTURANCE: A CASE STUDY OF AFRICAN PRIMARY HEALTH SCIENCE CURRICULUM DEVELOPMENT[1]

ROBERT SERPELL

This chapter advances a cultural perspective on applied developmental psychology that conceptualizes education as facilitating the appropriation of new ideas by learners through participating in socially organized activities. The benefits of literacy, mathematics, and health science to a community cannot be gauged by simple aggregation of individual competencies, since the cultural structure of technology involves socially distributed cognition. The technological characteristics of cultural resources, such as, a system of writing, are both constraining and empowering. The cognitive possibilities that they afford are mediated by co-constructive processes among participants in various socially organized activities. Rather than conceiving instruction as the 'de-contextualized' transmission of information, this perspective on education emphasizes the benefits of situating learning opportunities within the socio-cultural context in which the target student activity will be applied in everyday life. Not only does this obviate the problem of 'transfer' of learning that has often arisen in assessments of the impact of formal education, it also provides opportunities for multiple instructional supports within the learner's 'zone of proximal development', and acknowledges the mutually constitutive relationship between culture and cognition. This in turn provides a basis for recruiting the imaginative creativity of young learners in the appropriation of a dynamically evolving cultural system of meanings rather than treating them as passive recipients of fossilized knowledge. This chapter illustrates this perspective with a case study of health science curriculum development in a rural district of northern Zambia.

INVITATION TO PARTICIPATE: A PEDAGOGICAL APPROACH CONDUCIVE TO APPROPRIATION

Ideally, I think, in the field of behavioural development, the relationship between theory and practice should be mutually constitutive. Theoretical formulations should afford practitioners guidance on how to conceptualize their tasks and how to evaluate their actions; and engagement in practice should afford theorists insight into the adequacy of theoretical concepts and models for explaining human behaviour and experience. In this paper, I propose a theoretical conception of how pedagogical intervention can support and channelize personal development, and I argue for its validity by considering an illustrative example of successful educational practice. The central concept in my analysis is *participatory appropriation*.

The concept of participatory appropriation serves as a theoretical resource to explain and illuminate the nature of human development. As such it may serve as a guide to the design of intervention, because it accurately describes what is going on, because it can connect with moral expectations held by parents, teachers, health professionals, and other influential representatives of society, and because it informs the commitment to responsible social action by the research team of which I have been fortunate to be a member.[2] Furthermore, in addition to these general philosophical principles, I wish to claim some African cultural validity for the concept, insofar as indigenous Africans have endorsed it as researchers, teachers, health workers, parents, and indirectly also as children.

The interaction of context with development has been conceptualized in a number of different ways in formal theories of human development (Serpell, 1999a). Rather than regarding context as an external, detached environment that affords information and/or applies reinforcement contingencies, the socio-cultural perspective adopted in this paper construes context as an incorporating system of social activities (Bronfenbrenner, 1979), informed by a system of cultural meanings (D' Andrade, 1984). Developmental change within such a context involves a process of participatory appropriation: children enter a cultural activity as novices and develop by virtue of appropriating the system of meanings that informs the activity. Initially they participate in the activities peripherally, and/or under the guidance of experts or old-timers, and their developmental appropriation of the system of meanings enables them eventually to participate more centrally and with greater authority as full-fledged members of the community of practice who can now claim the culture as their own (Lave and Wenger, 1991; Rogoff, 1993; Serpell, 1997, 2001).

The cognitive development of children arises, as Piaget (1983) and his colleagues have shown, from active exploration. Much of what children learn about the material world as they explore it involves discovering 'affordances' of the environment (Gibson, 1982). In addition to discovering such properties of the physical world, children discover through verbal discourse and other forms of social interaction the other minds that populate their social world, and how to use the language of their culture to communicate about the physical and social world. The disposition to seek out inter-subjectivity with other minds is every bit as fundamental to human development as the desire to master and control the physical environment (Trevarthen, 1980). Moreover, the cultural system of meanings that children encounter as they begin to use language is dynamic and open-ended. Children do not simply adopt the language as they find it, but re-invent it, negotiating the right to transform their community's culture as they appropriate it (Ochs, 1990).

This theoretical view of child development as embedded in social interaction and cultural systems of meaning acknowledges their 'agency' as persons, over and above their behaviour as organisms. This focus of interpretation has moral and strategic implications for practice whose deeper significance is easily overlooked if a purely rhetorical attitude is adopted toward the proposal that the 'other' humans in psychological research be regarded not as subjects, but as participants (American Psychological Association, 1982). Children as newcomers to a cultural activity can be likened to 'apprentices'

(Lave and Wenger, 1991). As they progressively master the demands of the tasks confronting them, they gradually qualify as members of a community of practice, and by the same token acquire authority as owners of the system of cultural meanings that is shared by the community and informs its practices (Serpell, 1997).

The theoretical proposal, then, is that we construe children, not as a set of organisms to be moulded into a pattern of behaviour specified in advance as educational outcomes, but as newcomers to a community of practice, for whom the desirable outcome of a period of apprenticeship is that they would appropriate the system of meanings that informs the community's practices. By appropriating this system, students are expected to make those meanings their own, transforming them in the process, and co-constructing with the rest of the community a new, emerging set of cultural practices.

The opening move of such an enterprise is an invitation to participate. Productive discourse in search of enhanced understanding depends on an egalitarian set of premises—the conditions that the philosopher, Juergen Habermas characterized as the ideal communication situation (McCarthy, 1978). Each party must be in a position to adopt any one of the full range of dialogue roles, so that the outcome of discussion will be determined by the force of the better argument, and not by extrinsic factors of differential power and prestige. Although this idealization is open to criticism (McCarthy, 1976), it has the merit of highlighting some of the barriers to genuine understanding that tend to characterize a great deal of didactic discourse.

Teachers typically do not listen to their students with the same degree of respectful open-mindedness as they expect their students to bring to the interaction. Rather they seek to impose on their students' thinking a preconceived set of constraints, and provide feedback to their students' speech and writing acts primarily in terms of how well the student is conforming to their expectations. A very common form of this type of instructional interaction is the I-R-E routine, in which the sequence of verbal utterances is as follows: teacher initiates—student responds—teacher evaluates (Mehan, 1979). Such ritualized, factitious verbal exchanges have been described as prototypical of lessons in traditional American and European classrooms, and in many African primary schools (Koivukari, 1982; Pontefract and Hardman, 2005). As an alternative to this domineering type of discourse, which they term 'the recitation script', Tharp and

Gallimore (1988) have advocated the model of 'the instructional conversation', in which teachers seek to engage their students in a more authentic exchange of views, and inject their instructional contributions through 'in-flight responsiveness'.

The strategic power of this flexibly adapted style of intervention can be understood with reference to Vygotsky's (1978) concept of the 'zone of proximal development', or zoped, the zone between what a person can perform with the assistance of external support and what he or she can perform without such guidance. The zoped of each individual is different, so that when a pre-structured plan of instruction is addressed to a group of students, it is only likely to mesh with the needs of a small proportion of those within the group. For those whose mastery of the topic is relatively advanced, the instructional input will appear redundant and uninspiring, while for those who lack some of the foundational knowledge and/or skills, the same input will appear opaque and intimidating. In-flight responsiveness draws on a judicious use of questioning and observation to elicit evidence of each student's relevant pre-instructional understanding, and follows the student's orientation with a view to connecting with and recruiting his or her imagination and creativity. At its best, such instructional interaction not only expands the cognitive repertoire of the student, but also leaves the student's own mark on the very culture that s/he is learning about, transforming it in the very process of appropriation. As Cole (1985) put it succinctly, the zoped is thus a mutually constitutive nexus, 'where culture and cognition create each other'.

PARTICIPATORY HEALTH EDUCATION IN AN AFRICAN PRIMARY SCHOOL

Socially distributed cognition

The benefits of literacy, mathematics, and health science to a community cannot be gauged by simple aggregation of individual competencies, since the cultural structure of technology involves socially distributed cognition (Salomon, 1993). For example, in contemporary, cosmopolitan preventive and curative health practices, responsibility for the cognitive and practical work is distributed across many participants in activities that extend across time and space. Consider the task of maintaining healthy growth of an infant during the first five years of life.

Growth-charts

According to the strategy of growth monitoring (Morley and Woodland, 1988), the quality of the match between a young child's nutritional needs and the nutritional inputs that she or he receives can be significantly enhanced by regular weighing of the child and recording of her weight on a chart (see Figure 3.1). The slope of the line graph that emerges on this chart provides critical information for determining whether the child is growing at a normal rate of development. The slope is compared with that of averaged measurements over time of a large standardization sample. In order to make possible such a comparison, information known to the child's primary caregiver (such as the child's date of birth) has to be coordinated with statistical information that has been compiled and organized by scientists. Records have to be made accurately on the chart by people with relevant training, preserved by the child's family, and brought together with the child on a subsequent occasion, to a location where the child can be accurately weighed. And the whole complex of information must be synthesized and interpreted in accordance with scientific guidelines by a competent person and communicated to the responsible caregiver, along with appropriate advice on actions to be taken to maintain or ameliorate the child's current pattern of care.

Learning exercises for primary school students

Building on the work of Morley and his colleagues, Gibbs, and Mutunga (1991) have articulated a set of instructional modules in mathematics that are focused on practical aspects of primary health care, including the monitoring of young children's weight. The Child-to-Child Trust has also for a number of years promoted the idea of involving school-age children in the monitoring of younger children's weight and other indices of health (Hawes, 1988; Otaala, 1982). 'Child to Child' (often abbreviated as CtC) is a broadly conceived approach to the integration of education and health that seeks to mobilize the potential of children as agents of preventive health in their schools, their homes and their community. The educational philosophy expressed in CtC materials centres around respect for the child as a morally responsible member of the community with a basic right to health and education. The child is conceived as an active, exploratory agent who will learn best when she or he makes

Figure 3.1 CHILD-to-CHILD, Twinning Project: MATHEMATICS: Upper: TIMING BIRTHS and GROWTH CHARTS: PART 3

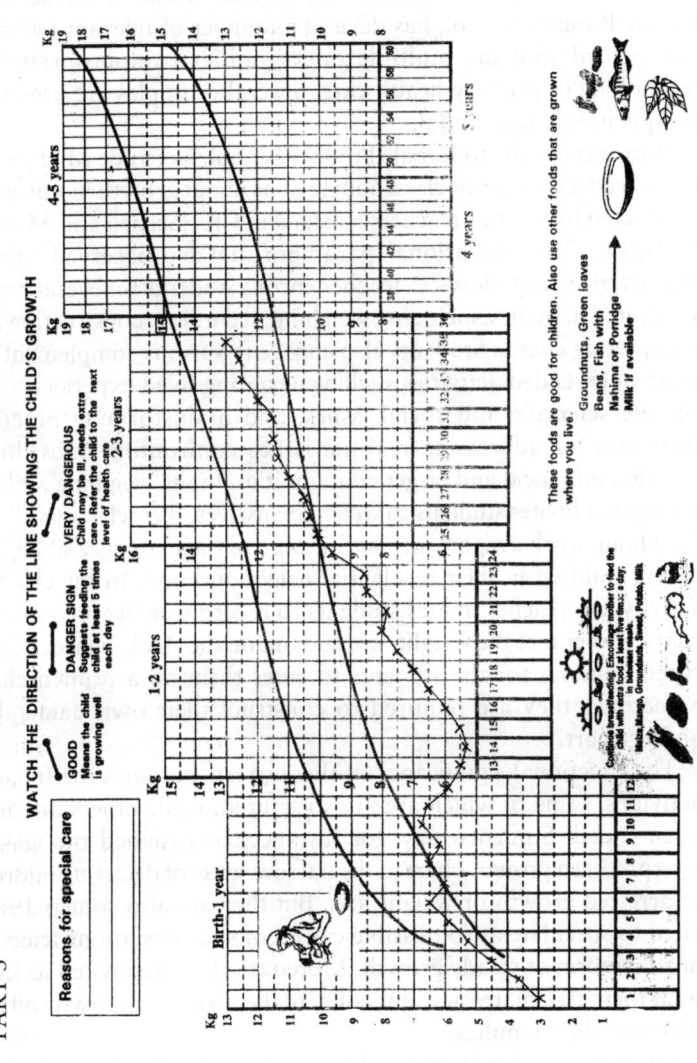

Source: Paul Mumba, Kabale Primary School, Mpika, Zambia.

discoveries—a principle derived from Piaget's (1983) influential theoretical perspective. Under the auspices of Zambia's CtC programme, a group of teachers in the Mpika District of Northern Province has systematically applied these concepts. Paul Mumba, a teacher at Kabale Primary School, has devised a number of relevant exercises that afford students multiple opportunities to appropriate the technology of primary health care. Several examples are presented in Appendices 1, 2, and 3.

During our visits to Kabale Primary School, Gertrude Mwape and I observed a number of classroom lessons about growth monitoring, conducted by various teachers engaged in CtC (Serpell and Mwape, 1998/99). The educational paradigm that we observed can be characterized as follows. A teacher enrolls students in several highly structured activities, including weighing, recording, constructing and interpreting charts. Students also engage in various complementary, more open-ended activities such as narrating lived experience, discussing scientific and social issues, and brainstorming practical strategies for addressing real-life issues confronting individuals, families, and local and larger communities. In the weighing activity, the teacher invites students to weigh themselves, their classmates, and (as a homework assignment) one or more of their younger siblings or young children in their residential neighbourhood. In the charting activity, the teacher invites students to record weights on a growth chart. Sometimes the weights are laid out on the chalk-board, or on a typed handout for the students to enter them on a printed chart. Sometimes they are required to construct their own data table, and/or chart.

The functional significance of these charts becomes the focus of activities, some of which are pre-structured, while others are more open-ended. Students may, for instance, be assigned the task of interpreting a growth-chart in the narrow sense of detecting episodes of arrested growth or weight loss. But they are also sometimes invited to speculate as to possible causes of such deviations from the healthy norm of steady growth. Moreover, they are invited to share with their classmates accounts of actual episodes of growth-related illness in their families.

Students are also invited to brainstorm possible action strategies to ameliorate the situation, both in the short-term with individualized intervention processes such as oral rehydration, and in the longer term with preventive, public health measures such as hand-washing, waste disposal, water purification, and even population planning. These possibilities for active, ameliorative intervention are not merely discussed in theory. The students take on responsibility for applying them in practice, through group projects. These include clearing the school grounds of refuse, and digging rubbish pits; rosters of shared responsibility such as bringing containers of clean water to class each day for students to wash their hands when returning from the latrine, and individualized service projects. Some of the students adopted a younger child and monitored his or her growth and other health indicators by escorting the child for regular check-ups at the local under-five clinic, and, when the occasion arose, assisting with the youngster's health care and supplementary nutrition.

Practical, social, and moral goals of education

The CtC approach at Kabale School stands in marked contrast to the standard paradigm of Institutionalized Public Basic Schooling (IPBS) that has been widely established across the world (Serpell and Hatano, 1997). This paradigm, with its emphasis on text-based classroom lecturing was originally designed for very different social, cultural and economic circumstances, exported to Africa under politically oppressive and exploitative conditions, and only minimally adapted by an indigenous bureaucracy, that now attempts to maintain it with dwindling resources and a set of product-oriented efficiency criteria that tend to constrain the socio-cultural sensitivity of their personnel. Those efficiency criteria derive their legitimacy partly from historical tradition, and partly from the advocacy of certain economically-oriented technical specialists and agencies (Hawes and Stephens, 1990). Several dysfunctional consequences flow from adhering to them. For instance, primary schools and the local communities they are supposed to serve tend to conspire in adopting an extractive definition of educational success as leaving one's community of origin to enter an outside, more privileged world (Serpell, 1993). This definition is fundamentally self-defeating, since it legitimates a stereotyped equation between intellectual progress and alienation from the indigenous culture. Moreover, preoccupation with input-output statistics serves to divert attention from questions of educational quality (Hawes and Stephens, 1990). For instance, the 'narrowing staircase model' of schooling, tends to overlook, and sometimes even to undermine, the cultivation of social responsibility (Serpell, 1993).

If the paradigm is to be reformed, one of the most important steps is for educators to legitimize parallel tracks to various valued outcomes of education, especially at the local level. The school needs to expand its public criteria of what constitutes a successful outcome of several years of enrolment: instead of defining the only index of success as passing an exam to proceed to the next level of the curriculum, schools and the communities they serve need to acknowledge as alternative indices of educational success more directly observable behaviours with ostensible relevance to local needs, such as food production, nutrition, and health (Serpell, 1999b).

In order to work toward such locally valuable outcomes, teachers and parents need to agree on dimensions of personal development that deserve promotion and recognition, other than those conventionally emphasized in the regular curriculum of IPBS. Some of our exploratory quantitative studies using questionnaires and rating scales with primary, basic and high school teachers suggest that teachers with exposure to CtC got to know their students better than non-CtC teachers on the following dimensions: practical problem solving, self-confidence, healthy lifestyle, taking responsibility, co-operating with others, and nurturance (Adamson-Holley, 1999).

Cooperative learning

In addition to the emphasis on health across the curriculum, and the explicit promotion of development toward practical, social, and moral goals, another striking feature of the pedagogical practice in several of the classes at Kabale Primary School is the organization of learning opportunities around group work. In Mumba's class of about 60 students, students were grouped for extensive periods of time in teams composed of six children of mixed gender and academic standing, to discuss questions posed by the teacher prior to plenary class debates, to complete written work assignments, and to design and execute projects in the community.

The significance of this instructional practice can be construed in a number of different ways. It has often been advocated as a pragmatic strategy for classroom management in large classes, freeing the teacher to attend more intensively to the needs of individual students in rotation. The importance of adjusting the form and pace of instruction to characteristics of the individual learner is a very widely agreed principle shared among the Behaviourist, Piagetian, and Vygotskian perspectives on learning and development.

The Vygotskian rationale has been well articulated, for instance, by Tharp and Gallimore (1988) in their account of the highly successful Kamehameha Early Education Program (KEEP) in Hawaii. In addition, some advocates of cooperative learning arrangements have argued that peer-mediated learning affords special opportunities for cognitive growth, although the key processes for achieving this remain a matter of controversy (Forman and McPhail, 1993).

Mumba (2000), himself, values these arrangements for their productivity of both social and personal progress. He construes the organization of his students into 'cooperative learning groups' as part of a strategic process of 'setting up of a participation atmosphere' conducive to 'democratization' of the learning community constituted by his class. Another component of this strategy was to introduce the students to an awareness of their rights as children. He describes a pedagogical focus on children taking responsibility for evaluation of their own performance, that of their peers, and that of the teacher; and for active participation in decision-making about activities to be undertaken by the class. He claims a number of positive outcomes for this strategy which has evolved over a period of several years of experimentation. It has, in his own words: 'created a good classroom climate; increased participation in learning built self-esteem in the students; improved interpersonal relationships; improved punctuality and lessened absenteeism; improved the performance and image of the girl child; improved the quality of teaching; helped to avoid "burn-out" by teachers; introduced the community to participate in their children's education; developed leadership qualities in the leaders of learning groups; and improved preventive maintenance of school structures, contents and environment' (Mumba, 2000).

A crucial condition for the success of this innovative approach to education, according to Mumba, is for teachers 'to build a genuine relationship with their pupils...a teacher should seek opportunities to interact with the pupils at all costs, and to enrich this relationship he must reach a level of joining their conversation without raising suspicions among the pupils' (Mumba, 2000: 32). In articulating his philosophical rationale for the form of practice that he has designed over the years, Mumba has increasingly drawn on published social, psychological and educational theory, appropriating ideas from the texts which the research team has introduced to him, and placing his own distinctive mark on them while reflectively interpreting his practical teaching experience.

Altough CtC was proclaimed in Zambia as a policy initiative in the mid-1980s to be introduced nationwide in all public schools (Sianjibu-Miyato, 1993), two independent assessments commissioned by the Zambian Government concluded that, in contrast to the vibrant enthusiasm we witnessed at Kabale Primary School, by the late 1990s the great majority of schools across the country had only very superficially appropriated the concept of Child-to-Child, reducing it to little more than an extra-curricular, voluntary club (Chiwela, 1996; Gibbs, 1997). Mumba (2000) argues that the main impediment to widespread effective implementation of CtC in Zambia has been resistance by teachers to the organizational change that it requires, namely democratization of class activities.[3] He attributes the resistance to democratization to both an indigenous African cultural tradition that prescribes authoritarian relations between adults and children and to a gap that has been created historically between parents and schools. He notes that inviting Kabale school students and their parents to participate in the design of the syllabus served to enhance the relevance of the curriculum to the felt needs of the community. By emphasizing the rights and responsibilities of children in their educational practices, primary school teachers can 'influence the larger society' and 'help to transform this nation for the better'.

Project activities in the home community

Another striking feature of the activities at Kabale Primary School is the emphasis on assigning students practical activities in their home community. A recurrent theme, derived from the CtC approach is termed 'twinning'. Contrary to what might be expected from the term, these pairings are generally between an older and a younger child, and involve some kind of explicitly asymmetrical, adoptive or mentoring relationship. The child to be adopted may be a younger sibling within the student's own family, a neighbour, or a student attending the same school. The focus is nurturant, with an overt emphasis on service by the older child to the younger child, but, as I will discuss later, the developmental benefits of such a relationship for the older child may also be considerable. In the case of growth monitoring, the assignment involves the older child taking responsibility for negotiating acceptance of his or her good faith by the younger child's parents, a task made easier by the existence of an indigenous cultural tradition of delegating caregiving responsibilities for young children to older children in the family or community.

At its best, the innovative approach to education spearheaded by the CtC teachers at Kabale Primary School affords opportunities for teachers and students to negotiate a shared understanding and appreciation of the significance of growth-monitoring. They co-construct an application of the technology to the life of the community that reflects their multiple, complementary perspectives. Ideally, through participation in this and other related activities, children will gradually appropriate the cultural practice of primary health care, including both the technology of growth charts, immunization, and so on, and the underlying meaning system of nutritional monitoring and disease prevention, as conceptualized in contemporary social medicine. The child will thus develop into an informed and responsible member of the community of practice of primary health care, and an owner of the system of meanings that informs the clinical practice as it evolves.

DISSEMINATION AND APPROPRIATION OF A SEMINAL IDEA: THE CHILD-TO-CHILD APPROACH

Cultural and historical origins

One feature of the successful educational approach at Kabale Primary School that seems to me to be of particular importance is the special attunement or receptiveness of indigenous African cultural practices and values to the emphasis of CtC on nurturant mentoring relationships between older and younger children.

Several child development researchers in Africa have stressed that the responsibility for nurturance is more widely shared in African family traditions than might be expected from the Western, middle-class paradigm of the nuclear family. Indeed, rather than delegation of a burden, the practice of involving children in the care of younger siblings is better construed in African cultural terms as a reflection of two principles: the sharing of responsibility for the young amongst all members of the family, and the socialization of the elder child through a priming process for learning adult roles (Nsamenang, 1992). Whereas UNICEF has at times tended to include the domestic participation of African girls in child care as an example of exploitative child labour, it is important to realize that in many African communities with a subsistence economy, child labour can be legitimately interpreted 'an indigenous educational strategy that keeps children in contact with existential realities and the activities of daily life—[that] represents the participatory component of social integration' (Nsamenang, 1992: 157).

Moreover, a child nurse 'is expected' not only to protect and feed, but also 'to sing to, play with, and entertain her or his young charge', an expectation which seems to acknowledge and capitalize upon 'a natural playfulness' (Harkness and Super, 1992). The channelization of that social playfulness towards infants and toddlers is probably less directly governed by disciplinary management than it is a product of pro-social attitudes cultivated in the earliest phase of socialization. Rabain (1979), for instance, has described for the Wolof tradition in Senegal how adults encourage even infants and toddlers to interpret their emotions in terms of sharing and nurturance.

So deeply entrenched are the cultural expectations of older children's participation in the nurture and care of their younger siblings, that as Weisner (1989: 89) suggests of the Aba-Luyia of Kenya, 'mothers use evidence that a child has the ability to give and receive social support, and assist others, as markers of a child's more general developmental level, much as an American parent might use literacy skills such as knowing the alphabet, or verbal facility, to show how grown-up or precocious his or her child is'. Traditionally, across many societies, 'children are socialized within this system both through apprenticeship learning of their family roles and responsibilities and through self-ascribed cultural standards and beliefs about their appropriate role behaviour according to age and gender'. (Weisner, 1997: 14).

Udell (2001) conducted a qualitative analysis of texts (many of them unpublished) to explore the various philosophical and cultural influences that have converged over time on different key actors in the promotion of the CtC approach. Both of the major originators of the CtC curriculum, Morley and Hawes, spent formative years of their lives in Africa and were profoundly influenced by what they observed there and elsewhere in the Third World. For Morley the key motivation was to promote early childhood health and nutrition as a public health intervention, while for Hawes a crucial value of the approach was its incorporation of Piaget's conception of child development as driven by active investigation of the world. For the

Catholic missionaries advocating the introduction of CtC in Zambia, an equally important motive may have been promotion of the Christian value of service. All of these complementary philosophical themes latched onto a set of indigenous cultural practices that informed the assessment by the indigenous Zambian teachers that CtC constituted a 'culturally compatible' form of curriculum (Jordan, 1992). This helped to inspire them to appropriate the concept and articulate its implementation in their schools.

Local parental views on the promotion of nurturance

One strand of our research in Mpika has been directed at documenting the current attitudes and beliefs of local parents in this regard, and their perceptions of how the CtC programme at the school relates to their sense of cultural tradition. A stratified sample of forty-one parents were interviewed in 1996 in the catchment population of the Kabale School.

Most parents said they regard the practice of children of primary school age caring for younger children as part of an old Zambian tradition and reported that they were expected to do this in their own childhood at home. But only about half of them recalled this being a theme at their own school. Most parents (of both boys and girls) said they require their children to do this at home. On the question of what benefits the older child derives from such activity, parents cited growth of a nurturant attitude, a sense of responsibility and preparation for parenthood, but also intrinsic pleasure and a sense of personal worth. While the pattern of these responses did not vary significantly according to the gender of the child, the more subjective benefits were especially apparent to parents of academically low-achieving students. Many, but not all, of the parents interviewed were aware of other aspects of the CtC approach and were generally quite supportive, although a few were skeptical of its relevance to their child's prospects of academic success.

Life-journeys of students after leaving primary school

One of the most widely known indices of academic achievement in Zambian society is the national Secondary School Selection Examination (SSSE), a centrally set, computer-marked exam composed of six multiple-choice papers, covering the subject area of English, mathematics, social studies, science, and special papers I and II, which are respectively verbal and non-verbal tests of reasoning designed to assess intellectual aptitude. Separate cut-off criteria are set each year for admission of boys and girls in each province based on the distribution of scores and the availability of places in secondary schools.

Using this measure of achievement, one of the two grade seven CtC classes at Kabale (taught by Paul Mumba) achieved an exceptionally high level of academic performance in November 1996, with twenty-one of the fifty-seven enrolled students (forty-eight of whom sat for the exam) qualifying for admission to secondary school, and a further twenty-one qualifying for admission to basic school.[4] When both types of grade eight class are combined, this yields an overall progression rate of 74 per cent, as compared with 43 per cent for the other CtC class, and 33 per cent and 29 per cent respectively for the two non-CtC grade seven classes at the same school. Two-thirds of Mr Mumba's successful candidates were girls. Although there is a policy of affirmative action in favour of girls' progression to secondary and basic school, implemented by setting a lower cut-off criterion for girls in each region than for boys, it is noteworthy that in this class, the average absolute score obtained by girls (692) was almost equal to that obtained by boys (691).

Relevance of psychosocial dimensions
to academic achievement

The significance of several of the dimensions of personal development emphasized by the CtC approach extends well beyond academic achievement, especially beyond those aspects of achievement that it is designed to assess. Qualities such as responsibility, cooperativeness, and nurturance are conventionally regarded by teachers as complementary to, and independent of, the qualities that are conducive to academic achievement, such as verbal and mathematical abilities, or intellectual curiosity. In CtC classes, however, we learned of efforts by the teacher to cultivate these non-traditional qualities both for their own intrinsic value and as resources for the successful mastery of academic topics by study groups. In the case of practical problem-solving, we also saw evidence of CtC teachers investing considerable effort in connecting the substance of the curriculum with real-life, practical problems confronted by the students and their community.[5]

Two years later, a sub-sample of the Kabale grade seven graduates were followed up in grade nine by Adamson-Holley (1999) at two local basic schools and two residential, single-sex High Schools. In the basic schools, teachers rated the girls who graduated from the CtC programme at Kabale significantly higher on average than their current classmates on nurturance, cooperativeness and taking responsibility. But these predictable, enduring consequences of exposure to the CtC approach were not confirmed for boys, nor for either gender among students enrolled in the high schools. CtC students appeared to have less opportunities at the secondary schools to apply the cooperative, pro-social skills and attitudes they had acquired at primary school than those enrolled in basic schools. Adamson-Holley (1999: 2) concluded that 'while the dominant culture of the educational establishment appears too conservative to incorporate CtC philosophy as a whole, elements of CtC could be incorporated, thus achieving some modest amelioration of the status quo'.

Life prospects outside the academy

Of equal interest are the future life journeys of the graduates of CtC curriculum who discontinue their schooling after grade seven. This pattern of behaviour, sometimes designated 'dropping out of school' continues to be the norm for the majority of children completing primary school in Zambia and elsewhere on the continent. I have discussed elsewhere (Serpell, 1993) the tragically demoralizing impact of public stigma on these young people, especially in the first few months and years after they learn of their academic 'failure'. Yet, many of them subsequently achieve satisfactory integration and contribute significantly to the welfare of their natal communities.

One likely implication of the cooperative learning arrangements used in the CtC classes at Kabale was suggested by Paul Mumba. He expected the CtC groups formed in grade seven to continue to function as a source of mutual support over the years to come. Confirmation of this prediction was reported by Adamson-Holley for a number of the adolescents who were continuing their schooling. Some of those she interviewed at the more prestigious local high schools had voluntarily established a practice of meeting regularly with their peers at local basic schools to share experiences and provide informal tutorial assistance with mastery of the grade nine curriculum.

Another impressive longer-term outcome came to my attention, when I had the opportunity to visit, together with a University of Zambia student, the home of a young woman of eighteen almost three years after she had completed grade seven and left Kabale school. We called on her without advance notice in her home, which was located in a very low-income neighbourhood of Mpika. She was now married and nursing her first child, and when asked what she remembered learning at school, she mentioned growth-monitoring and oral rehydration. So we pressed her for an example of how this had been of value to her community. She then recounted advising one of her friends, who also had a baby, on how to handle an episode of diarrhoea by means of oral rehydration using the home-made solution of sugar, salt and water they had learned about at school.

From a broader perspective, we may ask the question: how fundamental and intractable are the incompatibilities between the authoritarian, extractive staircase model of IPBS on the one hand and the key elements of the successful CtC approach, such as co-operative learning arrangements, outreach activities and nurturant mentoring relationships? The challenge is for education and health personnel to come together with parents in the community they aspire to serve, and convince them that these innovations do not jeopardize any of their crucial expectations of public schooling but that they have the potential to add to the traditional goals of imparting skills and knowledge, important empowering outcomes for boys and girls in the socio-emotional domain, and for the community as a whole by laying the foundations of a healthier future. The case to be made is that CtC is a 'win-win' formula that affords academically talented students an opportunity to learn to take responsibility and on the other hand enables the needy to be included and to receive support from their peers in the confident expectation of mutual benefit. Extrapolating these implications of a successful educational innovation for the wider system of public schooling rests on a conception of the activity of teaching as centered on the cultivation of personal growth, of which one defining dimension is social responsibility.

CONCLUSION

Several major developments have taken place since the Zambian CtC programme was first implemented. Indirect applications of the earlier work have centered on the systematic promotion of children's rights through the establishment of class and school councils, and on the involvement of preadolescent children in the design of play-based preschool programmes.

The class council programme has built on the principle of recognizing children's agency in their development through inviting their active participation in school activities which was articulated in Mumba's (2000) paper on democratization of primary classrooms. Further impetus arose from the joint participation of Mwape and Mumba in an international training programme in 2003–04 on 'Child rights, classroom and school management', which brought together at the University of Lund in Sweden multilevel national teams from eleven countries to conceptualize and plan a project in each country based on the UN Convention on the Rights of the Child. The Zambian team engaged in a consultative process at Kabale School that culminated in the establishment of class councils and a school council. Important inspiration for this initiative came from what the participants saw in place in Swedish primary schools. Subsequent elaboration has drawn on the model of school councils in UK. A national toolkit has been compiled drawing on the experience of Kabale and several other Zambian schools (Mwape et al., 2006), which articulates three principal objectives: giving voice to children's feelings and desires in opposition to those of adults, affirmation of gender equality, and promotion of structured participation in school governance. The toolkit offers a set of explicit rules and procedures for enabling class and school councils to address those objectives.

The emphasis of CtC on the cultivation of nurturance is not reflected in the school councils programme, but has continued to find a place at Kabale school in the participatory design by upper primary school children of play activities for stimulating the development of thinking in children of preschool and lower primary school age. Students are assigned to research such activities in consultation with their parents and report back in class on what they have learned. Reflecting on whether the cooperative learning theme of CtC has been sustained over the past decade, Mumba observed that 'students continue to visit each other and share common problems' (Mumba, personal communication, 2006). However, the focus of their cooperative activities has shifted somewhat. Due to the country's economic problems, most families are focused on ways of generating income, and include the children in this. So when the school teachers look for the best ways of helping their students, they focus more on income-generating activities in school that the children can take home, such as, making toys and simple artistic designs for sale, and shoe repair.

Together these developments represent a significant shift away from the integrative theme of participatory promotion of child health that informed the CtC approach that we observed in the 1990s. On the other hand, what has been retained is an emphasis of children's agency in the design of intervention programmes to foster and channelize their psychological development (Eckensberger, 2003), and on the need to connect the school curriculum with local cultural practices that acknowledge the legitimacy of children's participation in the domestic economy (Nsamenang, 2003).

APPENDIX 1

Instructional resources designed by Paul Mumba, Kabale Primary School, Mpika, Zambia

The road to health charts are important (see Figure 3.1). They help mothers know when their children need more nutritious food and special attention. They also help health workers better understand the needs of the child and its family. They also let the mother know when she is doing a good job. For example, for the health of both mothers and children, parents should wait until their youngest child is at least two years old before having another baby.

Questions

1. Study the chart and write answers for the questions below.
In the first year of the child's life, the mother stopped breast feeding her child:
   (a) Which month was this?
   (b) What do you think happened?
2. At ten months, the child developed diarrhoea.
   (a) What happened to his weight?
   (b) How would you have stopped the diarrhoea if you were the mother?
3. What caused the difference in weight between the tenth month and the twelfth month?

4. However, the mother learnt how important it is to give the nourishing food.
   (a) In which month did this happen?
   (b) What reason can you give for the answer above?
5. (a) How many times should a very small child feed in a day?
   (b) Give a reason for the answer above?
6. Find the child's weight at:
   (a) 2 1/2 years
   (b) 1 1/3 years
   (c) 1 1/4 years
7. Write in three ways a mother can be helped from the growth chart.
   Prepared by: Paul Mumba.

Reference and help from: *Children for Health*; Willam Gibbs/Mutunga Peter, *Health into Mathematics*; David Werner, *Where There is No Doctor*.

APPENDIX 2

Kabale primary school, child-to-child twinning project: mathematics. children's clinic (graphs)

The information below shows the number of children being brought to the under-five clinic on 14 November 1995. This information was provided by grade 6D of Kabale Primary School.

Table 3.1

Period	No. of children
0–1 year	83
1–2 years	62
2–3 years	9
3–4 years	0
4–5 years	1

Table 3.2

Upward	Downward	Static
60	57	38

Study the above tables and answer the questions below:

1. Show the information in Table 3.1 using bar graphs scale: 1 cm = 1 year across and 1 mm = 1 child up.

2. Why are there more attendants in the first year than the rest?
3. Find the total number of children who attended the clinic.
4. Show the information in Table 3.2 using the scale: 1 cm = 1 box across and 1 mm = 1 child up.
5. Give one reason why some graphs were static.
6. From the information in Table 3.2, find out the total number of children doing badly.
7. Most parents complained that the downward movements of their graphs was due to diarrhoea. List 3 causes of diarrhoea.
8. Suggest solutions to the above causes in your community.

APPENDIX 3

Kabale primary school child-to-child group twinning: upper primary English composition/controlled writing

The following topics on child-to-child methodology have been tried out by children in Grade 6, 1995.

1. You have received a letter from your auntie telling about the sickness of your (baby) cousin from a disease called kwashiorkor. Kwashiorkor comes when a child does not eat enough proteins. Your auntie suspects witchcraft at the neighbourhood. Reply to your auntie telling the causes of kwashiorkor and how it could be prevented. Mention the sources of proteins and what they do to the body.
2. A friend of yours has written to you. He wants you to tell him about tooth decay because his brother is suffering from it. Write in your letter explaining the causes of tooth decay and ways of avoiding it. Your former classmate who stopped school because of being pregnant has given birth to a baby boy. You feel she should know some information on breast feeding. Write a letter to her telling all you could on the importance of breast feeding. Tell the importance of colostrum.
3. Your pen pal has written to you and in his/her letter, he has mentioned that he began smoking cigarettes. Write to him immediately telling the dangers of smoking. Let him be aware of harmful chemicals such as tar, nicotine and carbon monoxide. You can make mention of the disease he could be at risk (danger) of.
4. Your friend in another country has heard about twinning within groups which is being done in your class. He wants to learn from you so that he with other pupils can adopt your ideas. Tell him about the good things about this method and how it has helped you.

5. There is an outbreak of diarrhoea in a town of Isoka among children. Write a letter to your sister in that district telling about the causes of diarrhoea and how it could be treated locally. (The same could be done for another disease like malaria, and so on).

6. Write a letter to your elder sister who wants to know more about immunization. In your letter tell about the six killer diseases and when immunization should be completed. Include the dangers of not immunizing children.

N.B. These letters could be easily written if pupils are prepared in terms of surveys in community, discussions in twinning within groups, poster making and other practical activities.

Prepared and tried out by Paul Mumba. Ideas adapted from Child-to-Child activity sheets and Children Health.

NOTES

1. An earlier version of this chapter was presented as a keynote address to the 4th African Regional Workshop, International Society for the Study of Behavioural Development, in Windhoek, Namibia: July 1998. The research described in this paper was initiated under a grant from the African Forum for Children's Literacy in Science, and Technology and the Rockefeller Foundation to the University of Zambia, where the author held an appointment as Visiting Professor in the Department of Psychology.

2. The research team was initially constituted in 1995 by the author and Ms Gertrude Mwape, Lecturer in the Psychology Department of the University of Zambia. On our first exploratory visit to Mpika, we were joined by two undergraduate students of the University of Zambia as Research Assistants, Ms Chisha Serpell and Mr Humphrey Washanga (both of whom are since deceased). Arising from our discussions in Mpika, the team was expanded to include Mr Patrick Kangwa, Mr Paul Mumba, and Mr Clement Mumbo, all Teachers at Kabale Basic School. In 1997 further data collection was undertaken in Mpika by another undergraduate student of UNZA, Ms Teza Nakazwe, and a recent graduate of the University, Ms Chimika Mwale. Following my return to Baltimore in 1996, two graduate students of Applied Developmental Psychology at the University of Maryland, Baltimore County joined the team: Ms (now Dr) Care Udell (who conducted documentary research on the origins of the Child-to-Child programme in Mpika for her Masters thesis), and later Ms (now Dr) Dorothy Adamson-Holley (who visited Mpika in 1998 to collect data for her doctoral dissertation study).

3. Mumba (2000) describes several complementary entry-points for the promotion of democratization: introduction of students to the notion of children's rights; creation of cooperative learning groups; engaging students in performance evaluation (of their own performance, that of their peers, and that of their teacher); involving students in decision-making (in relation to academic activities and preventive maintenance of school facilities).

4. All Basic Schools offer Grade 8 and Grade 9 classes attached to primary schools. A less stringent set of cut-off marks has been used for admission to 8th Grade classes at Basic Schools.

5. Indeed, using our rating scales, which were anchored with examples of relevant observable behaviour generated by Zambian teachers, we found, using multiple regression analysis, that in the two CtC classes at Kabale School, practical problem-solving ability was significantly predictive of SSSE scores and academic standing within the class only marginally so, whereas in the non-CtC classes only academic standing was predictive.

REFERENCES

Adamson-Holley, D. 1999. 'Personal Dimensions and Their Relation to Education: A Follow-Up Study of Students Graduating from the Child-to-Child Program in Mpika, Zambia'. PhD Dissertation. Baltimore, MD: University of Maryland Baltimore County.

American Psychological Association. 1982. *Ethical Principles in the Conduct of Research with Human Participants*. Washington, DC: American Psychological Association.

Bronfenbrenner, U. 1979. *The Ecology of Human Development*. Cambridge, MA: Harvard University Press.

Chiwela, J. M. 1996. 'Child-to-Child Programme Development and Mapping: An Assessment Report of the Developmental Level of Child-to-Child Program in Zambia', Lusaka: GRZ Ministry of Education/UNICEF.

Cole, M. 1985. 'The Zone of Proximal Development: Where Culture and Cognition Create Each Other', in J.V. Wertsch (ed.), *Culture, Communication and Cognition: Vygotskian Perspectives*, pp. 146–61. Cambridge: Cambridge University Press.

D'Andrade. R. 1984. 'Cultural Meaning Systems', in R.A. Shweder and R. Levine (eds), *Culture Theory: Essays on Mind, Self and Emotion*, pp. 88–119. Cambridge: Cambridge University Press.

Eckensberger, L.H. 2003. 'Wanted: A Contextualized Psychology: Plea for a Cultural Psychology Based on Action Theory', in T.S. Saraswathi (ed.), *Cross-Cultural Perspectives in Human Development: Theory, Research and Applications*, pp. 70–101. New Delhi: Sage Publications.

Forman, E. and J. McPhail. 1993. 'Vygotskian Perspective on Children's Collaborative Problem-Solving Activities', in E. Forman, N. Minick and A. Stone (eds), *Contexts for Learning: Sociocultural Dynamics in Children's Development*, pp. 213–29. New York: Oxford University Press.

Gibbs, W. 1997. *Evaluation of the Child-to-Child Programme in Zambia*. Limited Circulation Report. Lusaka: GRZ Ministry of Education.

Gibbs, W. and P. Mutunga. 1991. *Health into Mathematics*. London: Longman/British Council.

Gibson, E.J. 1982. 'The Concept of Affordances: The Renascence of Functionalism', in A. Collins (ed.), *The Concept of Development: The Minnesota Symposia on Child Development,*15: 55–81. Hillsdale, NJ: Erlbaum.

Harkness, S. and C. Super. 1992. 'Shared Child Care in East Africa: Sociocultural Origins and Developmental Consequences', in M.E. Lamb, K.J. Sternberg, C.P. Hwang and A. Broberg (eds), *Child Care in Context*, pp. 441–62. Hillsdale, NJ: Erlbaum.

Hawes, H. 1988. *Child-to-Child: Another Path to Learning*. Hamburg, Germany: UNESCO Institute for Education.

Hawes, H. and D. Stephens. 1990. *Questions of Quality*. Harlow, Essex, UK: Longman.

Jordan, C. 1992. 'The Role of Culture in Minority School Achievement', *The Kamehameha Journal of Education,* 3(2): 53–67.

Koivukari, M. 1982. 'Rote Learning, Comprehension and Participation by the Learners in Zairian Classrooms', *Jyvaskyla Studies in Education*, 49. Jyvaskyla, Finland: Jyvaskylan Yliopisto.

Lave, J. and E. Wenger, 1991. *Situated Learning: Legitimate Peripheral Participation*. Cambridge: Cambridge University Press.

McCarthy, J.A. 1976. 'A Theory of Communicative Competence', in P. Connerton (ed.), *Critical Sociology*, pp. 470–97. Harmondsworth, UK: Penguin.

———. 1978. *The Critical Theory of Juergen Habermas*. London: Hutchinson.

Mehan, B. 1979. *Learning Lessons: Social Organization in the Classroom*. Cambridge, MA: Harvard University Press.

Morley, D. and M. Woodland. 1988. *See How They Grow: Monitoring Child Growth for Appropriate Health Care in Developing Countries*. London: MacMillan.

Mumba, P. 2000. 'Democratisation of Primary Classrooms in Zambia: A Case Study of its Implementation in a Rural Primary School in Mpika', paper presented at International Special Education Congress 2000, University of Manchester, UK, July 24–28. Available online at http://www.isec2000.org.uk/abstracts/papers_m/mumba_2.htm (downloaded on 30 May 2008).

Mwape, G.K., H. Kafula and V. Tembo-Musonda. 2006. *Toolkit for Establishing Class and School Councils*. Lusaka: University of Zambia.

Nsamenang, A.B. 1992. *Human Development in Cultural Context: A Third World Perspective*. Newbury Park, CA: Sage Publications.

———. 2003. 'Conceptualising Human Development and Education in Sub-Saharan Africa at the Interface of Indigenous and Exogenous Influences', in T.S. Saraswathi (ed.), *Cross-Cultural Perspectives in Human Development: Theory, Research and Applications*, pp. 213–35. New Delhi: Sage Publications.

Ochs, E. 1990. 'Indexicality and Socialization', in J. W. Stigler, R. A. Shweder and G. Herdt (eds), *Cultural Psychology*, pp. 287–308. Cambridge, MA: Harvard University Press.

Otaala, B. 1982. 'The Child-to-Child Program in the Context of Educational Problems in Africa'. *Botswana Educational Research Journal*, 1(1): 39–51.

Piaget, J. 1983. 'Piaget's Theory', in W. Kessen and P. H . Mussen (eds), *History, Theory and Methods, Handbook of Child Psychology*, Vol.1, pp. 103–28. New York: Wiley.

Pontefract, C. and F. Hardman. 2005. 'The Discourse of Classroom Interaction in Kenyan Primary Schools', *Comparative Education*, 41: 87–106.

Rabain, J. 1979. *L'enfant du lignage*. Paris: Payot.

Rogoff, B. 1993. 'Children's Guided Participation and Participatory Appropriation in Sociocultural Activity', in R. Wozniak and K. Fischer (eds), *Development in Context: Acting and Thinking in Specific Environments*, pp. 121–53. Hillsdale, NJ: Erlbaum.

Salomon, G. (ed.). 1993. *Distributed Cognitions: Psychological and Educational Considerations*. Cambridge: Cambridge University Press.

Serpell, R. 1993. *The Significance of Schooling: Life-Journeys in an African Society*. Cambridge: Cambridge University Press.

———. 1997. 'Literacy Connections Between School and Home: How Should We Evaluate Them?' *Journal of Literacy Research*, 29(4): 587–616.

———. 1999a. 'Theoretical Conceptions of Human Development', in L. Eldering and P. Leseman (eds), *Effective Early Intervention: Cross-Cultural Perspectives*, pp. 41–66. New York: Falmer.

———. 1999b. 'Local Accountability to Rural Communities: A Challenge for Educational Planning in Africa', in F. Leach and A. Little (eds), *Education, Cultures and Economics: Dilemmas for Development*, pp. 107–35. New York: Garland.

———. 2001. 'Cultural Dimensions of Literacy Promotion and Schooling', in L. Verhoeven and C. Snow (eds), *Literacy and Motivation*, pp. 243–73. Mahwah, NJ: Erlbaum.

Serpell, R. and G. Hatano. 1997. 'Education, Literacy and Schooling', in J.W. Berry, P.R. Dasen and T.S. Saraswathi (eds), *Handbook of*

Cross-Cultural Psychology, pp. 345–82. Boston, 2nd edition, Volume 2. MA: Allyn & Bacon.

Serpell, R. and G. Mwape. 1998/99. 'Participatory Appropriation of Health Science and Technology: A Case Study of Innovation in Basic Education in a Rural District of Zambia', *African Social Research,* 41/42: 60–89.

Sianjibu-Miyato, H. 1993. 'History of Child-to-Child in Zambia', in S.M. Luswata (ed.), *Child to Child in Zambia Orientation Manual,* pp. xx-xx. Lusaka: GRZ Ministry of Education.

Tharp, R. G. and R. Gallimore. 1988. *Rousing Minds to Life,* Cambridge: Cambridge University Press.

Trevarthen, C. 1980. 'The Foundations of Intersubjectivity: Development of Interpersonal and Cooperative Understanding of Infants', in D. R. Olson (ed.), *The Social Foundations of Language and Thought: Essays in Honour of Jerome S. Bruner,* pp. 316–42. New York: Norton.

Udell, C. 2001. Educational Innovation: A Case Study of Child-to-Child in Zambia. Master of Arts Thesis. Baltimore, MD: University of Maryland Baltimore County.

Vygotsky, L. S. 1978. *Mind in Society: Development of Higher Psychological Processes.* M. Cole, V. John-Steiner, S. Scribner and E. Souberman (eds). Cambridge: Harvard University Press.

Weisner, T. 1989. 'Cultural and Universal Aspects of Social Support for Children: Evidence from the Abaluyia of Kenya', in D. Belle (ed.), *Children's Social Networks and Social Supports,* pp. 70–90. New York: Wiley.

———. 1997. 'Support for Children and the African Family Crisis', in T.S. Weisner, C. Bradley and P.L. Kilbride (eds), *African Families and the Crisis of Social Change,* pp. 20–44. Westport, CT: Bergin & Garvey.

4

SITUATED LEARNING AND COMPAGNONNAGE FORMATION: IMPLICATIONS FOR THE EDUCATION SYSTEMS OF POOR (AND RICH) NATIONS[1]

JOHN D. HERZOG

THE CURRENT IMPASSE IN EDUCATION

If one compares, in general terms, the education systems of the poor and the rich nations of the world, important and often discouraging divergences are evident. In the present chapter, I will focus on one such difference, a seldom-discussed contrast most clearly visible at the secondary; and university level. I ask the reader to regard this chapter as a preliminary attempt to focus attention on a nearly invisible and certainly neglected topic.

For many decades poor nations have sought to emulate the education systems of rich countries. They have often tried to make their own procedures as much like the latter's, as possible, on the assumption (shared by most people in the wealthier nations) that doing so will make theirs similarly productive of economic growth and personal development. In most poor countries, however, these attempts produced disappointing results. In overcrowded and physically inadequate classrooms, teachers superficially educated in the knowledge and ways of thinking of a more affluent culture try to disseminate an unavoidably lowest common denominator of the substance of that education. Given these circumstances, most students become modestly literate and numerate, and only a few master the intricacies of the wealthy society's knowledge and styles of thinking, link them with those of their own culture, and proceed towards elite university, professional, and civic careers. In the process, these 'successful' ones are often alienated from their indigenous traditions and communities of origin. The schooling received by the rest is usually inadequate to usher them into a self-sufficient and hopeful way of life.

The poor nations have, in fact, bought into a major sub-assumption of the wealthier ones: that it is beneficial, indeed natural, for all children, at least between the ages five to six and sixteen to eighteen, to spend the longest part of most days in school, separated from the adult world, because it is almost entirely in schools and classrooms that the desired education can be achieved. An alternative phrasing is that schools and classrooms are 'good' places; whatever the faults of a specific one, its advantages outweigh the negatives. Note that the growth of a world education ideology, within which the educational principles of the poor nations are coming to parallel those of the rich ones, is celebrated in Meyer et al. (1992), for example, and deplored in Ginsburg et al. (1990).

There are few signs that influential people in poor nations question this assumption, even as attendance rates in many places decline and young adults begin to question the usefulness and costs of schooling. Imaginative curriculum reforms, such as those described by Gasché (2004) and Teasdale (1994) are meant to adapt the basic institution to the local culture and to rescue it from irrelevance. In no sense do most of the reformers question the assumption that all children should spend the larger part of each day in a place called school.

On the other hand, during the last third of the 20th century, many people in the wealthier nations became dissatisfied with fundamental aspects of their schools, particularly secondary schools. Employers, parents, and professors complained and continue to complain about the supposedly inferior academic achievement, social skills, and professional capacities of graduates. This outcry has led to a variety of responses: tougher examinations, stricter behaviour codes, new emphasis on 'the basics', reorganized teacher training, and (counterintuitively) decreased funding. In short, schools in the wealthier countries have become less respected and more rigid institutions.

Parallel to this criticism from older adults, students and young adults have asserted for several decades that secondary schools (and universities) are for the most part inadequate learning environments, cut off from the 'real' world. The youth of the sixties and seventies were particularly strident about labelling high school 'irrelevant' and claiming that its atmosphere 'sucked'; many dropped or tuned out. Symptomatic of these decades were the manifestos of the 'de-schooling' movement (for example, Freire, 1996; Goodman, 1960; Illich, 1970; Reimer, 1971). These writers concurred that formal education in the West, especially at the secondary level, was ineffective and probably pernicious. Only Freire (see Mesquida, 2004) proved capable of inspiring, establishing, and sustaining new programmes based on his analyses and ideas.

Since then, however, the claims of the de-schoolers have been indirectly confirmed in accumulated research on adolescence (most of it done in the rich nations) by psychologists (cf. Berk, 1993; Csikszentmihalyi et al., 1993; Feldman and Elliot, 1990; Goethals and Klos, 1976; Lerner, 2001; Muus, 1995; Steinberg, 2001), sociologists (cf. Coleman, 1961; Hine, 1999), and anthropologists (cf. Cohen, 1964; Schlegel and Barry, 1991). But few, if any, of these academics take the next step, which would be to challenge the basic assumption that school is the proper place for youths to be, most of the time.

Many contemporary teens in the better-off countries continue to be temperamentally or philosophically anti-school. They insist that time spent in jobs, at the mall, with the media and computers, and especially in informal interaction with peers, is more interesting and applicable in adult life than school, and so far as they are able, they invest their energies in such settings. But the current atmosphere of achievement testing and behaviour codes makes acting in accord with these beliefs difficult. Unintentionally, such measures often increase the alienation and depression of the already restive students.

To be sure, an important minority of young people with academic or scientific interests remains loyal to the school and tolerates the segregation from adult affairs that it imposes. But many of these 'best' students approach classroom learning with a pragmatic attitude that distresses their instructors: they do what they think they must, without passion, in order to receive the grades they need to 'get ahead' later. These phenomena are, of course, not unknown in the schools of poor countries.

It is significant that serious criticism of the 'sit-listen-read-write' model of formal education scarcely existed until the last three or four decades, although a few reformers, among whom Dewey (1998) is perhaps pre-eminent, made proposals to reduce its inherent gloom and inefficiency. Thus, for centuries, adults have imposed lengthier and more complex requirements concerning school attendance on more and more youths, and have felt virtuous about doing so. Aside from a few dedicated 'home-schoolers', most people in the rich nations cannot picture a society without almost all adolescents in schools: this arrangement is, for them, a 'given'. In poor countries, the pressure continues to extend the classroom to more and more youth for progressively longer periods of time.

EDUCATION OUTSIDE OF SCHOOL

But there is a second trend that has taken root within the secondary schools and universities of the richer nations that has been hardly noticed, at least as a widespread 'movement', by scholars who analyze educational systems. (Indeed, it does not have a widely accepted collective name.) This is the proliferation of courses, programmes, and even entire institutions that allow or require their students to spend significant blocks of time, from a few hours per week to a year or more full-time, constructively engaged in activities *outside* the classroom and *outside* the school.

These opportunities include apprenticeship and aspects of vocational and professional education, but go well beyond them to innovations that have appeared in very many secondary and university programmes: internships, field-based education, work-study, clinical experience, community service education, experiential education, cooperative education, *alternance*, and so on—even the 'leaves of absence' now granted routinely these days by elite universities. How what is learned in these environments connects with traditional school subjects is often unclear, as is how many students are reached by them, because each variety defines itself differently and reliable international and national statistics are difficult to acquire. However, such programmes exist everywhere in the wealthier countries. To adapt the canny huckster's maxim, 'If you look for them, you will find them'.

Such programmes assume explicitly or implicitly that school is *not* necessarily the best place for *all or most* adolescents to be, *most* of the time, and that valuable learning can occur *outside* of the classroom. Note that most advocates of these structures reject only the widespread monopoly in education of classrooms and schools; they do not wish to abandon all instruction in this format. Each out-of-school model is a slightly different response to (*a*) students' expressed wishes, sometimes supported by parents, to escape schools and classrooms, at least some of the time, in order to learn in and experience the adult world, (*b*) employers' and other adults' beliefs that the effective education for maturity and employment best occurs on-the-job, and (*c*) many educators' convictions that supervised and analyzed real world experiences ultimately engage almost all students in the study of traditional school subjects, while also increasing their understanding of themselves and the adult world.

However, these forms of out-of-school education (part of a larger category of activities often called 'non-formal education'; cf. Dasen, this volume) scarcely exist, so far as I know, in most poor countries, except in vocational and professional education, which enrol very small proportions of the members of each age cohort. This is because (*a*) voc-tech schools are expensive to run, (*b*) most parents and the elite are wedded to the classroom-and-school model, and (*c*) many people in less wealthy nations regard life in the contemporary 'real world' of their own country as irrelevant to preparation for a better future, and thus wish to distance their children from it. Later on, I will suggest that this derogatory evaluation is not necessarily correct.

The point I want to emphasize here is that the systems of education in wealthy and poor nations are moving in opposite directions. In rich countries, adults, educators, and youth are approaching consensus that out-of-school, non-formal experience may be more effective for some purposes than school-and-classrooms. In poor countries, old assumptions about where young people learn best have a strong hold, perhaps increasingly so. If, during coming decades, non-formal education practices continue to be improved and more widely implemented in the wealthy countries, and are not adopted by the poorer nations, the latter may find themselves (once again) relatively less well off than they are now.

The idea that out-of-school settings could be used to educate young people finds support not only in the opinions of students and employers, but also in recent scholarship in the biological and social sciences. I will summarize only two strands of this research here, one from developmental psychobiology, the other from the study of 'everyday learning'. I believe that as we implement school and classroom instruction more rigorously, we unintentionally increase the discrepancy between scientists' emerging ideas about the types of environments in which young people best learn, and the settings that, with the best intentions, we set up. We seem to be wedded to the task of fitting square-pegs into round holes.

ADOLESCENT DEVELOPMENTAL PSYCHOBIOLOGY

During the last ten or fifteen years, scientists have learned an enormous amount about the development and functioning of the adolescent brain (much of the following is drawn from Steinberg, 2001; Strauch, 2003; Teicher et al., 1995). They formerly believed that the volume of the brain stops growing long before adolescence; that adults' and teenagers' brains are similar, if not identical, in how they operate and in what they can accomplish; and that environmental and unidirectional genetic factors determine both special abilities as well as aberrations. Today, each of these propositions is rejected by most neurologists, psychiatrists, psychologists, human biologists, and so on, as the result of recent research using non-invasive scanning techniques, computer programmes, and so on, that provide access to phenomena inaccessible until recently.

For example, this research shows that the cerebral cortex, especially the pre-frontal area in which most higher order transactions occurs, does not grow in volume uni-directionally, from birth to maturity: rather, it does so until puberty (age eleven or twelve), and then it actually decreases gradually until about age twenty, by which time it has lost upto 15 per cent of its earlier grey matter (that is, neurons). This is the outcome of a massive 'pruning' and reorganization of neurons and axons that occurs during this period, only partly in response to a youth's experiences in the environment. During the same years (twelve to twenty), myelinization ('insulation') of established pathways (axons) also takes place, ensuring that impulses are carried more reliably and speedily among the neurons. Both pruning and myelinization affect how complexly and efficiently a youth can analyze, reason, sense moral issues, empathize, plan ahead, and so on. These are skills that most secondary school and college teachers assume exist, in their 'raw' adult form, and that can be sharpened by appropriate instruction and practice, certainly during the second half of adolescence. But many such students are probably not as capable of 'abstract' thinking as we have assumed them to be, and as they likely will be after age twenty or so.

Further, we know now that dopamine levels in the brain rise during adolescence, then decline to previous magnitudes in early adulthood. Dopamine is neurotransmitter, experienced pleasurably by the organism, which tends to seek its increase. Production is stimulated by experiences of risk, novelty, physical movement, alcohol, nicotine, sexual activity, productive cooperation, and so on, to each of which adolescents are often attracted. Because the pre-frontal cortex remains somewhat immature during the years of pruning and myelinization, messages about dopamine-producing situations often are shunted to and mediated in another brain region, the amygdala. The amygdala's response repertoire is limited to 'fight' (aggression) or 'flight' (avoidance, or running away), both of which produce dopamine. This hook-up may have possessed survival value in hunting and gathering societies, where group welfare would, on balance, have been advanced if juveniles (rather than children nor adults) were especially active in, and curious about, physical and human phenomena beyond the campsite, and in which they often served as sentinels on the lookout for predators. But very few classroom experiences involve risk, movement, novelty, and so on, the stimuli that provoke production of dopamine. This paucity may partly explain many teenagers' distaste for the classroom and their parallel attraction to disruptive behaviour, sports, extracurricular activities, parties, jobs, the street corner, and so on.

There is also the provocative and relatively new notion of *intuitive ontology* (Boyer, 1998; Boyer and Barrett, 2005; Hirschfeld, 2002; Sperber, 1996), which suggests that human neonates and juveniles are genetically programmed to perceive and experience the world in species- and age-specific ways. Thus, almost all children inevitably use similar category systems to organize basic cognitive domains, such as number, persons, animals, and so on, as well particular inferential processes linked to each of them, whether or not the adults in their environment deliberately teach or model these categories and processes. According to Boyer, '[I]ntuitive ontology constrains the range of inferences to be derived (by the child) from available information, by triggering a set of definite intuitive expectations about the observable features and underlying properties of different types of objects [in the environment]' (1998: 879).

Hirschfeld (2002) adopts this perspective to propose an explanation of why and how young children everywhere classify and rank people into universal sets of cognitive categories: for example, by age, race, gender, social standing, and so on. He has done seminal work (Hirschfeld, 1996) using this approach to understand the early appearance of 'racial thinking' in children in many cultures around the world. Acting on Hirschfeld's findings, for example, we might with better prospects try to influence the specific qualities children impute to members of particular categories (for example, 'races', gender, and so on), than struggle to remove from their thinking the category systems themselves. I suggest that adolescents also may be influenced by innately-derived 'definite intuitive expectations', although Boyer and Barrett, 2005 do not discuss this possibility, that constrain them to perceive the world differently than teachers and other adults prefer them to.

I want to link the neuro-psychological and intuitive ontology perspectives by suggesting that the 'neural architecture' (Hirschfeld, 2002: 623) of (especially) the adolescent brain may include 'propensities' or 'cognitive dispositions' to learn both pleasurably and more readily things they are vaguely predisposed to learn, through bodily activity in novel mental and/or physical and/or emotional environments (that is, the adult social and physical world). Such tendencies are likely reinforced when the learning situation is meaningful to them, rather than routine in locales such as age and space segregated schools and classrooms. That is, the 'learnability' of almost anything increases if the teenager or youth encounters it while participating actively in a novel, emotionally-intense, real-life setting, rather than in what I think of as a 'holding pen' for adolescent learners (for a similar view, see Wilson, 1998). Schools, which offer mainly passive roles to learners, are recent inventions in human history and (within their own walls, except for athletic activities) are rarely capable of providing significant opportunities for authentic exploration and activity. Indeed, in rich and poor nations alike, novelty and challenge are experienced by adolescents for the most part with and in the peer group. Thus, much of what adolescents learn they acquire from each other, or in each other's company.

The slightly earlier work of psychologists and psychobiologists such as Damasio (1994), LeDoux (1996), Schore (1994), and Thomkins (in Demos, 1995) also questions the soundness of the standard school-and-classrooms model. Each emphasizes that efficacious learning environments require roughly equal involvement of the affective (emotional) and the cognitive systems of learners, reinforcing what the newer research concerning risk, novelty, movement, and so on, suggests. Affects are the 'primary motivators', Demos (1995: 190) says, and can operate as facilitators or impeders; they can partly determine if an individual will or will not persevere in a particular learning task, and what the outcome will be. In recent research, Tai et al. (2006) found that 34 per cent of eighth graders with average math scores but a declared interest in science went on to graduate from college with a degree in science or engineering, compared to 19 per cent of their age-mates who had above average math scores but no preference for science as a subject. In other words, feelings must be attended to, according to this and other studies and to the theorists, though they are relegated to background status in the dominant model of teaching and learning.

Granted that too-ready acceptance of imputed innate components of thinking and behaviour can lead to mistaken and dangerous conclusions about individuals and groups, similar to those advanced by some 19th and early 20th century psychologists and anthropologists. But simpler assumptions, that the neonate is a blank slate subject only to experiential and cultural influences, and/or that the genes operate unidirectionally and cumulatively, are no longer admissible. Effective teaching and learning for teenagers must be based upon accurate understanding of the likely characteristics of young people, not pre-scientific assumptions about the adolescent psyche.

SITUATED OR EVERYDAY LEARNING

The work of certain socio-cultural-historical theorists, such as Lave (1988); Lave and Wenger (1991); Rogoff (1995, 2003); Wertsch (1998); Wertsch et al. (1995), and so on, in the tradition of Vygotsky (1978), provides additional support for considering out-of-school experience as a potential major component of educational systems in both poor and rich countries. These ethnographers and cultural psychologists became interested in out-of-school learning as a result of their fieldwork in the United States, Latin America, and Africa. They observed that much of what ordinary people know, including fairly sophisticated skills and knowledge, is not acquired in school, nor is it always deliberately transmitted in other settings. Thus, Hutchins (1991) documented how new sailors learn to navigate large naval vessels; Rogoff et al. (1995) described the acquisition of organizational and cultural abilities by Girl Scouts conducting cookie sales; Lave (1977) showed how Liberian tailors acquire in their worksites the specialized arithmetic used in their trade.

These and other ethnographers demonstrated (as had Vygotsky, inter alia, much earlier) that learning and re-learning occur everywhere, and most of the time, even though formal roles of teacher and pupil(s) often cannot be identified; that both children and adults spend a lot of time watching, rehearsing, discussing, demonstrating, and so on (that is, learning), specific aspects of their culture, often (but not always) in multi-person settings where others are engaged in performing the same activities; and that 'activity' in a social setting seems essential to the learning process, as does 'mediation' (thinking) by the individual about what he/she is doing and has experienced.

Gradually these researchers have co-opted or invented a (not always felicitous) vocabulary and stance for studying and understanding what they call in different papers *distributed learning* or *situated learning,* or more simply, *everyday learning.* All three terms I understand to suggest learning that occurs in real-life situations, outside of school and frequently in the absence of deliberate instruction. They direct attention to the often impressive mental and physical development that occurs when a novice observes, and gradually enacts over time, the application by an expert, of complex skills and knowledge in an everyday setting. In the pages that follow, I will most often employ 'situated learning', because 'distributed' is a term used in some countries to describe school programmes that prepare young people for work in retail sales, and 'everyday learning' feels too broadly evocative.

In the circumstances these researchers have studied, the expert or master usually does little or no explicit teaching. (Lave and Wenger, 1991: 92) Novices 'learn mostly in relation with other [novices]' (1991: 93), that is, via *peripheral participation* in a *community of practice.* Lave characterizes situated learning as 'centripetal' (1991: 100), in that the longer it continues, the closer the learner, as he becomes more skilled, moves to the centre of a network of practitioners, and the more rapidly his/her learning occurs. These concepts are intended to provoke 'a more comprehensive view' (1991: 32) of everyday learning.

Rogoff's further elaboration of situated learning divides it into three interconnected 'planes', (1995: 141) or aspects. The first, the behavioural aspect, she calls *apprenticeship,* emphasizing 'the active roles of newcomers and others in arranging activities and support' (1995: 143) for neophytes' learning and development. The second she calls *guided participation*, including in it the 'system of interpersonal engagements and relationships involved in participation in activities' that leads to learning. (1995: 146). The third plane is *participatory appropriation*, or 'the process by which individuals transform their understanding and responsibility for activities' through their own efforts at meaning-making (1995: 150).

More briefly, the first plane spotlights activity at the site where learning occurs; the second focuses on social relationships among learners and practitioners; the third emphasizes development of personal identity. Rogoff's particular contribution, in my view, is her exposition of guided participation and participatory appropriation, which are often ignored even by educators, psychologists, and anthropologists who want to explore learning beyond school and classroom. Allied with 'apprenticeship', they are the sources of most or much of what people know, even in thoroughly schooled societies.

In summary, recently articulated positions in developmental psychobiology and socio-cultural-history seem to strongly reinforce each other. Both support the notions that the learning process is most efficient when the adolescent learner can be physically as well as mentally active in it, when the setting is in the 'real world', when efforts to learn occur in a group situation, and when the learner feels excitement and/or moderate pressure. These conditions schools and colleges are hard-pressed to provide. I conclude that the educational impact of schools and classrooms may be much less and very different than what we routinely assume.

AN OVERVIEW OF MODERN FRENCH COMPAGNONNAGE

For more than ten years, Dorothy Herzog and I have been studying French *compagnonnage*, a complex system of craft and technical apprenticeship/academic education/psychological development. In describing the programme, its leaders sometimes assert, 'We are NOT a school!'. Indeed, the programme could be interpreted as a deliberate demonstration of the situated learning model, rooted in the principles of psychobiology, except that its pedigree goes back more than 500 years, and its contemporary leaders probably are not acquainted with the concepts of pruning, dopamine, peripheral participation, and so on.

The idea that the neural architecture of the adolescent brain may include propensities to learn more readily and more pleasurably through bodily activity in a novel, peopled, and challenging environment first occurred to us during our initial observations of compagnonnage classrooms, workshops, and recreational areas, and in our conversations and interviews with the young participants. Both of us were accustomed to working with adolescents in other educational settings, and we were astonished to witness the verve and sense of purpose exuded by the compagnonnage youths. As a particularly well-developed system of situated learning, compagnonnage should be (in my view) of considerable interest to educators from both poor and wealthy nations who seek to soften the hold of the school-and-classrooms model in their countries, and to replace it, in part, with other forms of education better suited to the psychological characteristics of youth and to the needs of the economy.

I need to emphasize that contemporary compagnonnage is not merely an especially well-organized apprenticeship programme, similar to those in Germany (Hamilton, 1990; Schlegel, unpublished) and Switzerland (Dasen, personal communication), for example. As will be seen subsequently, compagnonnage goes well beyond these models, in a number of ways: overall length, number of job sites and employers experienced, total hours at work, residential requirements, sense of community, affective engagement (for example, rituals, myths, and interpersonal relationships), integration of age groups, elite status of the programme itself, potential lifetime membership, and so on.

Compagnonnage is a programme of education, personal development, and training (formation) that has evolved from the guild system of the Middle Ages. During that period, *compagnons* (qualified journeymen) ranked between masters and apprentices. Masters in the old sense do not exist today, but *compagnons* do. They now concentrate on preparing youths to be skilled artisans, conscientious citizens, and solid family men, and to be their successors in compagnonnage. Compagnonnage existed in most European countries hundreds of years ago, but it is a living force today only in France. Even in France, some people think it expired before 1900. (Sources in English on contemporary compagnonnage scarcely exist; see Icher (2000) and the papers by my wife and me, listed in the references of the present chapter. In French, see Guèdez (1994), Hautin and Biller (2000), Icher (1995; 1999).

A youngster typically enters compagnonnage at sixteen or seventeen as an *apprenti* (apprentice), one of about 4000 who do so each year, after finishing *collège* (middle school). The youth may have been placed in the bottom half of the class and decided that *lycée* (secondary school) would not be productive or enjoyable for him/her. Recently, increasing numbers of lycée leavers and graduates and even university students have joined the programme. Traditionally, compagnonnage was an all-male organization, but girls have been accepted as apprentices since the late nineties, and in 2004 the first women became *aspirants*. It is expected that during the next few years some of them will become compagnons.

The youth becomes an associate of one of the thirty or so major compagnonnage *maisons* distributed throughout France. A *maison* is like a small American college, housing forty to 150 youths, as well as workshops, classrooms, dormitories, dining hall, exposition hall, and so on. The novice immediately begins an entry-level job, negotiated by the compagnons, in the *métier* that he has chosen from the twenty-five or so available: carpentry, cabinet-making, masonry, automotive bodybuilding, metalworking, upholstering, pastry-making, and so on. Ideally, his *patron* (boss) is a compagnon, but often he is simply a well-regarded craftsman. He receives a training-level wage, like other French apprentices, only about 5 per cent of whom are in compagnonnage.

About half of the apprentices reside in the *maison*; the rest live with their parents or (if necessary) rent rooms near their place of work. However, during two weeks of every eight they come together in a *maison* for *stage* (intensive training), which includes vocational, academic, and moral components. *Stage* is led by a young *compagnon* in the *metier* called a *maître de stage*, who very recently concluded his own formation. After two (sometimes three) years, completion of a small but challenging *travail* (project in his trade), passage of the basic government exams in the *métier*, and a formal initiation, a youth becomes (if he wishes) an *aspirant*.

The young *aspirant* moves through five to eight of the 150 or so *maisons* in France, and probably also one or two in another country, such as, Switzerland, Germany, Italy, and the Netherlands. The typical *maison* projects a communal and goal-directed ambience, remarkable in that no one older than in their mid-twenties resides there. He/she is employed in successively more demanding jobs in his *metier*, for which he receives a skilled worker's pay. Every six to twelve months he changes job, city, and *maison*. For hundreds of years the compagnons have called this journey the *Tour de France*.

Life on the Tour is demanding: a combined total of fifty-five to sixty hours per week that includes time on the job, academic and professional classes, evenings and Saturdays, and skill-development projects in the *maison* workshop. At all times *aspirants* participate in teaching and mentoring, by and of fellow residents. The environment is Spartan, with little partying, early bedtime, infrequent dating with girls, and postponement of marriage. It is also communal, with shared chores, mutual support, and no hazing. There are many rituals: initiations, banquets on *metiers'* traditional saints' days, use of customary gestures and argot. The youth inhabits a pervasive interactional programme of moral socialization that transmits the values of compagnonnage. These include work as the primary means of personal fulfilment; tradition and progress as co-essentials in the practice of the *metier*; interdependence in professional affairs of activity, theory, and general knowledge; pride in one's efforts and products; compagnonnage as fraternity; and centrality of family in adult life. Religious instruction and proselytization are banned, although for complex reasons, members of France's ethnic and religious minority groups are under-represented among participants.

After five or six years, an aspirant may request to become a compagnon. If his skills and character are acceptable to his seniors, he executes a challenging *chef d'oeuvre* (masterwork) in his *metier* and undergoes a second initiation, during which he receives symbolic regalia and a full compagnonnage nickname. He is now an *itinérant* (unsettled compagnon), who will probably remain in a *maison* two or more additional years, teaching and mentoring the younger boys, perhaps as a *maître de stage*, while working outside in a well-paid job. After this, he selects a city or region in which to establish himself in his *metier*, as a small business-owner or as a well-paid employee, and becomes a *sédentaire* (settled). At age twenty-five or so, he is also ready for marriage.

French employers regard *compagnons* as the aristocrats of their *métiers*. They are sought after, expected to set standards for other workers, and deferred to in problematic circumstances. They belong to a network of craftsmen who share a common background, assist each other in obtaining jobs and/or clients, and participate in the affairs of their *metier* and the *maison* in their city. They may specialize in restoration (for example, of historic buildings, antique furniture, classic cars), but more often they practice their trade on building sites or in factories, or in their own small, businesses focused on the production of high-quality objects for the contemporary market.

COMPAGNONNAGE AND SITUATED LEARNING

Our lengthy, on-the-ground study of compagnonnage has helped us see a number of unexpected and complex elaborations of the situated learning model and the perspectives of psychobiology in the compagnons' programme. These occur in all three of Rogoff's planes: apprenticeship, guided participation, and participatory appropriation, but guided participation is most easily recognizable. The ways in which these components are used and elaborated in compagnonnage demonstrate that the Lave/Rogoff model may require further development.

First, the programme does much more than simply insert its teenagers into unskilled jobs (as do some European and American apprenticeship programmes) with only slight provision for continued academic learning, and does so at ages proponents of school-based education often regard as premature. Newcomers to compagnonnage, typically sixteen or seventeen and straight from *collège*, immediately enter beginning-level, low-paid, full-time jobs in real worksites where the *métier* they have chosen is practiced. As *apprentis*, they start out doing mostly 'donkey' work and watching their bosses and skilled co-workers, but during the first weeks and months they are asked and allowed to undertake increasingly difficult and useful tasks. As their skills, knowledge, and age increase, they move closer to the centre of the community of artisans with whom they work.

The full programme theoretically requires seven or eight years to complete. On-the-job experiences of trainees are complexly varied, in ways that enhance their centripetality as they move from worksite to worksite. Explicit teaching is episodic, and usually task-specific. *Patrons* (bosses) are typically *compagnons* themselves, participating because they like and are effective with young employees, and informally supervised by other compagnons while they employ trainees. During his years on the *Tour de France*, a youth works in six to ten different towns, for the same number of employers, each of whom has his own personal qualities, a particular specialty within the trade, and a different array of equipment, other employees, and style of working.

This multiplicity of employers and job sites enriches a youth's mastery of the skills of the trade, develops his social skills and adaptability, and reduces or eliminates competition among trainees for preferred jobs and for the attention of the master, both of which Lave mentions as inherent problems in situated learning (Lave and Wenger, 1991: 103–04). In most *métiers* the *patrons* regard their apprentice as future colleagues, rather than prospective competitors, which Lave also proposes as a common difficulty (1991: 114), because the bosses take seriously their mission of preserving and advancing the *métier*, and because skilled artisans in most crafts are in short supply in France. Further, during each of the initial years of apprenticeship the youths attend eleven or twelve weeks of intensive residential training (*stage*), during which they learn and perfect specific skills for which there is insufficient time or current need at their worksites. In Rogoff's terms, these arrangements blend a powerful strand of guided participation into the apprenticeship plane of situated learning.

Second, the *compagnons* deftly harness the affective dimensions of the learning process, an aspect of 'everyday learning' that Lave, Rogoff et al., do not much discuss, despite their interest in identity formation. For example, the *stages* are led by a young *compagnon* recently accorded this status. Typically, this *maître de stage* is marvellously skilled in his craft, an engaging role model, and wholly devoted to the progress of his twelve to eighteen trainees. He is an obvious and frequently chosen 'model' with whom the *apprentis* can easily identify, and thus a powerful influence in the participatory appropriation aspect of this situated learning system.

During the stages, apprentices reside in a compagnonnage *maison* (small residential college), where they mingle with other young men who are more advanced in their *métiers* and available as tutors and models. *Apprentis* and *aspirants* also experience frequent off-the-job, but professionally oriented, contact with mature *compagnons*, in their own trade especially, who counsel, evaluate, and befriend them, and who introduce them to the activities and goals of the regional and national organizations of compagnonnage. They thus profit from participating, 'legitimately', in multiple and overlapping settings where they interact with others in ways that promote their continuing development.

In contemporary technological society, schools are rarely capable of providing opportunities for authentic exploration and activity.

Novelty and challenge occur for the most part within the teenage peer group. In compagnonnage, the barriers between generations, and between adjoining age cohorts, are low and permeable. A seventeen-year-old recruit associates daily not only with age-mates, but also with trainees one to six or more years older than he, with his heroic *maître de stage*, with young *compagnons*, and with mature *compagnons* and co-workers aged twenty-five to sixty-five and older. Being with such 'older brothers' undercuts and partially neutralizes the potentially powerful adolescent cultures of both the *maison* and the youths' home neighbourhoods. As a result, the content of compagnonnage youths' social and cultural formation is very different from that of their peers in academic and professional *lycées*. They begin to perceive what it is to be a professional and an adult.

After the years of apprenticeship, changes of jobs occur every six or twelve months, in tandem with changes of residence from *maison* to *maison*. This moving about helps the young men become more autonomous and gives them experience in varied social settings. The *compagnons* also involve trainees in affect-arousing rituals of status change (apprentice to *aspirant*, *aspirant* to *compagnon*) and of solidarity with other participants, young and old. Eligibility for such rituals, especially those of initiation, explicitly requires character development according to compagnonnage norms, as well as proficiency as an artisan. The programme enlists the youths emotionally by means of these rituals, which are reinforced by strategic recounting of complex compagnonnage origin myths, and by pervasive emphasis in daily conversations on each youth's ultimate responsibility to help preserve both the traditions and the future of his chosen *métier*.

The residents of a *maison* live according to an interestingly French set of norms and values for communal living and for artisanal practice, some components of which have already been mentioned. Many of these standards are enumerated in an elaborately printed document, *la Règle* (the Rule), which is posted in a prominent place in each house. Some of the more accomplished youths tell us that at work and/or in the *maison* workshops they occasionally experience feelings akin to what Csikszentmihalyi calls 'flow' (Csikszentmihalyi et al., 1993); that is, they enter a period of joyful self-forgetfulness while absorbed in mastering a challenging task in the *métier*, which at the onset was well-matched to their sphere of competence.

In conversations and interviews, youths at all levels talk excitedly about the Tour (past, present, and future); they express delight that they have encountered (or will meet) many different people and cultures in *maisons* and in jobsites on the Tour; they express satisfaction about mastering personal chores such as getting their laundry done; they speak solemnly of their prospective roles as guardians of the *patrimoine* of their *metier*; their most common complaint is that their bosses do not give them sufficiently complex work. Clearly, they welcome the challenges and novelties they encounter, and they respond to them by learning how to cope. For more on this subject, see Herzog, 1991; Herzog, 2005; Herzog and Herzog, 1998; Herzog and Herzog, 2001, 2005.

Apprentis and *aspirants* have described to us, and we have observed, the sequence through which their perceptions of themselves change, typically from feeling insignificant in the world at large, confused about the future, dissatisfied with school, and regretful about disappointing their parents by not proceeding to *lycée*, to the sense that they are skilled, informed, committed, and admired practitioners of the skills, standards, and traditions of their *métier*, respected by their parents, and better prepared for life ahead than their *lycée* (or drop-out) peers. Personal growth of this sort occurs even during the two years of apprenticeship. We have partially documented these claims in several previous papers (cf. Herzog, 1992; Herzog and Herzog, 1997, 1999a/b, 2000). I think in the preceding paragraph we see the degree to which the trainees can be said to inhabit the participatory appropriation plane of distributed learning, as well as that of guided participation.

Third, the two-week residential stages for apprentices include serious amounts of didactic classroom instruction in the technology, aesthetics, and history of the *métier*, which topics they may encounter only haphazardly at work, and in academic subjects such as French, math, science, history, and a second language (usually English). Content, methods, and instructors to varying degrees are selected and adapted to the trade and to the intimate (for French secondary schools) *maison* classroom of twelve to eighteen students.

Most of the school-jaundiced youths who populate compagnonnage respond positively to this classroom instruction, although the *maison* workshop remains their favourite learning environment. In the *maison* they are surrounded by older youths whom they admire and who endorse the usefulness of all or most of the academic content to which they are exposed, and gradually they, too, see the relevance to future practice of most of the subjects. Further, as they approach the ages of eighteen and nineteen, perhaps the abstractions of math, history, science, and so on, become more accessible to them. Certainly compagnonnage *apprentis* pass the government's exams for initial certificates in their trade, which include academic and theoretical components as well as tests of 'practical' competence, in greater proportions and after fewer years of study than youths in non-compagnonnage programmes. It is interesting that Lave doubts that academic instruction (in her words, 'a teaching curriculum' (1977: 97) can be amalgamated to situated learning. The *compagnons* manage it for most of their youths, who are perhaps 'softened up' for it by their eye-opening experiences at the worksite and in the *maison*.

COMPAGNONNAGE/SITUATED LEARNING AS A MODEL FOR EDUCATION

I do not propose French compagnonnage as a template for the poor (or wealthy) nations to implement, component by component. I offer it, rather, as a well-developed, still evolving, and powerful example of what situated learning, built as it seems to be on an intuitive understanding of the psycho-neurological development of adolescents, can be and can do, and as the basis from which appropriate adaptations can be made for other environments. These other environments might well include the mainstream educational systems of both poor and rich countries.

Poor countries seem to offer both advantages and handicaps for the implementation of situated learning inspired by the compagnonnage model. For example, one of the difficulties which the French programme faces is recruitment and retention of sufficient numbers of adult compagnons to maintain the age-mix that I have described, without which the programme would lose much of its vitality. This problem is rooted in the increasing 'individualization' of French culture. Today, *compagnon* artisans, like most members of French society, experience considerable pressure to further their personal careers and businesses, to spend time with their children and family members, and to enjoy themselves in recreational activities, each of which may lessen their abilities to serve as *patrons* or *maitres de stage*, to worry about the future of their *metier*, and to participate in the fraternal and ritual affairs of the *métier*, each of which formerly had higher priority.

There is a difference between poor and rich countries that might make deliberately organized situated learning especially attractive and effective in the less wealthy nations. In many of them, a strong sense of community identity exists among people. Individuals often see themselves as belonging to something larger than the immediate nuclear family, and dedicated to more than a personal career. Thus, the difficulty of recruitment and retention of adult models might be lesser in these environments: an experienced practitioner who became a mentor might see himself as exercising a traditional role in a modern manner, benefiting the larger community, and assuring the continuity of the craft.

Another valuable tradition in many poor countries, today often denigrated, is indigenous apprenticeship. Many instances are described in Coy (1989) and Singleton (1998), for example. Such forms could be explored, publicly rehabilitated, and elaborated. Effective practitioners of various trades could be identified, certificated, and subsidized for their contributions as instructors. This would raise their status and that of their *métier* in the community and nation.

A further factor that could aid in the establishment of distributed learning is the relative scarcity of qualified artisans, especially in modern trades, in these nations. The initial goal of a youth's experiences in situated learning would be the attainment of a basic level of technical skill and general education adequate for him/her to function as a competent semi-skilled worker in a particular trade, on the basis of which he/she probably could obtain employment. After this, he/she could be offered additional part-time and full-time opportunities, in a situated learning context, to refine his skills and knowledge.

One of the limitations of contemporary compagnonnage, stemming from its medieval origins, is that it prepares young people for only the 'manual' trades. But this restriction is by no means an inherent characteristic of situated learning. In the poor and wealthy countries, its principles could be adapted for work and learning in 'white collar' fields as well, from clerical to professional. In poor countries great numbers of young people fail to flourish in professional and technical training programmes because they do not start them with an adequate idea of the nature of the work and of the daily routines of practitioners in the field they have chosen—for example, what an engineer actually does, how computers are used in an office, and so on. A sensitively organized programme of situated learning could reduce the amount of waste and pain these circumstances produce.

Finally, situated learning of all kinds could have the welcome impact, as it does in compagnonnage, of showing youth why knowledge and capabilities in subjects such as math, science, high level reading and writing, an international language, world history, and so on, are useful in contemporary life and in their *métier*, and will become more so in the future. This could help them make better sense of what they have been and will be asked to master in formal education sessions. It may also help educators and governments to prune and re-shape the content of what is taught in regular schools, particularly secondary institutions.

One of the difficulties to overcome in establishing formal situated learning in poor countries is the fierce prejudice, already mentioned, of the elites and many parents against something they perceive as inferior to the established academic curriculum that so richly benefited some of those who experienced it, at least until the last few decades. This challenge is parallel to that which existed in East Africa fifty or so years ago, when the colonized peoples rejected 'elementary' schools, because the term (and its clumsy implementation) suggested that the new schools would teach only those 'elements' of the colonizing power's curricula deemed suitable for Africans. This resistance was not overcome until the label 'primary' was introduced, and the curriculum enriched. However, today it is secondary education that is viewed with increasing scepticism. If situated learning were introduced gradually, and incorporated major components of the compagnonnage version, this sort of resistance might crumble quickly.

In the dissemination of their type of situated learning, especially in the building and other 'manual' trades, I suspect that the compagnons would be available to help. In their eyes, the traditional *Tour de France* has already metamorphozed into the *Tour du Monde*. More significantly, in the last few years the largest compagonnage organization, AOCDTF (*Association ouvrière des Compagnons du Devoir du Tour de France*), has signed contracts with governments in Latin America, Africa, and Eastern Europe focused on helping local artisans acquire modern skills and become better able to transmit their competencies to others. Readers interested in pursuing this idea could contact <international@compagnons-du-devoir.com> (but in explaining why you are inquiring, speak of your interest in 'compagnonnage', not 'situated learning'!).

NOTE

1. This chapter is an extension of an earlier version of a paper delivered at the annual meeting of the American Anthropological Association, New Orleans, 2002, and published in French in Akkari and Dasen (2004).

REFERENCES

Akkari, A. and P. Dasen. (eds). 2004. *Pédagogies et pédagogues du Sud*. Paris: Editions l'Harmattan.

Berk, L. 1993. *Infants, Children and Adolescents*. Boston: Allyn & Bacon.

Boyer, P. 1998. 'Cognitive Tracks of Cultural Inheritance: How Evolved Intuitive Ontology Governs Cultural Transmission', *American Anthropologist*, 100 (4): 876–89.

Boyer, P. and C. Barrett. 2005. 'Domain Specificity and Intuitive Ontology', in D. Buss (ed.), *Handbook of Evolutionary Psychology*, pp. 96–118. Hoboken, NJ: John Wiley.

Csikszentmihalyi, M., K. Rathunde and S. Whalen. 1993. *Talented Tenagers. The Roots of Success and Failure*. Cambridge: Cambridge University Press.

Cohen, Y. 1964. *The Transition from Childhood to Adolescence*. Chicago: Aldine.

Coleman, J. 1961. *The Adolescent Society*. New York: Free Press.

Coy, M. (ed.). 1989. *Apprenticeship: from Theory to Method and Back Again*. Albany, NY: State University of New York.

Damasio, A. 1994. *Descartes' Error*. New York: Avon Books.

Demos, E. V. (ed.), 1995. *Exploring Affects: The Selected Writings of Sylvan Thomkins*. Cambridge: Cambridge University Press.

Dewey, J. 1998. *Experience and Education*. West Lafayette, Indiana: Kappa Delta Phi.

Feldman, S. S. and G. R. Elliott (eds). 1990. *At the Threshold: The Developing Adolescent*. Cambridge, MA: Harvard University Press.

Freire, P. 1996. *Pedagogy of the Oppressed*. London and New York: Penguin.

Gasché, J. 2004. 'La motivation politique de l'éducation indigéne et ses exigences pédagogoiques Jusq'ou ou va l'interculturalité?', in A. Akkari and P. Dasen (eds), *Pédagogies et pédagogues du Sud*, pp. 107–37. Paris: L'Harmattan.

Ginsburg, M., S. Cooper, R. Raghu and H. Zegarra. 1990. 'National World-Systems Explanations of Educational Reforms', *Comparative Education Review*, 34(4): 464–99.

Goethals, G. and D. Klos. 1976. *Experiencing Youth: First-Person Accounts*. Boston, MA: Little, Brown.

Goodman, P. 1960. *Growing Up Absurd*. New York: Random House.

Guèdez, A. 1994. *Compagnonnage et apprentissage*. Paris: Presses Universitaires de France.

Hamilton, S. 1990. *Apprenticeship for Adulthood: Preparing Youth for the Future*. New York: Free Press.

Hautin, C. and D. Billier. 2000. *Etre compagnon*. Paris: Presses Universitaires de France.

Herzog, J. 1991. 'Supervision by "Near-Peers" in French Compagnonnage Apprenticeship', Paper presented at the 12th Annual Ethnography in Education Research Forum, Philadelphia, PA.

———. 1992. 'The Impact of Initiation: Preliminary Data from a Study of Compagnonnage', paper presented at the symposium in honour of Beatrice and John Whiting, Annual Meeting of the Society for Cross-Cultural Research. Santa Fe, NM.

———. 2005. 'French Practice-Oriented Education: The Compagnonnage Version', paper presented at the World Conference on Cooperative Education. Boston.

Herzog, J. and D. Herzog. 1997. 'The Integration of Ritual in Compagnonnage Education', paper presented at the annual meeting of the American Anthropological Association. Washington, DC.

———. 1998. '"We Are Not a School!" Compagnonnage Education as Valorization of Cultural Capital', paper presented at the annual meeting of the American Anthropological Association. Philadelphia.

———. 1999a. 'Initiations, the Tour, and the Maitre-De Stage: The Management of Affective Arousal in Compagnonnage', paper given at the annual meeting of the American Anthropological Association. Chicago.

———. 1999b. 'Silk purses: Adolescent Change in *Compagnonnage*', paper given at the biennial meeting of the Society for Psychological Anthropology. Albuquerque, NM.

———. 2000. 'The Shaping of "scripts" and "intuitive ontology" in French *Compagnonnage* Socialization', paper given at the annual meeting of the American Anthropological Association. San Francisco.

———. 2001. 'The Role of Metaphor in *Compagnonnage*', paper given at the annual meeting of the American Anthropological Association. Washington.

———. 2005. 'The Frailty of High School and the *Compagnonnage* Alternative', paper given at the annual meeting of the American Educational Research Association. Montreal.

Hine, T. 1999. *The Rise and Fall of the American Teenager*. New York: Avon Books.

Hirschfeld, L. 1996. *Race in the Making: Cognition, Culture, and the Child's Construction of Human Kinds*. Cambridge, MA: MIT Press.

———. 2002. 'Why Don't Anthropologists Like Children?', *American Anthropologist*, 104(2): 611–27.

Hutchins, E. 1991. 'The Social Organization of Distributed Cognition', in L. Resnick, J. Levine and S. Teasley (eds), *Perspectives on Socially Shared Cognition*, pp. 283–307. Washington: American Psychological Association.

Icher, F. 1995. *Les compagnons ou l'amour de la belle ouvrage*. Paris: Découvertes Gallimard.

———. 1999. *Les compagnons en France au XXème siècle*. Paris: Jacques Grancher.

———. 2000. *The Artisanal Guilds of France*. New York: Harry N. Abrams.

Illich, I. 1970. *Deschooling Society*. New York: Harper and Row.

Lave, J. 1977. 'Tailor-Made Experiments and Evaluating the Intellectual Consequences of Apprenticeship Training', *Quarterly Newsletter of the Laboratory for Comparative Human Cognition*, 1: 1–3.

———. 1988. *Cognition in Practice: Mind, Mathematics, and Culture in Everyday Life*. Cambridge: Cambridge University Press.

Lave, J. and E. Wenger. 1991. *Situated Learning. Legitimate Peripheral Participation*. Cambridge: Cambridge University Press.

LeDoux, J. 1996. *The Emotional Brain*. New York: Touchstone.

Lerner, R. 2001. *Adolescence*. Englewood Cliffs, NJ: Prentice Hall.

Mesquida, P. 2004. 'Philosophie et education: les influences européennes sur la penséé de Paulo Freire', in A. Akkari and P. Dasen (eds), *Pédagogies et pédagogues du Sud*, pp. 275–93. Paris: L'Harmattan.

Meyer, J., D. Kamens and A. Benavot. 1992. *School Knowledge for the Masses*. Washington, DC: Falmer.

Muus, R. 1995. *Theories of Adolescence*. McGraw-Hill: New York.

Reimer, E. 1971. *School is Dead*. New York: Doubleday.

Rogoff, B. 1995. 'Observing Sociocultural Activity on Three Planes: Participatory Appropriation, Guided Participation, Apprenticeship', in J. Wertsch, P. Del Rio and A. Alvarez (eds), *Sociocultural Studies of Mind*, pp. 283–307. Cambridge: Cambridge University Press.

———. 2003. *The Cultural Nature of Human Development*. Oxford: Oxford University Press.

Rogoff, B., J. Baker-Sennett, P. Lacasa and D. Goldsmith, 1995. 'Development Through Participation in Sociocultural Activity', in J. Goodnow, P. Miller and F. Kessel (eds), *Cultural Practices as Contexts for Development*, pp. 45–65. San Francisco: Jossey-Bass.

Schlegel, A. Unpublished. 'Learning Through Labor'.

Schlegel, A. and H. Barry III. 1991. *Adolescence: An Anthropological Inquiry*. New York: Free Press.

Schore, B. 1994. *Culture in Mind*. Oxford: Oxford University Press.

Singleton, J. (ed.), 1998. *Learning in Likely Places: Varieties of Apprenticeship in Japan*. Cambridge: Cambridge University Press.

Sperber, D. 1996. *Explaining Culture. A Naturalistic Approach*. Oxford: Blackwell.

Strauch, B. 2003. *The Primal Teen*. New York: Anchor Books.

Steinberg, L. 2001. *Adolescence*, 6th edition. New York: McGraw-Hill.

Tai, R., C. Liu, A. Maltese and X. Fan. 2006. 'Career Choice: Planning Early for Careers in Science', *Science*, 312(5777): 1143–44.

Teasdale, G. R. 1994. 'Education and the Survival of Small Indigenous Cultures', in L.F.B. Dubbeldam (ed.), *International Yearbook of Education. Development, Culture and Education*, XLIV: 197–224. Paris: UNESCO.

Teicher, M., S. Anderson and J. Hostetler, Jr. 1995. 'Evidence for Dopamine Receptor Pruning Between Adolescence and Adulthood', *Developmental Brain Research*, 89(2): 167–72.

Vygotsky, L. 1978. *Mind in Society: The Development of Higher Psychological Processes*. Cambridge, MA: Harvard University Press.

Wertsch, J. 1998. *Mind as Action*. Oxford: Oxford University Press.

Wertsch, J., P. del Rio and A. Alvarez. 1995. 'Sociocultural Studies: History, Action, and Mediation', in J. Wertsch, P. del Rio and A. Alvarez (eds), *Sociocultural Studies of Mind*, pp. 1–34. Cambridge: Cambridge University Press.

Wilson, F. 1998. *The Hand: How Its Use Shapes the Brain, Language, and Human Culture*. New York: Pantheon.

Section II

Culturally Appropriate Schooling for Aboriginal People

5
CURRICULUM LOCALIZATION: A VIEW FROM THE SOUTH

GEORGE ROBERT TEASDALE

INTRODUCTION

This chapter will explore some of the newly emerging pedagogies of the South, and introduce several of its pedagogues. The 'South' is referred to here in both its geographical and its metaphorical senses. I will focus in particular on the island nations of the South Pacific, on Papua New Guinea, and on South East Asia, describing how my colleagues in these contexts are trying to localize school curricula by developing pedagogies that are more in harmony with local languages, values, and cultural traditions.

The field of curriculum localization is one of the considerable contestation. The imposed curricula of the west have taken deep hold in the south, and have proved highly impervious to change, even more so than in the west itself. The legacy of the colonial period lives on, even in countries that have been decolonized for several decades; its hegemony being nowhere more apparent than in the content and processes of the school curriculum. This hegemony has been reinforced in recent years by the ever increasing influence of globalization (Teasdale, 1998).

Some of the earlier attempts to localize the curriculum, especially in indigenous settings in Australia, were based on the idea of domain separation. Advocates of this approach, especially Harris

(1990), suggested that Western and indigenous knowledge should be compartmentalized, with the former transmitted as a kind of 'giant role play' to be learned but not necessarily internalized. In recent years there has been a move away from this idea, the emphasis shifting from separation to syncretism. Curricula are now being localized through the blending of the local and the global.

THE ROLE OF UNESCO

The increasing emphasis on the local in many of the recent educational reforms in the south has been supported by the changing discourses of international agencies, especially those of United Nations Educational, Scientific and Cultural Organization (UNESCO). About ten years ago, for example, UNESCO brought together a group of fifteen scholars and thinkers from around the world, asking them to reflect on the future of education. They were constituted as the UNESCO International Commission on Education for the 21st Century. Their task was not so much to invent new ideas about education, but to evaluate what was happening at the cutting edge: to try and envision the future through the best of the past and the present.

At the end of 1996 the Commission produced a report that many of us consider one of the most important educational documents published in recent decades. It was given the title: *Learning—The Treasure Within* (Delors, 1996). The chair of the Commission was Jacques Delors, a former president of the European Union (EU). He prepared a substantive preamble to the report. It is a very visionary statement, and is deserving of careful reading and reflection.

One of his central themes is that, in the 21st century, humanity will need to resolve a series of tensions. In fact, he suggests that our very survival as a species depends upon how effectively we are able to do this. And he argues that education needs to play a central role here. Amongst the tensions he identifies are those between the spiritual and the material, between tradition and modernity, between the universal and the individual, and between the global and the local. The tension between the global and the local is, in fact, the first on Delors' list. He here asserts that for people to become true global citizens they must retain their own deep local values and identities: that the response to globalization must be an equal emphasis on the local; that is, the global and the local must be held in balance.

His idea of tension needs further analysis. We commonly think of tension when there is conflict between opposing sides: the kind of tension that leads to fights, or to war, and where only one side can win. We talk, for example, about tension in the Middle East, or between India and Pakistan. It is a highly negative and destructive tension. I'm quite sure it is not the kind of tension that Delors is referring to.

But there is another way of looking at tension. During my daughter's school days she learned to play the harp, one of the most beautiful of instruments. And we were able to buy a harp direct from a harp-maker, and watch it being made. Now the whole design of a harp is dependent upon tension. The curve of the timber and the positioning of the strings creates the tension that in turn produces the sound. Without the tension, the harp would be quite useless. The tension in the strings is a necessary tension, a functional tension, a creative tension. And I believe it is this kind of tension that Delors is referring to.

The great challenge, of course, is to get the tension right, and to keep it right. The tuning of a harp is a constant challenge. Each string has to be individually adjusted to ensure harmony. Even the act of playing the harp can change the tension, and make re-tuning necessary. Changes in temperature and humidity can have an even greater impact. One has to work constantly to maintain the right balance. And thus it is with the Delors' tensions, especially the ones between the global and the local. Even though the tensions might be functional, the world of education is never static, and constant re-adjustment is necessary if schools are to maintain any kind of balance between the two in their curricula. In fact, my colleagues in the south, who are seeking to develop pedagogies that are more in harmony with local cultures, find it a constant challenge to achieve any kind of balance, given the strength of the global. It is a big struggle. Global ways of thinking and knowing are very powerful indeed.

As noted earlier, there is a strong hegemony here, driven by economic rationalism, mass media, big multinationals, and by the Information and Communication Technology (ICT) revolution. It is very instrumental in its focus. It emphasizes preparation for the world of work; the acquisition of wealth, status and power; and the search for a secure future in an uncertain world. Another related phenomenon, especially in South East Asia, is the rapid globalization of the English language, and the proliferation of English as a Second

Language programmes; again driven by economic imperatives. Against these global forces it takes much determination to nurture local knowledge and languages, and to ensure their effective and balanced representation in the curriculum. Pedagogues in the south are at a relatively early stage in their attempts to achieve these goals. Nevertheless, as will be evident from the following accounts, new pedagogies are emerging.

EDUCATIONAL THEORIES AND PRACTICES OF THE MAJORITY WORLD

The South Pacific

The first and most significant lesson to have emerged from the South Pacific is that the blending of the local with the global cannot be imposed by outsiders. True curriculum localization can only be achieved from within. This was a dominant theme at the 1992 Rarotonga seminar, which affirmed that indigenous or local cultures must own all aspects of the education of their people. Six years later this principle was reaffirmed by a UNESCO workshop on cultural rights held in Apia, Samoa (Wilson and Hunt, 2000). Once again it was agreed that local cultures must be in control of the curriculum: 'First, the education system must be developed in the culture it serves and be owned by it and, second, it must provide the knowledge and skills necessary for the development of the culture' (Wilson and Hunt, 2000: 167).

These principles, however, have been very difficult to achieve in practice. It is easy to affirm that all educational decisions must be made by local communities, and that education must be a 'bottom-up' process. But the reality is different, especially when the 'local' is embedded in a small developing island nation dependent upon the support of aid donors. I have elsewhere given an account (Teasdale and Teasdale, 1999) that typifies the approach of many donor agencies, but the story is worth retelling here.

I was working on a development assistance project in a small Pacific island nation as one of a team of Western academics hired by a donor agency to assist with the start-up of a new post-secondary educational institution. Some members of the team were adamant that the programmes we were developing had to have a 'proper' conceptual framework, and had given some examples of these from their own experiences in Western institutions. Our local counterparts were very uncomfortable with this approach, and quietly resisted it. They found such theoretical models too cold, too clinical, too removed from reality.

Early one morning, Salote, one of the local staff members, arrived at work clutching a sheaf of papers, and looking very pleased with herself. 'I've got it! I've got it!' she said, 'It came to me last night. I've got the theoretical model they want'. And she spread her papers out on the desk. The model was not immediately apparent. There was no sign of neat boxes connected by multidirectional arrows. Instead there was a hastily drawn picture of a coconut palm, firmly embedded in the earth. However, looking closer, those around the desk could see that each element of the drawing—earth, roots, trunk, fronds, flowers, fruit, sunshine, rain—was labeled, and that each label referred to a process or product of the curriculum.

The 'coconut tree model' became the focal point of the next staff meeting, and was duly explained using an appropriately artistic overhead. It obviously resonated with the locals. They seemed intellectually excited by it. But not so some of the outsiders, one of whom got reluctantly to his feet: 'I'm sorry', he said, 'but this is not a model. A metaphor perhaps, but definitely not a model. You see it is not completely logical. Some of the categories are not mutually exclusive. It leaves some of the issues open, some questions unanswered. It contains conceptual ambiguities'.

Nothing was resolved at the meeting. But afterwards Salote and a few others met for a kind of post-mortem. Said one: 'They just didn't understand the spiritual significance of the coconut tree. Why, I can still go back to my village and identify the palm tree at whose base my father symbolically buried the placenta and umbilical cord after my birth. That is a profoundly significant and symbolic tree for me'.

'No', said another, 'nor do they understand that in our culture we cannot separate out the spiritual, the cultural and the intellectual. Things don't have to be logically consistent. But they do have to be culturally and spiritually consistent. It doesn't matter if there are ambiguities and discontinuities. They are part and parcel of the spiritual dimension, part and parcel of the way we think and live'.

'That's right', said a third, 'nor do they understand that we think holistically. Ideas are integrated, not compartmentalized into boxes'.

Then the first speaker again: 'The good thing about our model is that it keeps opening up new possibilities, new ideas. It challenges my thinking. The other way closes it up, boxes it in'.

Interestingly, in a subversive way, the coconut palm model did become the conceptual framework for the new institution and its programmes, although it was never accepted as such by most of the outsiders. And as it was used within the institution, and shared with students, it was further refined and developed. Ultimately it was shared with other Pacific island peoples at regional gatherings, and became something of a leitmotif for education in the region. More recently it was the focal point of a colloquium held at the University of the South Pacific (USP) in April 2001 on the theme, *Re-thinking Pacific Education*. The colloquium addressed a number of key issues confronting Pacific educators, the first of which was:

> [T]he lack of ownership by Pacific peoples of the formal education process. It was noted that, while the churches have succeeded in becoming fully integrated with the Pacific way of life, education remains an alien process and is viewed by Pacific peoples as something that is imposed from outside: an instrument designed to fail, exclude and marginalize the majority and therefore irrelevant and meaningless to their way of life. (Institute of Education, 2002: 2)

In responding to the challenge to reconceptualize education in the Pacific the participants revisited the above model, albeit shifting from the use of a coconut palm in deference to those from highland regions where such flora do not grow. Instead they developed the more generic idea of a 'Tree of Opportunity' as the most appropriate metaphor for rethinking education:

> The Tree of Opportunity encapsulates the new vision for Pacific education based on the assumption that the main purpose of education in the Pacific is the survival, transformation and sustainability of Pacific peoples and societies, with its outcomes measured in terms of performance and appropriate behaviour in the multiple contexts in which they have to live....

> Education, or the Tree of Opportunity, is firmly rooted in the cultures of Pacific societies. The strengths and advantages it gains from its root source will allow it to grow strong and healthy, and further permit the incorporation of foreign or external elements that can be grafted on without changing its fundamental root source or the identity of each tree. It can accommodate the best of both old and new, and can bear different fruits and be useful for a variety of purposes without destroying its roots or the new grafted elements.

Sustainable, self-help and self-managed education in the Pacific imply control and direction by Pacific people so that they own the processes. (*Tree of Opportunity*, 2002: 3)

One of the colloquium participants was Professor Konai Helu Thaman, who holds a UNESCO chair in Teacher Education and Culture at USP. Scholar, poet, educator and citizen of the Kingdom of Tonga, Thaman has made a remarkable contribution to education in the South Pacific in the thirty years she has taught at USP. One of her major projects has been a deep exploration of the Tongan notions of learning, knowledge and wisdom, and the values underlying these notions, using linguistic and cultural analysis. She has encouraged her graduate students to conduct similar studies of their own cultures and languages with the aim of enabling them to reclaim their education by '...looking towards the sources of their identities and developing philosophies and teaching and learning strategies that are rooted in their cultural values and practices' (Thaman, 2000: 49; see also Thaman, 1998, 2001).

Essentially, Thaman's work is grounded in a deep commitment to helping Pacific island peoples to understand and use their own ways of thinking, knowing and understanding as part of the processes of schooling and higher education. Her writings emphasize the importance of kinship and interpersonal relationships in learning, the role of the spiritual and/or supernatural dimensions, the need for a holistic approach to knowledge, and a commitment to the collective rather than the individual good. Translating these values and qualities into specific learning outcomes, Thaman has prepared a list relevant to her own Tongan context, suggesting that it might be a useful exemplar for other Pacific cultures. Among the learning outcomes she identifies are:

Understand and show facility in appropriate Tongan behaviour and etiquette.

Be able to maintain good interpersonal skills.

Demonstrate respect for persons of rank and in positions of authority.

Be able to work cooperatively with others for the purpose of achieving collective goals.

Have civic responsibility and respect for law.

Have skill in appropriate arts and crafts, and in planting food crops. (Thaman, 2002: 28–29)

As part of her role as a UNESCO Professor at USP, Thaman has initiated the development of a series of resource modules for teacher education in the region. In a low-cost but relatively durable format, they are designed for use by teacher educators and their students in the Pacific. An initial set of six modules deal with themes as diverse as: making sense of human development from a South Pacific perspective; ethnomathematics; incorporating local knowledge into the curriculum; the role of vernacular languages in the classroom; and learning from indigenous leadership (Thaman and Benson, 2000). They all have a common goal of assisting educators in the Pacific to understand and use their own ways of thinking, knowing and understanding in the classroom.

Papua New Guinea

Papua New Guinea (PNG) is a nation of immense diversity in cultures, languages and geography. With a population of approximately four million people, it has over 860 separate languages, together with numerous dialects (Nagai, 2000). As Nagai (2000: 79) explains:

> Each ethnic group from the small (300–900 people) to the large (up to 100,000 people) has developed a distinct way of life and pattern of culture. The language and cultural characteristics in one community will not necessarily be repeated in the village beyond the next mountain, or across the next river.

Most regions of PNG have a relatively recent history of colonization, predominantly during the past century, by Germany, Britain and later Australia, and during Word War II by the Japanese. The Western education system was introduced by various Christian missionaries, with English as the language of instruction. Between the end of World War II and independence in 1975, however, Australia played a dominant role in the provision of schooling and post-secondary education. The colonial legacy in PNG has been deeply resistant to change, and it is only in the past decade that significant educational reforms have begun to emerge, largely in the early years of schooling. Prior to the reforms, children generally started formal schooling at age six, entering a primary school where the language of instruction was English, or a combination of English and PNG Creole, or pidgin, that developed during the early colonial era.

The curriculum was little different from that of the pre-independence era, with didactic teaching and rote learning the norm.

In a genuine attempt to ground the education system in local knowledge and learning, a totally new level of schooling was introduced in the mid-1990s. Children now began school at age five, entering a vernacular elementary school where they would spend three years before moving on to primary school. The aim of the new vernacular elementary schools is to produce young people who are firmly rooted in their own languages and cultures, and who have a strong sense of their own cultural identity and associated cultural values. These children then can move on to primary school, with its more Westernized curriculum and use of English as the language of instruction, thereby learning to take their place in the modern, globalized world.

The development of the vernacular elementary school system was a major undertaking for a small developing nation, especially given its linguistic diversity. Many languages are specific to a particular village, or small cluster of villages. How does one find teachers fluent in the local language, and develop a curriculum that is grounded in the local culture? The challenge for education authorities in PNG clearly was to develop a 'bottom-up' approach to early education by drawing on the skills and resources of people within the village. This was done by asking a village to identify two or three adults who had the most appropriate cultural and status qualifications to assume the role of teachers, and who were prepared to accept this responsibility. These people then were given a six week programme of intensive training in a residential college to equip them to begin their work. At the same time the villages were expected to provide a simple structure within which schooling could take place. Generally these schools were built of local materials by the villagers themselves.

Once the school was operational, the teachers were supported in their work by a cadre of especially trained advisers who provided continuing professional development, both on-site and through small regional workshops. The teachers also continued their studies in distance mode, and attended further college-based intensive training programmes, until they had completed a teaching diploma. All instruction in the school was in the vernacular, community participation encouraged, and the curriculum localized both in content and process. The most significant challenge was the teaching of reading. How could literacy be introduced in a vernacular that had few, if any, print resources, or in some cases not even a developed written form and associated orthography? Fortunately many of the small languages of PNG have the latter, and have had at least some parts of the Christian Bible translated and produced in written form thanks to the work of the Summer Institute of Linguistics and other missionary organizations.

Using whatever local language resources are available, or can be developed by villagers, the teaching of vernacular literacy proceeds using the 'big book' approach. Instead of individual readers, teachers themselves, with community support, produce their own 'big books', using stories drawn from local traditions, events and experiences. Following carefully developed protocols in terms of level of complexity, introduction of new words, repetition of word forms, and so on, teachers produce written text on one side of a large page and, often with the help of children, illustrations to accompany the text on the facing page. Children then are taught to read the books by sitting on the floor around the teacher who displays the text and illustrations by holding the book in her/his lap. As each school develops a collection of big books, these became a resource for children in free reading periods, where they are allowed to read the books individually or in small groups. To facilitate the rapid deployment of big books in elementary schools across the nation, and to augment the supply of local material, 'shell' books have been developed as part of the reform process, and distributed widely to schools. These books provide a story written in pidgin or English inside the back cover, and black and white illustrations throughout. On receiving a shell book, teachers translate the story into the local language and record each segment opposite the matching illustration. The latter can then be coloured in by the children.

At this point it is appropriate to introduce another pedagogue, Yasuko Nagai, who has played an unobtrusive but effective role in supporting the reform process in PNG. A vernacular literacy consultant and educational anthropologist, Nagai was instrumental in facilitating the first vernacular elementary school in the nation, and in developing the use of the 'big book' methodology. Most of Nagai's work has been undertaken in Milne Bay Province at the Eastern end of the main island, and specifically at Maiwala village. Working with a group of three women who were selected by the Maiwala community as teachers, Nagai provided initial training and support which enabled the development of a localized curriculum. Having an unwavering commitment to 'bottom-up' development, she was able to develop a deep sense of local ownership and control of the processes and content of the elementary school programme at Maiwala. Having begun ahead of the reform process, the school subsequently became a demonstration site, and was used extensively for training purposes for teachers from other villages and regions, both through on-site visits and observation, and through the preparation of training videos. Many of the big books developed by the Maiwala teachers and community also were used in the preparation of the shell books described above. An impressive feature of Nagai's work in PNG is the extensive documentation of the processes and outcomes of her research and consultancy (see Nagai, 1999, 2000 and 2001 for recent examples).

Another pedagogue who has made a significant scholarly contribution in Papua New Guinea is Michael A. Mel, from the Mogei culture in the Melpa area of the PNG highlands, near Mount Hagen. Mel's initial work followed that of Thaman in exploring the linguistic and conceptual frameworks surrounding the processes of thinking, knowing, learning, feeling, understanding, remembering and living in his own culture (Mel, 1995). Using a holistic approach, he then applied the results of his analysis to reconceptualizing the content and processes of the school curriculum in PNG:

> Colonial practices placed an emphasis on subjects, knowledge and jobs, but not on the values and beliefs of the community. By shifting the emphasis, children will have closer contact with their own parents and relatives, and be able to participate more extensively in community life. The community will help and advise in varying degrees on curriculum content and process, on the location of schools ... and the language(s) of instruction. The community's values and beliefs will become an integral part of the children's education, enhancing their sense of place and identity. (Mel, 1995: 692)

In more recent years, Mel has taught at the University of Goroka (UoG), in the PNG highlands, where most of the nation's senior secondary school teachers are trained. His central project has been to decolonize the content and processes of the teacher education curriculum in line with the education reforms taking place in the school system. Mel (2000: 21) describes his work in the following way:

> The teacher education programs at UoG have relied far too much on ideas that have come from outside. Students are being trained in ways that seem very narrow and technical and exclude any real concern or

awareness of what it may mean to teach in an Indigenous context....
There is a clear and ever increasing gap between the dominant ideas from
outside and those from within.

The project sought to initiate a process of changing this system of teacher
training so that students could see the imbalance of ideas; ...(they)
could then begin to appreciate and acknowledge their own cultural
locations, including their own values, beliefs and languages, ... this in
turn would encourage them ... to engage with their own pupils and
encourage them to acknowledge and maintain their local cultural values,
beliefs and practices, and to grapple with the often powerful influences
from other cultures.

Eastern Indonesia

Indonesia is a large and complex nation: more than 13,000 islands,
and approximately 220 million people speaking over 700 different
languages. Having achieved independence at the end of World
War II, after 350 years of Dutch colonization followed by three
years of Japanese occupation, the task of bringing a sense of unity
and cohesion to such a disparate archipelago was a daunting one.
A centralized education system, with a common curriculum and
language of instruction, was one of the strategies used. Over the years
this led to an increasingly prescriptive and examination-dominated
curriculum in both primary and secondary schools, delivered using
didactic, teacher-centred methodologies. It was not until 1989 that
the national government finally recognized the limitations of this
approach, passing a new education law that allowed local groups to
develop a supplementary curriculum that included elements of their
own cultural values and practices. Even so, no more than 20 per
cent of the school curriculum could be localized, and, given the
lack of experience in curriculum development at local level, and the
hegemony of the national curriculum, the new law had little impact
overall. Nevertheless, a few scholars began to explore the possibilities of a more localized approach to schooling. One of these, Elias
Kopong, a Lamaholot person from the province of Nusa Tenggara
Timur in the east of the archipelago, began a series of pioneering
studies that have been reported in the Western literature (Kopong,
1995, 2000).

Kopong's initial work took the form of an ethnographic study of
learning amongst his own Lamaholot people. He found that children

acquire knowledge predominantly through active participation in the life of the home and community, by listening, by observation and imitation, and by parental modelling and advising in relation to specific skills and understandings. Kopong notes that the Lamaholot belief system permeates all knowledge, playing a unifying role. He continues:

> Within the extended family setting, knowledge is conveyed not so much to prepare the Lamaholot child for a better future life, but to preserve tradition.... Lamaholot culture emphasizes harmony and co-operation as important pre-requisites for survival, both in terms of co-existence with other people and with the physical surroundings ... the acquisition of knowledge and skills only becomes meaningful if it is applied to the benefit of the family and community, rather than simply being a means of establishing a sense of personal control over social situations. (Kopong, 1995: 644–45)

Kopong then went on to explore the implications of his findings for the contents, processes and contexts of the school curriculum, setting out a detailed framework for curriculum localization in Lamaholot settings. He believed that an integrated approach was feasible within the parameters of the Indonesian curriculum localization legislation. To demonstrate this, he subsequently sought and obtained Government of Indonesia research funding for a study at the senior secondary school level. A three-year study was planned in order to develop a culturally-based curriculum following an intensive programme of in-service training that attempted to change the attitudes and practices of teachers. A rigorous data collection and evaluation process was implemented throughout.

Initially Kopong worked with teachers and community leaders to identify the core values that formed their cultural identity. Three interrelated values emerged: hard work, cooperation and religious commitment. The national curriculum in all subject areas of the senior secondary school was reviewed from the perspective of these values, and the two-week in-service programme for teachers at the state high school in Larantuka focused on how these values might be built into teaching/learning processes during a three month implementation period. Kopong (2000: 40–41) takes up the story:

> Understandably, most teachers encouraged the value of hard work by regularly discussing with pupils the benefits of self-discipline and

persistence in their learning endeavours, and especially in their home-work. Examples were constantly given of good results achieved by con-sistent effort.

In order to promote the value of cooperation, teachers ... divided their classes into small work groups of four or five pupils and allocated learning tasks that had to be carried out collaboratively.... Another approach ... was the formation of study groups. Based on where they lived in the community, pupils were constituted in study groups that were expected to meet out of school hours to complete homework as-signments together.

From the perspective of religious commitment, most of the teachers de-cided to start and finish their lessons with prayer, thus reinforcing the value of religious observance in daily activities.

For many readers the approaches taken by the teachers may not seem particularly innovative.... However they need to be viewed against the background of secondary schooling in rural Indonesia, which is ex-tremely formal, didactic and teacher centred. It is most unusual for stu-dents to play any active role in their own learning.

Using nationally standardized tests, as well as classroom observa-tions and questionnaires, Kopong compared the performance and attitudes of students who participated in the study with control groups. Those who participated in the curriculum localization programme achieved significantly higher scores in most areas of school achieve-ment, showed more positive attitudes to local knowledge, and were more strongly motivated to implement local values in their daily lives. Kopong (2000: 41) concluded that, '...a fusion of the ... national and the local ... may actually enhance the acquisition of modern knowledge as well as enabling pupils to stand more firmly in their own cultural values and identities'.

Since Kopong began the latter study, the education laws in Indonesia have been further liberalized following the end of the Suharto era. As part of a national policy of political and financial decentralization, much greater autonomy is being given to local provinces and sub-districts in all areas of government activity, including education. Sig-nificant steps are being taken to localize the school curriculum, with up to 40 per cent of local content now permitted. At the request of the Government of Indonesia many donor agencies are focusing their development assistance in this area. One such development project is the Nusa Tenggara Timur Primary Education Partnership (NTTPEP) a major initiative funded by the Government of Australia in the island of Flores, in the eastern archipelago.

NTTPEP is working closely with teachers in the early years of primary school, initially in central Flores, assisting them to rebuild the curriculum from a centralized, top-down model, to one that is localized and 'bottom-up', with extensive community participation. Ownership of the content and processes of the curriculum by local communities is being encouraged. Regular workshops involving teachers, principals and school inspectors are seeking to identify local ways of thinking, knowing and learning, and are exploring how these might be incorporated into the teaching processes of the school. There is strong interest in the use of local languages in the early years of schooling, and a vernacular literacy programme has begun in some villages, using the 'big book' approach described earlier. Although NTTPEP has been running for little more than one year, significant changes already are evident. These are being shared widely throughout Flores and beyond through radio broadcasts and regular journals distributed as inserts in local newspapers.

CURRICULUM LOCALIZATION IN A WESTERN UNIVERSITY SETTING: A PERSONAL ACCOUNT

I would like to conclude this chapter by describing my own attempts in a Western university setting to allow post-graduate students from the south (and here I also include Indigenous Australian students) to draw on their own local knowledge and wisdoms in their scholarly work. These students bring with them the epistemologies, deep values, and learning approaches of their own local cultures as they enter the global world of the Australian university. There is an immediate tension between the global and the local. It is a tension that challenges many of their deeply-held ways of thinking, knowing and learning. They are expected to make a choice between two seemingly oppositional world views. And most staff expect them to choose the global, and to put the local on hold, presumably for the duration of their university studies.

In my own work, and in providing professional development programmes for my colleagues, I have started asking some quite radical questions: How can we help our students from the south to deal with the tensions between the global and the local? How can we enable them to live confidently and productively in our globalizing world and yet maintain, in a strong and dynamic way, their own cultures of primary identity? How can we affirm and celebrate their local identities, yet prepare them to engage effectively with the global?

The answer sounds simple, but in reality is complex: I believe we should meet them half-way, or at least part-way. Instead of expecting them to come 100 per cent of the way into our cultures of knowledge and learning, we should adapt just as much to theirs. Instead of using a process of assimilation, we should use one of accommodation, where we each adapt to the other. In other words, we should make adjustments to our teaching, and to our expectations of their learning, in response to their ways of thinking, knowing, and learning. We should, in other words, help them to achieve a functional balance—or fusion—between the global and the local.

Because every teaching and learning environment is different, there is no simple formula for doing this. And I'm not aware of many university teachers in Australia or elsewhere who are attempting it. So I cannot tell you what to do. I have no magical answers. But what I can do is share some stories based on my own experiences during the past fifteen years as I have sought to meet students half way—to meet them in terms of their own knowledge, wisdom, and learning. It has been a fascinating journey. I've made a lot of mistakes, and I certainly do not claim to have many of the answers. But the stories may provide some ideas and inspiration. To preserve anonymity, I have used pseudonyms throughout, and varied geographical locations.

Helen

Helen was an Indigenous Australian student who grew up on a cattle station in a very remote part of Western Australia. Her first degree was in visual arts. Now she was doing a Masters in Education. She had a remarkable visual capacity—both conceptually, and expressively. She struggled to put ideas into words and sentences. But ideas flowed powerfully from the end of a paintbrush. There was no way I could see her completing a conventional written thesis. Yet she was an outstandingly talented student. So we encouraged her to paint her thesis.

First Helen went back to the country of her childhood to talk with those who grew her up, and with those who grew up with her.

Then she came back to her studio and painted. Her studio became a laboratory where she tested and expressed her ideas. She prepared dozens of big canvases. And as she painted she talked into a tape recorder. As ideas developed on canvas, so she was able to express them in words, and to capture those words. She subsequently used edited transcripts of the words along with the pictures as the text of the thesis. The end result was an original and very powerful research report on the education of young Indigenous Australians.

Wani

Wani was from a small village on a remote northern island of Papua New Guinea. During her childhood she was regularly cared for and educated by her maternal grandparents, neither of whom had any contact with European cultures and languages. A particularly bright child, she was selected by her family to attend a secondary boarding school, from whence she was chosen for study at the University of Papua New Guinea. Now she was in Australia to do a Masters, which soon turned into a Ph.D, so effective was her academic work.

Wani struggled with the conceptual framework of her thesis, so we talked about how she might draw on the wisdom and knowledge of her own people, and in particular, the ways of thinking and knowing that she had acquired from her grandparents. Hers was an oral culture, where the story was the primary tool for the storage and analysis of knowledge. So she decided to use story telling as her primary method of analysis, blending it, where appropriate, with Western modes of thought.

Thus, Wani's theoretical chapters began with the telling of a story, a story that provided the conceptual framework for her thesis. The issues were not separately identified and dealt with in a linear or sequential way. Instead, Wani approached her research question by 'walking around it' in ever decreasing circles, using a holistic approach, and regularly coming back to her central story. At various stages other stories were used to clarify or explicate.

The end result of Wani's work was a very dynamic fusion of the local and the global. The syncretism of the two was somehow more powerful than either could have been on its own. And Wani certainly benefited in terms of affirmation of her own deep cultural identity.

Paulus

I have another Ph.D student from PNG named Paulus. He is currently back home completing his data collection, and he too has been given the freedom to blend the local and the global. He has gone back to his village to explore with the older men the oral literature of his people, so that his literature review can bring together both global and local perspectives. From this he has developed a conceptual framework based on an explanatory device—a kind of metaphor—that his people traditionally have used to understand the processes of growing up their children. But he has expanded and developed this through an exploration of Western theoretical perspectives. Again there is this creative fusion of the global and the local. I'm waiting with interest for his return.

Both Wani and Paulus bring a spiritual, or metaphysical dimension to their thinking and writing. Unlike the Western style, with its quite narrow focus on the empirical and the rational, they are comfortable with the subjective, and with spiritual explanations of reality. Like many indigenous peoples, they have a tolerance for ambiguity. One of the important lessons for me, as I seek to accommodate to their epistemologies, is to accept this ability to hold two seemingly incompatible ways of thinking at the same time.

Mike

Mike was one of my Ph.D students—a philosopher by training, and an Indigenous Australian. He too was given the opportunity to blend the local and the global. Like others, he took a holistic approach, traversing a number of themes in ever increasing intensity until he reached the nub or core of his ideas. He described it as 'talking it through to the end' or, 'talking it to death', likening the process to that used by Indigenous Australian groups when they meet to talk through a dilemma, or a matter of concern, and keep talking, however long it takes, until they have reached a resolution.

I was sharing my experience in supervising Mike with an indigenous Maori colleague. Instead of traversing in ever decreasing circles, he explained his way of thinking using a cross-section of a nautilus shell: he started with an initial idea, and then let it traverse outwards, in an ever expanding way.

CONCLUSION

The great challenge for educators in the south is to achieve an effective syncretism between the local and the global. Schools, colleges and universities in the south need to produce young people who are firmly grounded in their own local languages and cultures, and who have a real sense of who they are and where they belong. Yet these institutions also need to prepare young people to take their place in the modern globalizing world with ease and confidence.

This is a profound challenge given the hegemony of Western epistemologies. How can it best be addressed? Those of us working with students from the south who have chosen to study in Western countries face a similar challenge: how can we affirm and celebrate their local identities, yet prepare them to engage effectively with the global? This chapter has explored some of the newly emerging pedagogies of the south, and introduced several of its pedagogues who are seeking to address questions such as these. Theirs is a daunting task as they seek to develop approaches to teaching and learning that are more in harmony with the local. It takes much determination to nurture local knowledge and languages, and to ensure their effective and balanced representation in the curriculum. Pedagogues in the south are at a relatively early stage in their attempts to achieve these goals, although the momentum for change is growing. We in the west would do well to learn from their experiences and to support their endeavours.

REFERENCES

Delors, J. (chair). 1996. *Learning: The Treasure Within*. Report to UNESCO of the International Commission on Education for the Twenty-First Century. Paris: UNESCO.

Harris, S.C. 1990. *Two-Way Aboriginal Schooling: Education and Cultural Survival*. Canberra: Aboriginal Studies Press.

Kopong, E. 1995. 'Informal Learning: A Case Study of Local Curriculum Development in Indonesia', *Prospects: UNESCO Quarterly Review of Comparative Education*, XXV (4): 639–51.

———. 2000. 'Universities and Curriculum Localisation in Nusa Tenggara Timur, Indonesia', in G.R. Teasdale and Z. Ma Rhea (eds), *Local Knowledge and Wisdom in Higher Education*, pp. 33–42. Oxford: Pergamon.

Mel, M.A. 1995. 'Mbu: A Culturally Meaningful Framework for Education in Papua New Guinea', *Prospects: UNESCO Quarterly Review of Comparative Education*, XXV (4): 683–94.

———. 2000. 'The Indigenisation of Trainee Teachers in Papua New Guinea', in G.R. Teasdale and Z. Ma Rhea (eds), *Local Knowledge and Wisdom in Higher Education*, pp. 15–32. Oxford: Pergamon.

Nagai, Y. 1999. 'Developing a Community-Based Vernacular School: A Case Study of the Maiwala Elementary School in Papua New Guinea', *Language and Education*, 13 (3): 178–206.

———. 2000. 'New Approaches to University Research in Indigenous Settings: An Example from Papua New Guinea', in G.R. Teasdale and Z. Ma Rhea (eds), *Local Knowledge and Wisdom in Higher Education*, pp. 79–94. Oxford: Pergamon.

———. 2001. 'Developing Assessment and Evaluation Strategies for Vernacular Elementary School Classrooms: A Collaborative Study in Papua New Guinea', *Anthropology and Education Quarterly*, 32(1): 80–103.

Teasdale, G.R. 1998. 'Local and Global Knowledge in Higher Education: A Search for Complementarity in the Asia-Pacific Region', *International Journal of Educational Development*, 18(6): 501–11.

Teasdale, J.I. and G.R. Teasdale. 1999. 'Alternative Cultures of Knowledge in Higher Education in the Australia-Pacific Region', in F.E. Leach and A.W. Little (eds), *Education, Cultures, and Economics: Dilemmas for Development*, pp. 241–60. London: Falmer.

Thaman, K.H. 1998. 'Pillar 4: Learning to Be', in G.W. Haw and P.W. Hughes (eds), *Education for the 21st Century in the Asia-Pacific Region: Report on the Melbourne UNESCO Conference 1998*, pp. 71–77. Canberra: Australian National Commission for UNESCO.

———. 2000. 'Towards a New Pedagogy: Pacific Cultures in Higher Education', in G.R. Teasdale and Z. Ma Rhea (eds), *Local Knowledge and Wisdom in Higher Education*, pp. 43–50. Oxford: Pergamon.

———. 2001. 'Towards Culturally Inclusive Teacher Education with Specific Reference to Oceania', *International Education Journal*, 2(5): 1–8.

———. 2002. 'Towards Cultural Democracy in Pacific Education: An Imperative for the 21st Century', in *Tree of Opportunity: Rethinking Pacific Education*, pp. 22–30. Suva: Institute of Education, University of the South Pacific.

Thaman, K.H. and C. Benson (eds). 2000. *Pacific Cultures in the Teacher Education Curriculum*. Modules 1 to 6. Suva: Institute of Education, University of the South Pacific.

Institute of Education. 2002. *Tree of Opportunity: Rethinking Pacific Education*. Suva: University of the South Pacific.

Wilson, M. and P. Hunt (eds). 2000. *Culture, Rights, and Cultural Rights*. Wellington, New Zealand: Huia.

6
EDUCATION OF TRIBAL CHILDREN IN INDIA

RAMESH C. MISHRA

This paper describes some major challenges confronting the education of tribal children in India. The tribal context of India is briefly described. Cultural and psychological characteristics of tribal children are examined with a view to analyze how these can be used in meeting the challenges of education. Major issues related to the education of tribal children are described in some detail. The strategies adopted by the federal and state governments are discussed and critically evaluated. It is argued that the problems related to tribal children's education are very different from those of other cultural groups of the Indian society. For effective participation of tribal children in education, a culturally sensitive, ecologically valid and economically viable programme of education will have to be evolved and implemented.

THE TRIBAL CONTEXT OF INDIA

India represents a culturally plural society in all respects. A large number of ethnic, religious, and linguistic groups constitute the cultural mosaic of the country. These groups differ enormously in their overall socio-cultural features. Such a cultural diversity provides Indian researchers with an opportunity to carry out cross-cultural research next door for which researchers from other places (for example, Europe and USA) have to bear the trouble of travelling long distances, often to other nations. If we look at these diverse groups, we find that while some of them constitute the mainstream of Indian society, others exist as peripheral groups seeking entry (or being pushed to enter) into the orbit of the larger mainstream society. Mainstream Indian society is characterized by the existence of an inherent caste structure (traditionally called *varna*), which is vertical in nature and is generally unheard of elsewhere in the world. On the top of this structure are the Brahmins. The *kshatriyas, vaishyas* and *sudras* occupy the lower levels in this structural hierarchy respectively. The last ones, the *sudras*, are now designated as 'scheduled castes' (SC), because they have been scheduled under the Constitution of India for special privileges for a period of time. They represent about 15 per cent of the total population of the country. The tribal people constitute an outcaste group, as they do not form part of mainstream Indian society. They are popularly known as *adivasi,* which means the 'original inhabitants' of a country. They are regarded as the people indigenous to the soil. A majority of them live in naturally isolated forests and hilly regions, hence, they are also known as *vanbasi* (forest dwelling people). Constitutionally, these groups have been termed 'scheduled tribes' (ST) or *anusuchit janjati* after being scheduled in the Constitution of India for special privileges for a period of time, similar to the SC groups. They are more like the indigenous or native peoples in other parts of the world.

It may be noted that the term 'tribe' is nowhere defined in the Constitution of India. As a result, a lot of debate revolves around the use of this term for the groups of people we are referring to here. Maffesoli (1996) argues that all of us seem to belong to tribal groups in some respect. According to article 342 of the Constitution of India, the ST represents the tribes or tribal communities, which may be notified by the President. This means that the existing list of tribal groups cannot be taken as final. The Census of India enumerates only such tribal communities as are scheduled under the relevant constitutional order in force at the time of the census.

Reports indicate that India has the largest population of tribal people in the world. According to the 1991 census, the tribal population of India was about 67.8 million constituting approximately 8.1 per cent of the country's population. This figure does not include Jammu and Kashmir where the 1991 census enumeration did not take place. The census report indicates that the tribal population varies considerably from one state to another. The largest population was found in undivided Madhya Pradesh (approximately 16.40 million), followed by Orissa (approximately 7.03 million) and undivided Bihar (approximately 6.61 million). Their largest proportion to total population among all states is found in Mizoram (95 per cent), followed by Nagaland (88 per cent), Meghalaya (85 per cent) and Arunachal Pradesh (64 per cent). Among the Union Territories, Lakshadweep ranks first (93 per cent) (islands in the sea down south, west of Kerala) followed by Dadra Nagar Haveili (79 per cent) (in Gujarat).

Generally speaking, the term tribal, in India refers to a group of people who, (a) claim themselves as indigenous to the soil, (b) generally inhabit forest and hilly regions, (c) largely pursue a subsistence level economy, (d) have great regard for traditional religious and cultural practices, (e) believe in common ancestry, and (f) have strong in-group ties. However, none of these characteristics strictly applies to all tribal people. For all practical purposes, the term tribal today represents a 'federally determined and locally recognized category'. In some psychological research, however, they are also identified on the basis of 'strong tribal identity' just like any ethnic group in a multicultural society.

It is true that tribal people do not form a homogeneous group today. It is also true that a majority of them largely retains its traditional culture and identity despite having undergone many historical and cultural influences in earlier decades. Even today tribal people represent the most neglected group of Indian society (Sivanand, 2001). The centre- and state-level governments have introduced a variety of developmental programmes to bring about changes in different spheres of their life. As a result, tribal people currently witness several changes, some at the group and others at individual levels. However, their participation in various change programmes has been fairly diverse depending mainly on the place where they live in the country.

Based on several indicators of socio-economic development and cultural transformations in their life, tribal people have been classified in a number of ways. A dominant classification based on economic activities puts them in four distinct categories, namely hunting–gathering group, rudimentary agricultural group, irrigation–agricultural group, and urban, industrial, wage-earning group. In recent years, many individuals of irrigation–agricultural group have engaged in business or wage employment in a variety of organizations.

Such people are very different from those tribals who still pursue their traditional lifestyle. They have adopted many cultural and psychological qualities of the members of other groups. They participate in various spheres of life (for example, political, economic, religious, and educational) more or less similar to the members of the general population. On the other hand, the hunting gathering (for example, Birhor) and rudimentary agricultural (for example, Asur) groups display little impact of other cultural groups or of development programmes. These groups are labelled 'primitive' or 'backward' tribes not only by outsiders, but also in official records. It is the members of these groups that are in the main focus of educational and other developmental activities of the government. They have very low participation in programmes of education and wider economic activities.

People generally hold a negative view of tribals. Even in scholarly writings and official documents, terms like 'primitive culture', 'educational backwardness', 'cultural backwardness' and 'intellectual deficits' have often been used. These expressions suggest that tribals are culturally inferior, behaviourally unsophisticated and intellectually underdeveloped compared to members of other groups. Such conceptions held about tribal people do not have any logical basis or empirical support. The strengths of tribal culture and life generally go unnoticed by people who do not know them very closely. Hence, most evaluative judgements about them largely reflect the stereotypical perceptions of the larger population.

EDUCATIONAL STATUS OF TRIBALS IN INDIA

Some information about the educational status of tribal children in India can be obtained from the census data. The first census in 1951 did not provide any data on the literacy rate among tribal people. In later census reports, we find information about literacy rate not only in the general population, but also among scheduled castes and tribes. The census records indicate an almost three times increase in the literacy rate among tribals (from 8 per cent in 1961 to 24 per cent in 1991). The records also indicate that female literacy rate had increased four times (from 3.8 to 14.5 per cent) during the same period.

Inspite of the increase in literacy rate as reflected in the 1991 census, the tribals have a lower literacy rate than that of the general population (52 per cent). The tribal literacy rate is also lower than that of the scheduled castes (30 per cent), which is identified as another disadvantaged group of the Indian society. The literacy rate among rural tribals (21.81 per cent) is lower than that of the urban (46.35 per cent). The census also indicates wide differences in literacy rates according to tribal groups as well as according to regions. For example, the literacy rate among the Naga is higher than other tribal groups, whereas it is very low among the Bhil of Rajasthan and Santals of Bihar, although both are numerically large tribal groups.

These census records also indicate that the gross school enrolment ratio among tribals at the primary school level is almost similar to that of other groups of the population. In the case of tribal boys, in fact, the enrolment ratio (125.6) is slightly higher than that of the scheduled caste (121.4) or the general population (115.3) (these figures are derived per thousand of the population). The situation changes drastically between grades six and eight, and we find lesser number of tribal children in schools than those of other groups. This suggests that schools are not able to retain tribal children to the same level, as is the case of children of other groups. High rate of 'drop out' of tribal children from schools is a characteristic feature of tribal education even today. Ensuring school 'enrolment' of tribal children has been a major agenda of the 'universalization of education' programme during the last few years. As a result of this programme, almost all children are now enrolled in one school or another, although many of them may have never attended it. However, many of those who go to school somehow do not find it attractive and decide to leave it at some point of time. Preventing 'drop out' of children from schools is a serious challenge for the educational authorities. A number of incentives (for example, scholarships, free supply of books, uniform, and midday meal, and so on) are being tried out with tribal children. Unfortunately these plans have not been very successful in retaining children in schools owing largely to a poor delivery system.

PSYCHOLOGICAL STUDIES WITH TRIBAL CHILDREN

The effect of day-to-day activities of tribal children and socialization experiences during childhood on the development of their cognitive abilities or competencies has been reported in several anthropological writings. In spite of these favourable reports many people, including teachers, cast doubt on the competence of tribal children for school achievement. They believe that tribal children are not as 'educable' as the children of other groups. As a result, a number of studies have been undertaken to assess the personality and cognitive characteristics of tribal children. Among others, psychologists have tried to study these competencies more systematically. They have directly assessed some of the skills and abilities of tribal children in a variety of settings. These empirical studies provide us with some understanding of the cognitive life of tribal children.

Broadly speaking, the studies on tribal children have tried to assess their performance in *school settings* and *test settings*. Since these studies inform us about the cognitive strengths of tribal children we will examine them in some detail before moving on to the various issues confronting education of children of the tribal groups.

Studies carried out in school settings generally focus on the overall achievement of tribal children in the classroom as compared to those of other groups. A general finding of these studies is that tribal children perform poorly in schools and demonstrate a lower level of achievement in comparison to children of other cultural groups. Singh (1996) and Singh and Jayaswal (1981) have argued that low levels of parental education, occupation, income, and deprivation characteristics of home and neighbourhood are mainly responsible for poor performance of tribal children at school. They have also analyzed the characteristics of the family of tribal children. These analyses reveal that factors like negative parental attitude to education, less parental support in schoolwork, and educationally less encouraging patterns of parent–child interaction largely account for poor school performance of tribal children. Low levels of motivation and poor self-concept of children have also been considered as important factors in poor school performance.

None of these studies provides evidence of any cognitive or intellectual deficiency on the part of tribal children. They clearly suggest that familial, social, economic, and motivational factors are largely responsible for poor educational achievement of these children. Sinha and Mishra (1997) have argued that tribal children can perform fairly well in schools if the intervention programmes directed at them can overcome their deprivation conditions. Tribal parents generally lack motivation for sending children to school. In day-to-day life they interact with children in a manner that would not at all encourage them to participate in the process of school education. In the school, they are taught various skills (for example, use of language and mathematics) in a setup that is far removed from their real life context. No effort is made to link school education with the skills and abilities that are strongly placed among children (perceptual differentiation, tactual abilities). All these factors create a context in which schooling turns out to be an uninteresting goal both for the community and the child. Encouraging appropriate motivations and patterns of parent–child interaction in the home and the use of abilities that are highly placed among tribal children for educational purposes can also ensure their optimal performance in schools (Sinha and Mishra, 1997).

Studies of tribal children in test settings are many. However, only few have used psychological tests in which real life situations of tribals find adequate representation. In these studies the contents of the tests are carefully drawn from the local natural context of tribal children and the functions required in tests match fairly well with those represented in children's performance of activities in day-to-day settings. These studies indicate that the cognitive qualities of tribal children can be reliably understood, assessed and evaluated by examining their 'functionality' or 'utility' in day-to-day life. Abilities of perceptual differentiation, learning and memory, categorization, conservation, and spatial orientation are mainly examined in these studies. We will briefly describe here some of the studies related to these abilities.

Perceptual differentiation

In an early study, Sinha (1979) worked with two subgroups of the Birhor tribal culture of Bihar (now Jharkhand). One of these led a nomadic hunting-gathering life; another had made the transition to a sedentary agricultural life. A long-standing agricultural group of the Oraon tribal culture was also included. Boys and girls of eight to ten years, sampled from each of these groups, were administered Sinha's (1978, 1984). Story Pictorial Embedded Figures Test (SPEFT). This test was modelled on the Children's Embedded Figures Test (CEFT) by embedding local familiar stimuli (for example, squirrels, snakes, and butterflies) in larger organized natural scenes (for example, forests, and gardens). Findings revealed that children of the hunting-gathering group disembedded a significantly greater number of stimuli in comparison to those of the agricultural group. In another study, Sinha (1980) compared tribal and non-tribal samples with a view to analyzing sex difference in performance of the SPEFT.

The difference between boys and girls in the tribal sample was not significant. On the other hand, a clear gender difference (favouring boys) in the non-tribal sample was noted in the four to five, seven to eight and nine to ten year groups. The results indicated that hunters and gatherers were psychologically more differentiated than agriculturists.

G. Sinha (1988) studied the role of schooling as well as exposure to industrial and urban environment in perceptual differentiation among children of the Santal tribal culture. The effects of all these variables on SPEFT scores were found to be in the predicted direction (greater differentiation in the schooled, industrial, and urban samples). This shows that differentiation can be influenced both by traditional and acculturation factors. There was also evidence for a stronger influence of industrialization than schooling or urbanization on performance of the SPEFT. A less pervasive effect of schooling was attributed to some qualitative features of schools found in the Santal region. While these schools did not function regularly due to the absence of teachers, the quality of teaching and learning was also poor and functionally ineffective.

Mishra et al. (1996) carried out a large-scale study in parts of the State of Bihar (now Jharkhand) in India, focusing on children and adults of the Birhor (nomadic hunter-gatherer group), Asur (recent settlers pursuing a mixed economy of hunting, gathering, and agriculture), and Oraon (long-standing agriculturists) tribal cultural groups. In each group, sampling variations were obtained with respect to a number of objective and subjective measures of contact-acculturation. The test-acculturation of individuals was also assessed. SPEFT, TEFT (Tactile Embedded Figures Test), and Kohs Block Designs Test were used as the measures of cognitive style.

Findings with regard to the effect of ecology and acculturation on cognitive performance of adults and children were in the predicted direction. Hunter-gatherers were cognitively more differentiated than agricultural samples. The interaction between ecological background and acculturation revealed the effect of the latter, largely for the Oraon sample. Although test acculturation appeared to be an important predictor of people's test-performance, it could not displace the effect of the long-standing eco-cultural adaptation of groups. Mishra and Mishra (in prep) obtained support for these results in another study with children of predominantly hunting-gathering, agricultural and wage-earning samples of the Tharu culture drawn from the northern Himalayan region.

Mishra (1996) adopted another strategy in a study of unschooled children of the Birjia cultural group in Jharkhand. Distances travelled away from home either in the forest or within the village and self-directed activities of children were assessed to develop ecological parameters. Children were administered the SPEFT and the Indo-African EFT as tests of perceptual differentiation. The findings revealed that children moving into the forests (called forest-children) generally travelled longer distances and engaged in more self-directed activities than did those moving in the village surroundings. Forest-children also scored significantly higher than village-children on both the measures. These findings were explained in terms of greater exploration opportunities and high differentiation demands placed on children in the ecology of the forest.

These findings bring out the 'adaptive' quality of cognitive abilities. They suggest that abilities developed among individuals are significantly related to their utility and functionality in a given ecological or cultural context.

Learning and memory

Learning and memory play important roles in the life of each one of us. It is true that we do not learn and remember everything that we encounter in this world. We learn only those things that seem to be important for successful living in our environment. Similarly we remember only those things that seem to be important for us. The environment in which tribal people live is very different from ours, and so are the demands of their environment. Therefore, one can expect several differences between tribal and non-tribal children both in the contents as well as ways of learning and remembering.

The difficulties of learning identified with tribal children in school settings seem to reflect an ethnocentric bias. Researchers have rarely attempted to assess the tribal context of learning and memory while studying these in school settings. When due attention is paid to these contexts in the tasks and test situations, supposed deficiencies of tribal children's learning and memory often disappear.

Shukla (1991) and Mishra et al. (1999) assessed the learning and memory of Tharu childern living in the north Himalayan region of India, and compared their performance with those of the non-scheduled and scheduled castes. Lists of unrelated, phonetically related, and conceptually related words were given to children. A free recall procedure was used to assess learning and memory.

The analyses revealed that on unrelated and conceptually related tasks, Tharu children demonstrated poorer learning and memory than the other two groups. On the phonetic task, they demonstrated not only slightly better learning than other groups, but also significant evidence of clustering in recall, which was faintly evident on the conceptual task. This evidence clearly reflects the influence of cultural practices of singing and dancing, which are primarily based on rhythmic principles. Singing and dancing are an integral part of the Tharu cultural life, and these are greatly admired and valued in the community. From a very early age, a Tharu child is socialized into these arts through regular participation with adult members of the community. Thus, the child is fully exposed to a cultural environment in which attending to rhythmic qualities of stimuli is imperative. These experiences not only predispose Tharu children to use their cognitive processes on the task that requires processing according to phonetic features of verbal items, but also serve as aids to learning and memory.

Studies also reveal that tribal children seem to have an amazing memory in some spheres. Mishra and Singh (1992) compared the recall memory of Asur children of Jharkhand for 'pair' and 'location' of objects, using a culturally appropriate task especially designed for those children. Children remembered the 'location' of pictures far better than the 'pair' of pictures even in the absence of explicit instructions to do so. The authors indicated that the Asur are in the habit of managing life during nights without lamps or other sources of light. Such a life dictates on them that various objects are placed at fixed places in the home and remembered accurately so that they could be easily reached in the hours of need even during nights when there was no source of light. Such cultural practices predispose them to learn and recall the location of objects better than the pair of objects. Instructions in this case helped only in learning of the pair of pictures.

Thus, the findings of research in this domain indicate that the abilities, which are functionally salient in the cultural life of a group, are highly developed and competently displayed in test situations by individuals who negotiate their life in that particular culture.

Conservation abilities

Studies carried out in the Piagetian research tradition suggest that in the course of development, children acquire the ability to conserve the properties of various objects. Conservation of mass, weight, volume and spatial concepts have been particularly investigated in the Indian setting. Poor ability of conservation on the part of tribal children has often been reported (see Mishra, 1998). Many researchers have taken this as reflecting a low level of cognitive development of tribal children as compared to that of the non-tribal.

On the other hand, some studies reveal a very different story. They suggest that even these universal processes need to be examined in the context of their utility in day-to-day life of tribal children. Mishra (1994) compared the conservation abilities of the Birhor and Oraon of Jharkhand by using locally available objects as test materials. He found a higher level of volume conservation in the Oraon group as compared to that of the Birhor, and a high level of spatial conservation in the Birhor as compared to that of the Oraon. Volume conservation task included small and big wooden pots of narrow and large diameter. Spatial conservation tasks required the judgement of ropes of different lengths put in different configurations, judgement of area, distances of objects, and spatial memory of objects. The functional utility of these concepts in the life of the two cultural groups was clearly demonstrated. In the hunting-gathering life of Birhors, spatial understanding is of prime importance because it helps in knowing one's location and organizing hunts and traps in the forest. In the agricultural life, on the other hand, understanding of volume is of prime value, because farmers must be skilful enough to estimate the amount of rice in order to work out the number of vessels in which it could be safely stored. Such conservation qualities represent an important dimension of cognitive development, and the evidence suggests that tribal children are fairly competent in these cognitive operations. However, a comparison of these abilities of tribal children with those of the non-tribal populations is strongly warranted.

Classification of objects

The external world around us presents us with such an enormous set of stimuli that some kind categorization of those stimuli becomes essential to organize and retain them for future use. Categorization represents a relatively higher form of cognitive activity, because it requires individuals to go beyond the information contained in stimuli. How do tribal children go about using it?

Mishra et al. (1996) presented to tribal children an array of objects for putting them freely into categories that they thought was most appropriate. They found that the Birhor children demonstrated this complex cognitive behaviour. While conceptual (for example, all are animals) and structural (for example, all have four legs) properties of stimuli formed important bases of classification, function or utility of objects was used more frequently as the basis of classification of objects. Some researchers argue that functional categorization represents a less advanced form of cognition from a developmental point of view. If we adopt this viewpoint, then we may interpret this result as indicating that tribal children are cognitively less advanced than children of other groups. Contrary to this, Mishra et al. (1996) argue that there is no question of greater or lesser advancement of cognition. The evidence only suggests that cognitive activities of tribal children are largely governed by a utilitarian principle.

Mishra et al.'s (1996) study also indicates that tribal children, even of the nomadic group, possess remarkable ability for making fine judgements of shape and size of stimuli. Their tactual ability is highly developed and the sense of direction, spatial orientation and grasp of spatial relations are unparalleled. All these cognitive qualities are in consonance with the demands of their day-to-day life. These cognitive qualities have allowed tribal people to survive in their respective eco-cultural contexts facing many kinds of challenges of life.

EDUCATION OF TRIBAL CHILDREN

In spite of the fact that psychological studies indicate that tribal children possess several cognitive strengths, their schooling has not met a desirable level of success. Participation of tribal children in formal education is not optimal. For a long time it was believed that longer distances of schools from tribal settlements were a major hindrance in children's school attendance. During the last decade, however, a number of schools have been established in remote tribal villages to cater to the primary educational needs of the communities. Many of these schools are fairly small (less than fifty students) often confined to one room, and a single teacher managing grades one to five. These schools also lack the basic minimum facilities of instruction (for example, chalk and blackboard) and stand nowhere in competing with other schools in non-tribal rural or urban areas.

However, the establishment of schools in tribal areas has led to the analysis of educational processes in these schools. A common assumption is that the tribal groups served by such schools are almost homogeneous and governed by common educational goals. Since the tribals share many common economic and social characteristics, it is also assumed that a common curriculum will be able to meet the educational requirements of all groups. Empirical studies, however, do not support these assumptions. In a study of tribal children and adults, Mishra (1996) found that different tribal groups not only hold different ideas about education, but they also perceive very different outcomes of schooling.

On the other hand, there are still tribals who hold the view that school education places children in a culturally marginalized state. Similar observations have been made by others who have worked with issues of school education of the tribal communities (for example, Jabbi and Rajyalakshmi, 2001). The government seems to have a full commitment for education of children of all tribal groups including those who still continue to live in forests as nomads. The greatest irony of this situation is that psychological dimensions have remained generally ignored not only in research on educational processes, but also in educational planning and policy. For example, we still don't know what the forest dwelling groups think about schooling of children. What kind of attitudes do they have about schooling? How will the schooling needs of such children be fulfilled whose families do not stay at a fixed place? What will be the content of their curriculum, and who will teach them? What will be the language of instruction? Other such questions need to be answered before a policy for education for these tribal groups is evolved and the process of school education initiated.

The psychological characteristics of tribal people, especially of those living in remote areas, are not much understood. Sinha and Mishra (1997) reviewed Indian studies related to personality, motivational and cognitive characteristics of tribal children. They found only a handful of studies; and these were considered too inadequate to form the basis of policy of tribal education. The dominant needs of tribal communities and their expectations from education were generally not examined at all in such studies. Mishra (2001) has attempted to analyze these aspects in the context of education of the Kharwar tribal group. Detailed analyses are still awaited, but the findings broadly suggest that participation of Kharwar children in education can be predicted to a considerable extent from an understanding of the needs of the community and the level to which people believe that education would serve as a means of fulfilling those needs.

MAJOR ISSUES OF TRIBAL EDUCATION

Efforts towards the education of tribal children in schools have brought out a number of issues that need to be seriously addressed both by researchers and policy makers. These relate broadly to teacher, curriculum, pedagogy, and language of instruction (Mishra, 1999). No appropriate answer to any of these issues has been discovered so far. In order to provide insight into these issues, we will briefly discuss them here.

Teachers

We all know that teachers occupy the most important place in all educational processes. In countries like India, where a teacher is respected as god, people expect considerably more from them with respect to children's education than elsewhere. A major problem of tribal education is the lack of interest of teachers in working in tribal areas. This applies to both tribal and non-tribal category of teachers. These areas are fairly remote, generally not easily accessible, and involve many problems (for example, poor physical facilities and living conditions, food), which discourage even teachers of tribal origin to work in those regions. Hence, the first priority of such teachers is to arrange an early transfer to a school in the city area. As long as this does not happen, they generally stay on leave or abstain from attending school. Even if they are physically present there, they take no interest in teaching. The non-tribal teachers find themselves placed in a new cultural setting, which has got no attractions for them. There is also a major problem of education of teachers' own children who come to work in the tribal regions. This forces teachers to leave their families all alone somewhere in a city. Their problems keep teachers mentally occupied most of the time. On the whole, the tribal setting turns out to be totally unattractive for teachers.

In order to overcome this problem several state governments have evolved the policy of sending the newly appointed teachers to serve in tribal areas for initial few years. A major issue related to this policy is: who should teach the children of tribal groups? A tribal teacher who knows about tribal culture, life and the demands of education for children, or a non-tribal teacher, who is alien to the place and has no sensitivity to tribal culture, life or the needs of tribal children. Should tribal children be taught by a newly recruited, inexperienced teacher or by an experienced teacher? To what extent will an unwilling teacher contribute to the quality of education in a school where serious commitment and sense of responsibility are required? What kind of controls can be developed for unwilling teachers to ensure the quality of education for tribal children? Even the very policy of forcing new teachers to work in remote tribal areas is questionable. Should teachers be forced for this, or other options (for example, incentives) be evolved that may attract more experienced teachers to work in tribal areas?

Studies suggest that teacher motivation contributes more to teaching-learning processes than teacher competence (Vaidyanathan and Nair, 2001). In an evaluative study Sarma, Dutta and Sarma (1992) found that almost 50 per cent trained teachers did not apply their teaching skills in the classrooms. How can teachers be motivated to practice the learnt skills in their classroom? This is a perpetual problem that bothers not only education administrators, but also people in general whose children attend schools.

Curriculum

Perhaps no issue is more seriously debated upon in the field of education than the curriculum that is to be taught to children in schools. The issue assumes greater significance in the context of tribal education. In the past the emphasis was on a 'common' curriculum for all children. It was based on the belief that school education as a means of change is closely linked with curriculum. Since the national goal was integration of tribal people with the larger society, a common curriculum was thought to facilitate this goal by providing tribal children with the same set of experiences to which children of other groups were exposed in their respective schools. During the last decades, many researchers have questioned the utility of uniform curriculum for tribal children. A plea has been made to develop culturally sensitive programmes of school education that can ensure 'dignity' of tribal groups by providing them with economically viable options for life (Sinha and Mishra, 1997).

As a result, some attempts seem to be evident for linking curriculum with the local needs of the communities. This has been done mainly in schools that are managed by NGOs in the tribal regions. Imparting knowledge about local environment and its resources represents an important part of the child's curriculum in such schools. It is believed that such a curriculum would make tribal children more sensitive to local contexts, and sustain them in their respective environments instead of forcing them to move out in search of another life.

Since such efforts have been made in a sporadic manner, they have not been able to influence the general run of tribal education. The policy planners have not seriously addressed the type of school education that will be more relevant for tribal children. How such education can be imparted has also not been addressed. Efforts in these directions seem to carry great relevance in the face of evidence that a majority of tribal children (as high as 70 per cent in some groups) drop out of schools within a few months of their enrolment. Comparative evaluations of traditional and the new curricula in terms of their flexibility, relevance and outcomes seriously require research attention (Dave, 1997) in respect of overall primary education in India. This is even more urgently needed in the context of tribal education.

Pedagogy

How something is taught to children in schools is perhaps more important than what is taught. The way teaching-learning processes are managed in schools has far-reaching consequences for a child's later life. Teaching technology is a highly debated issue in India today. For tribal children, direct experience and activity-based learning has been the traditional way of acquiring knowledge about various aspects of life including the skills that are needed for managing day-to-day affairs. This learning often took place in informal settings through participation of children in various activities with more skilled people of the community, who would correct any mistakes the child committed.

The learning sessions would continue as long as the child would not achieve an optimal level of perfection. A number of cultural practices were evolved to reinforce children's mastery. For example, in the hunting-gathering communities, a male will not be considered for marriage unless he has demonstrated his skill of managing a major hunt.

In the formal educational system, 'learning by doing' does not find a respectable place. Children are generally forced to commit to memory a prescribed curriculum, which is largely divorced from their real life situations. Tribal people often question the utility of such curriculum for development of their children. At the same time, learning such curriculum also requires children to concentrate on techniques through which they can pass or obtain high scores in examinations. This system does not provide children with opportunities to develop and master the skills required for effective functioning in vital spheres of life (for example, at home or in the workplace). As a result, schools are generally viewed as 'certificate distributing agencies' rather than as 'centers of learning' (Mishra, 1999). Since the schools in tribal areas lack even basic facilities, the use of modern technology as an aid to the teaching-learning process is beyond imagination. As a result, oral teaching and rote learning processes largely characterize the teaching-learning processes of tribal children in schools even today.

Some people have made efforts to exploit this situation by opening private schools at several locations in tribal areas. They use a market approach to education, in which 'profit' is granted a legitimate status. The overall set up of these schools appears quite impressive. Their appearance fits well with the fascinating image of schools that is projected to the minds of tribal people through various sensitization programmes of the government (for example, in posters and film shows). As a result, we find a phenomenal increase in the number of private schools not only in tribal areas, but also elsewhere in the country. Tilak (1998) has discussed in detail the maladies of private schools in general. Yet such schools have proliferated tremendously over the years to meet the educational challenges of an increasing number of children. The few tribal people, who can afford the cost of child's education in such schools, have granted acceptance to these schools. Some accommodation of experience and activity-based teaching and learning processes in these schools make them fairly distinct from government schools. However, more innovations in pedagogy are needed to generate and sustain the interest of tribal children towards learning in schools and to make this learning more effective.

Language

Language is the most essential component of communication and interaction processes. Unfortunately the policy on language use in schools is quite burdensome for many children. In some states of India, children can go through their entire school career in their mother tongue (for example, Hindi in Uttar Pradesh or Madhya Pradesh). In other states children begin with their mother tongue, but at some point of time, switch to another language. In many states, children have to acquire mastery in at least three languages (a regional, a vital, and a foreign language). This is particularly true for a tribal child, who often starts in school with mother tongue (a tribal language), but has to switch to a vital language (for example, Hindi) at the end of the primary level of education, and possibly to a foreign language (that is, English) during the college years of education.

The appointment of non-tribal teachers in schools of tribal children creates a major problem in education. They do not know the language the children speak, and children do not understand the language the teachers use. Given this situation, one can only imagine the kind of interaction going on between teachers and children in the school. Thus, the purpose that a non-tribal teacher would enrich the knowledge base of tribal children by sharing the experiences of the outside (non-tribal) world remains altogether unfulfilled. On the other hand, the language barrier also makes teachers and children disinterested in each other. This, in turn, results in the loss of motivation on both the sides, and jeopardizes the teaching-learning process in schools.

Studies indicate that a tribal child spends quite a lot of its energy on the learning of languages. A failure in the mastery of language leads to the child's failure in schools. While the hierarchy and dominance of languages is a major issue of discussion in its own right, it creates several problems with respect to the school education of tribal children. Many children, who fail to cope with the demands of language mastery in schools, develop disinterest in education and drop out of school.

The issue of language use in schools is still alive in the context of tribal education. While some researchers argue for a uniform policy with respect to language use in schools, others perceive it as a constraint in the process of schooling. The research evidence is more in favour of bilingual (or even multilingual) schooling in view of its positive consequences for cognitive development and social interaction processes (Mohanty, 1994; Mohanty and Perregaux, 1997). However, there are several complex issues related to bilingual or multilingual schooling that need careful research for evolving a sound policy on language use in schools. At the top of it is the dominance of English medium schooling, and the value placed on it by a smaller segment of the population that seems to control the wider economy and resources of the country.

CONCLUSION

The discussion presented above gives us two important lessons. One is that the cognitive qualities of tribal children have to be viewed and evaluated taking into consideration their ecological and cultural contexts that place very different demands in day-to-day life. Because of differences in the demands of tribal ecology, the patterning of their cognitive abilities shows considerable variation from those of other groups. A related and more important lesson is that tribal children are neither culturally inferior nor cognitively less competent than the children of other groups. Instead many of their skills and abilities are highly developed and extremely sophisticated.

The implications of these findings for schooling of tribal children are clear. A programme of schooling, that does not pay attention to the ecological, cultural and psychological characteristics of tribal children, is highly unlikely to make any significant impact. The educational system of the dominant non-tribal population is of very limited value in the tribal cultural milieu, because it does not match with the lifestyle of individuals and the needs of the tribal community. Linking school education with life in general, and the needs of the tribal communities in particular, is the step that requires serious attention.

Researchers have described several qualities of tribal people, which are highly desirable not only for participation in and success at school, but also outside the school. For example, tribal students appear to be more assertive, venturesome, imaginative, experimenting, emotionally stable and practical (Srivastava, 1983) than non-tribal students. They also have an accepting, emotionally supportive and positively involved family (Singh, 1996), which has significant linkage with higher academic achievement and creativity among children.

These evidences suggest that tribal children possess the basic cognitive abilities and psychological dispositions for successful participation in schools. Yet evidence suggests very low level of participation and success of tribal children in the programmes of school education. It points to our failure in evolving a sensitive model of tribal education rooted in the psychological strengths of tribal children. Studies indicate that, in comparison to other groups, hunters and gatherers possess a high level of visual and tactual differentiation, they demonstrate capacity for fine judgement of shape and size of stimuli as well as spatial relations, and produce fine categorization of an array of objects (Mishra et al., 1996). These abilities are greatly required for success in science, art, music, dance, athletic activities, and vocations like carpentry, tailoring, wood, and stone crafts. These skills need to be utilized not only for education of tribal children in schools, but also in the broader economic spheres of tribal life. Such attempts will be helpful in generating and promoting the sense of competence, self-efficacy, self-respect, and positive self-image among tribal children in general.

Such attempts are also highly likely to provide tribal children with a culturally meaningful, ecologically valid and economically viable alternative to life by reinforcing the dignity of their culture and identity. Ever increasing contact of tribal people with the outside world over the years has introduced several changes in their culture and life. These changes are reflected in their psychological characteristics also. Studies (for example, Mishra et al., 1996) indicate that their ways of perceiving the world, categorizing objects, interpreting pictures, and strategies of learning and memory become more similar to those with whom they interact and negotiate their life in these changed circumstances. This suggests that tribal children can acquire all those skills that members of other groups in society possess. What is important on our part is to develop a positive frame of mind about tribal children. This is possible only through sensitivity to tribal culture and life, recognition of the cognitive strengths of tribal children, and appreciation of their personality qualities. Efforts in these directions will be greatly helpful in organizing the programme of tribal education as well as promoting economic and other aspects of tribal development.

At the governmental level, certain steps need to be solidified. Analyses indicate that the incentives introduced by the government for increasing participation of poor tribal children in schools serve as great attractions for parents. Not only do these incentives often reach them quite late, their delivery is also highly irregular. Regular availability of these incentives can boost both enrolment and retention of tribal children in schools. The scheme of midday meal has been most effective in this respect. However, the quality of these meals has to be ensured in order to win the confidence of the community. Similarly a clear policy for language use in schools has to be evolved. Research evidence suggests that schools in which the language of tribal groups is used for instruction at the primary level of education not only draw large number of children, but also witness a low level of drop out. Development of primers in the tribal dialect involving contents from the local contexts is also likely to encourage children's active participation in the teaching-learning process at school.

Changes are necessary at the level of schools as well. While there is a general need for improvement in physical facilities in all schools located in remote tribal regions, change in perception and outlook of teachers about tribal children is equally important. They have to be profusely sensitized about the cultural and behavioural strengths of tribal children, and motivated for delivering their best to them in schools. Incentives have to be initiated to attract effective teachers to work in tribal schools and to retain them there. Only such motivated teachers are likely to generate interest among tribal children towards school education by attempting to link the contents of the curriculum with the existing realities of tribal communities through the use of innovative technologies.

REFERENCES

Dave, P.N. 1997. 'Primary Education', in National Council of Educational Research and Training (ed.), *Fifth Survey of Educational Research*, Vol. 1, pp. 273–312. New Delhi: NCERT.

Jabbi, M.K. and Rajyalakshmi, C. 2001. 'Education of Marginalised Social Groups in Bihar', in A. Vaidyanathan and P.R.G. Nair (eds), *Elementary Education in Rural India: A Grassroots View*, pp. 395–458. New Delhi: Sage Publications.

Jayaswal, M. 1981. 'Familial Correlates of Academic Achievement in Tribal School Students', Doctoral Thesis. Ranchi: Ranchi University.

Maffesoli, M. 1996. *The Time of the Tribes*. Thousand Oaks, CA: Sage Publications.

Mishra, R.C. 1994. Unpublished MS. 'Conservation Abilities Among Nomadic Birhors and Sedentary Oraons', Benaras: Department of Psychology, Banaras Hindu University.

———. 1996. 'Perceptual Differentiation in Relation to Children's Daily Life Activities', *Social Science International*, 12: 1–11.

———. 1998. 'Cognitive Processes', in NCERT (eds), *Fifth Survey of Educational Research*, Vol. 1, pp. 128–46. New Delhi: NCERT.

———. 1999. 'Research on Education in India'. *Prospects*, 29: 335–47.

———. 2001. 'Some Psychological Barriers to the Education of Kharwar Children of the Naugarh Region'. Unpublished Report. Benaras: Department of Psychology, Banaras Hindu University.

Mishra, R.C. and K. Mishra, Unpublished MS. 'Cognitive Style of Tharu Children in Relation to Daily Life Activities and Experience of Schooling', Benaras: Banaras Hindu University.

Mishra, R.C. and T. Singh. 1992. 'Memories of Asur Children for Locations and Pairs of Pictures', *Psychological Studies*, 37: 38–46.

Mishra, R.C., D. Sinha and J.W. Berry. 1996. *Ecology, Acculturation and Psychological Adaptation: A Study of Adivasis in Bihar*. New Delhi: Sage Publications.

Mishra, R.C., S.N. Shukla and A. Mishra. 1999. 'Development of Recall Memory for Conceptually and Phonetically Related Words', *Social Science International*, 15: 14–25.

Mohanty, A.K. 1994. 'Bilingualism in a Multilingual Society: Implication for Cultural Integration and Education', Keynote Address at the International Congress of Psychology, Madrid, Spain.

Mohanty, A.K. and C. Perregaux. 1997. 'Language Acquisition and Bilingualism', in J.W. Berry, P.R. Dasen and T.S. Saraswathi (eds), *Handbook of Cross-Cultural Psychology*, Vol. 2, pp. 217–54. Boston: Allyn & Bacon.

Sarma, H. N., S. Dutta and D. Sarma. 1992. 'Identification of the Problems of Primary Education'. Jorhat: State Institute of Education (Technical Report).

Shukla, S.N. 1991. 'Learning and Memory Among Socially Deprived Groups. A Developmental Study'. Unpublished Doctoral Thesis, Avadh University.

Singh, A.K. 1996. 'Improving the Educational Status of the Tribals in India', paper presented at the National Seminar on Research in Tribal Education, National Institute of Educational Planning and Administration, New Delhi.

Singh, A.K. and M. Jayaswal. 1981. 'Correlates of Scholastic Achievement in Socially Disadvantaged Students', *Social Change*, 11: 23–28.

Sinha, D. 1978. 'Story-Pictorial E.F.T.: A Culturally Appropriate Test of Perceptual Disembedding', *Indian Journal of Psychology*, 53: 160–71.

Sinha, D. 1979. 'Perceptual Style Among Nomadic and Transitional Agriculturalist Birhors', in L. Eckensberger, W.J. Lonner and Y.H. Poortinga (eds), *Cross-Cultural Contributions to Psychology*, pp. 83–93. Lisse: Swets and Zeitlinger.

———. 1980. 'Sex Differences in Psychological Differentiation Among Different Cultural Groups', *International Journal of Behavioral Development*, 3: 455–66.

———. 1984. *Story-Pictorial E.F.T. and Indo-African E.F.T.* Varanasi: Rupa Psychological Corporation.

Sinha, G. 1988. 'Exposure to Industrial and Urban Environments and Formal Schooling as Factors in Psychological Differentiation', *International Journal of Psychology*, 23: 707–19.

Sinha, D. and R.C. Mishra. 1997. 'Some Personality, Motivational and Cognitive Characteristics of Tribals and Their Implications for Educational Development of Children', *Journal of Educational Planning and Administration*, 11: 283–95.

Sivanand, M. 2001. 'The Good Doctors of Sittilingi', *Reader's Digest,* 159: 110–17.

Srivastava, R.K. 1983. 'Psychological Characteristics of Tharus and Non-Tharus: A Cross-Cultural Study', paper presented to the 70th session of the Indian Science Congress, Tirupati.

Tilak, J.B.G. 1998. *Changing Patterns of Financing Education.* Occasional Paper No. 26. New Delhi: National Institute of Educational Planning and Administration.

Vaidyanathan, A. and P.R.G. Nair. 2001. *Elementary Education in Rural India: A Grassroots View.* New Delhi: Sage Publications.

7

THE DECOLONIZATION OF ABORIGINAL[1] EDUCATION: DIALOGUE, REFLECTION, AND ACTION IN CANADA

MARIE BATTISTE

It is only through the decolonization of our minds, if not our hearts, that we can begin to develop the necessary political clarity to reject the enslavement of colonial discourse that creates false dichotomy between Western and Indigenous knowledge

Donald Macedo, 1999

INTRODUCTION

Education is not just in a state of crisis for Aboriginal peoples, but in a state of crisis for Canadians in general. This chapter offers an analysis and conclusions regarding these crises, raising issues and questions I consider necessary for educational reform in Aboriginal education in particular and in education in general. Each crisis can benefit from an ethical and inclusive decolonized practice of education.

Several themes in my paper diverge into three different currents, but then converge in one stream. The first theme deals with the educational context in which Aboriginal students in Canada are situated and points to a critical failure in Canadian education. The second focuses on the curricula or the knowledge base of education that Canadians receive and the false assumptions that create the foundations of colonial thought and its destructive practice. The last theme, politically grounded in reflection, dialogue, and action, urges conscientization and collective action to transform theory and practice in education to make cogent educational policies and reform in Indigenous education.

The struggles to unravel colonial education will require multiple responses in multiple sites. It will require individuals and groups to engage in conscientization, resistance, and transformational praxis (Smith, 1997), not just in areas where peoples are dispossessed of their voice, cultural identity, and heritage or are in poverty, marginalized, and powerless. More importantly, reform and change will require everyone involved in policy, leadership, and educational practice to acknowledge and re-examine the foundations of their cognitive dependencies on Eurocentric ideologies, opening themselves to a wide range of knowledge and perspectives drawn from diverse experience and cultures. I also challenge commonly held assumptions that Indigenous knowledge is not compatible and relevant to a contemporary education system and has no benefits for the transformation of Aboriginal and Indigenous peoples at large. Finally, I urge a process of respect in the dialogue and in the development of postcolonial strategies for Aboriginal and Indigenous peoples at large and for non-Indigenous educators.

ABORIGINAL EDUCATIONAL CONTEXT

Imagine that for hundreds of years your peoples' most formative achievements and traumas, your daily suffering and pain, the abuse you live through, the terror you live with are ignored and silenced. Then, these experiences and the compelling voices and stories are cast in romance novel stereotypes, occasionally brought forward as evidence of the backwardness of your people, or used to sanction some proposed programmatic innovation or to support some theory of opposition or resistance. Finally, they are re-positioned in the margins of knowledge and curricula.

Consider that for more than a century, your children have been part of a forced assimilation plan. Your language is ridiculed, your heritage and knowledge is rejected and suppressed, and all are ignored by the education system. Imagine the consequences of this powerful plan being supported by the government and the churches, which were complicit in an initiative of assimilation, colonization, and cognitive imperialism! This has been the experience and context of education that the First Nations peoples of Canada have had, as a result of their negotiating a treaty of services for education in return for the use of their ancestral lands and for peace in those contexts.

After more than a century of forced assimilation and coercive residential schools among First Nations students in Canada, the Auditor General of Canada concluded that the federal government had failed to educate First Nations children at par with other Canadians (Auditor General of Canada, 2000). An audit of the federal government's education programme for First Nations people in the year 2000 revealed that the Department of Indian and Northern Affairs' programmes are the most costly of all its programmes—currently at C$1.3 billion annually. However, they found that the record of academic achievement of First Nation children living on reserves is 'much worse than that of other Canadians' (p. 7).

The Auditor General of Canada's report of the education programme of Indian and Northern Affairs Canada (INAC) noted that it would take more than twenty years of accelerated and restorative education programmes for First Nations students to catch up to the Canadian average of 65 per cent of high school graduates (p. 8). The report also asserted that while INAC has had the responsibility and authority to take an active role in First Nations education, INAC has chosen to rely on provincial governments to provide a 'solution to problems related to school curricula, teacher qualifications, school buildings involving a process of transfer of funds through tuition agreements, and other financial arrangements to offset the costs of Indigenous education' (p. 8). In 1972, First Nations urged the federal government to undo the years of neglect and destructive practices and turn to the parents and communities to develop education for their children, much in the same way as the provinces had with public schools (National Indian Brotherhood, 1972). Since 1973, federal policy has held a delegation of responsibilities to turn educational control of local schools to First Nations governments. Only a few schools currently remain under federal control. First Nations governments and school boards are managing local schools, hiring teachers and carrying out administration of those schools, while provinces that are responsible for the education of all other citizens of Canada continue to provide the foundations of the basic curricula, teacher certification, schools standards, and textbooks. This citizenry divide is the result of the treaties and Indians being assigned by the provinces to federal jurisdiction. Therefore, Indians, now characterized as First Nations, are educated under federal responsibilities and contracts with the provinces. Each of the provinces, on the other hand, has constitutional responsibilities for education, both secular and Catholic and legislate their curriculum, standards, certification requirements, and funding. Because of federalism, the division of the federal government and the provinces, the provinces create education without systematic First Nations or federal input. As such, the federal branch overseeing First Nations education, the Indian and Northern Affairs Canada (INAC) has had no assurance that the province has been or is appropriately and routinely meeting the educational needs and aspirations of First Nations elementary and secondary students (p. 5). With approximately 68 per cent of First Nations in the provincial schools (RCAP, 1996), INAC's ongoing approach to turning over their fiduciary responsibility of education to provinces and to contractual obligations with First Nations, has compromised the federal government's investment in the future economic well-being of Canadian Indigenous society.

First Nations students who are enrolled in provincial schools are not treated as provincial citizens with free public education. Rather, the federal government, through the First Nations bands, pays the provinces at 100 per cent of the charge of tuition of each student living on First Nations reserves and attending public schools. From one end of Canada to the other, these students are immersed in Eurocentric, nationalistic curricula developed outside of Indigenous contexts. The conventional provincial curriculum ignores First Nations languages, traditions and knowledge, their rich ecological and spiritual understanding, and their ways of knowing in the humanities and sciences. With a higher birth-rate than the average Canadian population, Aboriginal youth show the highest demographic growth. 'One third of the Aboriginal population is under fourteen years of age (Avison, 2004: 2)'. It is significant then that in 2004, the Council of Ministers of Education in Canada agreed to make Aboriginal education a priority in each province and territory in Canada with an aim to build a skilled and highly qualified workforce (Avison, 2004). However, the Anglo-centric majority in Canada increasingly contests these policies. With only two colonial languages being made official languages of Canada, that is, English and French, the educational outcomes of 'success' of First Nations students have also as a consequence that Aboriginal students lose their ancestral language and culture, their identity connected to their place, and their connections to their family and community.

Also troubling is the attendance record of First Nations youth. Only one in five First Nations children of school age (6–16) was in school in the year 1999 (Auditor General of Canada, 2000: 8). For youth who do not go to school, there are not many non-formal learning environments that nourish their intellectual, emotional, and spiritual spirit, and are also enabling and empowering. The loss of ancestral language has also resulted in many First Nations peoples losing connections to the Elders[2] and to the ancient knowledge and skills embedded within the land and the unique prescription for living, which they create. The lack of a thriving economy in First Nations communities and the persistent discrimination in hiring practices within the province further restrict learning opportunities for First Nations people and youth. Instead, the streets, organized crime, child prostitution, and youth gangs have framed a chilling learning environment for youth who search for nourishment, purpose, and guidance, having lost Aboriginal languages, norms, cultures, and participation in a supportive community (Chartrand, 1999).

Knowledge about the current educational crisis is not new. In the last century, many studies conducted by federal and provincial governments or university academics have sought to unravel the underlying issues facing Indigenous people. A cursory reading of some of these, summarized in reports of the Royal Commission on Aboriginal Peoples (RCAP), reveals a consistency of conclusions over the years. Literacy and schooling have not been, and are not now, relevant or connected to the experience of Aboriginal peoples. The educational gap between Aboriginal peoples and the rest of Canada is significant and progress in closing the gap has been unacceptably slow (Auditor General of Canada, 2000). The Auditor General (2004) reports that it will take twenty-eight years at the present rate before First Nations students reach parity with other provincial students.

As part of its initial research, RCAP did an inventory of research studies conducted prior to 1990 on Aboriginal peoples. RCAP found that most of these studies were conducted by non-Aboriginal researchers and academics, who used similar ethnographic type methodology and drew on varying statistical measures regarding population. Ethnographic accounts of cultures relied on testimonies and insights among non-Aboriginal informants and their experiences with Aboriginal people. Few studies had actually involved Aboriginal people themselves in the research or had them interpret the findings. In a departure from the other previous studies, RCAP sought to address the deficiency they had found in the multiple levels of research and studies—most notably in their methodology. Choosing meaningful and extensive collaboration and consultation with Aboriginal people throughout Canada, RCAP's methodology involved extensive travel to communities, with face-to-face meetings, hearing testimonials from thousands of Aboriginal people in formal and informal hearings and meetings, leading up to over 4,000 pages of transcripts from the community discussions held in over 100 communities; consultations with leading Aboriginal scholars; policy consultation teams in diverse areas with Aboriginal leaders and people; and the inclusion of Aboriginal peoples' own analysis of their research, their reviews of documentation, and their reports. The Commission addressed these issues from a holistic, and, wide range of Aboriginal perspectives, taking into account the whole lives and histories of First Nations people and the institutions and societies with which they have intersected (RCAP, 1996: Vol. 5: Appendix).

The Commission's mandate was to unravel the effects of generations of exploitation, violence, marginalization, powerlessness, enforced cultural imperialism, and racism on Aboriginal peoples. In addition, they were to make recommendations to Canada on how to make effective changes and reform that would significantly transform the lives of Aboriginal peoples. Their voluminous reports and written documents offer the most current and comprehensive understanding of the nature of the colonial problem, a wealth of historical records, which offer insights into how these have affected Aboriginal peoples, together with some tested solutions and promising practices. These understandings and recommendations represent the largest research project ever undertaken in Canada, and the recommendations are foundational to this century's mandate in all aspects of Aboriginal peoples' lives.

The RCAP report concludes that the painful legacy of our colonial history bore heavily upon Aboriginal people in the form of cultural stress and that the time has come to correct false assumptions in all their manifestations, especially in education. Education, they asserted, is the key to escaping poverty and a significant strategy essential for change (1996: Vol. 2: 958–69). However, they observed that educational reform is not achieving the needed breakthrough. The Aboriginal population is growing at twice the national rate, and now totals 3.8 per cent of the national population, that is, 1.3 million people. Half the Aboriginal population is under the age of 25 and in some provinces, like Saskatchewan for example, predictions are that by the year 2016, Aboriginal children will make up 46 per cent of all school-aged children (Tymchak, 2001: 8).

Against this backdrop, conditions in many Aboriginal communities are appalling:

1. Infant mortality rates in Aboriginal communities are nearly double those of other Canadians.
2. The youth suicide rate is seven times higher than the Canadian average.
3. The unemployment rate on reserves is three times the Canadian average.
4. Literacy rates are half the Canadian average.
5. Most Aboriginal people live below the poverty line (RCAP, 1996).

This state of affairs has arisen from conditions that have existed for more than fifty years and government policies have made little progress to correct them. The problems continue to escalate, as does the call for urgent innovative education reform (Auditor General of Canada, 2000, 2004).

Little data gathering has occurred in provinces across Canada with regard to Aboriginal children and youth, with one exception being British Columbia, which has tracked First Nations student's progress in the schools. The BC study, 'How Are We Doing?: Demographics and Performance of Aboriginal students in BC Public Schools, 2001–2002' published their findings, some of which are offered in the Council of Ministers of Education in Canada (CMEC) report *A Challenge Worth Meeting: Opportunities for Improving Educational Outcomes* (Avison, 2004) as follows:

1. First Nations graduation rate is at 30.7 per cent in Canada overall and 42 per cent in British Columbia compared to 78 per cent in the general population (p. 4).
2. Of those who graduate, only 31.3 per cent of Aboriginal students in British Columbia take and pass provincial examinations in Grade twelve English (p. 4).
3. Fewer graduates participate in sciences, of whom only 5.2 per cent take and pass the Mathematics twelve (p. 4).

4. BC offers grade assessments starting at Grades four, seven and ten, using the Foundation Skills Assessment that show Aboriginal students at 55.6 per cent in reading and 66 per cent in numeracy and Non-Aboriginal at 81.7 per cent in reading and 86.9 per cent in numeracy (p. 4).

The Council of Ministers of Education concluded its report with several recommendations:

1. Recognize early childhood education as a key to improved literacy (p. 6).
2. Provide clear objectives and a commitment to report results, including working closer with the Government of Canada and Aboriginal communities (p. 6).
3. Implement strong teacher development and recruitment (p. 8).
4. Improve the accountability arrangements with Aboriginal parents and communities (p. 9).
5. Share learning resources (p. 9).
6. Support the elimination of inequitable funding levels for First Nations schools (p. 10).
7. Create a National Forum on Aboriginal education (p. 11).

Neither the assimilation approaches of residential schools and day schools in the first half of the last century nor the integrative approaches of the past second half of the century have succeeded in effecting successful outcomes for Aboriginal students. At present, little more than 9 per cent of the 35 per cent of First Nations students who complete high school enter university and only 3 per cent of them complete their degree programme (RCAP, 1996: Vol. 3: 440). These statistics indicate a significant failure as students enter the critical years of employment or higher education. The educational gap between First Nations students and non-First Nations students represents a significant challenge and a crucial test of the resolve of many educators, policy makers, and First Nations people.

While much of the criticism has been levelled at elementary and secondary schools, universities are also implicated in this failure. Assimilative education continues throughout post-secondary education, where often the only academic content that reflects Aboriginal peoples' experience is found in courses that provide sociological analysis of societies, in native studies courses or specially-designed courses around cross-cultural or Aboriginal themes in literature, history, anthropology, or education. Yet, these few courses have not effectively provided a systematic remedy, for they offer a fragmented and, more often, Eurocentric analysis of Aboriginal experience. For the most part, university policies have not yet addressed the Auditor General's report or the RCAP recommendations, and universities are not likely to take up Aboriginal curricula or support for Aboriginal students without the support from their ministries (Battiste et al., 2003). While there is a growing interest in Aboriginal education and learning in Canada, the knowledge, research and practice have not been adequately assessed to determine exemplary or promising practices and on what theories that should rest. Not coincidentally, the RCAP report entitled *Gathering Strength* has been gathering more dust than strength, as few mainstream educators know of its contents or value for shaping new programmatic solutions for Aboriginal education.

Many Aboriginal scholars and writers have been imagining new restorative education programmes, well before 1973, when the federal government accepted the National Indian Brotherhood's proposal entitled *Indian Control of Indian Education* (National Indian Brotherhood, 1972). Under this policy, the federal government provided funds to First Nations' bands[3] to manage and direct their own programmes. Yet, even under this regime, the schools were required to adhere to the policies outlined by the federal government and use provincial educational standards, curriculum, teacher certification, and school standards. Since 2004, INAC has begun reviewing its roles and responsibilities for education as the fiduciary for First Nations; however, it is far from making the anticipated inroads as the Auditor General of Canada's report confirms. Like RCAP authors, Aboriginal scholars and writers have recognized that education is the key matrix of all disciplinary and professional knowledge and central to alleviating poverty in Aboriginal communities. But they also recognize that education and literacy have not been benign processes, because cognitive imperialism, licensed by dominant colonial languages and Eurocentric discourse, has tragically diminished Aboriginal languages and knowledge. It has further contributed to the discontinuity and trauma Aboriginal peoples continue to experience (Battiste, 1986, 1998, 2000; McConaghy, 2000; Smith, 1999). Most Aboriginal people understand the crisis they live in and feel the urgency for reform. Some have begun to address their crisis in a discourse of postcolonial education, or a decolonized education that reconciles contemporary education with the past and eliminates the colonial model.

Postcolonial studies, however, have been a contested terrain, as the analyses of colonial education have resulted in multiple ways to understand the oppression, its consequences, and its strategies for transformation. It does not offer a common methodology or solution and is mired in discourses of difference. To Aboriginal peoples, the term 'postcolonial' is also an aspirational practice, goal, or idea used to imagine a new form of society they desire to create—a symbolic strategy for shaping a desirable reality that they recognize currently does not exist (Battiste, 2000). The conceptualization of postcolonial is an act of hope, a light in the darkness of educational failure. Yet, what are the social and cultural requirements for this dreamed about or idealized version of education? Moreover, what role do schools, universities, teachers, and faculties have in helping to effect that change?

DISPLACING THE COLONIAL LEGACY IN INSTITUTIONS

All citizens of Canada rely on the State to provide them with access to fair and balanced centralized knowledge and personal capacity building transmitted through its educational institutions. Yet, as a professor teaching pre-service teachers at the University of Saskatchewan, I am most aware of the sanitized and one-sided version of history and knowledge most pre-service teachers of Saskatchewan and beyond receive. They are not aware of the history of their country and the treaties that give meaning to their location in Canada, and the differential negative treatment of Aboriginal peoples and its consequences for their economies and stature in Canada. In the last decade, the teacher training programmes in Canada have begun to make efforts to correct this foundation. With the introduction of postcolonial and post modern studies as cornerstones of change, the once grand theories of analysis and change have given way to understanding the local, the voices of people from the margins, and the significance of race, class, and gender as significant factors to academic accessibility and achievement in Canadian education. At the University of Saskatchewan, graduates of the teacher education programmes have now an introductory awareness to these issues and in particular, how to understand their own locations and how these can interfere with their assessments of their students' capacities and environments. When presented with an historical context of diverse groups of people in Canada, many pre-service teachers feel a sense of betrayal that their own education has not provided them with a balanced portrayal and analysis of the Canadian educational experience, nor has it offered remedies drawn from diverse perspectives and experiences of Canadian peoples or helped to address the critical issues that poverty, racism, and culturalism have created.

Bringing to pre-service teachers the experiences of those marginalized in Canadian society has not prevented other students and teachers from continuing to assert their privilege, questioning educational equity and the need for transformation in educational content and processes, and they have a large audience in Canadian society. Anti-racist educators St. Denis and Schick (2003) offer a description of the opposition they faced among their predominantly white students who were exposed to and asked to consider their silence to inequity and their lack of knowledge of realities of racism, prejudice, poverty, and their strategy of blaming the victims for what they perceived as their faults for perceived bad behaviours. These seemingly open-minded students used their ignorance or their perceived lack of complicity in racism to maintain and justify their dominance in society. Yet, these same student teachers are those who will enter the school system and continue to teach according to the 'silent curriculum of Eurocentric knowledge'. The 'silent' curriculum persists and each year, more Aboriginal students are harmed by education systems that purport to help them. Canadian universities are not doing enough to educate future teachers on issues of power theory, cognitive imperialism, and anti-oppressive education.

Since 1972 when Canada adopted multiculturalism as Canadian domestic policy, an era of developing respect for diversity and equality among all groups have been common themes in education. Yet in the last two decades, cross-cultural and multicultural research has not adequately provided the needed framework to deal with the context of diversity in Canadian education, nor has it been able to erode the base of Eurocentric dominance and colonialism entrenched in contemporary knowledge and curriculum and educational discourses. The context of racism and the resulting legacy of oppression among Aboriginal peoples continue to affect them in adverse ways and have not been significantly acknowledged or examined especially in the area of public education (St. Denis, 2002).

Aboriginal teachers themselves have not been supported adequately in schools, where they are deemed responsible for doing the work of supporting Aboriginal students, and being bridges for students or parents, or called on for assisting other non-Aboriginal teachers in building appropriate content and materials. What was more significant to them was that they had felt the blunt edge of racism in Saskatchewan public schools (St. Denis et al., 1998). In this research study we conducted a survey among eighty Aboriginal teachers and interviewed twenty of them in Saskatchewan to identify their perceptions, experiences, and relationships in the public schools. In examining their personal goals and visions and the influences on them, including the role and impact of culture and identity on their roles as teachers, we uncovered the rich and varied knowledge and experiences held among Aboriginal teachers. Yet, most of the teachers reported that in their workplace their supervisors and peers often treated them as a homogeneous 'other', despite their wide range of experiences, knowledge, skills and tribal affiliations. With more than six language groups represented in the study group, we found quite diverse identities, experiences, and socializations, yet in the schools, they were expected to have similar experiences and knowledge as First Nations or Métis teachers and were expected to share with other teachers and students this perceived knowledge and experience. Often the loss of the identities and languages, because of residential schooling or assimilation polices integrated into their homes and communities created a deep sense of loss among them, and even guilt or ambivalence about their heritage. They were also frequently called upon to educate everyone in the schools on all issues affecting Aboriginal peoples, although 'Aboriginal' in Saskatchewan includes three constitutional groups (First Nations, Inuit and Métis), six different tribal affiliations, seventy five First Nations communities, and six languages in three language families, covering a huge land base in the prairies.

Many of the Aboriginal teachers interviewed perceived that the stereotyping of Aboriginal people among the non-Aboriginal teachers went hand-in-hand with negative perceptions, such as having low expectations of Aboriginal students and Aboriginal teachers themselves, as well as assigning negative caricatures to Aboriginal parents. Yet, their school administrators expected them to fulfil the role of classroom teacher and cultural broker on a full range of issues that arose in schools concerning Aboriginal student populations.

These have included contributing to policy issues, curriculum content, extra programming, and counselling or mediation between the school and Aboriginal parents regardless of the level of talents, skills, or knowledge (St. Denis et al., 1998).

Many non-Aboriginal teachers had called on these Aboriginal teachers to help them to teach content related to Aboriginal people's knowledge, as they had too little information about Aboriginal peoples and their experience and knowledge. Yet, Aboriginal teachers acknowledged that their own lack of experience and knowledge also presented them with barriers to this seeming specialized knowledge, which they were unable to provide since many of them had quite different life and school experiences. The Aboriginal teachers recalled that many of their Elders had often remarked that Aboriginal knowledge is not gained as a feature of being 'native' or living in a particular community or from having an interest in the topic, but is gained by living, observing, working, and sharing with Aboriginal peoples. Despite the core required course of Native Studies provided at the University of Saskatchewan that provided some colonial history of Aboriginal peoples, they did not have the requisite knowledge to create informed curricula on the Aboriginal experience. The need, then, for professionals to help in meeting the needs of Aboriginal peoples and integrating their knowledge into conventional knowledge is far from being achieved. In this study, Aboriginal teachers reported preferring professional development with trained educational consultants who specialized in Aboriginal knowledge and were knowledgeable about Aboriginal communities, histories, pedagogies, ethics, and protocols. This knowledge and these skills were basic requirements to support all teachers as they seek to implement the policies of integration and inclusion, especially dealing with Aboriginal knowledge and perspectives (St. Denis et al., 1998).

Although educational equity has largely been a discourse of feminist activism, in Saskatchewan, the Human Rights Commission has developed educational equity in a programme launched in 1985 in 'response to studies showing that up to 90 per cent of Aboriginal students left school before completing grade twelve. It asked school divisions to address this crisis by adopting education equity plans' (Saskatchewan Human Rights Commission, 2006). As a result, educational institutions can devise their own strategies and timetables for change and the Commission works with sponsors to develop resources, best practices and indicators of success. Educational equity has since been an important social political vehicle for change in Aboriginal education in Saskatchewan, and in other provinces as well, particularly for school divisions with high populations of Aboriginal students. The provincial body responsible for overseeing the legislative responsibility for education in Saskatchewan has developed laudable initiatives for Aboriginal education since 1985; however, our study highlighted the fact that they had not communicated those initiatives adequately to the schools and to teachers. As such, the meaning of educational equity, its purpose, and its processes remained elusive to many interviewed teachers. Some interpret educational equity as additive and supplementary—a unit or lesson dealing with Aboriginal content, a field trip to a local reserve or site, or an Elder or cultural resource visitor to the school. Others saw it as recruiting and hiring of First Nations, Métis, or Inuit teachers. Still others interpret it as connecting the school to the community with its activities, communications, and curriculum content.

How these initiatives affect the political and cultural climate of schools and relationships among teachers, students, and communities have been inadequately addressed. Racism remained the primary persistent issue facing Aboriginal teachers in public schools in Saskatchewan (St. Denis et al., 1998; St. Denis and Schick, 2003; Schick, 2000). While many teachers recognize their lack of preparation and knowledge of Aboriginal peoples and need the support of the small number of Aboriginal consultants provided by the province, Aboriginal teachers alone cannot solve the persistent historical Eurocentric education contradictions, cultural exclusion, and systemic discrimination.

In the last three decades, Canadian universities have made some progress in making Canadian post-secondary education accessible to Aboriginal students. In education, we have witnessed the success of the Aboriginal Teacher Education Programs (ATEPs) across Canada, developed as a response to the 1972 policy for Indian Control of Indian Education (National Indian Brotherhood, 1972). Since then, a significant number of Aboriginal teachers has been trained, and there is now much literature focusing on cross-cultural, Aboriginal awareness and teaching methods. Anti-racist education has inspired an important critique and even has begun to affect the consciousness of many incoming pre-service teachers. Yet, in order for institutions to live up to their mission statements and alleged priorities for Aboriginal peoples, it is necessary for policy makers and leaders to confront the colonial history of education and its baggage, inherent in the Eurocentric curricula, and the attitudes of superiority that continue to demean the role of Aboriginal knowledge and people in education. This is especially evident in the public perception that Aboriginal ownership, custodianship, and management of their territory and resources—indeed, their knowledge and education—is conflict-prone and incompatible with contemporary standards of education and society.

The hope of a postcolonial education for Aboriginal faculty and students offers some sign of change away from the cognitive imperialism of Eurocentrism. Decolonization of existing Eurocentric thought is already underway in the work of many scholars. The experiences of Indigenous peoples throughout the world hold that decolonization can be achieved in multiple ways but it is achieved in a distinct manner, particular to Indigenous people. Maori educator and scholar Linda Tuhiwai Smith, one of the leading Indigenous theorists of decolonization of the Maori in New Zealand, clarifies the nature of the task when she writes: 'Decolonization is about centring our concerns and world views and then coming to know and understand theory and research from our own perspectives and for our own purposes' (Smith, 1999: 39). These interrelated strands weave solutions not only to decolonize education built on cognitive imperialism, but also to sustain the Indigenous renaissance and empower intercultural diplomacy, two essential features of the postcolonial movement. It is not a movement to reject all theory or research of Western knowledge, but to create a new space in which Indigenous peoples' knowledge, identity, and future is factored into the global and contemporary equation.

GENERATING POSTCOLONIAL EDUCATION: GETTING FROM HERE TO THERE

Decolonizing moves in a negative and a positive proactive direction. Past chairperson of the United Nations Working Group on Indigenous Peoples, Erica Irene Daes, at the Summer Institute on Cultural Oppression of Indigenous Peoples at the University of Saskatchewan, noted:

There is an expression, 'You cannot be the doctor if you are the disease.' What I am saying is the Europeans themselves have had the disease of oppressed consciousness for centuries, and, as a result, they have grown so used to this experience that they do not always appreciate the fact that they are ill. Indigenous peoples, by comparison, are much closer in time to the experience of spiritual independence and therefore are generally far more aware of the extent to which the symptoms of the disease persist, even after the formal institutional machinery of alien domination has been dismantled and replaced by the appearance (at least) of renewed self-government and self-determination (Daes, 2000: 4).

What is becoming clear to educators is that any attempt to de-colonize schools and actively resist colonial paradigms is a complex and daunting task. The colonial model that offers students a frag-mented and distorted picture of Indigenous peoples in curricula must be rejected. Also, students require a critical perspective of the historical context that has created that fragmentation. Under-standing Eurocentric assumptions of superiority within the context of history and their continued dominance in all forms of con-temporary knowledge is foundational to any change (Duran and Duran, 1995).

To understand why Indigenous knowledge is marginalized is to unravel Eurocentric diffusionism. As a theory that has been the dominant artificial context for knowledge during the last five centuries, Eurocentrism postulates the superiority of Europeans over non-Europeans. Eurocentrism is not just an opinion or attitude that can be changed by some multicultural or cross-cultural exercise, workshop, or course, for Eurocentrism is an integral foundation of all dominant scholarship, opinion, and law. As an imaginative and institutional context, Eurocentrism is the dominant consciousness and order of contemporary life (Blaut, 1993).

Eurocentrism is an ultra-theory in modern thought. It is the context for many smaller theories—historical, geographical, psychological, sociological, and philosophical—which are integral parts of Euro-centric diffusionism. In its classic form, the basic framework of dif-fusionism depicts a world divided into the two categories—one is historical, invents, and progresses (Greater Europe, Inside); the other is ahistorical, stagnant, and unchanging and receives progressive innovations by diffusion from Europe (non-Europe, Outside). From this platform, diffusionism asserts the difference between the two polarities represented in this dialectic as some intellectual or spiritual factor, something characteristic of the 'European mind', the 'European spirit', 'Western man', and so on, that leads to creativity, imagination, invention, innovation, rationality, and a sense of honour, or ethics, or 'European values'. The reason for non-Europe's non-progress is a lack of this intellectual or spiritual factor. This proposition asserts that non-European people are bereft, or partly so, of 'rationality'— that is, of ideas and proper spiritual values.

All Eurocentric scholarship is diffusionist since it axiomatically accepts the Inside-Outside model—the notion that the world as a whole has one permanent centre from which culture changing ideas tend to originate. Eurocentric thought has always claimed to be universal and general. Often, this claim of universality is a cloak for the projection of Eurocentric beliefs onto other cultures that possess different worldviews, 'inner logic', or localized knowledge. Claiming universality often means aspiring to domination. Universality is the underpinning of cultural and cognitive imperialism, which establishes a dominant group's knowledge, experience, culture, and language as the universal norm. Dominators or colonizers reinforce their culture and values by bringing the oppressed and the colonized under their expectations and norms. Because Eurocentric colonizers consider themselves the ideal model for humanity and carriers of superior culture and intelligence, they believe they can judge other people and assess their competencies. In short, Eurocentric academics believe they have the power to research and interpret differences, and this belief has shaped the institutional and imaginative assumptions of colonization and modernism. Using the strategy of differences, they believe they have the privilege of defining human competencies and deviancies such as sin, offence, and mental illness. They also believe they have the authority to impose their tutelage over Indigenous peoples and to remove from them the right to speak for themselves.

Given the assumed normalcy of the dominators' values and identity, the dominators construct the differences of the dominated as inferior and negative. Thus, Memmi (1965) shows the development of a binary consciousness and society of the immigrant–colonizer and the Indigenous–colonized, something which the colonized have to accept if they are to survive. This binary consciousness of a universal Eurocentrism has been used to justify the separation of Indigenous people from their ancient rights to the land and its resources, and the transfer of wealth and productivity to the colonialists and their mother country.

Typically, to succeed in creating this sense of objectivity, colonizers must erase Indigenous memory and knowledge. Without significant exception, the universal discourses of Eurocentric thought forces silence on Indigenous peoples: they lose their language, cultural continuity, and histories. Silence strips Indigenous people of their heritage and identity, while the Eurocentric education and legal system induce a collective amnesia that alienates Indigenous people from their elders, linguistic consciousness, and order of the world. In this outlook, only 'superior peoples' can be the agents of progress, either by the will of God or by the law of nature. European learning or white Canadian learning, then, is conventionalized as the universal model of civilization that must be imitated by all others groups and individuals and which monopolizes history, progress, and interpretation, creating an alienation to Aboriginal peoples. Noël (1993) aptly notes: 'Alienation is to the oppressed what self-righteousness is to the oppressor' (p. 70).

The universality of Eurocentrism creates a strategy of difference that leads to racism that allows the Europeans and colonialists to assert their privileges while exploiting Indigenous people in an inhuman way. Memmi (1969) outlines this strategy most clearly:

> Racism is the generalized and final assigning of values to real or imaginary differences, to the accuser's benefit and at his victim's expense, in order to justify the former's own privileges or aggression. (p. 185)

In this definition, Memmi identifies four strategies which have been used to maintain colonial power over Indigenous people: (a) stressing real or imaginary differences between the racist and the victim, (b) assigning values to these differences to the advantage of the racist and the detriment of the victim, (c) trying to make these values absolute by generalizing from them and claiming that they are final, and (d) using these values to justify any present or possible aggression or privilege (p. 186).

Linguistic ecologist Robert Phillipson (1992) demonstrates that many of the basic terms used in English and French analyses of Indigenous peoples and their knowledge are ideologically loaded with Eurocentric diffusionism tenets. The descriptions of complex and diverse Indigenous peoples continue to reflect a European way of conceptualizing the issues and tend to reinforce colonial myths, racism, and stereotypes. Noël offers her reasoning for stereotyping: 'A too complex victim escapes as victims must be made to correspond to the sketch, whether they like it or not' (Noël, 1993: 109). Many English concepts therefore establish a pattern of Eurocentric self-exaltation that creates an idealistic image of itself and a devaluation of Indigenous other and any other aspects of them. For example, European nations have 'languages', while tribes have 'dialects'. European nations have 'knowledge', while tribes have 'culture.' Canadians have governments; First Nations have band administration. These perspectives have shaped a broad understanding of non-Eurocentric knowledge systems. Most international documents and most academic definitions are not aware of their Eurocentric biases or traditions. The systemic biases are integral and hidden in their language systems.

In assessing the current state of research on Indigenous knowledge, researchers must understand the context of the historical development of Eurocentric thought, as well as the Indigenous contexts. A body of knowledge differs when viewed from different perspectives. Not only will the interpretations or validations of Indigenous knowledge depend on the researcher's attitudes, capabilities, and experiences, but they will be also based on their understanding of Indigenous consciousness, language, and order. Indigenous knowledge may be utilitarian, non-utilitarian, or both; it may be segmented or partial depending on Eurocentric reductionistic analysis. Indigenous knowledge needs to be read and interpreted based on form and manifestation, as Indigenous people understand it.

According to Noël, domination and oppression are grounded in intolerance. The fact that the modern intolerance is Eurocentric consciousness itself has profound implication on how to liberate Indigenous knowledge. In terms of getting educated, finding knowledge, doing research, finding research ethics, where are Indigenous people to find those experts who can rise above the value contamination of their consciousness? Where are they to be trained? By what faculty are they to be taught? Because of the persuasiveness of Eurocentric knowledge by colonization, Indigenous peoples do not have at their disposal today any valid search for truth.

Every structure of university research, discourse, or discipline has a political and institutional stake in Eurocentric diffusion and knowledge. Every university has been contrived for the interest or ease of their interpretation of the world, which is still opposed to Indigenous knowledge. The faculties of the contemporary university are created to influence their students to be the gatekeepers of Eurocentric knowledge in the name of universal truth. Yet, it is no more than a philosophy of Europe invested in history and identity to serve a particular superior interest. Its research is methodologically flawed with multiple forms of cognitive imperialism when it approaches Indigenous issues or peoples.

From a sociological perspective, all peoples have knowledge; the transformation of knowledge into a political power base has been built on controlling the meanings and diffusion of knowledge. Different groups in society use knowledge, and control of knowledge and its meanings, in order to exercise their power and privilege over others. The controlling agents of education have linked these diffused meanings with economics; thus, ensuring that some knowledge is diffused with rewards and others not.

English literacy and the schools that diffuse literacy and knowledge are not neutral sites. Using the sanctions of the state, the ruling government can channel knowledge to their own interests, using vague notions of 'standards' and 'public good' to control what counts as knowledge, how it is diffused, and who benefits from it. In all cases, those holding the colonial power control what counts as knowledge, and Indigenous knowledge is excluded from the curriculum as it is regarded as too local or too particularistic, or inferior to universal knowledge. Only recently have scientists dealing with biodiversity, ethno-botany, and pharmacy begun to see the value in commodifying Indigenous knowledge. They have seen the potential and value in buying or appropriating Indigenous knowledge, patenting the results, and selling it back to Indigenous peoples. This appropriation of Indigenous knowledge follows the logic of linking knowledge to power and economics (Battiste and Henderson, 2000). This takes me to the final theme, one that is found at the intersection of the political realm and the voices and visions of Indigenous peoples.

CREATING THE INDIGENOUS RENAISSANCE

A postcolonial framework cannot be constructed without Indigenous people renewing and reconstructing the principles underlying their own worldview, environment, languages, communication forms, and how these construct their humanity. I have explored this reclaiming process in a recent publication *Reclaiming Indigenous Voice and Vision* (Battiste, 2000). It is a renaissance of Indigenous people and non-Indigenous allies who are providing critical frameworks for addressing these issues while acknowledging excellence through the proper valuing and respectful circulation of Indigenous knowledge across and beyond Eurocentric disciplines. They are seeking to heal themselves, reshape their context, and affect reforms based on a complex arrangement of conscientization, resistance, and transformative praxis.

Through collaborative work with scholars in Canada, Australia, New Zealand, and the United States, Indigenous scholars and leaders have illustrated the strength of this renaissance movement in their multidisciplinary foundations essential to remedying the acknowledged failure of the current system. They are achieving this in many disciplinary and community sites where a diverse range of problems must engage innovative strategies, strategic goals, and broader politics.

Indigenous peoples' struggles cannot be reduced to singular solutions or a best practice taken from one location. Rather Indigenous scholars and community catalysts are envisioning the work to grow organically in place, in multiple sites, using multiple strategies simultaneously (Smith, 1997). It is now in the interest of universities, schools, and society, at large, to affirm the idea that Indigenous knowledge is important and transformative. That work is complex and daunting but the work of everyone, for 'In working together across difference, the Indigenous humanities acknowledge that we all have a stake in dismantling colonial structures and oppressive singularities while reimagining and rebuilding practices and institutions and telling stories otherwise' (Findlay, 2003: 4).

Among important contributions is the work being done at the United Nations by Indigenous peoples working in many lobbying bodies who have raised the consciousness to the plight of oppressed peoples around the world. Against the confident and rock-hard forces of assimilation and Eurocentrism, Indigenous peoples have achieved over the course of a generation a stunning transformation but that is still little understood or appreciated. The transformation achieved at the end of the 20th century is the beginning framework of the Indigenous renaissance. Despite being born into indignity, in societies that were oppressed, hopeless, confused, and resigned to extinction, and being educated in Eurocentric systems, these educated Indigenous people resisted Eurocentrism, seized the initiative, brought forth their grievances and proposed solutions, and, more often than not, accomplished the kind of progress and cultural restoration that they dared to dream and seek. Their dreams, visions, and actions created the framework of an educational transformation. This framework was initiated by the state, as it was only reluctantly accepted by governments through the weight of their dialogue, even when acceptance ran counter to widely held assumptions and premises.

The self-determination movement of Indigenous peoples displayed the depth and power of their humanity, its noble commitment to empower the powerless and dispossessed to lead better lives and overthrow the chains of racism, assimilation, and Eurocentrism. It showed an ability to learn how to use the political and legal systems to create new frameworks within which progress could be made in small or incremental steps. They put their heritage and knowledge to work, to dream, and painstakingly build creative and effective institutions and programmes for the powerless and dominated; in a reluctant, suspicious majority. They generated noble and virtuous visions of justice and equality in displacing colonialism.

The United Nations has offered an effective forum for acknowledging the concerns of Indigenous peoples, although the struggle to recognize Indigenous peoples as peoples with rights and protections has yet to be addressed fully. Indigenous peoples remain the only peoples in the world without a declaration or covenant embracing or urging standards to protect them, as has been achieved for women, children, refugees, cultural minorities, and people with disabilities. The Decade of Indigenous Peoples came to a close in 2004, with Indigenous peoples agreeing to an 'Indigenous Declaration on the Rights of Indigenous peoples' consistent with international human rights covenants, but the nation states resisted ratifying it. Through continued dialogue, however, the revised UN Human Rights Council approved of the Indigenous Declaration. The General Assembly of the UN voted to affirm the Declaration (United Nations Human Rights Council, 2007), with 133 nation-states approving, and four states dissenting: Canada, USA, New Zealand, and Australia.

The UN Declaration affirms that Indigenous peoples: have the right to the full enjoyment, as a collective or as individuals, of all human rights and fundamental freedoms (art. 1); have the right to be free from any kind of discrimination, in the exercise of their rights, in particular those based on their indigenous origin or identity (art. 2); Indigenous peoples have the right of self-determination to freely determine their political status and freely pursue their economic, social, and cultural development (art. 3). The Declaration affirms they have the right not to be subjected to forced assimilation or destruction of their culture (art. 8); to revitalize, use, develop and transmit to future generations their histories, languages, oral traditions, philosophies, writing systems and literatures, and to designate and retain their own names for communities, places and persons (art. 13); to establish and control their educational systems and institutions providing education in their own languages, in a manner appropriate to their cultural methods of teaching and learning (art. 14); to the dignity and diversity of their cultures, traditions, histories, and aspirations which shall be appropriately reflected in education and public information (art. 15).

This is a significant step, a long hard dialogue to assert the value of Indigenous humanity and cultural dignity. At this time, we need to rethink the underlying values of our educational and social systems on which contemporary society has built its knowledge and institutions, the mythical portraits that have been assumed from a biased knowledge base, and the neglected rich diversity of our nations. The knowledge base of Indigenous peoples, as well as others, can be sources of inspiration, creativity, and opportunity and can make contributions to humanity, equality, solidarity, tolerance, and respect. The United Nations has been providing exemplary opportunities to educational institutions to confront their ethics, methodologies, and lessons of Indigenous knowledge, and heritage, as in the *Principles and Guidelines for the Protection of Indigenous Heritage* (Wiessner and Battiste, 2000), in UN Year of Dialogue among Civilizations (2001), and in the Decade of Indigenous Peoples (1995–2004). As the work remains unfinished, a second decade, the International Decade of the World's Indigenous Peoples (2005–2014) has also been established. The resulting educational and cultural rights of Indigenous people in the United Nations framework and international law are further summarized in Battiste et al. (2005, 2006).

In Canada, the RCAP has also commented on this long-delayed dialogue to engage suppressed knowledge among Indigenous civilizations. The educational significance and justification for these respectful dialogues cannot be over emphasized as a basis for arriving at a decolonized educational agenda. This should take us beyond the prior processes of cross-cultural awareness and inclusion and bridging programmes to a new perspective and process that support Indigenous knowledge, communities, languages, and self-determination in a new decolonized way.

These rights need to be recognized and implemented by national and local educational authorities. So many Indigenous peoples around the world continue to suffer trauma and stress from genocide and the destruction of their lives by colonization. Our work at the international level is to initiate dialogue, advance a postcolonial discourse, work actively for a transformation of colonial thought, and advocate for the Indigenous humanities (Battiste et al., 2003; Battiste and McConaghy, 2005). Our efforts are to reveal the inconsistencies of policies and practices with the emergent consensus of national and international educators and policy makers, challenge the assumptions, and the taken for granted, expose the ills, and search from within ourselves and our Indigenous heritage for the principles that will guide our children's future to a dignified life. The international rights of Indigenous peoples include our right to learn and teach Indigenous humanities as well as Indigenous science. In other words, we have a right to create an educational transformation and the necessary Indigenous Renaissance.

While educational institutions have a pivotal responsibility in transforming relations between Indigenous peoples and Canadian society, the RCAP has firmly held that all institutions should respect Indigenous knowledge and heritages as core responsibilities rather than a special project undertaken after other obligations are met (Vol. 3: 515). To date, a growing emergence of collaborative work has offered new transcultural, interdisciplinary coalitions across education, humanities, social sciences, and law, as well as in physical sciences, particularly ecological diversity, biodiversity, and environment. Globalization has pressured institutions to seek new innovative and holistic solutions to ecological and global problems using Indigenous knowledge. However, respect for Indigenous knowledge must be one that begins with Indigenous peoples providing the standards and protections that accompany the centring of Indigenous knowledge. Again, many Indigenous peoples have taken up this challenge in many forms and forums.

Despite the painful experiences Indigenous peoples have had for more than a century, they still see education as providing hope for their future, and they are determined to see education fulfill its promise (Vol. 3: 433–34). This has been made clear among many groups—the Indigenous peoples themselves in many media and forums, especially in RCAP's Final Report, in the dedicated efforts of the UN Working Group on Indigenous Populations, and among Indigenous researchers and postcolonial scholars and leaders. No longer can institutions be inactive, based on the notion that 'We don't know what they want' (Havemann, 1999: 70).

We must examine a process of respect in the dialogues and in the development of postcolonial strategies for both Indigenous peoples and non-Indigenous educators. We must seek the appropriate protocols and methodologies that will help us to enter into a sustained dialogue of respectful relations. Finally, to achieve this outcome will necessarily require Canadian people and its institutions to view Indigenous peoples not as disadvantaged racial minorities, but as distinct, historical, and socio-political communities within Canada with collective rights (Chartrand, 1999).

In the Canadian Constitution of 1982, the principles of maintaining respect for Aboriginal rights and treaties have been articulated. Canada has a responsibility to live up to its reputation as a compassionate and innovative nation on the way to becoming a truly just society. We can arrive at a truly just society by acknowledging our dependencies on Indigenous knowledge, values, and visions and our renewed investment in holistic and sustainable ways of thinking, communicating, and acting together.

NOTES

1. Aboriginal is a term in Canada that constitutionally recognizes three distinct Indigenous groups in Canada: Indians, Inuit, and Métis peoples. Since these are distinct groups of peoples with treaty and constitutional rights in Canada, the capitalization of the terms recognizes and honours their national status. This convention holds for Indigenous as similar to 'European', 'Asian' and other national and international terms. 'First Nations' is a term used among most Indian nations to counteract the 'Founding Fathers' concept expressed in the 1960's nationalism campaign in Canada to develop English and French bilingualism as a national policy. This paper will use the terms 'Indigenous', 'Aboriginal',

'Indian', and 'First Nations' to refer to the first peoples of Canada and, with the exception of 'First Nations,' which generally refers to Indians who have 'status' under the *Indian Act*, are inclusive of Indians as defined in the Canadian constitution—Indian, Inuit, and Métis people. Inuit peoples originally live in the circumpolar tundra area and Métis are peoples of mixed origin, typically French and First Nations who live in recognized Métis communities. Indigenous is a term used in the international context to describe tribal peoples within a country who are characterized by the distinctive identity, values, and history that distinguishes them from other peoples in the country and who retain some or all characteristics of the original pre-colonial inhabitants of that land, and who despite their legal status hold some or all of their social, economic, cultural, and political institutions.

2. 'Elder' is a capitalized term to respect conventional protocol among Aboriginal writers who write in English.
3. Since 1965, the federal government has created local administrative units called Indian Bands, and communities elect their chief and councils to manage local activities and oversee the disbursement of local funds from the federal government. They have replaced the previous Indian agents, formerly used to manage these local activities. Currently more than 600 bands among First Nations communities exist in Canada.

REFERENCES

Auditor General of Canada. 2000. *Indian and Northern Affairs Canada—Elementary and Secondary Education*. Report submitted to the House of Commons, Chapter 4. Ottawa: Minister of Public Works and Government Services, Canada.

———. 2004. *Indian and Northern Affairs Canada—Elementary and Secondary Education*. Report submitted to the House of Commons, Chapter 4. Ottawa: Minister of Public Works and Government Services, Canada.

Avison, D. 2004. *A Challenge Worth Meeting: Opportunities for Improving Aboriginal Education Outcomes*. Report of the Council of Ministers in Education. Ottawa: Council of Ministers of Education.

Battiste, M. 1986. 'Micmac Literacy and Cognitive Assimilation', in J. Barman, Y. Hébert and D. McCaskill (eds), *Indian Education in Canada: The Legacy*. Vol. I, pp. 23–44. Vancouver: UBC Press.

———. 1998. 'Enabling the Autumn Seed: Toward a Decolonized Approach Toward Indigenous Knowledge, Language and Education', *Canadian Journal of Native Education*, 22(1): 16–27.

———. (ed.). 2000. *Reclaiming Indigenous Voice and Vision*. Vancouver: UBC Press.

Battiste, M. and J. Barman (eds). 1995. *First Nations Education in Canada: The Circle Unfolds*. Vancouver: UBC Press.

Battiste, M. and J. Y. Henderson. 2000. *Protecting Indigenous Knowledge and Heritage: A Global Challenge*. Saskatoon, SK: Purich Press.

Battiste, M. and C. McConaghy. 2005. 'Thinking Place: The Indigenous Humanities and Education', *Australian Journal of Indigenous Education*, 34: 1–6.

Battiste, M., L. Bell and L.M. Findlay. 2003. 'Decolonizing Education in Canadian Universities: An Interdisciplinary, International, Indigenous Research Project', *Canadian Journal of Native Education*: 26(2), 82–95.

Battiste, M., L. Bell, I. M. Findlay, L. Findlay and J. Y. Henderson. 2005. 'Thinking Place: Animating the Indigenous Humanities in Education', *Australian Journal of Indigenous Education*, 34: 7–19.

Battiste, M., L. Bell, Findlay, L. M., L. Findlay and J. Y. Henderson. 2006. 'Animating the Indigenous Humanities in Education', *Australian Journal of Indigenous Education*, 35: 7–20.

Blaut, J. 1993. *The Colonizer's Model of the World: Geographical Diffusionism and Eurocentric History*. New York: Guilford Press.

Chartrand, P. 1999. 'Indigenous Peoples in Canada: Aspirations for Distributive Justice as Distinct Peoples', in P. Havemann (ed.), *Indigenous Peoples Rights in Australia, Canada, and New Zealand*, pp. 88–107. Auckland, NZ: Oxford University Press.

Daes, E. 2000. 'Prologue: The Experience of Colonization Around the World', in M. Battiste (ed.), *Reclaiming Indigenous Voice and Vision*, pp. 3–8. Vancouver: UBC Press.

Duran, E. and B. Duran. 1995. *Native American Postcolonial Psychology*. Albany, NY: State University of New York Press.

Findlay, I. 2003. 'Working for Postcolonial Legal Studies: Working with the Indigenous Humanities', *Law, Social Justice and Global Development Journal*. Available online at http://www2.warwick.ac.uk/fac/soc/law/elg/lgd/2003_1/findlay (downloaded on 21 July 2008).

Havemann, P. (ed.). 1999. *Indigenous Peoples Rights in Australia, Canada, and New Zealand*. Auckland, NZ: Oxford University Press.

Macedo, D. 1999. 'Preface', in L. M. Semali and J. L. Kincheloe (eds), *What is Indigenous Knowledge? Voices from the Academy*, pp. xi–xvi. New York and London: Falmer Press.

McConaghy, C. 2000. *Rethinking Indigenous Education: Culturalism, Colonialism and the Politics of Knowing*. Flaxton, Queensland, Australia: Post Pressed.

Memmi, A. 1965. *The Colonizer and the Colonized*. New York: Orion Press.

———. 1969. *Dominated Man: Notes Toward a Portrait*. Boston: Beacon Press.

National Indian Brotherhood. 1972. *Indian Control of Indian Education.* Ottawa: National Indian Brotherhood.

Noël, L. 1993. *Intolerance: A General Survey.* Kingston and Montreal: McGill-Queens University Press.

Phillipson, R. 1992. *Linguistic Imperialism.* Oxford: Oxford University Press.

Royal Commission on Aboriginal Peoples. 1996. *Report of the Royal Commission on Aboriginal Peoples,* Volumes 1–5. Ottawa: Canadian Communications.

Saskatchewan Human Rights Commission. 2006. 'What is Educational Equity?' Available online at http://www.gov.sk.ca/shrc/equity/what_is_equity/what_is_education.htm (downloaded on 20 May 2008).

Smith, G. H. 1997. 'Kaupapa Maori: Theory and Praxis', Ph.D. Thesis. Education Department, the University of Auckland. Monograph. Auckland, New Zealand: The International Research Institute for Maori and Indigenous Education.

Smith, L. 1999. *Decolonizing Methodologies: Indigenous Peoples and Research.* London: Zed Books.

Schick, C. 2000. 'By Virtue of Being White': Resistance in Anti-Racist Pedagogy', *Race, Ethnicity and Education,* 3(1): 83–102.

St. Denis, V. 2002. *Exploring the Socio-Cultural Production of Aboriginal Identity: Implications for Education.* Unpublished PhD Dissertation, Stanford, CA: Stanford University.

St. Denis, V., R. Bouvier and M. Battiste. 1998. *Okiskinahamakewak Aboriginal Teachers in Saskatchewan's Publicly-Funded Schools: Responding to the Flux: Final Report.* Regina, Saskatchewan: Saskatchewan Education.

St. Denis, V. and C. Schick. 2003. 'What Makes Antiracist Pedagogy in Teacher Education Difficult: Three Popular Ideological Assumptions', *Alberta Journal of Educational Research,* XLIX (1): 55–69.

Tymchak, M. 2001. 'School Plus: A Vision for Children and Youth. Toward a New School, Community and Human Service Partnership in Saskatchewan', Final Report submitted to the Minister of Education, Government of Saskatchewan. Available online at http://www.artssmarts.ca/media/schoolplus.pdf (downloaded on 20 May 2008).

United Nations Human Rights Council. 2007. 'United Nations Declaration on the Rights of Indigenous Peoples', UN Doc. A/61/L.67

Wiessner, S. and M. Battiste. 2000. 'The 2000 Revision of the United Nations Draft Principles and Guidelines on the Protection of the Heritage of Indigenous Peoples', *St. Thomas Law Review,* 13(1): 383–90.

8
ISSUES AND CHALLENGES FOR INTERCULTURAL AND BILINGUAL EDUCATION (IBE) IN LATIN AMERICA[1]

ANAHY GAJARDO, GIOVANNA CARRARINI, JOSÉ MARÍN, AND PIERRE R. DASEN

INTRODUCTION

While the indigenous peoples of the world live in different environments and practice a great variety of languages and cultures, they do share nonetheless a common history of domination, exclusion, and subordination. In the field of education, this has led to the denial of cultural and linguistic diversity. In the past few decades, however, the education systems for indigenous peoples have changed considerably, and gradually, some programmes attempting to consider their languages and cultures have been developed.

In Latin America, it is only relatively recently that the ethnocentric methods used to teach indigenous peoples have been challenged, and this mainly through the involvement of these populations themselves. Since the 1970s, there has been a growing mobilization of indigenous peoples attempting to have their rights recognized, at the national as well as international levels. A number of their demands relate to education.

Educational indicators show a correlation between indigenous origin, socio-economic poverty and failure in school. In most countries of the world, indigenous peoples belong invariably to the most disadvantaged and socio-economically marginalized segments of the population and to those showing the highest rates of failure, of repeated classes and of drop out, as well as the highest rates of illiteracy (Perez, 2003b).

In view of these facts, some have questioned the learning capacity of indigenous peoples. However, most studies and surveys show that this is not the problem. Indigenous peoples have the same abilities and faculties as the rest of the population (Mishra, this volume), but their way of life and their belief systems follow types of logic and sets of values that foster knowledge and learning that differ from those used by the official education systems, which are usually governed by a mono-cultural and monolingual logic. Moreover, formal education is not homogeneously offered in all the areas populated by indigenous peoples. Therefore it is not the learning potential of these populations that is in question, but the capacity of the education systems to meet the challenges of cultural and linguistic diversity.

CULTURAL AND LINGUISTIC DIVERSITY

Indigenous peoples represent some 4 to 6 per cent of the world population, or about 250 million in over 70 countries. In Latin America, in spite of all the policies set up during the last five centuries to assimilate indigenous peoples and homogenize nation-states, there remain today over forty million indigenous peoples or about 10 per cent of the American sub-continent population (López, 1999). Except for Uruguay, where the indigenous population has been totally exterminated, all Latin American States are, to some extent, facing indigenous issues. They can also be considered, in various ways, as multilingual and multicultural societies, since they have all been populated through old and more recent migrations from Europe, Asia, and Africa.

One of the most important expressions of the cultural diversity of Latin American indigenous peoples is language. Policies and education programmes for indigenous peoples have largely been designed and implemented on the basis of language. If one considers indigenous languages only (excluding Spanish, Portuguese, all Creole languages and some of the languages spoken by small migrant groups), some 400 to 450 languages are spoken in Latin America today, as well as a vast number of dialects.

At the heart of the problem...a question of definitions

Who are the 'indigenous peoples'? A multitude of terms has been used to describe these populations, according to the times, the topics and national and regional contexts; they are often heavily derogatory and revealing of the way these populations are perceived. Indigenous peoples in general have suffered from these definitions imposed by others and reflecting the way the non-indigenous populations consider them.

While the cultural diversity and wide geographical distribution of the indigenous peoples makes it difficult to develop a universal definition, international organizations tend to use a definition to cover all cases, without mentioning national, ethnic, or cultural origin. Today, the Working Group for Indigenous Peoples (offshoot of the defunct UN Commission for Human Rights, which met in Geneva between 1982 and 2006) includes peoples as culturally different and geographically distant as the Saami of Sweden and Finland, the Mapuche of Chile and Argentina or the Masai of Kenya.

Most of the definitions approved by international organizations agree on the following points (Cobo, 1986; ILO, 1989; Sanders, 1999):

1. Indigenous peoples are groups that are culturally different from the rest of the population and have maintained their own social, economic, cultural, and political institutions.
2. On a semantic level, terms such as indigenous, aboriginal, first nations, and so on, underline the fact that these societies inhabited an area before the groups who came at a later date from other regions, following various migratory patterns, and who settled on the same land.
3. Indigenous peoples maintain specific material and spiritual links with the territory they live on. The relationship of indigenous peoples with their territory is increasingly recognized as the element that distinguishes these populations from the rest of society. For indigenous peoples, nature has a spiritual dimension that goes far beyond the Western world's purely material concept of land as a means of production: the land is one's habitat, territory and basis of socio-political organization and socio-cultural identification. The Western concept of private property gives one the right to own and benefit from the land, and to dispose of it as an individual possession. The relationship of indigenous peoples with the land is by nature collective and sacred. The land cannot be owned and exploited: 'Mother-Earth' has to be respected and preserved.

4. Indigenous peoples are characterized by their determination to conserve, develop and pass on to future generations the territories of their ancestors and their ethnic identity, which are the very foundation of their continuing existence as a people.
5. The relationship of indigenous peoples with the nation-states in which they find themselves is colonial in nature. They are dominated by the social and political structures of the country.
6. The group's self-identification and recognition mean that the individuals themselves have to determine if they belong to an indigenous group, provided that this group identifies them as indigenous.

Peoples or minorities? The issue of the right to self-determination

In international law, the discussion on the definition of 'indigenous' raises the issue of the terms 'peoples' and 'minorities', that have important implications for the right to self-determination, a right given only to 'peoples'. Self-determination is the only internationally-recognized right that would ensure that indigenous peoples have control over their territory and their destiny. It includes all aspects of indigenous reality, and this includes the right to choose the type of education corresponding to their aspirations. In this regard, Article 3 of the UN Declaration on the Rights of Indigenous Peoples (United Nations, 2008) states: 'Indigenous people have the right of self-determination. By virtue of that right they freely determine their political status and freely pursue their economic, social, and cultural development'. And Article 15: 'Indigenous children have the right to all levels and forms of education of the State. All indigenous peoples also have this right and the right to establish and control their educational systems and institutions providing education in their own languages, in a manner appropriate to their cultural methods of teaching and learning'.

In some writings within comparative education (for example Perez, 2003a/b), preference is given to the use of the term 'minorities', that also seems to carry more weight in the recommendations of the Council of Europe. Many nations seem to fear that indigenous groups would ask for independence if they were recognized as 'peoples', with the right to self-determination; however there are three basic differences between minorities and indigenous peoples:

1. Prior land occupation is not an essential criterion for identification as a minority group.
2. The link with the territory of origin is one of the bases of indigenous identity.
3. While they are sociological minorities (situation of non-domination within the nation-state), the indigenous peoples are not necessarily a numerical minority.

Furthermore, the indigenous groups who want national independence are rather rare; usually, they demand some form of territorial, political, and economic autonomy within a multinational and multicultural State.

Until such time as the Declaration on the Rights of Indigenous Peoples (United Nations, 2008), frozen because some countries were unhappy with Article 3, was accepted, the ILO convention 169 on indigenous and tribal peoples (ILO, 1989) constituted the most important legal framework concerning the rights of indigenous populations. This convention, ratified by numerous Latin American countries, defines minimal norms below which the rights of indigenous peoples should not fall. As far as education is concerned, it states, in particular, the right of indigenous peoples to control the curricula and contents of programmes, their right to set up their own institutions and means of instruction, their right to learn to read and write in the indigenous languages, as well as access to one language of the national community.

FROM BILINGUAL EDUCATION (BF) TO INTERCULTURAL AND BILINGUAL EDUCATION (IBE)

At the beginning of the 1960s, Latin American governments started developing education programmes for indigenous peoples. Over time, these were modified according to the progress of educational research, national and regional contexts, political whims and changes in the representations of cultural and linguistic diversity. However, all these models have one thing in common: they give a prominent place to indigenous languages, whatever their educational or political orientations.

Transitional bilingual education

Implemented during the 1960s and 1970s, the so-called transitional bilingual education model was aimed at assimilating indigenous peoples. This type of programme used indigenous languages in the first few years of schooling for indigenous children, in order to facilitate their passage to the colonial language (Spanish or Portuguese). The indigenous languages were only used insofar as they represented a bridge, a way towards the national language. The programme content remained the same and the fact that the indigenous learners have a different history and different traditions was not recognized. The partial use of the indigenous language was therefore placed in a perspective of domination, which was depriving the indigenous population of its own knowledge and characteristics.

During that time, several education projects based on this model were developed, especially in Peru, Guatemala, and Bolivia. They were characterized by a strong presence of churches, in particular evangelical groups, and by international cooperation. The programme of the Summer Institute of Linguistics (SIL) is a case in point. Created in the 1940s in the United States, the SIL is a religious evangelical institution which, under cover of academic purposes (the study of indigenous languages and their teaching by linguist-missionaries) aims to translate the Bible in all the world languages in order to better evangelize populations. The influence of SIL in Latin America was particularly strong in the tropical belt of the Amazon forest. In several cases, the SIL had the support of governments who considered it as an ally in their efforts to assimilate the indigenous populations (Marín, 1992, 1994a/b, 2000, 2001).

Maintenance bilingual education

A second model was developed in Latin America in the 1970s–1980s, in a context of 'Indian awakening' and indigenous demands. The indigenous groups, organized as federations or associations demanded, in particular, a more egalitarian access to schooling and complained that they were the victims of linguistic discrimination. They were demanding an upgrading of the indigenous languages in the schools and an access to the national language. Indeed, mastering Spanish or Portuguese is one of the conditions of social and economic integration in the national society, without which the indigenous peoples remained marginalized, with no opportunity to participate in civil society.

In this model, reading and writing are taught in the indigenous languages, and Spanish is taught as a second language, but does not dominate.

Bilingual and bicultural education

The third model was developed during the 1980s at a time when it was recognized that a cultural dimension was missing in all the education models intended for indigenous populations and it aimed (in words at least) to recognize both the culture and the language of the indigenous peoples. In this sense, it was the first attempt to integrate indigenous culture in the curricula. However, critics of this model note that the various curricula inspired by it generally integrated only fairly superficial aspects of the culture such as habitat, food, or clothing, and gave a stereotyped image of the indigenous cultures considered as isolated enclaves incapable of change. Some authors think that this model follows a similar logic to that of transitional bilingual education and is intended as a bridge towards the dominant language and culture.

Intercultural and bilingual education (IBE)

A fourth model was finally developed during the 1990s and is still being implemented. It is based on a premise that considers culture not as a fixed reality with clear boundaries, but as a dynamic, evolving entity, closely associated with the interactions happening between individuals. Because it considers indigenous cultures in their interactions not only with the national culture but also with the rest of the world, this model promotes an education rooted in the culture of reference of the learners, but open to elements and knowledge from other cultural horizons, including a 'universal' culture. On a pedagogical level, this model emphasizes the need to go beyond a purely linguistic level and to adapt the curricula, taking into account the indigenous skills and knowledge. Therefore, it entails major changes in the teaching programmes, in order to embed them in the realities experienced by the learners. The idea is to reinforce the indigenous languages and cultures as well as to create a new paradigm that would include both indigenous and Western knowledge. A long term ambition of the IBE model would be to expand and to apply to non indigenous populations, to the rest of the population groups of Latin America, so that indigenous cultures and languages would also be represented and recognized, from an indigenous perspective, in the national school curricula.

A TRAINING PROGRAMME FOR INTERCULTURAL AND BILINGUAL TEACHERS IN THE PERUVIAN AMAZON (FORMABIAP)

This programme was started in Iquitos, Peru, in 1988 by some indigenous representatives of the federations of the Interethnic Association of the Peruvian Forest (AIDESEP) and a multidisciplinary team from the Centre for Anthropological Research on the Peruvian Amazon, including foreign experts. Their goal was to design an alternative school curriculum adapted to the ecological, socio-economic, and cultural context of the region that met the needs of the indigenous peoples, as well as promoted their languages and cultures. The programme was set up after negotiations with the Ministry of Education through the Loreto Higher Education Institute (ISPL) and the Italian NGO Terra Nuova (Gasché, 1989).

In this programme, the trainers are recruited according to national criteria, but with a measure of autonomy given to AIDESEP and ISPL. The teachers are not necessarily indigenous and their training is multidisciplinary: education, history, anthropology, linguistics, mathematics, agronomy, fine arts, and physical education. However, care is taken to ensure that the recruited teachers identify with and follow the objectives of the programme.

For the students of a particular indigenous group to access the programme, the group must be a member of a federation affiliated with AIDESEP. The regional federations have two tasks: elect the elders or indigenous specialists, one for each language and culture per ethnic group, and organize the entrance exam of the students. The indigenous communities of each federation choose their candidates according to the interest they have shown for their society and their language. They are kept informed of the students' progress and of any problems of discipline. The students commit themselves, in writing, to work within their region and for their community at the end of the training (Rougemont, 2006).

This training programme associates traditional and Western education, without using a single system and opposing 'traditional' and 'modern' education. It is not considered enough to just translate Western culture into two languages, but learning Spanish as a second language is encouraged. This type of education is associated with local ecology and with the local socio-economic, political, and cultural realities (AIDESEP/ISPL/PFMB, 1988).

For the creators of the programme, a multicultural approach may contribute to a true dialogue between ethnic groups and nations and redress the present situation of discrimination, dependence, and submissiveness. But some problems remain:

1. How to obtain a collaboration between teachers trained in a Western university and indigenous specialists in their own language and culture in order to develop the contents of an intercultural education programme?
2. How to avoid imposing ready-made curricula?
3. How to coordinate practical experience in two cultures with a view to share knowledge and skills?
4. How to deal with the central issue of self-depreciation felt by the students and find ways to develop self-esteem, which is essential to the re-valorization of their knowledge, their language and their way of life?

The involvement of indigenous organizations in this programme paved the way to a discussion of the issue of land ownership, without which these societies are doomed. In the past few years, the governments of Latin American countries have become aware of this fact and have offered a few concessions and recognized some rights. There are also political demands linked to education and several initiatives are now being developed (Amadio, 1990; Amadio and López, 1993; Gasché, 2004; Godenzzi, 1996; López, 1990). Gasché (2004), for example, used his experience with FORMABIAP to respond to a request from Chiapas Indians in Mexico, who are struggling to obtain the right to their own territory and to a measure of autonomy from the Mexican State (Campa Mendoza, 1999; Varese, 1990).

THE TRAINING PROGRAMME IN INTERCULTURAL AND BILINGUAL EDUCATION FOR THE ANDES COUNTRIES (PROEIB-ANDES)

This programme is a regional strategy for training in IBE, with head-quarters at the Universidad Mayor de San Símon (UMSS) in Cocha-bamba, Bolivia. Its first decade of operation was made possible by a bilateral technical cooperation agreement between the Bolivian Government (through UMSS) and the German Government (through its technical cooperation agency, GTZ). Five other countries joined through their ministries of education: Colombia, Ecuador, Peru, Chile, and Argentina. Around twenty universities and indigenous organiza-tions in the region are also participating. The next step in the process was to create the foundation for education in multilingual and multi-cultural situations—FUNPROEIB-Andes—which is the new institu-tional framework implemented in March 2006.

The objectives of PROEIB-Andes are to support the sustainable development of IBE initiatives in Andean countries. The programme was set up along four axes: human resources development; research; creation of national centres for documentation and publications; and development and strengthening of a regional training network (PROEIB-Andes, 1997; OEI, 1997). The *Maestria* in intercultural and bilingual education is one of the multiple processes of training in human resources set up by PROEIB-Andes and it is aimed at pro-viding partner countries with IBE-trained executive staff and at setting up a permanent exchange of educational experiences carried out in communities for and by indigenous populations. The interest of this double training perspective is to move academic training closer to the needs of the primary schools, so that they can benefit from the results of research on the culture, language and education of indi-genous societies and improve the quality and equality of education where indigenous languages are spoken.

The *Maestria en EIB* is a university degree obtained after four semesters, intended for indigenous language speakers with uni-versity training and several years of practice in IBE. Since 1996, 105 students from several indigenous groups have followed this programme.

The link between training and research is one of the concerns of this programme. The practical application of the theoretical ideas through a scientific research done at the end of the course is always carried out in the area of origin of the students. The continuing interaction between the students and their society of origin, especially with the local, regional and national indigenous organizations is one of the key points of this training.

The training process itself provides a time to think about and develop a culturally-appropriate education system based on the experiences of each individual student and the knowledge of his/her community. Each participant learns on the basis of the recognition of belonging to a particular indigenous group. Specific knowledge linked to one group is thus continuously confronted with the knowledge of other ethnic groups. The students experience the concept of interculturality on a daily basis. It is in fact an experience that is constructed through interaction, even at the scientific level.

A community of learning is constituted between students, teachers, indigenous experts and leaders, and foreign researchers. Individuals become conscious of their identity and particularities, but not as separate entities to be safeguarded in closed spaces. Conflictual relations are examined in a historical, socio-political, and economic perspective (Godenzzi, 1996; Moya, 1998; Zúñiga, 1999), where the linguistic, cultural and educational issues are analyzed and interpreted in a comparative fashion, in order to spot differences and commonalities. Horizontal interpersonal relationships are promoted. A multidisciplinary spirit gives the training a holistic perspective.

Knowledge is built from each participant's individuality and experience as an individual and as a member of a group, having often experienced subordination and cultural devalorization. Thus, the process of re-appropriation of what has been denied is a pre-condition for the introduction of new knowledge (López and Küper, 1999). This fact is all the more important that this re-appropriation of cultural knowledge is allowed in a formal and official institution. A 'dialogue between types of knowledge' is encouraged and sustained throughout the course of study.

The use of indigenous languages in this training is part of the re-appropriation of cultural knowledge that has been previously denied. One week in every semester is devoted to teaching the students their first language. Indigenous experts, whether academically certified or not, who have a real and acknowledged command of the language and culture of the group they represent are incorporated into the teaching team. The purpose is to foster both an oral and written command of the indigenous language. Later on, an indigenous language module includes discussion in small groups of issues linked to IBE, sometimes at a very high level of abstraction, in the indigenous languages, with a translation into Spanish whenever needed. This is an institutional attempt to recover through these languages and their cognitive contents, an educational space from which they have always been excluded. To encourage this activity, *cooperative learning* is an essential teaching practice. Indigenous cultures are never presented as folklore, but the purpose is a process of revalorization and development of ethnic and intercultural identities.

INTERCULTURAL AND BILINGUAL EDUCATION (IBE): NEW CHALLENGES

It is interesting to note that these programmes are not limited to countries with large indigenous populations (Mexico, Guatemala, Ecuador, Peru, Bolivia), but exist also in countries such as Brazil, Columbia, and Chile, where they are a minority (D'Angelis and Veiga, 1997; Moya, 1990; Tedesco, 1990). These peoples become the actors of their own history, after having been the objects of forced assimilation policies imposed by nation-states. IBE is conceived as a democratic project within educational policies, but it permeates the whole society and makes it more democratic, in a very broad sense (Arratia, 1994). According to Godenzzi (1996), this perspective in the Latin American context takes into account the following observations:

1. The goal of this intercultural approach is to foster equitable relationships in the economic, social, political, and cultural sphere.
2. The change to a situation of equality comes from a process of social negotiation during which the participants—mainly the most marginalized indigenous peoples—manage to fight for their autonomy and define their rights as citizens.

The challenges raised by IBE projects are numerous and complex. Gasché (2004) underlines a few of them. In particular, he wonders about the concrete achievements of such programmes, versus their utopian or even angelical (Pollyanian?) dimensions. He also raises the difficult issue of transferring indigenous knowledge to a written form. How can one include in the curriculum the knowledge of oral societies, for which neither the history, nor the techniques, value systems or aspirations are ever put in writing, except, and from their own points of view, in the publications of anthropologists?

Various authors (Gottret, 2001; Montoya, 2001; Pérez, 2003b) show concern about the discrepancy between the theoretical concepts behind IBE and the practical applications, and about the variety of educational practices that hide behind the label of 'intercultural'. In particular, the persistence of practices that contribute to assimilate and homogenize while claiming to be part of IBE is a reminder of how difficult it is to change paradigms, especially when they consist of models that have marked social reality for several centuries and that tried to justify the domination of European cultures. For example, most of the programmes continue to be concerned mainly with linguistic matters and neglect the cultural aspects.

Gottret (2001), who was one of the persons in charge of IBE in the national reform of the education system in Bolivia that was proclaimed in 1992, mentions that, in theory, IBE 'is not reserved for indigenous ethnic groups, but should concern—on principle—all the children of the country (as much the city children as the rural ones)' (pp. 247–48). This vision has remained a utopia. Gottret's main conclusion concerning this educational reform is that it is necessary to understand 'that the curriculum should not be conceived *for* indigenous peoples, but *with* them and starting *from* them' (p. 245).

Montoya (2001) shares with Gottret the ideal of an IBE run by the State:

> Without decisive government support, without in fact the commitment of the heads of State themselves, IBE remains a very weak proposal. A poor quality IBE that does not live up to the parents' aspirations is sure to lead to its downfall. It would indeed be sad if the parents were to refuse IBE because of its poor quality. Indigenous people certainly deserve better. (p. 267)

The author thinks that most of the NGOs do not have the means to develop quality programmes. Although he has been advocating IBE in Peru since the 1990s (Montoya, 1989, 1990), he seems rather pessimistic. In his analysis of the Peruvian situation a decade later (Montoya, 2001), he mentions only five relatively minor positive points, such as 'one step towards a better learning of Spanish' (p. 252), which in fact turns IBE back to a model of transition. On the other hand, he lists ten major problems, among which are:

The structural hypocrisy of the States and their governments; the opposition of dominant classes and groups at the regional and local levels; the internalization of domination by the indigenous people themselves; ... the very difficult living and working conditions of the IBE teachers, and their poorly valued public image. (p. 252)

Indeed, Montoya (2001) describes teachers trained for IBE as feeling undervalued, often being given only temporary jobs, poorly paid, many of them choosing this profession without any calling, only because they are out of a job. Their training is often minimal. 'Several of these teachers have a minimal command not only of Spanish, but also of their own language' (pp. 258–59). According to Montoya's observations, they often do not speak a pure Quechua, but frequently intermix Spanish words. This, he thinks, is 'because they want to show, consciously or unconsciously, that they do know Spanish. Diglossia as a phenomenon of domination of a more prestigious language over another appears to be an important process' (pp. 257–58).

Rougemont (2006) has carried out research interviews with various actors involved in the FORMABIAP programme and in particular with teacher-trainees. She speaks of the many paradoxes linked to the fact that the programme seems to be a utopia that is far from being shared by all indigenous communities, which are marked by a too long-standing denial of their language and culture. Some of the young people sent to the training programme said that they did not speak their indigenous language, and did not identify with their indigenous culture, but were forced to do so in order to be accepted in the programme. When they had to return to their communities (since the training alternates theory and practice), they felt compelled to defend the values of the programme almost against their own people. 'What happens after this short experience, which will have lasted only one year, is that they will no longer feel at home anywhere' (p. 196).

Thus, Rougement (2005) seems to be rather dubious about this programme, even though it is presented as a success story. According to her analysis, the difficulty for the students to get their communities to identify themselves with pride as indigenous 'comes from five emblematic figures of influence: the colonial master, the employer or trader, the *mestizzo* teacher, the Christian evangelist, and local authorities' (p. 169). This makes one wonder whether the deleterious impact of assimilation can ever be reversed!

Pérez (2003b) also mentions a series of difficulties with IBE programmes, notably that indigenous populations are not convinced of the interest for their children to learn the local languages, because they know that learning Spanish is more useful to get a job. She also remarks that the rural population tends to seek work in towns, and therefore gets exposed to cultural homogenization. 'Nevertheless, IBE is very often, developed only in the rural areas and not in the urban ones, which leads to the marginalization of these programmes' (p. 224). Furthermore, 'to be efficient, IBE should continue at the secondary school level, but most often the teaching of subjects at higher levels is done in Spanish and not in the indigenous languages' (p. 226).

In opposition to Gottret (2001) and Montoya (2001), Pérez (2003b) argues that the best IBE programmes are likely to be privately funded, in particular through international public aid. This is because she sees a fundamental contradiction between the interests of the local communities fighting for their autonomy, and those of the nation-states, that remain cultural homogenization imposed from top, and this despite any political discourse to the contrary.

All of these criticisms, stemming from educational researchers who are more or less close to IBE programmes, should be taken seriously, or it is likely that the enthusiasm for these innovations will gradually fade. Some solutions to these problems may be found through comparative research, taking into account the experience accumulated in different contexts.

EDUCATION FOR INDIGENOUS PEOPLES IN OTHER REGIONS

While this chapter has not attempted to deal with this issue on a worldwide level, it is clear that the question of specific education for minorities or indigenous populations is not particular to Latin America. Mishra (this volume) deals with education for *adivasi* (also called 'tribal') populations in India. The Indian Constitution acknowledges that these groups have rights and even privileges in the form of positive discrimination. However, in spite of a quota system and efforts made to open schools in isolated areas, the quality of these schools is often very poor and school attrition is very high. The problems mentioned by Mishra show that India has not yet found the best solution to these problems.

According to Teasdale (1994, 1995, this volume; Teasdale and Little, 1995), innovations seem more promising in Oceania. In 1995,

Teasdale described several interesting projects in New Zealand and Australia, which allowed a growing involvement of the indigenous peoples in the management of their educational systems. In New Zealand, he describes one of the rare examples where a secondary school redesigned by and for the Maoris is also attended by Pakehas (white New Zealanders). In the 1990s, Australia started a 'two-way' system, in which indigenous and Western knowledge were taught separately, so that Aborigines could become familiar with the dominant system in order to be able to profit from it, but without necessarily accepting it, since its values are, in part, contradictory to the traditional Aboriginal values. Teasdale (this volume) shows that this slightly schizophrenic design has now been abandoned and a more syncretic approach is being implemented. He also mentions several innovations in Papua New Guinea, for example, which demonstrate that adequate solutions can be found even in the absence of massive funding.

The formal Western schooling model has become the unique system throughout the world to such an extent—Serpell (1993; Serpell and Hatano, 1997) calls it a 'hegemonic imposition'—that few people now dare suggest alternatives. Therefore few authors attempt to challenge schooling as an institution (but see Herzog, this volume). Battiste (2002; this volume) does take a very radical stance, insisting on the need to decolonize education as far as indigenous peoples are concerned. In the next few years, we could well see a quest for alternative systems more akin to informal education (Dasen, 2000; this volume).

CONCLUSION

According to Brandão (1991), there are two ways to analyze cultural interactions, a socio-political one centred on power, and a symbolic one, centred on knowledge. The first considers culture as a way to respond to its needs for self-reproduction and social organization, as an instrument of the power that justifies the existing social order. Culture transforms itself in order to reproduce itself. The second way to consider culture is to see it as a collective creation around a consensus, which allows people to agree about the meaning of codes and worldviews. These two perspectives co-exist, and point to the important issues that have to be taken into account in cross-cultural research and applications.

Cultural decentration in teacher training seems to be an essential step, which posits the refusal to accept stereotypes, and seeks changes in attitude. It avoids the reproduction of the mental schemes of categorization and the hierarchization of values, and corresponds to a constant effort to understand the common elements that unite us as members of a single human species. To create the necessary conditions for living together, despite our differences, should become a collective challenge. The indigenous peoples representing the many multicultural societies of different regions of Latin America will find in the wealth of their diversity the building materials for a democratic social construction that respects their human dignity.

The problems encountered by the indigenous peoples of the Americas can shed light on those of other continents, among which Europe, which is confronted with the integration of its national or ethnic minorities, such as Gipsies. Thus, comparative education and intercultural education are united in common goals (Perez et al., 2000). An intercultural perspective, beyond education and psychology, can help to understand the urgent need to respect cultural diversity despite the current process of globalization (Marín and Dasen, 2007; see also Marín, and Akkari and Dasen, this volume).

NOTE

1. This chapter was originally published in French: Gajardo, A., G. Carrarini, J. Marín and P. R. Dasen. 2008. 'Enjeux et de l'éducation interculturelle bilingue (eib) en amérique latrine', in S. Hanhart, A. Gorga, M. A. Broyon and T. Ogay (eds), *De la comparaison en éducation*. Hommage á Soledad Perez, pp. 282–314. Paris: L'Harmattan.

REFERENCES

AIDESEP/ISPL/PFMB. 1998. *Programa curricular diversificado de educación primaria intercultural bilingüe para los pueblos amazónicos*. Iquitos, Pérou: AIDESEP-ISP.

Amadio, M. 1990. 'Two Decades of Bilingual Education in Latin America', *Prospects*, 75: 305–309.

Amadio, M. and L. López (eds). 1993. *Educación bilingüe intercultural en América Latina: guía bibliográfica*. La Paz: UNICEF-Centro de Investigación y Promoción de las Culturas Autóctonas.

Arratia, M.I. 1994. 'Una experiencia piloto en educación intercultural en la región aymara del norte de Chile', *Pueblos indígenas y educación*, 29–30: 193–212. Quito: Proyecto EBI y Ediciones Abya–Yala.

Battiste, M. 2002. *Indigenous Knowledge and Pedagogy in First Nations Education: A Literature Review with Recommendations*. Available online at http://www.ainc-inac.gc.ca/pr/pub/krw/ikp_e.pdf(downloaded on 20 May 2008).

Brandão, C. 1991. 'A arca de Noe. Aportamentos sobre sentidos e diferenças a respeito da ideia de cultura', in P. Suess (ed.), *Culturas e evangelição*, pp. 21–40. São Paulo: Ediçoes Loyola.

Campa Mendoza, V. 1999. *Las insurrecciones de los pueblos indios en México. La rebelión Zapatista en Chiapas*. Durango, México: Ediciones Cuellar.

Cobo, M. 1986. *Study on the Problem of Discrimination Against Indigenous Populations*. New York: United Nations.

D'Angelis, W. and J. Veiga (eds). 1997. *Letura e escritura em escolas indígenas*. Campinas, Brazil: Mercado de letras.

Dasen, P. R. 2000. 'Développement humain et éducation informelle', in P. R. Dasen and C. Perregaux (eds), *Pourquoi des approches interculturelles en sciences de l'éducation?* pp. 107–123. Bruxelles: DeBoeck Université Collection, Raisons éducatives, vol. 3.

Gasché, J. 1989. 'A propos d'une nouvelle expérience d'éducation bilingue au Pérou. L'indigénisation d'un programme, sa critique de l'anthropologie', *Bulletin de la Société Suisse des Américanistes*, 53–54: 131–42.

———. 2004. 'La motivation politique de l'éducation interculturelle indigène et ses exigences pédagogiques. Jusqu'où va l'interculturalité?', in A. Akkari and P. R. Dasen (eds), *Pédagogies et pédagogues du Sud*, pp. 107–38. Paris: L'Harmattan.

Godenzzi, J. (ed.). 1996. *Educación e interculturalidad en los Andes y la Amazonía*. Cusco: Centro de Estudios Regionales Andinos Bartolomé de las Casas.

Gottret, G. 2001. 'La réforme éducative bolivienne. Une expérience qui se veut interculturelle', in C. Sabatier and P. R. Dasen (eds), *Cultures, développement et éducation. Autres enfants, autres écoles*, pp. 237–49. Paris: L'Harmattan.

International Labour Organization. 1989. Convention No. 169 Concerning Indigenous and Tribal Peoples in Independent Countries. Geneva: ILO.

López, L. E. 1990. 'Development of Human Resources in and for Bilingual Intercultural Education in Latin America', *Prospects*, 75(3), 311–19.

López, L. E. and W. Küper. 1999. 'La educación intercultural bilingüe en América Latina: balance y perspectivas', *Revista Ibero-americana de Educación*, 20(mayo-agosto): 17–85. Available online at 2005 dans: http://www.campus-oei.org/revista/rie20a02.htm (downloaded on 15 November 2005).

Marín, J. 1992. *Peuples indigènes, missions religieuses et colonialisme interne dans l'Amazonie péruvienne.* Uppsala: Missionsfornkning, Uppsala University.

———. 1994a. 'Dimension historique de l'ethnocentrisme européen dans le processus de la domination coloniale et post-coloniale de l'Amérique', in J. Blomart and B. Krewer (eds), *Perspectives de l'interculturel,* pp. 123–34. Paris: L'Harmattan.

Marín, J. 1994b. 'Ethnocentrisme et racisme dans l'histoire européenne dans le cadre de la conquête de l'Amérique et perspective actuelle', in C. Allemann-Ghionda (ed.), *Multikultur und Bildung in Europa,* pp. 181–96. Berne: Peter Lang.

———. 2000. 'Une éducation appropriée aux peuples autochtones d'Amérique latine', in P. Dasen and C. Perregaux (eds), *Pourquoi des approches interculturelles en sciences de l'éducation?* pp. 261–80. Bruxelles: De Boeck Université.

———. 2001. 'Histoire de l'Etat-Nation: De La Politique D'intégration En Amérique Latine et en Europe', in C. Perregaux, T. Ogay, Y. Leanza and P. R. Dasen (eds), *Intégrations et migrations: regards pluridisciplinaires,* pp. 141–58. Paris: L'Harmattan.

Marín, J. and P. R. Dasen. 2007. 'L'éducation face à la mondialisation, aux migrations et aux droits de l'homme', in M. C. Caloz-Tschopp and P. R. Dasen (eds), *Mondialisation, migration et droits de l'homme: Un nouveau paradigme pour la recherche et la citoyenneté,* vol.1, pp. 285–320. Brussels: Bruylant.

Montoya, R. 1989. *Multiculturalidad y Política. Derechos indígenas, Ciudadanos y Humanos.* Lima: Sur Casa de Estudios del Socialismo.

———. 1990. *Por una educación bilingüe en el Perú. Reflexiones sobre cultura y socialismo.* Lima: Mosca Azul editores.

———. 2001. 'Limites et possibilités de l'éducation bilingue interculturelle au Pérou', in C. Sabatier and P. R. Dasen (eds), *Cultures, développement et éducation. Autres enfants, autres écoles,* pp. 251–68. Paris: L'Harmattan.

Moya, R. 1990. 'A Decade of Bilingual Education and Indigenous Participation in Ecuador', *Prospects,* 75(3): 331–43.

———. 1998. 'Reformas educativas e interculturalidad en América latina', *Revista Iberoamericana de Educación,* 17: 105–87. Available online at http://www.rioei.org/oeivirt/rie13a11.pdf (downloaded on 17.07.2008).

OEI. 1997. 'II Congreso Latinoamericano de Educación Intercultural Bilingüe', *Revista Iberoamericana de Educación,* 13: 271–79.

Perez, S. 1996. *L'éducation rurale à petits pas. Etude comparative en Equateur.* Paris: L'Harmattan.

———. 2003a. 'Minorités', in D. Groux, S. Perez, L. Porcher, V. Rust and N. Tasaki (eds), *Dictionnaire d'éducation comparée,* pp. 364–65. Paris: L'Harmattan.

Perez, S. 2003b. 'Minorités et Amérique andine: quelles chances pour une éducation bilingue?', in A. Gohard-Radenkovic, D. Mujawamariya and S. Perez (eds), *Intégration des "minorités" et nouveaux espaces interculturels*, pp. 209–28. Bern: Lang.

————. 2004. 'Femmes et éducation préscolaire non formelle en Equateur', in A. Akkari and P. R. Dasen (eds), *Pédagogies et pédagogues du Sud*, pp. 139–60. Paris: L'Harmattan.

Perez, S. D. Groux and F. Ferrer. 2000. 'Education comparée et éducation interculturelle: éléments de comparaison', in P. R. Dasen and C. Perregaux (eds), *Pourquoi des approches interculturelles en sciences de l'éducation?* pp. 85–104. Bruxelles: DeBoeck Université Collection « Raisons éducatives » vol. 3.

PROEIB Andes Since. 1997.: Web page: Available at http://cgi.proeibandes. org/boletin/index.html (downloaded on 17 July 2008)

Rougemont, H. 2006. *Le troisième monde. Analyse compréhensive d'un programme de formation bilingue et interculturelle en Amazonie péruvienne.* Université de Genève: Cahiers de la section des sciences de l'éducation, no. 109.

Sanders, D. 1999. 'Populations autochtones: problèmes de définition', *Revue électronique du Centre de ressources de Planète autochtone.* Accessed November 2005: http://www.dfait-maeci.gc.ca/aboriginalplanet/resource/ canada/documents/sanders-fr.asp

Serpell, R. 1993. *The significance of schooling. Life-journeys in an African society.* Cambridge: Cambridge University Press.

Serpell, R. and G. Hatano. 1997. 'Education, Schooling, and Literacy', in J. W. Berry, P. R. Dasen and T. S. Saraswathi (eds), *Handbook of Cross-Cultural Psychology, Basic Processes and Human Development*, Second Edition. Vol. 2, pp. 339–76. Boston: Allyn & Bacon.

Teasdale, G. 1994. 'Education and the Survival of Small Indigenous Cultures', *International Yearbook of Education*, 44: 197–223.

————. 1995. 'Education and Culture: Introduction', *Prospects*, 96(4): 587–92.

Teasdale, G. and A. Little (eds). 1995. 'Education and Culture', *Prospects*, 96(4).

Tedesco, J. (ed.). 1990. 'Dossier: L'éducation interculturelle bilingue en Amérique Latine', *Perspectives*, 75(3): 335–426.

United Nations. 2008. Declaration on the Rights of Indigenous Peoples, Document 07–58681. Available online at http://www.un.org/esa/socdev/ unpfil/documents/DRIPS_en.pdf

Varese, S. 1990. 'Challenges and Prospects for Indian Education in Mexico', *Prospects*, 75(3): 345–55.

Zúñiga, M. 1999. 'Interculturalidad Educación Intercultural: conceptos y viabilidad en Latinoamérica', in D. Quilaqueo (ed.), *Educación Intercultural Bilingüe. Actas segundo seminario latinoamericano*, pp. 45–64. Témuco, Chile: Universidad Católica de Temuco.

Section III   Education and Religion

9

SOCIALIZATION, LEARNING, AND BASIC EDUCATION IN ISLAMIC CONTEXTS

ABDELJALIL AKKARI

The aim of the first section of this chapter is to show how a Koranic school presence has remained constant in spite of the sudden emergence of Western-style schooling introduced by colonization. The second section of the chapter revisits the problem of terminology in the study of the Koranic school. In the third section, using the perspective of situated learning, we will try to analyze the pedagogical system of Koranic schools by describing the social and cognitive processes employed by this institution. In the final part, we hope to show how the current educational situation in several Islamic contexts could be better served through closer interactions between Koranic and Western schools. Research conducted in Africa was primarily used for this text.

INTRODUCTION

A thorough knowledge of non-Western educators and educational theory remains inadequate in spite of several recent studies

(Akkari and Dasen, 2004; Reagan, 2000; Thanh Khoi, 1995). It should be noted that the opposition between Western and Koranic schools has been contested by Lecomte (1954), who underscored the continuity from the Byzantine school to the Koranic one. Reagan (2000), for his part, considers that the Western and Koranic educational traditions draw from the same religious sources. It is also necessary to add that the Koranic school undertook profound transformations towards the end of the 19th century, such as the introduction of secular subjects. These changes were halted by colonization. Makdisi (1981) has argued convincingly for a major Islamic contribution to the emergence of the first universities in the medieval West, showing how terms such as having 'fellows' holding a 'chair,' or students 'reading' a subject and obtaining 'degrees,' as well as practices such as inaugural lectures and academic robes, can all be traced back to Islamic concepts and practices. Indeed the idea of a university in the modern sense—a place of learning where students congregate to study a wide variety of subjects under a number of teachers—is generally regarded as an Arabic innovation, developed at the al-Azhar university in Cairo. Makdisi has demonstrated that cities bordering the Islamic world (Salerno, Naples, Bologna, Montpellier) developed the first European universities.

Koranic school systems[1] represent an interesting educational model not only because of its longevity but also because of its widespread geographical diffusion throughout the world. Up until now an understanding of Koranic school systems has suffered because of the lack of a deep anthropological study treating Islam as a religion with a novel cognitive system (Colonna, 1984; Institut International de planification de l'éducation [IIPE], 1984).

Even if comparative education has been open to including culture in its conceptual frameworks, this inclusion has not gone far enough concerning important theoretical debates on the concept of culture in any analysis of educational institutions (Hoffman, 1999: 466). The comparison of different educational traditions poses a problem of cultural identity[2] as research undertaken within education or anthropology has the following dilemma:

> ... (1) Anthropologists cannot adequately describe, let alone explain, any culture different from their own. (2) For any culture to be adequately described and understood, it must be investigated by an

anthropologist who himself has been acculturated in it. (3) For the latter to adequately convey the ideas and institutions of that culture, they must be reported in the native language, for there is no way of rendering the conceptual systems of one culture by the concepts of another...All science is ethnoscience. (Spiro, 1984: 345)

In spite of these difficulties, inherent in any comparative analysis, taking into account 'other' conceptions is necessary. As Geertz (1994) pointed out, this goal necessitates entering into an alien turn of mind. This is what we will try to accomplish in this text devoted to an analysis of the educational foundations of the Koranic school.

THE CHARACTERISTICS OF KORANIC SCHOOL

The history of Islamic teaching and research on Koranic schooling have been the subject of studies in the Maghreb (Colonna, 1981, 1984; Eickelman, 1978; El-Sayed Darwish, 1981; Lecomte, 1954) as well as in sub-Saharan Africa (Brenner, 1993; Delval, 1980; Désalmand, 1983; Lange, 2000; Meunier, 1997; Santerre, 1973; Santerre, C. mercier-Tremblay (eds), 1982). Taken as a whole these studies show that the pedagogical model of the Koranic school contains six basic characteristics which are more or less stable according to the historical period referred to: (*a*) openness, (*b*) ritualization, (*c*) permanence, (*d*) flexibility, (*e*) resistance, and (*f*) diversity.

Openness

Admission into a Koranic school is a right for any child of a Muslim father with no restrictions connected to birth, age, intellectual level or physical integrity.[3] The normal age of entrance into a Koranic school is around five years. Once the step towards adherence to Islam has been made, opening of the Koranic school to all social groups and cultures makes this an institution of 'basic education' intended for all, and thus by definition, egalitarian. The openness of the Koranic school represents an initiative of cultural integration and of full socialization, and also represents an essential characteristic that differentiates it from any other school system. This ease of access (automaticity), of course, goes with the inevitable corollary: the impossibility of using the Koranic school as a means of social differentiation (Colonna, 1984). The Koranic school embodies a horizontal distribution of basic knowledge that all Muslims are expected to possess.

Ritualization[4]

The intensive demands on memory, mobilization of the body by rhythm and voice are exterior signs of the pedagogy of the Koranic school. It is completely permeated by the respect of form and the central role of repetition, both a key category and a central practice of this learning method, which consists in ceaselessly repeating the same recitations, the same motions (Colonna, 1984). 'Learning by heart' larger and larger sections of the Koran have remained a central process of Koranic school pedagogy in spite of a progressive abandonment of this method in other educational traditions. Introduction of reading and writing during apprenticeship of the Koran, executed in Arabic characters irrespective of teacher's and pupil's primary language, is organized around an analytical and progressive approach: letter, word, sentence, and meaning.

According to the terminology used by Freire (1993), the Koranic school is essentially 'depository' since it treats students as potential 'recipients' of the Koran. They must immerse themselves in Islamic culture, conform to the established norms and values, and those who wander from these are quickly and severely brought to order. Koranic school can be considered as one in which the students gain access to the universality of the Koran by a transmission based approach. By imposing constraints (submission/*adhesion*) it puts in place conditional reflexes, habits built on repetition of a firm programme: the mastery of the Koran. Thus, traditional Islamic education is characterized by rigorous discipline and a lack of explicit explanation of memorized material (Eickelman, 1985).This rigid pedagogy has certain advantages: speed, low cost, and rapid teacher training.

Permanence

The permanence of the Koranic school through the ages should not be explained simply as an archaic cultural heritage. How then can one explain that the Koranic school has been able to survive through many centuries while being present in such a vast geographical area? One possible hypothesis regarding this permanence is the absence in Islam of a hierarchical clergy as within the Catholic Church. In fact, the opening of a Koranic school has no connection to a regulatory institution. The 'authority' to teach depends exclusively on the local community of faith. In the last section of this paper we will discuss the current vivacity of the Koranic school, most notably in Western Africa.

Flexibility

The flexibility and shifting of the Koranic school back and forth from one cultural system to another is realized by an optimal and subtle combination of oral and written language. This mixed nature allows the Koranic school to come in contact as easily with the greater culture (the written tradition) as with the oral, traditional ones (Colonna, 1984). This ability helps explain the quick implantation of the Koranic school in Western Africa. As Santerre (1973) explained, teachers in Koranic schools in northern Cameroon are not impeded by their lack of Arabic, as in no way does this lack keep them from playing an important role in the religious socialization of the children under their responsibility. The mode of operation at the Koranic schools is non formal and revolves around the individual operator. Progress of pupils depends on individual ability; they are allowed to progress at their own pace without hindrance. The pupils are first taught the Arabic letters and how to recite the Koran. They then study Islamic jurisprudence and other facets of Islamic education (UNICEF, 1999).

Resistance

The sudden development of the colonial educational system created a situation in which the Koranic school found itself, for the first time in its history, in a position of being dominated. Thus, in North African countries, a duality has been developed, with Western school in charge of educating the children of European settlers and the urban elites and the Koranic school being reserved for the indigenous population and the rural poor. This duality could be seen throughout the colonial period in Northern Africa (Colonna, 1984; Sraeïb, 1974). Even in this inferior position, however, the Koranic school was mobilized in the fight against colonization. While colonial schools (either public or controlled by foreign religious missions) were essentially mobilized for domestication,[5] the Koranic schools were engaged in a process of cultural resistance against colonization (Brenner, 1993; Coulon, 1993; Khayar, 1976; Turin, 1971). Richard-Molard (1954) found that even if the colonization was able to diminish the influence of Allah, too often, this only created people deprived of their cultural roots.

The resistance-transformation of Koranic schools continued into the postcolonial period where the expansion of modern schooling had become the 'priority of all priorities' of those Western educated elites newly in power. We can note that it took different characteristics according to the situation:

1. Devalued in face of a strong and generalized state system (Tunisia, Turkey).
2. Incorporated into the state system or at least tolerated within (Iran, Pakistan, Egypt, Morocco).
3. Complementary with the state system and responding to the needs of marginalized socio-cultural groups (Mali, Senegal, Gambia, Nigeria, Kenya).
4. Replacing a deficient or totally absent state system (Somalia, Afghanistan).

Diversity of the curriculum, goals, space, and time

To show the curricular diversity of Koranic schools, Colonna (1984) contrasted different types of schools:

1. 'Classical' Koranic school where only the Koran is taught/modernized with a varying degree of secular subjects.
2. 'Independent' Koranic school under the control of the community/ Koranic school under the control of the state and of village powers (religious confraternities).
3. 'Spiritual supplement' Koranic school (similar to Christian catechism)/ 'Single class Koranic school' which, in certain contexts, remains the only educational institution.

After the development and spread of Western-style schooling throughout the 20th century, the Koranic school lost its central role in a majority of Islamic regions. It retains, however, a certain influence in the socialization process. This influence differs in intensity and degree according to the region, the degree of urbanization, and the strength of what is officially offered as basic education. In the cities in Northern Africa it offers preschool, before children enter public school, and later weekly catechism classes. Its influence declines when going up the social scale. In rural zones, to the north as well as to the south of the Sahara, the Koranic school remains a central institution in education, sometimes the sole actor because of the deterioration of government services.

In Western Africa, the Islamic educational system has a many-levelled structure, less rigid than Western-style schooling. Currently there exists a traditional branch (Koranic studies only), a formal branch or its 'modern' equivalent (Franco-Arabic schools, often called *madrasa*) and intermediate or hybrid forms often called 'improved Koranic instruction'. While professional training is not an explicit part of the goals of Koranic education, most of the students who continue their studies beyond the elementary level end up working in the community as apprentices with a *marabout*, a craftsman or a shopkeeper (Easton, 1999).

The diversity of the Koranic school can also be seen at the level of:

1. The management of class space: Koranic schooling can take place in a mosque, in a single-family home, under a tent, in a shed or under a tree in the open air.
2. The management of class time: the temporal organization of the school does not interrupt the economic and social activities of the community.

As stated in Table 9.1, Koranic schooling may be considered as an original form of learning which is situated between the case of a society without schooling and society with Western-style schooling. As an original form of learning, the Koranic school thus deserves to be the subject of future studies in comparative education and anthropology.

Table 9.1 Comparison of educational forms

	Representation of the learner	Methods of learning	Age-space-time of learning	Social reproduction
Society without schooling	Ethnotheories	Empiric participation in the learning process	Everywhere in the social settings	Limited social reproduction through education
Koranic school	Potential believer	Teaching content coming from divine will	Koranic school and social settings	Limited social reproduction through Koranic school
Society with Western-type schooling	Representations of the child, the adolescent and the adult	-Imposition of goals and teaching methods -Teaching content coming from scientific rationality	Age-space-time of education are centred in schools	-Strong social reproduction through the school -Social change through the school

THE PROBLEM OF TERMINOLOGY IN THE STUDY OF THE KORANIC SCHOOL

The diversity of Koranic schools discussed in the last section can be also analyzed at the linguistic level.

We observe an enormous multiplicity of denominations: *Kuttab* (Tunisia, Algeria, Egypt), *Katatib* (Kuwait), *Msid* (Morocco), *Mahadara* (Mauritania), *Dox* (Somalia), *Khalwa-Zawia* (Libya, Sudan), *Madrasa* (Pakistan, West Africa), *Pesantrens* (Indonesia), and so on. Thus, a terminological clarification is required even if it is difficult to simplify the complexity of a long standing institution.

Let us notice initially that the translation of the term 'Koranic school' in Arabic (language of reference in Islamic education) does not make sense. Indeed, nobody speaks about *madrasa kurāniya*. Eickelman (1985) used the expression 'Koranic education'. The common use of 'Koranic school' is probably the consequence of an Eurocentric portrayal of the most stable local, non-formal education providing basic religious and moral instruction to a large number of children in the Islamic context.

As stated in Table 9.2, we distinguish three major terms used in different Islamic settings in Africa to refer to the so called 'Koranic school': (*a*) Kuttab, (*b*) Madrasa, (*c*) Zawia (Khalwa)

Table 9.2 Koranic schools

	Geographical area	Age scope	Size localization
Kuttab	North Africa Middle East	Young children-basic education	Small units Rural and Urban areas
Madrasa	North Africa West Africa South Asia	Life span	Big structures Urban areas
Zawiya	North Africa	Life span	Small and isolated units Rural and Urban areas

Kuttab

In Arabic, the root *k-t-b* is expressed as a verbal infinitive as *kataba*, meaning 'to write'. From that basic root we can then get the words *Kuttab*, *Kitab* 'book' (with a metaphorical meaning of 'Koran'), *Katib* 'writer', *Maktub* 'written' (with a metaphorical meaning of 'predestined') and *Maktaba* 'library'. The use of the term *Kuttab* is clearly linked to the development of a culture of literacy. *Kuttab* is generally used to name a small learning unit (single classroom) for relatively young children. It is the basic education in Islamic contexts before the intrusion of Western-style schooling.

Madrasa

The word *Madrasa*[6] generally has two meanings in Arabic. In a common literal and colloquial usage, it means 'school'. This term indicates the current modern schools in Arab countries. In addition, a *Madrasa* is an educational institution offering instruction in Islamic subjects including, but not limited to the Koran. Within this religious school, students learn Islamic theology and others philosophical or profane subjects. Generally, the students receive a scholarship and live in the school. *Madrasa* is an institution of education which is bigger, better organized and more structured that the *Kuttab*. It offers secondary as well as tertiary education.

Historically, the term *madrasa* is an institution intended for religious elites. It is a 'school of spiritual thinking'. Well known *madrasa*s such as Al-Azhar in Egypt or A-Zeitouna in Tunisia have been a major instrument for imparting interest in and fostering acquisition of scholarly knowledge and skills in Muslim societies for centuries. As a key element of the social fabric, they also played a major role in shaping the moral and spiritual development of the students in these societies. Eickelman (1985) analyzed specifically the Madarasa Yusufia (the Mosque-University in Marrakech) and traces the transformation of this type of traditional school into what he terms the 'Religious Institute'.

With the interplay of internal and external forces, the role and prerogatives of *madrasas* have changed in many Muslim societies, blurring somewhat the common sense perception of these institutions. An analysis of *madrasa* could have different implications within various cultural, political, and geographic contexts.

Zawia (Khalwa)

These expressions usually indicate a small room connected to a mosque used specifically for meditation and to learn the Koran. A *Zawia* is usually founded by a Sufi mystic of sufficient piety. His presence attracts followers forming an informal Islamic study group. In the case of a Sufi saint, his students often confine themselves to the monastic enclave and retreat, devoting themselves to prayers, education and charitable works.

Grandin and Gaboricau (1997) show that beyond local and regional specificities, Islamic teaching obeys everywhere and from immemorial time to the same logic. It never seems an autonomous system, but it is included in the general socialization system. Before the European colonial domination, knowledge (religious or profane) is an art whose transmission follows a single track, founded on apprenticeship or *Suhba* where written teaching and oral teaching are narrowly overlapping. In other words, the process of learning is based on a personal relationship between a master and his disciple. The master initiates the disciple at the same time with contents of the knowledge and the chain of the guarantors of the knowledge. The itinerancy is the second characteristic of this traditional Islamic education, the disciple moving in the Islamic space in the search of new Masters with the aim of perfecting initiation.

After the colonial domination of Islamic countries and regions, the Islamic educational system fell under a strategy of survival in the context of cultural and political domination, with the adoption of some aspects of Western schooling: system of organization, formalization of the master-pupil ratios, establishment of levels of qualification sanctioned by examinations and diplomas, introduction of new subjects, teaching of foreign languages, edition of religious works in vernacular languages, development of the education of women.

The definition of the ideal type of Koranic school is not possible without taking to account the context in which one wants to explain it. This context is determined by three main factors:

1. Colonial and post-colonial educational policies.
2. Space left by the current formal education system.
3. The degree of strength of local religious communities.

In most Islamic contexts, the State manages to control the recent revival of Islamic schools by tracking the *Wakf*[7] and fixing the curriculum of Islamic schools. The recent creation in Morocco of a department of traditional education within the Ministry of Islamic Affairs aims at extending state control to the network of Islamic schools. El Ayadi (2004) observes that teachers in the public sector play a major role in these new centres of religious training. Today, in the framework of a policy implementation following the development of radical Islamism and the appearance of religious terrorism in the country, the Moroccan authorities are determined to extend the State's control to this private sector.

Luckens-Bull (2001) explores one way in which the classical Islamic community in Java, Indonesia, seeks to negotiate modernization and globalization through the interface of an Islamic boarding school (*Pesantren*) and higher education. This negotiation requires imagining and (re)inventing both modernity and tradition.

The two first sections of this paper show that Koranic schooling is a paradoxical educational model that is difficult to analyze. On the one hand, we find an archaic and depository cognitive system distinguished by extreme ritualization, rigid discipline and the exclusive focus on rote and decontextualized learning of the Koran, a sacred work, the mastery of which is difficult even for Arabic-speaking children (who represent a decided minority in Koranic schools!); on the other hand, one finds a great diversity in its organizational methods, a flexible arrangement between the written and the oral and a largely successful socio-cultural embeddedness in the local community.

KORANIC SCHOOL: A SITUATED LEARNING?

It would seem that situated learning theory is a pertinent educational model with which to analyze and explain the socio-cultural rootedness and lasting quality of the Koranic school. Instead of considering learning as the acquisition of specific knowledge, Lave and Wenger (1991) place learning at the centre of *social relations and co-participatory situations*. In other terms, instead of wondering about which *cognitive processes* are mobilized in any learning activity, they tried to identify which type of social engagement provides the best learning context. Learning automatically implies a commitment in a 'community of practice'. Lave and Wenger's model suggests the predominance of the social over the psychological in any act of learning:

> The central grounds on which forms of education that differ from schooling are condemned [in conventional educational argument/ policy/discourse] are that changing the person is not the central motive of the enterprise in which learning takes place [...]. The effectiveness of the circulation of information among peers suggests, to the contrary, that engaging in practice, rather than being its object, may well be the condition for the effectiveness of learning. (Lave and Wenger, 1991: 93)

The 'legitimate peripheral participation' and the community of practice (or learning community) are at the centre of the model initiated by Lave and Wenger. The *practices* constitute the whole of social and individual conduct in relation with the norms, content and context of a field of expertise. We are then dealing with the enculturation of novices which easily exceeds the objective of the instilling of a specific knowledge. We can attempt to apply the situated learning model to Koranic school, where the field of expertise covers the mastery and comprehension of the written Koran. Master and students sit together on the floor in a semi-circle with no desks or other barriers between them; the best regarded seats are those closest to the teacher. Books and writing equipments are viewed as sacred and distinguished tools of knowledge due to the fact that God swears by them in the Koran. Anything that God swears by is regarded in high esteem (Makdisi, 1981). Is learning in Koranic school a legitimate peripheral participation?

Legitimate: Because all participants (students, teachers, parents, local community) accept the position of the children-novices as potential members of the community of Koranic experts (community of believers).

Peripheral: The learners settle in around the teacher by tirelessly repeating the required tasks. In the beginning these tasks are peripheral: preparing the tools (reeds, wooden board, ink, and so on), repeating the words of the teacher. The tasks progressively become more important: reading, writing, reciting longer and longer verses of the Koran, comprehension-commentary of the Koran and the application of its precepts in everyday life.

Participation: It is through action that the knowledge is acquired. Knowledge is situated in the praxis of the community of practice and not in a curriculum to be found outside of the community. The dynamics of knowledge acquisition in early Muslim civilization provided for a concept of Islamic education that placed no barrier between 'religious' and 'secular' learning (Douglass and Shaikh, 2004).

Moreover, Koranic school teaching is fundamentally a form of 'differentiated' teaching since the learner goes at his own speed and is only in competition with himself. The pedagogical division of the group/class is based mainly on the degree of expertise of the student and not on the basis of age or degree. The organization into the large group/class clearly recalls the single-room, rural classroom. The teacher divides the classroom into several levels, which are led by an advanced student. The habitual division consists of two or three groups: novices, less experienced and experienced, which curiously happens to correspond to the 'learning cycles' which are in vogue in many current school reforms in Europe. Novice students should not be overburdened, but progress should be systematic. Experienced students should not be stuck with easy material. The masters attend to the needs of students, assisting all students, not just the outstanding ones (Makdisi, 1981).

In Koranic school we can state that:

1. Knowledge is defined through doing: 'recite, read, write and understand the Koran', and to behave outside of the school in a way respectful of the precepts of Islam;
2. The Koranic school model rejects the separation into social and religious training, religious learning and exercise of the Koran;
3. Evaluation and accreditation work towards the command and consolidation of competences.

More precisely, the procedures of accreditation involve the whole community. Mastery of a part of the Koran (subdivided in sixty sections called *Hizb*) is subjected to oral notification to the parents, who praise the student and the teacher. If the student is able to read and write a substantial segment of the Koran, a ceremony of ratification of his competences is organized. If the student becomes an expert and is thus able to recite, read and write the Koran in its entirety, the family offers the teacher a remuneration in relation to their economic standing and in relation to the importance of the event for the community. Understanding and higher-order thinking are gradually introduced as the student advances. Because of the level of mastery required, teachers adjust the level of instruction to meet the individual abilities of the students. Students vary in ages and rates of instruction. Students 'graduate' when they are able to demonstrate complete mastery over the subject matter to the satisfaction of the teacher. Obviously this makes education a highly personalized experience wherein every teacher and student are acquainted with one another at an intimate level (Makdisi, 1981).

One needs also to keep in mind that the knowledge gained at the Koranic school is theoretically used daily for the five prayers and for other religious ceremonies. It is thus not knowledge for 'professional life' but for 'daily life.' The focus is on the ways in which learning is an evolving, continuously renewed set of relations. In other words, this is a relational view of the person and learning.

Bernstein (1996) uses the metaphor of a mirror and a resonance chamber in which many positive and negative images are projected. The central questions are:

1. Who sees oneself as having a *value* in these images?
2. In the same vein, one must also ask whose voices are being listened to at school.
3. Who speaks?

According to Bernstein, Western school clearly reflects a hierarchy of social class values and a specific distribution of knowledge, which is reflected in the resources, access, and acquisition of school culture.

The characteristics of the Koranic school do not enter into Bernstein's analysis as it consists of a non-extractive method of schooling (Serpell, 1999). Thus when, after many years of Koranic study, a student returns to his village, he will be respected since he will be capable of reading and reciting the holy book of the Muslims. This person will then be able to share his knowledge with younger children and thus continue the Koranic tradition.

Nor does the Koranic school model fit with the distinction proposed by Resnick (1987). This author contrasts, on the one hand, individual cognition in school, versus shared cognition outside of school, and on the other hand pure mentoring in school versus tool manipulation outside of it.

Briefly, despite the seemingly archaic cognitive system (rote memorization and recitation of the Koran), what is at stake in the Koranic school is the entry into a 'community of Islamic believers'. The knowledge of the Koran is of interest only if the individual is recognized as being worthy of the confidence of the local community.

Coming back to the situated learning model it should be noted that this model postulates the examination of a type of social engagement favourable for the learning context rather than for cognitive processes. In other words, everything happens as if, in the Koranic school, *the archaism of the cognitive process* is compensated by *the strength of the social engagement*. Looked at it in this way, the understanding of literacy mechanisms in the Koranic tradition should be connected to the general debate on the variety of ways to learn, to read, and to write (Goody, 1979; Serpell and Hatano, 1997). According to Gough and Juel (1989), the act of understanding the written word necessitates the mobilization of two essential components, the first being the recognition of written words and the second, the ability to give meaning to language, both written and oral. To put it in Freire's words 'to read the words and the world' (Freire, 1993). Koranic learning, as identified in many studies, is very far from using this pedagogical productive paradigm advocated by Freire.

The most important weakness of the Koranic school is its inability to put meaning and critical thinking at the centre of learning.

Fiske (1997) observed in Koranic schools in Burkina Faso, boys learning the Koran by rote memorization in Arabic; sometimes memorizing major segments of the text without any exegesis or discussion of its meaning, and, it appears, often without much understanding of the Arabic language. So, while certain kinds of schooling may entail a dramatic shift from imitation toward explicit conceptual transmission of declarative knowledge and certain formal skills, the shift may be limited within Koranic schools, and may not transform the mimetic transmission of more fundamental cultural practices outside of school.

While the fruitfulness of literacy methods based on 'meaning' needs no more proof, it seems that certain authors push us not to forget that 'access to the meaning of a text depends on the proper functioning of certain mechanisms and especially of their automatism' (Chardon, 2000: 116). It is precisely on this second component that Koranic school pedagogy is based. One can thus easily understand how, in spite of the numerous criticisms that can be addressed to Koranic school, it has shown itself to be very effective in literacy training (Wagner and Lotfi, 1983).

In this vein, in this post-September 11, 2001 period where everything having to do with Islam has become suspicious, it would be useful to come back to the supposed links between 'Koranic school' and 'Islamic Fundamentalism'. As mentioned in the first section, the Koranic school is characterized by an extreme diversity. The hypothesis which sees the Koranic school as the assimilation of the ancestral educational system for the preparation of future generations of fundamentalists does not hold up against a sharp analysis of the political, sociological, and economical contexts in which contemporary radical fundamentalism has developed (Algeria, Afghanistan, and so on). This is not to say that certain radical groups have not taken advantage of the chaotic situation of certain Islamic countries or of the confusion of the Islamic diaspora to take advantage of Koranic schools for their violent, politico-religious proselytizing.

Concerning the habitual exclusion of females from the Koranic school, it should be kept in mind that this is not original to Islam but can be found in all the principle religious traditions (Christianity, Judaism, Hinduism). Reagan (2000) pointed out that traditional Hindu education excludes not just girls but also inferior castes. Certain historical studies even go against common sense about Islamic education. Marty (1921), thus noted that girls are quite numerous in Koranic schools in Foutu in Guinea. They made up a third and sometimes half of the class. It is quite common for wealthy families to send girls for a year, and even for two or three, to learn the *Fatiha* (introduction to the Koran) and the *surats* (different chapters of the Koran) of the end of the book, and to learn proper prayer techniques. In Northern Nigeria, a survey by UNICEF (1999) found that there are 16,648 Koranic schools with 1,145,111 pupils. Only 184,592 or 16.1 per cent are attending primary school, out of which 38.1 per cent are female.

To conclude this section aimed at exploring the links between Koranic school and situated learning, we must recognize that situated learning depends on two claims difficult to find in Koranic schools:

1. It makes no sense to talk of knowledge that is decontextualized, abstract or general.
2. New knowledge and learning are properly conceived as being located in communities of practice.

TOWARDS A MOBILIZATION OF THE KORANIC SCHOOL FOR BASIC EDUCATION

In many countries in Western and Northern Africa one can witness how the recent expansion of the Koranic school has reduced the phenomena of non-schooling delineated by official statistics and international experts. According to Easton and Kane (2000), the search for alternative solutions has taken many forms: community schools sponsored by the state or by an NGO, pilot schools sponsored by the state (generally traditional elementary schools chosen to try innovative, community-based methods), an increase in interest in Koranic instruction or in hybrid forms that combine Muslim and Western instruction and also private schools created by independent businessmen, especially in urban zones.

In Mali, for example, school attendance figures have been in continual decline since the 1980s (30 per cent in 1980, 23 per cent in 1990). This loss of interest in public schooling has been counterbalanced by the growth of 'private' schooling. Koranic schools, *madrasa* (schools which give both secular and religious instruction) and community schools have proliferated and have seen their attendance numbers rise in the last ten years (Etienne, 1997). In the rural area of Kangaré in the southwest of Mali, where Etienne (1997) did his research, the number of *madrasa* quadrupled in ten years. While attendance rates in the public sector continually went down over more than a decade, nearly half (49.6 per cent) of all students in the area took Islamic instruction. Unlike Koranic schools which deal only with religious instruction, the *madrasa* have the distinctive feature of presenting a syncretical and bilingual instruction: given in both Arabic and French, both religious and secular. This type of instruction conveys not only Koranic precepts, but also French, reading, writing, and mathematics. This combination responds to a double necessity, on the one hand placing the child 'on the road to God' and on the other on the road to 'progress and modernity'. The weakness of the formal educational system, founded exclusively on the Western model, led to the development of an original education, both religious and secular, in which tradition and modernity come together in a new pedagogical and cultural syncretism.

In Niger, the number of Koranic school was estimated at around 40,000 in 1990, which number easily surpasses the number of public schools (Easton, 1999). In reality this type of instruction constitutes an alternative to the official, Western-style schools and presents a 'hidden culture' of knowledge that goes against official school culture but which also integrates certain of its elements.

This reorientation of the social demand for education cannot solely be explained by a repudiation of public schooling. Considered in the past as a way towards social promotion, public schooling, founded on the extractive, Western model inherited from colonization, no longer fits the expectations of parents. Public schools seem incapable of giving their children a useful base for obtaining a job or instilling them with techniques that they can count on in the future. This observation was made by a working group on informal education, Association for the Development of Education in Africa (ADEA). The credibility granted to the Koranic school has greatly increased in the past few years. Parents choose Koranic schooling because they consider it to be a factor of social integration because of what it teaches (the laws of the Koran and Islamic morality in particular). In a way it would appear that, by means of the educational strategies of the Koranic school, the populations of Western Africa are 'reinventing' basic education. In addition, this school adapts itself to the lifestyle of the population it serves. Thus, in Mauritania, the Koranic school is perfectly established in nomadic life. The educational situation of the country draws its novelty from the association of modern and traditional instruction (Ould Ahmadou, 1997).

Educational difficulties are often connected to the management style of Western-style schools, generally centralized and unconnected to village communities. In addition, as Gatti (2001) correctly points out, the greater and more diverse the participation of the community in school management, the easier the children can access the school and the higher the quality of education.

According to Easton (1999), the practical outcomes of Koranic instruction in Western Africa can be summarized in three points:

1. An introduction to writing, and to a lesser degree mathematics, to a large proportion of the population, men and women, of which a large number would otherwise have had no access to such instruction. Those who continue long enough to learn how to read, write and count well enough for practical daily use (generally in an African language, as a functional understanding of Arabic remains fairly limited) make up a minority, a large minority in certain cases. Among other things, literacy in Arabic has become a point of reference in many small towns and rural areas, largely considered illiterate according to Western criteria.
2. Training for local leaders, since a solid Muslim education is generally accepted as an indication of morality, honesty and discipline, thus a basic, necessary qualification for holding functions of responsibility in the community.
3. Economic and social promotion, which has always been the case, but even more so recently given the lack of interest for formal instruction. This is possible because of the close connection between relational networks of Koranic schools and traditional commercial networks of the region. Koranic school graduates are better able to find work or to find an apprenticeship with traditional businesses and in the informal commercial sector.

In Morocco, the revival of the Koranic school is connected to the inability of the state to extend basic education. Thus, Koranic schools make up the most widespread form of preschool in the country. They provide instruction of a 'renovated traditional' style. Koranic schools serve 67 per cent of all preschool children However, the percentage of girls is only 27.1 per cent against 44.6 per cent in modern preschool (Ministère de l'éducation [Maroc], 2000). Numerous studies on Moroccan village communities and the relationships between teachers and villagers shows that in this rural area the modern school is viewed with distrust and with scepticism regarding its usefulness. schools and teachers are not chosen by the local community and are clearly seen as cultural outsiders. They are imposed by the state and then proceed to spread their lifestyle and their way of thinking, which can be very different from that of the local way (Zouggari, 1991). In Tunisia, rural farmers show the same mistrust towards agricultural technicians who are supposed to be helping them (Akkari, 1993). In a recent study in the North of Morocco, Tawil (2006) shows that the Koranic school plays an essential role in the education of the rural poor. It alleviates the absence of official schooling more than it expresses a cultural refusal against this school.

All the signs of a revival of the Koranic school should push states with large Muslim populations, especially those facing difficulties at developing basic education, to make attempts to integrate Koranic schools into their educational structures or to gain inspiration from the pedagogical and social experience, often secular, accumulated by such institutions (Colonna, 1984). Such a position in no way rules out an attentive and critical examination of this form of education, and of how it relates to the local culture and the larger society, in such a way as to create the possibility for 'another school', one which would be socio-culturally appropriate (Wagner, 1988).

Looking at forms of modern schooling introduced in non-Western parts of the world, with very few exceptions, the model is similar to the one that has already been in place since the 19th century in Europe. This model exhibits centralizing and urban hegemony, specifically designed to do away with differences, not just at a linguistic level, but more importantly at the level of representations (representations of the world, or time and space and of social relations), thus constituting a form of violence against villagers and also against the developing urban proletariat (Colonna, 1984). Taken outside of the West[8], these models, while new national powers and the local elite endorsed them, were no less distant from the cultures upon which they were imposed. The Western-style schooling is an extractive model, particularly in Africa, where children who succeed, go away from their local communities (Serpell, 1999).

By comparison, a Koranic school, and the village in which it is located, would appear to have a symbiotic relationship, with its temporal rhythm and spatial structure, much more so than the best intentioned modern school could hope. Tawil (2004) pointed out, on the basis of field research in Northern Morocco, that local communities are resisting the supply of 'secular' basic education from the state, and, when asked, declare that they would send their children to public schools if the curriculum took more account of Islamic values and if teachers were hired from within their own communities. The strength of Koranic schools rests on its community support and the high level of commitment of both parents and teachers. To address the problem of basic education in Northern Nigeria, UNICEF (1999) recommends a state policy deliberately and directly addressing the problems of Koranic schools in terms of integrating elements of basic education, funding and management. Adequate learning materials and equipment should be provided, for both Koranic literacy as well as basic education programme.

As pointed out by Kadi (2006), the picture of education in Islam is very complex, with truth mixed with myths. Islamic institutions have arisen out of the postcolonial landscapes that conceive of themselves not as alternatives to secular, government-run schools, but as complementary to them.

CONCLUSION

The Koranic school is a traditional mode of schooling and an introduction into the culture of literacy, an aspect which is usually not taken into account by public education policy. It can be regarded as an alternative to public schooling in some Islamic areas, in particular when the State does not have the human and financial capacities of mass schooling. In some Islamic contexts, Koranic schools offer formal education which either replaces or complements state-run education. Beyond the apparent pedagogical archaism of Koranic schools (memorization, fixed curriculum, and so on), this form of education is making schooling more accessible to local communities. It is a highly personalized experience wherein every teacher and student gets acquainted with one another at an intimate level. It is certainly possible that the phenomenon of Koranic school revival, in multiple Islamic contexts, is linked to the efficiency of this institution in the development of literacy skills in the least educated layers of society. For researchers in comparative education, schools linked to the Islamic tradition in many parts of the world may represent, a new, more rooted, form of learning in and through revitalized communities, a kind of 'no man's land' neither narrowly 'Westerner' nor 'traditional' (Luckens-Bull, 2001; Morah, 2000). Emerging here, is a 'pedagogy of place', a theoretical framework that emphasizes the necessary interpenetration of culture, school, community, and environment, whether urban, suburban, or rural (Akkari and Dasen, 2004; Sobel, 2004).

NOTES

1. Unless otherwise noted in this chapter, the term *Koranic school* refers to Islamic schools at the primary and secondary levels.
2. Being an Arabic speaker and a former Koranic school student, I purposely did not use any 'autobiographical' elements in the writing of this text. It is however likely that the tone of this text has been influenced by the researcher's personal experience.
3. One finds a large presence of partially sighted or blind persons among the best 'readers' of the Koran.
4. It should be noted that this ritual dimension is present in other religious educations, for example in Buddhist pedagogy (Gurugé, 1982).
5. It should be noted that this domestication did not always give the desired results for the colonizers. While the first generation of resistance fighters, against the colonization in Algeria and Tunisia, were taught in Islamic schools, the second generation, which gained independence in Tunisia and which started the war for independence in Algeria, was the product of a double education, 'Arab' and 'French'. A typical example is Bourguiba, who completed his secondary studies in a traditional high school in Tunisia and then went on to obtain a law degree in Paris.
6. See 'Madrasah,' in the Oxford Encyclopaedia of the Modern Islamic World (1995. New York: Oxford University Press).
7. Wakf is a religious foundation dedicated to collecting funds in local communities. As an Islamic foundation under the control of local communities, the Wakf provides resources to sustain and develop and adapt Islamic schools to modernity. Wakf is a social, legal and religious institution which played an important role in the social, cultural and economic way of life of the Islamic world, especially the period, from middle of the 8th century until the end of the 19th. The Islamic Wakf (called habous in North Africa) can be defined as an action of a member of a Muslim society motivated by an element of the Islamic culture to transform some or all of his personal assets into pious foundations which will serve the public.
8. Many scholars pointed out that modern schooling in the West contribute to separating children from adults and to make instruction a meaningless activity (Charlot et al., 1992; Vincent, 1994).

REFERENCES

Akkari, A. 1993. *Modernisation des petits paysans. Une mission impossible?* Tunis: Éditions Éducation and Cultures.

Akkari, A. and P. Dasen. 2004. (eds). *Pédagogies et pédagogves du Sud.* Paris: L'Harmattan.

Bernstein, B. 1996. *Pedagogy, Symbolic Control and Identity. Theory, Research, Critique.* London: Taylor & Francis Ltd.

Brenner, L. 1993. *Muslim Identity and Social Change in Sub-Saharan Africa.* London: Hurst & Company.

Chardon, S.C. 2000. 'Expérience de soutien en lecture auprès des élèves faibles lecteurs de fin de cycle 3'. *Revue française de pédagogie,* 130: 107–19.

Charlot, B., E. Bautier and Y. Rochex. 1992. *École et savoir dans les banlieues et ailleurs.* Paris: Armand Colin.

Coulon, C. 1993. (ed.) *Da'wa, arabisation et critique de l'Occident.* Paris: Karthala.

Colonna, F. 1981. 'La répétition. Les Tolba dans une commune rurale de l'Aurès', in Ch. Souriau (éd.), *Le Maghreb musulman en 1979,* pp. 187–203. Paris: CNRS Editions.

———. 1984. *Le kuttab "école coranique". Prime éducation islamique et diversification du champ éducatif.* Paris. Institut International de Planification de l'Éducation.

Delval, R. 1980. *Les musulmans au Togo.* Paris: Publications orientalistes de France (CHEAM).

Désalmand, P. 1983. *L'histoire de l'éducation en Côte-d'Ivoire, Volume 1: Des origines à la conférence de Brazzaville.* Abidjan: CEDA.

Douglass S. L. and M.A. Shaikh. 2004. 'Defining Islamic Education: Differentiation and Applications', *Current Issues in Comparative Education* [Online], Available online at http://www.tc.columbia.edu/CICE/articles/sdms171.htm (downloaded on 20 May 2008).

Easton, P. 1999. Education et alphabétisation en Afrique de l'ouest grâce à l'enseignement coranique. *Notes sur les connaissances autochtones,* 11: 1–4.

Easton, P. and L. Kane. 2000. Les savoirs locaux et l'école. Le potentiel et les dangers de l'enseignement communautaire dans les régions de l'Ouest du Sahel. *Notes sur les connaissances autochtones,* 22: 1–3.

Eickelman, D. F. 1978. 'The Art of Memory. Islamic Education and Its Social Reproduction', *Comparative Studies in Society and History,* 20(4): 485–516.

———. 1985. *Knowledge and Power in Morocco: The Education of a Twentieth-Century Noble.* Princeton: Princeton University Press.

El Ayadi, M. 2004. Entre l'islam et l'islamisme. La religion dans l'école publique marocaine. *Revue internationale d'éducation, Sèvres,* 36: 111–21.

El-Sayed Darwish, K. 1981. 'Developing Koranic Schools to Meet the Educational Needs of the Young Child', in Notes, Comments. UNESCO-UNICEF, WFP, NS-86, August 1981. Paris: UNESCO. Available online at http://unesdoc.unesco.org/images/0004/000475/047585EB.pdf (downloaded on 30 May 2008)

Etienne, G. 1997. *La tentation du savoir en Afrique. Politiques, mythes et stratégies d'éducation au Mali.* Paris: Karthala-IRD.

Fiske, A. P. 1997. Learning a Culture the Way Informants Do: Observing, Imitating, and Participating. American Anthropological Association Panel, Washington, DC, November, 1997.

Freire, P. 1993. *Pedagogy of the Oppressed.* New York: Continuum.

Gatti, C. 2001. *Ecoles coraniques au sud du Sahara face à la "patrimonialisation" de l'UNESCO: problème ou ressource ? L'exemple de Djenné (Mali).* Actes du VIIIème Congrès de l'Association pour la Recherche Inter Culturelle (ARIC), Université de Genève, Geneva, September 24–28. Available online at http://www.unifr.ch/ipg/sitecrt/ARIC/8eCongres/Actes. htm (downloaded on 20 August 2003).

Geertz, C. 1994. 'The Uses of Diversity', in R. Borofesky (ed.) *Assessing Cultural Anthropology*, pp. 454–76. New York: McGraw.

Goody, J. 1979. *La raison graphique. La domestication de la pensée sauvage.* Paris. Minuit.

Gough, P.B. and C. Juel. 1989. *Les premières étapes de la reconnaissance des mots. L'apprenti lecteur.* Lausanne: Delachaux et Niestlé.

Grandin, N. and Gaborieau, M. 1997. (eds). *Madrasa. La transmission du savoir dans le monde musulman.* Paris: Arguments.

Gurugé, A.W.P. 1982. *The Miracle of Instruction.* Colombo: Lake House.

Hoffman, D.M. 1999. 'Culture and Comparative Education: Toward Decentering and Recentering the Discourse', *Comparative Education Review*, 43(4): 464–88.

IIPE. 1984. *Les formes traditionnelles d'éducation et la diversification du champ éducatif: le cas des écoles coraniques.* Paris: Institut International de Planification de l'Éducation.

Kadi, W. 2006. 'Education in Islam—Myths and Truths', *Comparative Education Review*, 50(3): 311–24.

Khayar, I. 1976. *Le refus de l'école. Contribution à l'étude des problèmes d'éducation chez les musulmans du Ouaddai (Tchad).* Paris: Maisonneuve.

Lange, M.F. 2000. 'Naissance de l'école en Afrique Subsaharienne', *Pour*, 165: 51–59.

Lave, J. and E. Wenger. 1991. *Situated Learning. Legitimate Peripheral Participation.* Cambridge, MA: Cambridge University of Press.

Lecomte, G. 1954. 'La vie scolaire à Byzance et dans l'Islam', *Arabica*, 1(3): 330–31.

Luckens-Bull, R. A. 2001. Two Sides of the Same Coin: Modernity and Tradition in Islamic Education in Indonesia. *Anthropology and Education Quarterly*, 32(3): 350–72.

Makdisi, G. 1981. *The Rise of Colleges: Institutions of Learning in Islam and the West*. Edinburgh: Edinburgh University Press.

Ministère de l'éducation (Maroc). 2000. *Statistique Scolaires*. Rabat: Ministère de l'éducation.

Marty, P. 1921. *L'Islam en Guinée: Fouta-Djallon*. Paris: Editions Ernest Leroux.

Meunier, O. 1997. *Dynamique de l'enseignement islamique au Niger. Le cas de la ville de Maradi*. Paris: L'Harmattan.

Morah, E. U. 2000. 'Old Institutions, New Opportunities: The Emerging Nature of Koranic Schools in Somaliland in the 1990s', *International Journal of Educational Development*, 20(4): 305–22.

Ould Ahmadou, E.G. 1997. *Enseignement traditionnel en Mauritanie: la mahdara ou l'école "à dos de chameau"*. Paris: L'Harmattan.

Reagan, T. 2000. *Non-Western Educational Traditions: Alternatives Approaches to Educational Thought and Practice*. Mahwah, NJ: Erlbaum.

Resnick, L. B. 1987. 'Learning in School and Out', *Educational Researcher*, 19(9), 13–20.

Richard-Molard, J. 1954. *Islam ou colonisation au Fouta-Djalon*. Paris: Présence Africaine.

Sanneh, L. 1997. (ed.) *Crown and the Turban. Muslims and West African Pluralism*. Boulder, CO: Westview Press.

Santerre, R. 1973. *Pédagogie musulmane d'Afrique noire. L'école coranique peule du Cameroun*. Montréal: Les Presses de l'Université de Montréal.

Santerre, R. and C. Mercier-Tremblay (eds). 1982. *La Quête du savoir. Essais pour une anthropologie de l'éducation camerounaise*. Montréal: Presses de l'Université de Montréal.

Serpell, R. and G. Hatano. 1997. 'Education, Schooling, and Literacy', in J.W. Berry, P.R. Dasen and T.S. Saraswathi (eds), *Handbook of Cross-Cultural Psychology*, Second edition, Volume 2, pp. 345–82. Boston: Allyn & Bacon.

Serpell, R. 1999. 'Local Accountability to Rural Communities: A Challenge for Educational Planning in Africa', in F. E. Leach and A. W. Little (eds), *Education, Cultures, and Economics: Dilemmas for Development*, pp. 111–39. New York and London: Falmer Press.

Sobel, D. 2004. *Place-Based Education: Connecting Classrooms and Communities*. Barrington, MA: Orion.

Spiro, M.E. 1984. 'Some Reflections on Cultural Determinism and Relativism with Special Reference to Emotion and Reason', in R.A. Shweder and

R.A. LeVine (eds), *Culture Theory: Essays on Mind, Self and Emotion*, pp. 323–46. Cambridge: Cambridge University Press.

Sraieb, N. 1974. *Colonisation, décolonisation et enseignement, l'example tunisien*. Tunis: Publications de l'Institute National des Sciences de l'Education.

Tawil, S. 2006. 'Qur'anic Education and Social Change in Northern Morocco: Perspectives from Chefchaouen', *Comparative Education Review*, 50(3): 496–517.

————. 2004. Basic Education, Exclusion and Development: Change, Crisis and Reform in Moroccan School Education. Doctoral Dissertation. Geneva: Graduate Institute of Development Studies, University of Geneva.

Thanh Khoi, Le. 1995. *Education et civilisations*. Paris: Nathan.

Turin, Y. 1971. *Affrontements culturels dans l'Algérie coloniale: Ecole, médecines, religion*. Paris: Maspéro.

UNICEF. 1999. *Baseline Survey of Qur'anic Schools in Katsina, Kebbi, Sokoto and Zamfara States*. New York: UNICEF.

Vincent 1994. (ed.). *L'éducation prisonnière de la forme scolaire*. Lyon: Presses universitaires de Lyon.

Wagner, D. 1988. '"Appropriate Education" and Literacy in the Third World', in P. R. Dasen, J. W. Berry and N. Sartorius (eds), *Health and Cross-Cultural Psychology: Towards Applications*, pp. 93–111. Newbury Park, CA: Sage.

Wagner, D. and A. Lotfi. 1983. Learning to Read by Rote. *International Journal of the Sociology of Language*, 42, 111–21.

Zouggari, A. 1991. *Stratégies des agriculteurs en matière d'éducation. Jbala-Histoire et société: Etudes sur le Maroc du nord-ouest*. Paris: CNRS.

10
SANSKRIT SCHOOLING IN INDIA

RAMESH C. MISHRA AND APARNA VAJPAYEE

INTRODUCTION

India is one of the ancient lands where worldly and spiritual realities of life have been found to live in a state of 'coexistence'. Very few countries in the world can offer such an enormous diversity in the philosophy of life as India.

Language represents an essential ingredient of the culture of a group of people. The foundation of Indian culture and its heritage is laid on the ancient Indian language Sanskrit. It is one of the world's oldest languages and has been the medium for deepest contents of thought and most pleasant realizations of human creations. The glimpses of greatness of this language can be found not only in its literature, but also in a variety of art and dance forms.

Sanskrit is also a language that embeds a variety of rituals and yogic practices that a large number of Indian people observe for the elevation of individual selves. It is a language of dreams and romance, of science and technology, and of a whole system of medicine. It contains a precise, advanced and finely tuned grammar, and is extremely rich in philosophical speculations. The concepts of 'zero' and 'decimal' have evolved out of it. In this way, Sanskrit language has lent enormous colour to wisdom and knowledge that has developed in this subcontinent over the past several thousand years.

HISTORY OF SANSKRIT LANGUAGE

Formal use of any language can be traced in the history of writing in that particular language. From this point of view Sanskrit language seems to be very old. Historical accounts of Sanskrit language and Sanskrit schools are available in several sources (Burrow, 1995; Filliozat, 2000; Raghavan, 1957; Upadhyaya, 1999; Vaidya, 1986). A chief difficulty in presenting this history is its temporal and spatial organization. Most Sanskrit writings do not provide us with a chronological account of their composition. Time and place, the two essential components of history, have always been a matter of debate among scholars in the context of Sanskrit literature. The difficulty of chronological arrangement of Sanskrit literature is further compounded by the belief that the Vedas the most ancient Sanskrit texts are eternal, and they were revealed at the beginning of creation.

Western scholars have generally divided the history of Sanskrit literature into Vedic and post-Vedic period, which appears quite sketchy to Indian scholars. Vaidya (1986) argues that the history of Sanskrit literature can be reasonably divided into at least three periods: (a) the Vedic and post-Vedic period about 4500 BC–1800 BC, called *Shruti* period, (b) the classical period about 1800 BC–800 BC, called *Smriti* period, and (c) the modern period about 800 BC–1500 AD, called *Bhashya* period. The first period represents a time when Sanskrit was the language of all people. During the second period, it was superseded by *Prakrit* a softer form of Sanskrit language. During this period men of higher classes mainly used Sanskrit; women and people of the lower classes generally used *Prakrit*. During the third period, Sanskrit became a non-vital language relegated to a marginal status and sheltered in some corners of the country. The literature created during the first period is recognized as 'sacred'; that created in the second period is considered to be thoughtful but less sacred. The literature of the last period is mostly scholastic, full of powerful reasoning and forceful expression.

SANSKRIT EDUCATION

Even in the early days of evolution of Sanskrit, the concern for Sanskrit education was quite explicit in the minds of Indian thinkers. Several scholars (for example, Altekar, 1934; Biswas and Agrawal, 1986; Chatterjee, 1999) have presented a detailed account of education in ancient India. While the historical account of Sanskrit schools presented here is largely based on these sources, we have also used the knowledge contained in the original texts of Sanskrit to describe the nature and status of Sanskrit education in ancient days.

It may be noted at the very outset that the goal of education at that time was more self-oriented than job-oriented. Thus, education in those days was concerned not only with providing factual knowledge to individuals and shaping their personality for worldly achievements, but also with the development of their physical, mental, spiritual and social aspects of life. The individual as a whole was the focus of education with the main emphasis of education being on grasping the philosophy of life that is, the meaning, purpose, and goals of life. The ultimate aim was to engage individuals with internal discoveries in order to realize their hidden potentials and the mysteries of life. It was believed that the seed of wisdom was contained inside individuals themselves, and that the divine light of education would enable them to direct the search inward, and spirituality could awaken the super-intellectual and other subtle planes of human consciousness. Thus, inner experience was considered a major source of knowledge and the guiding principle of moral development. The same was laid down as a major goal of education.

INSTITUTIONS OF SANSKRIT EDUCATION

In the traditional educational system one finds enormous emphasis on balanced development of intellectual, emotional, and practical aspects of life. The goals of such development were fulfilled by two potential centres of education: the *mandir* temple and the *gurukul* literally meaning the family or home of the teacher.

Temples served as smaller but important centres of education in India in ancient days. Even today many temples function as the centre of education. Sanskrit literature is full of the description of temples for education in Yoga, *sadhana* meditation, philosophy and religion, music, dance, and several other art forms for example, painting and sculpture, which were practised and performed as a way of realizing the diverse manifestations of the Almighty. The involvement and concentration these pursuits generated were considered as different forms of *upasana* ways of sitting close to the God and, hence, the easiest ways to realize the one that could not be reached otherwise.

On the other hand, the *gurukul* represented a vital educational institution. The guru teacher here was a scholar of repute in a particular stream or several streams of knowledge. Children were taken to different teachers according to their orientations in various fields of knowledge. These institutions were generally set up in the forest, away from the main habitation of populations. The secluded and peaceful life of the forests provided children with an ideal environment for practicing meditation and setting the mind to the desired level of concentration.

Almost all such institutions had some agricultural land, domestic animals for example, cows and horses, orchards, places for special worship, and residential huts for teachers and students. *Gurukul* was usually a single person managed programme of education, but often the senior disciples of the guru also shared part of the burden of teaching and training the younger students. Some of the *gurukuls* in ancient India had achieved the status of fairly big centres of education. The *gurukuls* of Takshashila and Nalanda now in the State of Bihar in northern India that comprised around 10,000 students and 2000 teachers were fairly well known centres of education during the Buddhist period around AD 600.

The teacher in traditional institutions

Whether in a temple or in a *gurukul*, the guru was perceived as gifted with the divine light of wisdom. He was the main transmitter of knowledge and wisdom among students. The knowledge and the psychic energy of the guru acquired specially through *tapasya* meditation and concentration were considered enough to open the doors of wisdom in a *shishya* sincere student. As a result, the guru was elevated to the level of supreme divine trinity Brahma, Vishnu, Mahesh; that is, the gods of creation, nurturance and destruction, respectively and granted the status of the living God. As such, he commanded high respect from his students as well as society at large. The royalty often consulted him not only for framing rules, regulations and administrative policies, but also in matters pertaining to justice, welfare and development of the kingdom and its people.

It may be mentioned here that a sincere student could accept someone as the guru even without being physically proximal to him. In that case, the student would have a symbolic representation of the guru for example, an idol and practice a variety of arts like, dancing or archery believing that the guru was there to guide and correct him. Sanskrit literature is full of such stories in which the guru stands as a symbolic figure, and is granted a higher status than that of a guru that is physically present.

CURRICULUM IN TRADITIONAL INSTITUTIONS

Education in *gurukul*-like institutions covered a long range of subjects that included not only grammar, literature, philosophy, and similar other disciplines of knowledge, but also sciences like mathematics, astronomy as well as practical disciplines like political science, administration, and martial arts for example, archery. On the one hand, these studies led to the great discoveries of 'zero' and 'decimal' system, and the principles of functioning of the solar and other planetary systems. On the other hand, they also led to an elaborated medicinal system called *Ayurveda*, which has got its own unique methods of diagnosis and treatment. Astrology and various art forms for example, music and dance including martial arts were an integral part of education in these institutions. All these were considered essential for leading a healthy, happy, and successful worldly life.

Techniques of concentration, meditation, *samadhi* trance and self-extension as means of promoting spiritual development constituted a major agenda of education in the *gurukul* system. Development of moral reasoning and behaviour was achieved through personalized and carefully supervised education in these institutions. Stories played a vital role in this process. Hence, they were freely created and narrated to students, especially to the young and less intelligent ones, to promote their grasp of abstract and difficult themes of instruction. Long-term stay in the *gurukul* enforced among students an eco-friendly behaviour, which continued even when they no longer stayed there. All in all, the curriculum of the *gurukul* was intended to make the child a moral, responsible and productive citizen, and thereby fulfil the need of comprehensive education.

PEDAGOGY

In the preceding pages we have mentioned that education in *gurukul* was intended to address a number of goals relating to worldly and spiritual life. A variety of age-specific and domain-specific strategies were adopted for achieving these goals. It was believed that the first awakening of consciousness happened around the age of seven. Hence, this was considered as the appropriate time to send the child to a *gurukul* or temple for the nurturance and promotion of his mental and spiritual potential. Prior to entry in a *gurukul*, an eligibility test was conducted. The criterion for the test slightly varied from one teacher to another. After admission to the *gurukul*, every child was initiated into three basic yogic practices: *nadi shodhan* purification of nervous system, *pranayam* meditation with specific patterns of respiration, and *surya namaskar* praying to the Sun with specific postures. *Gayatri mantra* prayer verse of the goddess of wisdom was also taught to them at this age to ensure a balanced growth of body and mind.

The next step was to teach students the methods of self-control, self-awareness and self-discipline. After induction into these practices, the *guru* would re-test the student before the commencement of formal education. If the child turned out capable of fulfilling the moral demands of education, then alone would the *guru* consider him *adhikarin* eligible candidate for formal education. Thus, satisfaction of the *guru* was essential in order to achieve the eligibility status for formal education. Level of concentration, involvement, and moral development were the major factors determining the nature and type of education. Perfection as a human being and basic eligibility for learning were the main criteria for providing higher education. This could, to some extent, ensure the right use of knowledge for community welfare. Thus, responsibility to community was of prime concern in higher education in a *gurukul*.

Teaching in a *gurukul* was carried out mainly in the oral tradition following a dialectical approach, with appropriate use of mnemonics in some courses. For example, Vedic education involved the unique use of hand beats according to the demand of specific pronunciations involved in chanting the Vedic *mantras* verses. This uniqueness has been preserved till the present days in the chanting of Vedic mantras with the same kind of pronunciation by different language speaking communities of India.

Life in a *gurukul* was very simple and disciplined. All students had to live the same kind of life and observe the norms of *gurukul* irrespective of their social background. The inmates put on unstitched clothes. *Sutra* the sacred thread across the neck and *shikha* few long hair on the back of skull on completely shaved head marked the general features of the pupils of *gurukul*. Ornaments were prohibited, but the use of powder or paste of sandal, turmeric, camphor and saffron were permitted. The teacher and students would generally sleep on mats spread on the ground. Students were prepared to be physically and mentally strong so that they could easily live with all the vicissitudes and hardships of life. Cutting and chopping woods for fire, tending cows, fetching water, cleaning habitation, and cooking, etc., were the collective responsibilities of the inmates of *gurukul*. Thus, the child received a comprehensive education at the *gurukul*, and the society in turn received a balanced, capable and responsible citizen. The end of education at *gurukul* was marked by a convocation ceremony in which the *guru* would make the last remarks about the pupil's achievement, and pass on a few essential tips for the use of knowledge acquired at the *gurukul*.

DOWNFALL OF SANSKRIT EDUCATION

Sanskrit education enjoyed a highly respectable status of being the only formal system of education in Indian society for several thousand years, but by early 15th century it was relegated to an almost marginal status. However, it received a further setback during the later centuries when the Mughal had fully established themselves in the northern part of India. They also imposed supremacy of their language and culture over the traditional Sanskrit-based culture that prevailed at the time. The larger population did not easily yield to this cultural invasion and resisted it. Then the British took over the reigns of the country from Mughals. This marked the beginning of colonial culture in India. Kumar (2000) considers colonial culture as a major force in the downfall of Sanskrit education especially in Varanasi, known as the seat of Sanskrit learning, because it dispensed with many ideas and practices underlying Sanskrit education. For example, Sanskrit education had ascribed a natural superiority to the *guru* by organizing a variety of rituals and symbolic practices to support and reinforce his sacredness. With the larger social and economic changes introduced by the British in the country the supremacy of the *guru* and many of the cultural practices and ideas behind Sanskrit education for example, the non-eligibility of women and lower classes for Sanskrit education were put to question (Kumar, 2000). These changes forced even the practitioners of Sanskrit education *pandits* to search for an alternative self-definition. The wider system of education introduced by the British and formal schools established in different parts of the country swept away the dominant influence of Sanskrit schools on education.

Inspite of these changes in the overall scenario of education, many scholars of Sanskrit often called *pandits*, (see Michaels, 2001) continued with their pursuit of knowledge in traditional ways. Their scholarship was not so much rewarded by people in general as by wealthy persons and aristocracies. They were often engaged in exposition, composition, and scholarly debates *shastrartha* on the meaning of scriptural texts, particularly in the courts. The last one was not only the shortest way to name and fame, but also the easiest means to manage offers for teaching positions and patronage. The history of Sanskrit literature is full of such anecdotes when a Sanskrit scholar was able to earn name, fame, wealth, respect and patronage for his whole life just by defeating an established scholar in a public debate (see Kumar, 2000 and Michaels, 2001 for some such real stories of scholars of the recent past). The patronage went to the extent of setting up a *vidyalaya* non-residential school, literally meaning the home/centre of learning or knowledge for that Sanskrit scholar. Such schools were established almost in all major Hindu kingdoms at that time, providing an easy option to *gurukul* education of the ancient days. These schools were called Sanskrit *pathshala* (place of Sanskrit lessons), which kept multiplying over the years as more and more Sanskrit scholars ventured to offer education to children. We feel that many such schools were probably set up to divert children from attending Western-type schools that were also being established at the same time in an ever increasing number.

It may be noted here that *gurukul, vidyalaya,* and *pathshala,* all refer to the institution of Sanskrit learning. While *pathshala* and *vidyalaya* are synonymous meaning school, *gurukul* is a broader institution of which school is just a part. In ancient days, schools were not independent from the *gurukul,* but later on they acquired independent status. In *pathshala* and *vidyalaya,* students can come as day scholars, but in gurukul, cohabitation of teacher and students was essential. A similar distinction has to be maintained between a *pandit* and *guru.* A *pandit* is a well-educated person characterized by wisdom, great skill for memorization, and an oral knowledge of Vedas, or one or several *shastras* a special tradition of writing. A *pandit* may or may not be a teacher. On the other hand, *guru* is certainly a teacher, but also something beyond that. He is the one who illuminates all aspects of one's life relating to physical as well as spiritual worlds. While a teacher exists only physically, a *guru* can also exist symbolically.

During the late 19th century, certain radical changes took place in Sanskrit schools, particularly in some operating in the cultural capitals of India. For example, in Varanasi a Sanskrit school was founded, which had its major emphasis on the teaching of *dharmashastra* that is, the code of conduct for Hindus. The British needed such experts who could help their judges dispense with Hindu law. For some time, this school ran along the indigenous line. Later on British principals, who were experts in Sanskrit and Western literature and science, were appointed at these schools with a view to expand their concerns beyond the knowledge of Indian classics (Dalmia, 1996). This effect spread to other schools as well, and that is how English got introduced into Sanskrit schools as a part of their curriculum. With this change, Sanskrit could be recognized as a strong cultural system that was capable of reflecting and creating both a social structure and an ideology. On the other hand, it also became an important means of economic and political exploitation that finally resulted in the weakening of the indigenous culture and its replacement by Western cultural values. For example, scholars with 'big titles' offered by the British could now be hired as regular teachers on paid salaries. Some scholars consider this change as the downfall of Sanskrit education in particular, and of overall education in general (Biswas and Agrawal, 1986).

CONTEMPORARY SANSKRIT SCHOOLS

We have noted earlier that the British opened a large number of schools that operated parallel to Sanskrit schools. The main purpose was to cultivate a group of people who could be loyal to the British government and hired locally to help the functioning of the government. Since education in these schools carried a variety of job opportunities, and there was less discrimination in terms of caste, class or gender, it gained more popularity than education in Sanskrit schools. After the end of the British rule in 1947, the government greatly realized the importance of these schools to serve the multifarious developmental needs of the independent nation. Hence, such schools multiplied, and as the population grew exponentially over the years, the government set up schools even in remote rural areas to fulfil the educational needs of individuals and developmental needs of the nation. Because these schools linked individuals with larger social, national, and international contexts, they seemed to serve the vital needs of society by providing people with job opportunities in a number of settings. Although these schools seem to carry great attraction today for people in general, the interests of Sanskrit schools have not been altogether ignored in the national policy of education.

Government support for Sanskrit schools

Tracing the history of Sanskrit education in Varanasi (Kumar, 2000), noted that during the late 19th and 20th century, there were four kinds of reaction from the *pandits* Sanskrit scholars to British intervention in Sanskrit schools: (*a*) full co-operation, (*b*) co-operation with difficulty, (*c*) indifference, and (*d*) active protest. As a result, we find a variety of Sanskrit schools today. A major distinction can be drawn between person-controlled and government-controlled schools. Several schools patterned on the model of traditional temple school or *gurukul* still continue to function without any support from the government. On the other hand, a large number of Sanskrit schools receive either partial or full financial support from State governments. These schools provide education in traditional areas like literature, grammar, philosophy, and astrology that have been popular in Sanskrit schools since ancient days. At the same time, there has been an effort to organize education in these schools much similar to that imparted in other government schools up to the primary level of schooling. Thus, subjects like English, geography, history, mathematics, social studies and basic sciences are now included in the course curriculum of Sanskrit schools, reflecting a kind of 'modernization of courses' of Sanskrit schools.

No reliable statistics for government supported Sanskrit schools is available at the national or provincial level. In the State of Uttar Pradesh (UP), however, an association of Sanskrit schoolteachers has been formed. This association has documented various categories of Sanskrit schools that presently exist in UP. According to a leaflet of the association, there are thirteen primary schools grades one to eight, 950 secondary schools grades one to twelve and 246 degree colleges offering Bachelor's and Master's level courses along with primary and secondary level courses. In addition to this, thirteen degree colleges are registered with the University Grants Commission, which provides grants to all Indian universities. On the whole, about 1,222 Sanskrit schools with more than 6,000 teachers seem to manage education of about 45,000 students of Sanskrit schools in UP.

The association has been concerned with a number of issues relating to Sanskrit schoolteachers. These include: categorization of Sanskrit schools, as primary, secondary and degree colleges, salaries and other facilities to teachers, promotion and appointment to higher positions, creation of non-teaching positions in Sanskrit schools, grants for building, furniture and equipments, etc., scholarships for students at various levels, filling up vacant positions in schools, provision for city allowance, group insurance and transport allowance, timely payment of salaries, and establishment of a separate secretariat for Sanskrit education. Unfortunately the voice of the association has not been able to generate any impact on the government.

Introduction of degrees

The establishment of Sanskrit universities in some parts of the country has marked another process of modernization of Sanskrit education. These universities differ from other universities in two major respects: (*a*) their course curriculum is traditional and much typical of traditional Sanskrit schools, and (*b*) the medium of instruction and examination is Sanskrit. Almost all Sanskrit schools and colleges today are affiliated to these universities for recognition of the education they provide. For different levels of education these universities have introduced separate degrees (Michaels, 2001), which are recognized by the state and central governments as equivalent to other similar level of degrees offered by universities in general for example, BA, MA, Ph.D. With these degrees the students acquire the minimum eligibility to apply for a large variety of jobs available in the government sector, and compete with those who hold degrees from other kind of universities.

PHILOSOPHY OF SANSKRIT EDUCATION

A second major change has taken place in the overall philosophy that teachers and students of Sanskrit universities and colleges nurture about them and their education. In ancient days, Sanskrit learning essentially dictated a way of life, which was much different from that of the individuals who did not attend these schools. In recent years, the idea of 'professionalism' has gradually emerged in Sanskrit schools. A majority of Sanskrit schoolteachers believes that 'profession' and 'life' should be dealt with separately. The point has been particularly explicit in our interviews and discussion with teachers working in Sanskrit schools. They often mentioned that they should not be expected to live a life completely different from that of its members educated in other schools. These influences have filtered down even to the lower levels of Sanskrit education. One can easily notice the effect of such changes in perceptions, attitudes, motivations and values among teachers and students, especially in government schools. Comparative studies in these areas are greatly needed.

Adaptations made by traditional Sanskrit schools

The modernization processes described above have partly failed to challenge the existence of traditional Sanskrit schools. Even today they exist side-by-side subscribing to all values and practices of traditional *gurukul*-type Sanskrit schools. These traditional schools differ from the modernized ones in the following respects:

1. They do not follow the syllabi and directives of the government with respect to education.

2. They do not hold any formal examination to determine student's grade or level of education.
3. They have no provision for degrees, and have no fixed curriculum for teaching.
4. They do not require formal degrees even for teachers.
5. There is no requirement for teaching fixed subjects in predetermined ways; teachers and students enjoy complete freedom to develop their own programmes and routines of teaching and learning.

Thus, the old system of teaching and learning as practised in the *gurukul* is still being honoured even today, at least in some schools. Several contemporary teachers in other Sanskrit schools seem to consider this a superior system of Sanskrit education, yet their number in the country is severely limited. Several probable answers can be given for the decline in their number. The most important reason seems to be the value of this kind of education in the present day job market. Since there are only few jobs outside the government network of schools and colleges, and all of them require government degrees as basic eligibility conditions, the students of traditional Sanskrit schools have very limited opportunity to avail suitable employment for them. As a result, even those students who pursue their studies in such schools out of their natural interest for Sanskrit learning, often appear at various levels of examinations from other Sanskrit institutions to acquire formal degrees. In one sense, this strategy is quite useful, because it provides a student with an opportunity for deeper study of Sanskrit at a traditional institution and acquiring a degree from the government supported Sanskrit institutions of higher education.

Women in Sanskrit schools

Other changes in Sanskrit education are also evident. In earlier days, women were not granted eligibility for Sanskrit education; they learnt it mainly from the members of their family. Today we find numerous *gurukul*-like Sanskrit schools set up for girls in several major religious cities of India. These institutions are managed exclusively by women. The major emphasis of these schools is on the learning of Panini *Vyakaran* (grammar) developed by Panini and the Vedas.

Born in South-West India in 4th century BC Panini fixed the form of Sanskrit grammar once and for all. This grammar consists of some 4,000 aphorisms of the greatest brevity, which is achieved by the invention of an algebraic system of notation of a kind not found outside the grammatical school. This grammar allows a great degree of freedom for playing with morphemes, because in this system, transformations made in the sequential arrangement of morphemes do not change the meaning of the sentence. Co-educational institutional of Sanskrit learning are yet to be seen.

Women Sanskrit schools have major problems with grants to manage the cost of education. Donations, charities and a little fee charged from students not compulsorily constitute the major sources of income of these schools. A community like living characterizes the life in such schools. The teachers and students live together inside the same campus, and they participate in all activities related to school, including cooking and cleaning of the premises. The inmates speak Sanskrit in all kinds of interactions. The girls are allowed to marry and live a family life after the completion of education if they so desire. Some of these girls take up teaching positions in Sanskrit schools, or in other schools as Sanskrit teachers.

Sanskrit schools in rural areas

Sanskrit schools for girls are lesser in number than those for boys. The latter can be found even in remote rural areas, although with very limited strength of students. As employment options are very limited, it is rather difficult now to convince people about the advantages of Sanskrit education. Most of the Sanskrit school students become priests, but for this, one has to belong essentially to the Brahmin community. Since this profession is not much valued in society today, even those Brahmin families that have traditionally worked as priests, refrain from sending their children to Sanskrit schools. The importance seems to have gone down to the level that even teachers of Sanskrit schools prefer to send their children to a non-Sanskrit school in the hope that with that kind of education, they would be able to competently work with children of other groups of society.

Sanskrit schools in cities

As compared to rural settings, the situation seems to be slightly better in big cities, especially those linked to Hindu religion. Pilgrimage to these places is still a popular pursuit of people from all social classes. Sanskrit scholars are needed for a variety of purposes in these places, such as offering worships, performing *yajna* or other rituals, discourse on religious texts, as well as making and reading horoscopes, and so on. Even young pupils of Sanskrit schools would receive invitations from families for performing a variety of rituals or religious activities on their behalf. In return for these services they get moderate offerings both in cash and kind. Although there are some special occasions when Sanskrit students are in high demand, a variety of ceremonies and activities are organized around Sanskrit scholars all through the year. With these options available their livelihood remains almost guaranteed. Such a situation attracts more students, especially from the rural poor Brahmin families that lack agricultural or other economic resources to fulfil the basic needs of children for example, food, clothes, education. Big religious centres like Varanasi and Haridwar attract such students more than do relatively smaller centres where the prospects of managing livelihood with Sanskrit schooling are not very high. Thus, we find fairly variable distribution of Sanskrit schools across different regions of the country including the number of students participating in them.

PSYCHOLOGICAL STUDIES WITH SANSKRIT SCHOOL CHILDREN

Very little psychological or educational research has been done exclusively with children attending Sanskrit schools. However, in a few studies, a comparison of some behavioural qualities of Sanskrit school children with those attending other traditional or modern Western-type schools has been attempted. This opens the possibility of developing research programmes for those who have interest either in a comparative analysis of educational processes in different types of schools, or in examining the effects of Sanskrit schooling on psychological, social, or other aspects of children's development.

Learning and memory

Much research has been done in cross-cultural psychology on the effect of schooling on cognitive development of children. Several detailed reviews of these studies are available (Mishra, 1997, 2001; Mishra and Dasen, 2004; Rogoff, 1981). Comparisons are often made between children who attend schools and those who do not. There are also a few studies examining the effect of form of schooling for example, Koranic on cognitive particularly memory development of children (Wagner, 1993). A general conclusion drawn from these studies is that Western-type schooling promotes the development and deployment of certain cognitive skills for example, use of organizational strategies or mnemonics in learning, whereas Koranic schooling does not exercise any major effect on the development and use of these skills. What happens to learning and memorization strategies with Sanskrit schooling is not much known.

Mishra (1988) compared learning and memory of children attending modern and traditional Sanskrit schools in a village of north India. Children of grades two to five were asked to learn a list of unrelated verbal items through a free recall procedure. Analysis of recall protocols revealed that children from Sanskrit and modern schools did not differ significantly in terms of the amount of recall, although the mean scores of Sanskrit school children were slightly higher than those of the modern schools. Analysis of the mean recall position of items, a measure of subjective organization in terms of order transformation in recall indicated that, for recall, although the tendency to rely on the order of word presentation was slightly stronger in Sanskrit school children, in none of the schools did children really attempt serial or raw learning. Sanskrit school children also presented evidence of lesser semantic confusions another measure of subjective organization than children of the modern schools did. Lastly, the semantic relationships involved in the recall of words were studied by preparing a 'matrix of distances' that is, the number of words intervening between the pair of words. The analysis revealed that for the Sanskrit school group *cow, bread, house, pitcher* and *book* appeared relatively more proximal items than others. For the modern school group *girl, door, house, bread* and *rain* were more proximal than other words.

These observations suggested that both groups tended to resort to organizational schemes, but using different principles. Sanskrit school children demonstrated organization in recall that was based on 'importance of objects' in their life these objects are often donated by households to Sanskrit scholars or priests. On the other hand, the organizational scheme of modern school children seemed to be based on the experience of 'specific events', which often form part of their storybooks. It was concluded that Sanskrit schooling influenced the 'scheme of organization' rather than the process of learning or the amount of recall.

Psychological differentiation

Psychological differentiation is another process that has been studied on children of Sanskrit schools. Witkin's 1978 theory proposes that psychological development of an individual proceeds from a less differentiated global to more differentiated articulated state of functioning, which is manifested in a number of behavioural domains. A less general construct of differentiation theory is cognitive style, generally known as field independent (FI) - field dependent (FD) style. FI and FD individuals tend to differ in their ways of relating to the environment and to themselves. More FD individuals tend to be global perceivers characterized by a passive acceptance of the environment, whereas more FI individuals tend to act on the given environment in an analytical manner (Witkin, 1978).

While cognitive style develops in adaptation to the ecological demands placed on individuals or groups, research studies indicate that Western-type schooling tends to promote the development of FI style (Berry, 1976; Mishra, 1997, 2001). What happens to this style in other forms of schooling is not much known. Mishra and Agrawal (2002) compared perceptual differentiation of children from traditional Sanskrit and Koranic and modern Western-type schools. Story Pictorial Embedded Figures Test (SPEFT) (Sinha, 1984) and Kohs Block Designs Test (BDT) were administered to 240 children of five to thirteen years of age.

A number of interesting findings emerged from the study, but we will report only the findings relating to the role of Sanskrit schooling. In general, the analyses revealed higher scores on the SPEFT with an increase in the age of children, however, the scores of Sanskrit school children were significantly lower than those of the modern schools at all age levels. Analyses of time scores on the SPEFT revealed that Sanskrit school children took more time in disembedding objects from the complex background as compared to modern school children. A similar pattern of results was noted on the BDT, with modern school children scoring higher than Sanskrit school children.

One may interpret this finding as indicating that perhaps Sanskrit school children were perceptually less differentiated than those in modern schools. This interpretation may also fit very well with the findings of those studies in which context-free use of analytical skills and transfer of learning from school to test context have been identified as universal empirical phenomenon taking place with formal Western-type schooling (Cole, 1996; Scribner and Cole, 1973). However, viewing these findings from an eco-cultural perspective Berry et al., 2002), we find that the overall environment of Sanskrit schools, the curricula and method of teaching adopted in these schools emphasize on social context and connectedness of units. Less differentiation found among Sanskrit school children in this study has been attributed to less importance of differentiation in the overall setting of Sanskrit schools. Whether these children will demonstrate greater development of interpersonal skills than those of the Western-type school, needs to be studied to validate the conclusion drawn above.

Social identity and prejudice

Enormous literature exists in developmental psychology to suggest that social development of children in denominational and non-denominational schools takes place in a different manner. The former kind of school provides children with an opportunity to interact only with the members of their own group. Hence, the probability for developing a glorified social identity in these schools remains higher than in other schools where children have the opportunity to meet and interact with members of other groups. Since social identity and prejudice are closely linked, it is also generally assumed that children in denominational schools will be more prejudiced to the members of other groups than those attending non-denominational schools.

In a large-scale study, Bano and Mishra (2006) attempted to examine these hypotheses. Two hundred Hindu and Muslim children, aged three to twelve years were drawn from modern and traditional schools in Varanasi and tested with a Model Identification Task and a Projective Prejudice Task especially designed for children.

The Model Identification Task presented children with two identical human models, one of which was dressed like a conventional Muslim, and another like a conventional Hindu. Children were asked a number of questions relating to the identity and behavioural patterns of those models, including their general liking and preference for one of them for a variety of interpersonal activities. Correct recognition of Hindu and Muslim models, and identifying them as belonging to one's own group were used as measures of awareness of social identity.

The Projective Prejudice Task presented children with pictures that depicted Hindu and Muslim children in situations that involved some degree of ambiguity. The children were shown the picture and told a background story about it. Each child in the story was given either a Hindu or a Muslim name and described as the initiator of certain actions that led to positive for example, winning a trophy or negative for example, stealing consequences. After listening to the story, the children were asked to guess the child of the picture who might have initiated the action, and also to tell the one who should be rewarded or punished. Recommending reward and preventing harm for the member of one's own group were used as measures of prejudice defined as in-group favouritism and out-group discrimination.

From a set of several interesting findings, we will describe here only those that relate to children of Sanskrit schools. All Sanskrit school children were aware of their social identity, whereas only 90 per cent children of the modern school knew their social identity. The basis of social identity in the case of Sanskrit school children was predominantly 95 per cent the internal features behavioural qualities of individuals; in the case of modern school children, both internal 49 per cent and external for example, dressing features 39 per cent characterized their social identity. Family was the main source of knowledge about social identity for both groups. While children of both groups showed equal preference for members of their own group, there were significant differences in the nature of their preference. The dominant preference of Sanskrit school children was primarily in terms of interpersonal activities, whereas the preference of modern school children was based on both interpersonal activities and general liking almost to the same extent. Further, Sanskrit school children preferred the members of their own group largely due to 'food habits' vegetarian in this context, which did not find a place in the choice of modern school children.

Findings on the Projective Prejudice Task revealed that although the children of Sanskrit schools generally showed slightly greater concern about positive outcomes rewards than negative outcomes punishment in comparison to those in the modern school, the differences between the two groups were not significant for either outcome.

Tendencies for allocation of reward and prevention of punishment for one's own group were equally dominant in both the school groups. In general, the findings indicated that development of social identity and prejudice was not much influenced by the type of schooling received by children. This finding can be interpreted in two ways. In the first place, it may be argued that formation of social identity is a universal process, and it takes place at home in the same manner among children of all kinds of schools. On the other hand, it may also be argued that glorification of social identities starts later than the age limit twelve years used in this study.

CONCLUSION

Sanskrit schools, which occupied a very respectable place in the traditional Indian society, have lost much of their importance in recent years, specially with the availability of other possible options of education that seem to make greater economic promises to the larger section of the Indian population. Although several of these schools are still surviving in rural areas and smaller townships, they run a high risk of losing their existence in the forthcoming years. On the other hand, schools located in big urban religious centres have a greater likelihood of existence there.

Some studies have been carried out to examine how Indian people generally deal with situations of culture change (Mishra and Chaubey, 2002; Mishra et al., 1996; Sinha, 1988). The findings reveal that Indian people often adopt a strategy of keeping the elements of their own culture as well as those of other's in a state of 'coexistence'. That is how the Indian society has been able to maintain its cultural heritage till today without getting into conflict with inroads from other cultures in contact. While many individuals of the Indian society do appear quite modern, their traditions still remain largely free from the influences of modernization. In fact, on several occasions, these modern people can be found to glorify traditions more than less modern people. Thus, as long as the traditions live, the life of Sanskrit schools is not in danger. However, their importance for common people is likely to diminish more than what we observe today.

During the last few years the government of India has felt a need for the revival of Indian traditional knowledge and wisdom. Scholarly debates persist on what and how to revive. There are certain areas of knowledge where a mutual interaction and dialogue between traditional scholars and modern scientists is seemingly possible. Time is one such area where traditional scholars of Sanskrit and modern scholars of physics and astronomy are working together. Space and motion of planets is another potential area. Astrology has always been in the centre of debate between traditional and modern scholars. Vedic mathematics, which is lot easier and precise in calculation than the mathematics generally taught in schools today, is also a potential area for mutual research and application. Several other frontier areas are being identified where traditional and modern scholars can make significant contributions. If such efforts continue, the importance of Sanskrit knowledge is likely to increase with the past glory of Sanskrit schools re-established. As far as the present is concerned, Sanskrit schools exist in a marginalized state in spite of the fact that Sanskrit texts still constitute the only valid source of all philosophical and religious knowledge, and mythological beliefs are strongly held by Indian people in general irrespective of whether or not they know Sanskrit.

Moving towards research, we find a very limited number of psychological or educational studies with children of Sanskrit schools. While teaching and learning processes represent potential areas of research in their own right, various dimensions of human development for example, perceptual, cognitive, intellectual, social, emotional, moral, personality also await research in relation to Sanskrit schooling. Challenges faced by teachers and students of Sanskrit schools in the context of socio-cultural changes taking place in Indian society, and the manner in which they are trying to adapt to these challenges, constitute other interesting areas of research. Comparative studies on all these educational and psychological dimensions are welcome in order to place this ancient system of education in an appropriate perspective.

REFERENCES

Altekar, A.S. 1934. *Education in Ancient India*. Varanasi: Indian Book House.
Bano, S. and R.C. Mishra. 2006. *Schooling and the Development of Social Identity and Prejudice in Hindu and Muslim Children, Indian Journal of Community Psychology*, 2: 168–82.

Berry, J. W. 1976. *Human Ecology and Cognitive Style*. New York: Sage Publication/Halstead.

Berry, J. W., Y.H. Poortinga, M.H. Segall and P.R. Dasen. 2002. *Cross Cultural Psychology. Research and Applications (Second Revised Edition)*. Cambridge: Cambridge University Press.

Biswas, A. and S.P. Agrawal. 1986. *Development of Education in India: A Historical Survey of Educational Documents Before and After Independence*. New Delhi: Concept Publishing Company.

Burrow, T. 1995. *The Sanskrit Language*. Delhi: Motilal Banarasidas.

Chatterjee, M. 1999. *Education in Ancient India*. New Delhi: D.K. Printworld.

Cole, M. 1996. *Cultural Psychology: A Once and Future Discipline*. Cambridge: Harvard University Press.

Dalmia, V. 1996. 'Sanskrit Scholars and Pandits of the Old School: The Benares Sanskrit College and the Constitution of Authority in the Late Nineteenth Century', *Journal of Indian Philosophy*, 24: 321–37.

Filliozat, P. 2000. *The Sanskrit Language: An Overview*. Varanasi: Indica Books.

Kumar, N. 2000. *Lessons from Schools: The History of Education in Banaras*. New Delhi: Sage Publications.

Michaels, A. 2001. *The Pandit: Traditional Scholarship in India*. New Delhi: Manohar.

Mishra, R. C. 1988. 'Learning Strategies Among Children in Modern and Traditional Schools', *Indian Psychologist*, 5: 17–24.

———. 1997. 'Cognition and Cognitive Development', in J.W. Berry, P. R. Dasen and T.S. Saraswathi (eds), *Handbook of Cross-Cultural Psychology*, Volume 2, pp. 143–75. Boston: Allyn & Bacon.

———. 2001. 'Cognition Across Cultures', in D. Matsumoto (ed.), *The Handbook of Culture and Psychology*, pp. 119–35. New York: Oxford University Press.

Mishra, R.C. and A. Agrawal. 2002. 'Perceptual Differentiation in Hindu and Muslim Children of Traditional and Modern Schools', *Social Science International*, 18: 16–25.

Mishra, R.C. and A.C. Chaubey. 2002. 'Acculturation Attitudes of Kharwar and Agaria Tribal Groups of Sonebhadra', *Psychology and Developing Societies*, 14: 201–20.

Mishra, R. C., and P. R. Dasen. 2004. 'The Influence of Schooling on Cognitive Development: A Review of Research in India', in B. N. Setiadi, A. Supratiknya, W. J. Lonner and Y. H. Poortinga (eds), *Ongoing Themes in Psychology and Culture. Selected Papers from the Sixteenth International Congress of the International Association for Cross-Cultural Psychology*, pp. 207–22. Yogyakarta: Kanisius.

Mishra, R.C., D. Sinha and J.W. Berry. 1996. *Ecology, Acculturation and Psychological Adaptation: A Study of Adivasis in Bihar*. New Delhi: Sage Publications.

Raghavan, V. 1957. *Modern Sanskrit Literature*. Delhi: Sahitya Akademi.

Rogoff, B. 1981. 'Schooling and the Development of Cognitive Skills', in H. C. Triandis and A. Heron (eds), *Handbook of Cross-Cultural Psychology*, Volume 4, pp. 233–94. Boston: Allyn & Bacon.

Scribner, S. and M. Cole. 1973. 'Cognitive Consequences of Formal and Informal Education', *Science*, 182: 553–59.

Sinha, D. 1984. *Story-Pictorial E.F.T. and Indo-African E.F.T.* Varanasi: Rupa Psychological Corporation.

———. 1988. 'Basic Indian Values and Behaviour Dispositions in the Context of National Development: An Appraisal', in D. Sinha and H.S.R. Rao (eds), *Social Values and Development: Asian Perspectives*, pp. 31–55. New Delhi: Sage Publications.

Upadhyaya, B. 1999. *Sanskrit Sahitya Kaa Itihaas*. Varanasi: Sharada Niketan.

Vaidya, C.V. 1986. *History of Sanskrit Literature*. Delhi: Parimal Publications.

Wagner, D.A. 1993. *Literacy, Culture and Development: Becoming Literate in Morocco*. New York: Cambridge University Press.

Witkin, H.A. 1978. *Cognitive Styles in Personal and Cultural Adaptation*. Worchester MA: Clark University Press.

11

SANSKRIT SCHOOLS IN VARANASI BETWEEN TRADITIONS AND TRANSITION

MARIE ANNE BROYON

INTRODUCTION

Like other forms of traditional schooling, the Sanskrit school is not very well known in the West. The few documents that do exist deal mainly with historical and philosophical aspects, and somewhat skim over the pedagogical aspects, and, apart from Protopapas (1998) and Michaels (2001), nobody has studied its adequacy or inadequacy for the needs of contemporary Indian society. Therefore, it seemed important to us to take an interest in these aspects. The study of two Sanskrit schools, one only for girls and the other only for boys, will allow us to have a better understanding of educational practices still in use in these schools. It will also enable us to grasp what is behind the public or private funding of these institutions. The historical background and philosophy of Sanskrit education are largely discussed in the chapter by Mishra and Vajpayee this book, so this chapter will develop only the aspects of the historical background and philosophy, which are most significant to the educational practices.

THE INDIAN SCHOOLING SYSTEM

India is a federation (twenty five states and seven union territories) and the educational system takes the form of a partnership between the central government and the governments of the different states. The funding of education is ensured mainly by the central and provincial governments, and to a certain extent, by the local governments. Funds that come from various private sources also contribute significantly to the financing of the system (Clark, 2006). The main peculiarity of this educational system is the preservation and partial funding of a form of education that is traditional. The schools are grouped in two parallel channels that go from primary school level to reach the university level, and they are:

1. Modern schools like the ones in the West (derived from the English system), which are far from being the most numerous. This category includes the municipal schools, the government-run schools, the private and semi-private schools, among which are the *English medium* schools where English is the medium of instruction.
2. Traditional schools which include the Sanskrit and the Koranic schools (most numerous), as well as Jain and Buddhist schools.

The quality level of Indian schools differs greatly from one category to another and from one school to another. The involvement of the management and the teachers of the establishment and the financial means at their disposal are the elements that determine good quality (Mishra and Dasen, 2004). There are instances where teachers are able to perform miracles with very little resources (we encountered some), but these remain rare. This rule applies as much to modern schools as to the traditional schools.

In the modern schools, whether public or private, it is not rare to find classes of more than fifty students. Lecturing and rote learning are common practices, which do not leave much room for reflection and innovation. The English medium schools, reserved for students from rich families, are of better quality (Mishra, 1988). They employ teachers who are motivated and better trained and practice new methods of teaching. There is little absenteeism (absenteeism of teachers is the biggest problem in the public system), the classes are smaller and the students have access to new technologies.

In specialized literature, the traditional schools are often blamed for emphasizing learning by rote and consequently, for failing to encourage the development of cognition. However, it would be very belittling to think of Sanskrit schools in this way. It is true that the learning of the Vedas (religious texts), which represent an important part of the teaching in the Sanskrit schools, is done by memorization but this can be explained, among other things, by the fact that during rituals, the precision of texts and gestures is essential, errors being considered as major faults (Renou, 2001) and a catastrophe for the community (Pollak, 1982). But this learning by heart does not take place as we tend to think of it generally: reciting of the Vedas takes place in eleven different ways, which implies a comparison and a reflection on their different uses (Filliozat, 2002). On the other hand, there exists a form of memorization, which is the memorization of the contents of the text (it is not a memorization of the words, but of the content that is touched upon, the order of the presentation of the content, the placement of ideas and information from the texts) (Filliozat, 2002: 82). Some of these teaching and learning techniques, which are mostly centuries old, are, to our eyes, innovative in many ways.

TRADITIONAL EDUCATIONAL PRACTICES

Indians have always linked education to religion. Sanskrit education is supposed to bring about material and spiritual well-being during life on earth as well as in the life beyond. Right from the beginning, this kind of education has been the object of much reflection and of a surprising awareness, which have contributed to the spread of Sanskrit during close to three thousand years in the entire Indian subcontinent (Filliozat, 2002). The educational practices, for example, are already discussed in detail in the *Upanishad*[1] (Reagan, 2000). Given the long history of Hinduism, it is normal that education has been considered differently across the ages. Authors like Mookerji (1969) and Pollak (1982) describe the evolution of Sanskrit education with reference to different periods. However, Reagan (2000) and Filliozat (2002) state that over the years, there is a great continuity of intellectual activity and that it is possible to observe examples of transmission of knowledge, from master to disciple, over many centuries. Another constant must be pointed out: the perpetual search for a link between intellectual and spiritual development. The three stages of Hindu educational practices described by Reagan (2000) demonstrate this well. The first stage *Shravana* is the memorization of entire texts, of grammatical techniques, exegesis, and arguments; this stage is the basis of knowledge, essential to all education. This first stage is followed by *Manana*, which implies a reflection on what has just been learned (what one must know from the first stage *Shravana*). For Reagan, this process is more intellectual than spiritual. This second stage is followed by *Nididhyasana*, a stage of meditation, which leads to an awareness of oneself. Besides, Indian philosophers understood very early the role of the unconscious and sought to develop the personality by exerting an influence on the unconscious (Filliozat, 2002). The basic idea is that all experiences that are lived (action and cognition attached to this action, feelings, concept, and so on) never die irremediably: they always leave traces in the psyche. The philosophers compared the psyche to a box where an odorous substance had been kept and then removed (the perfume remains). In the same way, experiences that are lived, leave traces that are invisible, but real, called *vāsanā*; these traces get organized amongst themselves, to make up an individual, and prepare him/her to receive new experiences, which make him/her capable of new psychological activities—this process is called *samskāra*.

Today we are constantly talking about 'lifelong education', as if it were a new concept. However, since the most ancient times, Sanskrit education has always been considered a lifelong learning process. Pollak (1982) remarks that Sanskrit education had always been thought of as an art of perfecting, which was meant to be followed till the end of one's life (you had to spend thirty six years learning the Vedas, an ideal rarely achieved). In this line of thinking, she explains that only a teacher who remained a good learner all his life was considered a true teacher.

Even though they are, for the most part, in a transitional phase, the Sanskrit schools still have recourse to certain ancestral learning and transfer of knowledge techniques. Oral teaching, for example, is still very privileged in these schools. Filliozat (2002) explains this preference by demonstrating that oral teaching favours contact with the teacher because the difficulty of memorization based on hearing requires constant attention to the teacher's words. On the contrary, reading favours isolation and you can turn away from writing at any point and then return to it; that's why certain teachers take pride in not using books. Moreover, the favoured relationship between a teacher and a student (described in this book by Mishra and Vajpayee) is very strong even today. Lastly, use of debates (*sāstra*) and discussions to promote learning are still dominant in certain schools. Thus, from a young age, these students must constantly defend what they have learned in front of their peers and their professor (later, they will do this in public). For Filliozat (2002), this intellectual exchange is conceived as an efficient way of sustaining knowledge that has already been acquired and enriching it further.

Contrary to some beliefs, women have also been successful in Sanskrit education but during an ancient era and for a brief period in time. Although some authors thought of this access as being very limited or quasi inexistent (Bose, 2000; Kumar, 2000; Walker, 1983), others are not of this opinion. Biswas and Agrawal (1986), for example, explain that at the time when Vedic literature was composed, each person (man and woman) had to follow the *Bhramacharya* discipline in order to initiate himself/herself to the sacred literature. The father of the family generally imparted this education up to the *Upanishad-Sutra* stage, when the complexity of rituals and of sacred literature led to teaching becoming a profession. As for Pollack (1982), she maintains that for many centuries, education for girls was as common as education for boys. She explains that young girls were generally educated at home and by a member of the immediate family. Women had the right to teach, sometimes even to teach young men. The author illustrates this by referring to certain stories narrated in the Puranas, which would lead us to understand that in certain cases, Sanskrit education could be co-educational (Pollak, 1982: 20). Referring to ancient religious texts, the author shows that women had the right to study the Vedas and perform sacrifices until 2200 BP; they had even composed certain hymns of the Rigveda. L'*Atharvaveda* (XI5.18), for example, mentions women who have followed the discipline of the *brahmacārin* (chastity and learning of the Vedas at a guru's house) and the Laws of Manu (Manu, II: 66) consider the sacrament of initiation as a compulsory ritual for girls.

Two thousand five hundred years ago, the position of women abruptly deteriorated and the education of women stopped being in vogue up to the point of becoming non-existent five centuries later. Pollak (1982) thinks that this loss of interest for education among women was probably due to the fact that they had to be married off at a younger age, which was not possible if they were still students. Gombrich Gupta (2000) explains that women were suddenly considered impure, up to the point where they were relegated to the same level of impurity as the *sudra*.[2] The priests, basing themselves on the myth of Indra,[3] progressively usurped their positions in the temples and excluded women from religious tasks. This distance, justified by impurity, originated from the fact that the lineage (*jāti*) being transmissible by males, the males must always be able to ascertain their paternity. Also, the Hindu men progressively put in place a system of laws that entirely controlled the sexuality of women: they were married before puberty, contact with men during their puberty was forbidden, and they were isolated during a certain period after childbirth. It is to be noted that the caste system was put in place at the same time. For Gombrich Gupta the more this system was reinforced, the more women were considered a source of danger for the social status of men and male domination exerted itself that much more.

In India, the caste system, 2000 years old,[4] still defines the place of individuals in society according to their birth. Did Sanskrit education play a role in preserving this system? For Kumar (2000), the most interesting facet of Sanskrit education is its hidden curriculum. For her, Sanskrit education contributed to the reproduction of the social hierarchy by consolidating its inequalities, by reinforcing the power of the guru and especially, by guaranteeing an implicit value system shared by many social strata. Due to this, it is evident that Sanskrit education strongly participated in the establishment of a Brahminical hegemony in Indian society. Students who attend these kinds of schools were, and still are, for the most part Brahmin, even though it was attested that some *Baniya*s and a few *Kayastha*s had access to this kind of education and that it was even possible to find certain *Kayastha* gurus (Kumar, 2000).

However, it would be wrong to believe that the educational system was solely in the hands of the Brahmins. The castes were traditionally associated to a profession or to a precise ritual task, and most of them had their own education system. In fact, hereditary specialization demanded that the work be divided by guilds and that the work procedures be preserved from one generation to another. Also, learning was imposed within the family, and normally the son continued the father's profession (Bouglé, 1935). Children of artisans were familiarized from their early days with the tools of their fathers and *Rajput* sons grew up with the idea that they were born to go to war. Baniyas, who were members of the traders' community, took their sons everywhere with them: they taught them how to count and kept them informed of their affairs. A report by Henry Stewart Reid,[5] published in 1852 and cited by Kumar (2000), describes many forms of trade learning which range from training within the family (brothers, cousins, and so on) at the trader' house to a form of schooling which was very formal (school building, teachers, experts, precise curriculum). This 'specialized and professional' education has undoubtedly contributed largely to hinder social mobility.

However, it must be highlighted that in the beginning of the 19th century, traditional education, Sanskrit or Muslim, was important and well organized in certain districts, such as those of Madras or Bengal (Biswas and Agrawal, 1986) and that it was open to all castes. In fact, referring to a series of studies meant to establish an inventory of the Indian education system and launched in 1822 by the tax collectors of the British[6] districts, Nivedita (1998) and Kak (2001) state that at that time, Bengal and Bihar had 100,000 village schools and in the district of Madras, each village had its school. Professors and students of all castes went to these indigenous schools where teaching was generally imparted in the students' maternal language.

TWO SANSKRIT SCHOOLS IN VARANASI

This study is based on interviews with directors and teachers conducted in March 2003 during a research on the development of space orientation and cognitive development.[7] This study of two Sanskrit schools in Benares: *Panini Kanya Mahavidyalaya,* a school for girls only, and *Mumuksha Bhawan,* a school for boys shows the complexity of Sanskrit education today. Actually, even if we find a certain number of similarities between these two schools, especially with regard to the importance of teaching Sanskrit today and religious instruction, there are a number of differences at other levels—a disparity which originates largely, but not only—because of the difference in the sex of their students.

Panini Kanya Mahavidyalaya

This institution is an oasis of greenery and serenity situated in one of the four corners of the city, near a small lake tarnished by garbage where herds of buffaloes come to drink. An enclosure surrounds the campus, which consists of many buildings: the students' dormitory, professors' apartments, the library, the kitchen, the armoury, the stable, and a large vegetable garden and playground surrounded by greenery. The buildings are freshly painted with pastel colours and most of them have an exterior arcade under which small groups of children study, shaded from the sun. The classrooms are simple, but clean and welcoming. This school is known for its high level Sanskrit classes and for its classes in Indian classical music. Seventy young girls of all castes, hailing from middle to upper socio-economic families (fathers being engineers, traders, professors, politicians, policemen, and so on), from six to twenty years of age, receive a strict education, without vacations or family visits and this, until the end of their studies (the children are even encouraged to refuse to attend phone calls from their parents). These young girls come from different parts of the country and communicate exclusively in Sanskrit amongst themselves. The school offers classes from the first year of primary school up to a Master's degree at the university level. Entrance exams are organized at every level (lower and upper pri-mary, high school, BA and MA). University level students (from the eighth year *prathama* up to the Master's level *acharya*) are also registered at the Sanskrit university of Benares where they go once a year to sit for their exams.

Up everyday at 4 a.m. the young girls start the day by reciting Vedas and doing the rituals around the fire. At 8 a.m. they have their breakfast. After that begins a long day, during which they have classes in English, math, geography, Sanskrit, music and knitting or embroidery, as per the season. The evening is dedicated to learning subjects associated with religion (religious texts, philosophy, traditions, rituals, sacrifices, and so on), classes which are generally taught by the principal of the school. The young girls do most of the housekeeping tasks (in groups and by turn) and each activity lends itself to learning. Thus, with every change of season, the teachers explain the diseases associated with that season, how to avoid them, which are the plants and ailments that could cure them, how much water to drink every day to avoid falling ill, which are the sports and yoga exercises that correspond to the season, and so on. Good manners, culinary specialties, and hospitality are also part of the education in this school. There is a focus on sports—the young girls play football and badminton, practice forming human pyramids and martial arts. To our great surprise, the students at this school receive real military training (club, spear, sword and real shooting); the principal justifies this training in these words: 'It is so that they can defend themselves and become independent, so that they can defend and help others and so that they can face threats in society if such a need arises'. It must be noted that during parades organized in the school courtyard, rifles under their arms, these students were filmed singing nationalistic and fundamentalist songs,[8] which is rather disturbing, especially since we know that the school is in the hands of one of the most fundamentalist missionary movements of the Indian sub-continent. Finally, the only link for these young girls with the outside world is a television, but they can only watch the news from time to time.

Mumuksha Bhawan

This school is established inside an ashram dedicated to a saint. This place of pilgrimage is also a place where life ends for some men and women who have decided to give up everything to come and spend their last years in this holy town. The ashram is separated from the road, which is bustling with life, by a thick wall and a watchman guards the door day and night. The buildings are not very well maintained, the paint is peeling off a little bit everywhere, but the place is clean. There is little greenery, and little open space for sports and games. Every day, at the end of the morning, and during more than forty-five minutes, about fifty young Brahmin adolescents, between twelve to seventeen years of age, dressed in traditional clothes (the dhoti, a kind of long skirt with two sides, and a kurta, a red/orange tunic with a Mao-style collar tied across the chest), a spot of vermillion in the middle of their forehead, recite, the same prayer by articulating each word with a hand movement. Even though they have all woken up at dawn to go to the temple and study the *sûtras* (grammar formulae), this collective prayer marks the beginning of formal non-religious classes (Sanskrit, English, political science, math, history, geography), which last until the end of the afternoon when they close with a session of yoga. These young people are housed, fed and educated at no cost for two years, generally the time after which they should have reached the level of *pathasala* (seventh and eighth year of schooling) or the level *maadhyamik* (intermediary level). As is the case for the young girls, the higher levels are reached after appearing for a university exam. These adolescents come, for the most part, from the neighbouring towns, and although they are all Brahmin (the highest caste), they come to this school, for the most part, for economic reasons: their fathers are priests, teachers at the primary school or farmers, and they don't have the means to continue to pay for their studies after the primary level. Also, for these young people coming from government-run schools, Sanskrit education is often the only way to access secondary schooling. On the other hand, even if the school offers courses up to the bachelor's level (BA degree), very few students continue their studies beyond secondary school. This is explained by the fact that after the first two years free of charge at this school, the students have to find accommodation elsewhere outside the ashram and they must begin to fund their own education. When they leave school, the young people who have a bachelor's degree turn to professions linked with public service: teaching (the majority, about 30 per cent), government service, the military. Those who do not achieve this degree, often head for *karmakanda* (practice of religious ceremonies, ritual sacrifices), but it is mainly because they do not find another way to meet their needs and those of their family.

In this institution, the young people have greater freedom to come and go than the girls of the other Sanskrit school. But this is not really a peculiarity of this school, because in India, the young girls are often confined to their homes after school. The boys can return to their families once a month and they are allowed visits from relatives. The ashram being located a few minutes away from Assi Ghat,[9] a very lively place with many tourists, the young people try to go there as soon as they get the opportunity, that is, every Sunday and every time school is closed for a religious holiday (which is often the case). Only the principal lives on campus with his family and his three children (two little girls and one young boy), who seem to be very close of the boarders. The young people are authorized to go to his house to watch cricket matches on television. Certain boarders are also in contact with the elderly people who live in the other part of the ashram. These people are often former pundits (teachers, doctors, professors) and can help students solve their emotional or intellectual problems.

The biggest problem that the management of the school has to face is the lack of teachers. The government has allocated eight posts to them (this school is funded by the State), but as of today, they only have four. They complain a lot about this situation, which prevents them, they say, from making progress. The principal, for example, must teach most of the modern subjects by himself, something that is not easy for him. He comments on the situation by saying that the professors are not willing to teach in institutions where the timetable is not fixed, and where there are so many levels. But maybe the explanation lies elsewhere. Protopapas (1998) states that since 1990 (year when a positive discrimination law was implemented to help the lowest castes), the Sanskrit schools that are funded by the State have to employ teachers who are not Brahmin. That is why, even if the teachers of lower castes have the required degree, these institutions prefer not to fill these positions.

CURRENT EDUCATIONAL PRACTICES

At the Panini Kanya Mahavidyalaya boarding school, the young girls receive a comprehensive education, therefore, every moment of the day is appropriate for learning. The students have little time that is unplanned (and uncontrolled). The professors at this school have dedicated their life to teaching and to the smooth running of the school, so that they have a very high opinion of their roles as teachers. The school has a good reputation and a large number of young girls want to go there. Yet, the principal does not want to increase the number of students, because she would not be able to personally keep track of each student if there were more than seventy of them. When she has to recruit new students, she selects them on the basis of their intellectual abilities, their social behaviour, their values and their age (between nine and eleven years).

The students are separated into classes by level and the classes are much more formal than in the boys' school. In all classes, there is an emphasis on discussions and debates. The material is read and prepared in class, and then the students are asked to exchange their ideas: first they learn, then they get together and they discuss. In the higher classes (Bachelor's and Master's), the students prepare the lesson and take turns to teach the class. During the class, the other students must pay great attention to their colleague, and at the end, everyone has the right to express their opinion and to share their doubts and difficulties. Then, they discuss the issue together to arrive at a conclusion for the subject. This is their way of advancing in a given field. In this institution, teaching Sanskrit is very advanced.

The founder of the school developed a method for beginners called 'how to learn Sanskrit without memorizing in six months', which is still used to quickly integrate the new arrivals. The teachers mainly rely on the Pānini method for teaching Sanskrit; a method which uses explanations and ensures, according to them, a happy and internalized learning process. Thus, the young girls must learn 4000 sûtras (grammar formulae) of Ashtādyāy (The eight lessons)[10] by heart in four years. In order to do this, the teachers begin by teaching small sûtras by breaking them up (each word and each phonetic aspect is explained). Then for each sûtra, the teachers explain the seven principal elements such as the separation of the words, the mode, the inflection and the ending, and so on. Then they make the connection between the various elements so that the students can learn to make inferences and reach a conclusion. For these professors, 'learning followed by a good explanation and an analysis remains engraved in the memory whereas memorization remains as a burden on the brain'. The young girls are also introduced to the Patañjali Mahābhāshya (a sort of debate on the interpretation of the sûtras by Pānini, developed by the grammarian, Pantañjali) that helps the students to increase their capacity for reflection and analysis. The Vedas (sacred texts) are also approached in an explanatory manner. Other classes are held on the teachings of the Vedas with relation to daily life and their implications on family and society. From time to time, a very famous poet comes to teach Hindi to the young girls for about twenty days. He is an old man, who is thus considered respectable and 'harmless'.

For these, female professors have to struggle[11] to make others recognize their rights to practice ancestral rituals, to read the Vedas and to teach Sanskrit. According to tradition, it is very important to emphasize the lessons, which teach young girls how to become independent and confident. They are taught how to defend themselves in the world, whether they are alone or accompanied by a man, how never to be scared, and how to earn a living later on.

When we ask these teachers, what are the qualities, that make a good student, they reply without hesitating that it is the person who is in agreement with their ideas, who has internalized the values taught at the school, and who thinks like them, who obeys their orders, who respects their wishes, and who is willing to study. It seems that the teachers reach their goals, because once their studies are over, a certain number of students choose to dedicate their lives to teaching at this school or at another school of a similar kind. Others become priests, yoga professors or they get married as they wish or as their family decides.

The first lesson that the boys learn when they arrive at Mumuksha Bhawan is how to maintain total silence. Then, the professors teach them the best way to sit on the ground in class, and how to listen carefully to the teacher. We were surprised to see how fast these young boys learn to resolve problems: they have a capacity to listen to directions that are given orally, without interrupting the person who is giving them, and then asking all kinds of questions in order to resolve any problem in the least amount of time. At Mumuksha Bhawan there is no bell to indicate the end of classes. The teachers are free to conduct their classes and the students are free to come and attend. All the levels are mixed and there is no difference between the students of different levels. The boys come and go from one class to another. Some classes remain empty while others are full. The young people explained to us that two professors (of whom one is the principal) are very good teachers and that they (the students) often have a preference for attending their classes.

In this establishment the professors never deliver lectures, and learning by rote, which is practiced in most Indian schools and also in some Sanskrit schools (according to them), doesn't occur here. The teachers stress individual teaching:

> The most important thing in our school is that in spite of the fact that they are in one class, *we teach each boy as if he were our own son*. We explain and then we ask the question: have you understood? And if the boy says no, we explain to him for a second time. In the primary classes we sometimes hold their hand to make them write and we ask, with reference to each word, whether they have understood, and if so, what they have understood.

Nothing is imposed, not even writing, but the teachers are happy if the boys themselves take the initiative to write down what is being said during the class and show it to the teachers. For them, it is proof that the lesson has been well internalized. While teaching the Vedas, the hand movements and the tone of voice play an important role. First the teacher does it himself, then he makes the students repeat each movement accompanied by each word. According to the professors, learning the movements and the tone of voice are essential to learning Sanskrit. For the principal of this school, learning Sanskrit is linked to human life and he thinks, *if someone has not studied Sanskrit he cannot really be a man* (*generically speaking*); he would be very proud if his son were to choose this path. However, he will leave the choice to him and will try to guide him according to his abilities. For this teacher, learning Sanskrit must be understood as a holistic (comprehensive) learning. Thus, it is not merely about learning a language and speaking it, but learning about all the traditions that are linked to it, because a great science underlies these traditions. He gives many examples such as the act of washing one's hands and face before eating, that of placing the plate at the level of the hands, and not on the ground, which prevents the insects from entering and polluting the dish, or that of wetting one's head to calm oneself, actions which are taught today on television and which have scientific recognition, while they were actually advocated in the ancient texts.

The teachers at Mumuksha Bhawan do their best to connect their teaching to contemporary society. They wish to extract everything that is good from the ancient system of education in order to combine it with certain modern teaching practices. Themes from current events, for example, are often discussed in class and linked to the teaching of ancient texts. They think it is of utmost importance to train the students to fend for themselves in modern society: for this the young people must be able to develop their character (intelligence, good behaviour) to learn to survive in society, to get integrated and to progress; the final goal of Sanskrit education being, according to these teachers, to make the students good pundits, respectable men and good citizens.

New challenges for Sanskrit education

Knowing the sacred language allowed some elite Indians to maintain a social and religious status that are enviable even today. For thousands of years, reciting the Vedas was the prerogative of men from the three superior castes. Brahmins are known as the 'twice-born', because they receive the initiation (*upanayana*), which allows them to undertake religious studies under a guru (Renou, 2001). However, for about ten years, we have been witnessing a real revolution: Sanskrit education is again accessible to women and, moreover, to women of all castes. This opportunity has unbelievable consequences for the traditional Indian society because some of these women become nuns (priestess) and are then able to conduct wedding ceremonies, morning ceremonies and *pujas;* certain clients even prefer them to their male counterparts.[12]

However, it must be noted that these schools for young women are not very common. Thus, in Varanasi, there is only one school of this kind whereas Protopapas (1998) listed 157 Sanskrit schools there. The young girls start when they are nine to eleven years old, which means that they have already spent some time in a modern school, sometimes even in an English medium school before coming to Varanasi. What could drive parents of a upper-middle socio-economic standing, living in big cities, to send their daughters to such a school? The Sanskrit school is subsidized by donors but the parents still have to pay school fees, even though it is not a significant amount. The fact that the young girls who come to this establishment have been initiated, that they wear the sacred thread (*janeu*) like the twice-born, and that they change their family name to 'Arya'[13] (respectable) could be an indicator. Indeed, in this school, the Brahmin students are a minority. Therefore it is possible that parents of lower castes, who wish to move up the social ladder, imitate the higher castes (Brahmin) and send their children to a school of this type. In specialized literature, this attempt at social mobility is called *sanskritization* (Deliège, 1993). On the other hand, this school educates the girls up to the BA level and a large number of them become teachers and stay in this 'monastic' system; and therefore the parents do not have to provide them with a dowry, because they will not get married. Lastly, knowing that the school is mainly funded by a fundamentalist group (Arya Samaj), it is possible that parents who share the same opinions send their daughters to this school to perpetuate the tradition or to promote a more orthodox Hinduism.

The public funding of a large part of the Sanskrit schools, already discussed in the article by Mishra and Vajpayee (this volume) seems to be changing the course of traditional education in India in an irreversible manner. In order to survive, most of the Sanskrit schools have to tie up with universities, thus becoming dependent on their administration and their subsidies (Protopapas, 1998). So, the teachers of traditional schools who used to be respected in the past are now nothing more than government employees, whose sole mission is to prepare their students to succeed in a series of exams, which will make them competitive on the job market. The teachers merely go over the syllabus and no longer have the time to develop anything. Pundit Joshi, interviewed by Protopapas (1998: 202), describes this situation well: 'Our biggest problem is that we are no longer well educated in our traditions, nor are we receiving an acceptable Western education. It's more like a mix of both...we have reached the point of a half-baked education'. For Protopapas, this hybrid Sanskrit education is wearing itself out trying to serve two educational systems, which are wholly contradictory: one trying to develop the personality of the youth at an intellectual and spiritual level and the other seeking to give them financial autonomy and material well-being. According to her, Sanskrit education seems to be directing itself, more and more, towards teaching a Western kind of curriculum, thus losing its ties with tradition and religion.

CONCLUSION

Previously, we have seen that there is a great choice of schools and pedagogical institutions in India and that public schooling is far from being standardized. With these two case studies, we realize that Sanskrit education is also a very complex phenomenon, which is in the midst of a transformation. On the one hand, we have a school that is meant only for girls, which blends fundamentalism and feminist activity and which teaches the girls how to use arms as well knitting needles. On the other hand, we have a school that is trying its best to face administrative and financial problems simultaneously trying to keep its spirit alive. It is very difficult in these conditions to foresee what the future of Sanskrit education will be. Veer Bhadra Mishra, a highly respected pundit in Varanasi, who is also a hybrid of both forms of education (he is in charge of the *Sankat Mochan* temple and is also the engineer who developed the system of purification of the Ganges), doubts the effectiveness of Sanskrit education in contemporary society. For him, Sanskrit education is incapable of competing with the humanist and scientific approach of modern Indian education and it does not prepare the youth in any way for the world that surrounds them. However, the wealth of the educational practices, whether they be individualized teaching, the practice of concentration and silence, the link between current events and ancient texts in the boys' school or working in groups, the use of debates and discussions as a form of learning, learning Sanskrit with the Pānini method in the girl's school, all seem much more appropriate to us for the development of young Indians than the education that is imparted in many modern schools (learning by rote, classes of more than fifty students, absent teachers, lecturing, and so on). Researchers in educational sciences would also have a lot to learn from these ancient practices, adapted and perfected over thousands of years.

NOTES

1. Group of texts belonging to the Vedic Revelation, that preach the release from rebirths and show the path to the absolute (Biardeau, 1995: 300).
2. One of the lowest castes. In the hierarchy of the castes, this comes just after the untouchables dalits. Besides, it is forbidden for the *śûdra* to listen to or to recite the Veda.
3. Myth explaining the origin of menstruation amongst women.
4. Deliège (1993: 32) thinks that in the beginning of the Christian era, the system was already in place in its current form.
5. Henry Stewart Reid, Report on Indigenous Education and Vernacular Schools, Agra: Secundar Orphan Press, 1852.
6. Study by Sir Thomas Munro for the province of Madras, published in 1826 and study by W. Adam for Bengal and Bihar published in 1835. These two studies have been largely described in the work of Shri Dharampal (1983), *The Beautiful Tree*, Delhi: Biblia Impex. Nivedita, Biswas and Agrawal probably refer to it, even if they don't quote it.
7. Directed by Professor P. Dasen FAPSE, University of Geneva in collaboration with Professor R.C. Mishra, Banaras Hindu University, subsidy of Swiss National Research Foundation.
8. In the documentary 'On the road to Ganga', aired by Arte, a French and German cultural TV channel on 22 April 2003.
9. The *ghats* are made up of large terraces and stairs, alongside the river Ganges where pilgrims come to bathe.
10. This work of the famous grammarian being divided into eight parts (Filliozat, 2002).
11. The vice-principal has the habit of challenging the male pundits when she represents the school during religious debates on topics such as the practice of *sati* the woman sacrifices herself on the *pyre* of her dead husband or the right of women to become pundits.
12. See article 'Women Priest for the Jet Age', *Times of India*, New Delhi, 8 September 2003. Available online at http://timesofindia.indiatimes.com/cms.dll/html/uncomp/articleshow?art_id=13804983 (downloaded on 21 May 2008)
13. The name *Arya* allows them, once they have finished their studies, to perform rituals outside the school.

REFERENCES

Biardeau, M. 1995. *L'hindouisme*. Paris: Flammarion.
Biswas, A. and S.P. Agrawal. 1986. *Development of Education in India: A Historical Survey of Educational Documents Before and After Independence*. New Delhi: Concept Publishing Company.

Bouglé, C. 1935. *Essai sur le régime des castes.* 3ᵉ édition. Paris: Presses universitaires de France.

Bose, M. 2000. *Faces of the Feminine in Ancient, Medieval, and Modern India.* Oxford: Oxford University Press.

Clark, N. 2006. 'Education in India. World Education News and Reviews (WENR).' Available online at http://www.wes.org/ewenr/06feb/practical. htm (downloaded on 16 October 2006).

Deliège, R. 1993. *Le système des castes.* Paris: PUF, collection Que sais-je?.

Filliozat, P.S. 2002. *Le Sanskrit.* 2nd édition. Paris: PUF, collection Que sais-je?

Gupta Gombrich, S. 2000. 'The Goddess, Women, and Their Rituals in Hinduism', in M. Bose (ed.), *Faces of the Feminine in Ancient, Medieval, and Modern India,* pp. 87–106. Oxford: Oxford University Press.

Kak, S. 2001. 'The Beautiful Tree', *Sulekha Columns,* 22 May 2001. Available online at http://www.geocities.com/ifihome/articles/sk003.html (down loaded on 14 July 2008).

Kumar, N. 2000. *Lessons from Schools: The History of Education in Banaras.* New Delhi: Sage Publications.

Michaels, A. 2001. *The Pandit: Traditional Scholarship in India.* New Delhi: Manohar.

Mishra, R.C. 1988. 'Learning Strategies Among Children in Modern and Traditional Schools', *Indian Psychologist,* 5: 17–24.

Mishra, R.C. and P.R. Dasen. 2004. 'The Influence of Schooling on Cogniture Development: A Review of Research in India', in B.N. Setiadi, A. Supratiknya, W.J. Lonner and Y.H. Poortinga (eds), *Ongoing Themes in Psychology and Culture,* pp. 207–222. Yogyakarta: Kanisius.

Mookerji, R. 1969. *Ancient Indian Education.* Delhi: Motilal Banarsidass.

Nivedita, K.B. 1998. *The Destruction of the Indian System of Education.* Paper adapted from a speech given under the auspices of Vivekananda Study Circle, IIT-Madras, Madras, January 1998. Available online at http://www.geocities.com/ifihome/articles/kbn001.html (downloaded on 14 July 2008).

Protopapas, J. 1998. 'Tradition in Transition: Sanskrit Education in Varanasi, India', *World and I,* 9: 200–03.

Pollak, S. 1982. *Traditional Indian Education.* Papers from the Bernard Van Leer Foundation Project on Human Potential. Cambridge, MA: Harvard Graduate School of Education.

Reagan, T. 2000. *Non-Western Educational Traditions.* Mahwah, NJ: Lawrence Erlbaum.

Renou, L. 2001. *L'hindouisme.* 14th édition. Paris: PUF, collection Que sais-je?

Walker, B. 1983. *Hindu World.* Delhi: Munshiram Manoharlal.

12
BUDDHIST EDUCATION AS A CHALLENGE TO MODERN SCHOOLING

NILIMA CHANGKAKOTI AND MARIE ANNE BROYON

INTRODUCTION

> *Whether a religion or a philosophy, Buddhism is*
> *most certainly an education.*

The legend has it that Buddha was born with a wheel imprinted on the sole of his feet and the palms of his hands, which indicated his predestination to be either a great conqueror or a great educator (Eckel, 2003). A wise man predicted that the child would grow up to be a holy man, rather than following his father in being a ruler. Suddhodana, father of Gautama Buddha, tried to prevent this from happening by making sure that the prince lived a sequestered, protected life, ignorant of the world outside. The discovery of the outer world and the 'four signs': old age, illness, death, and asceticism led him to renounce home and family and leave following the path of a beggar monk (*Shramana*). This departure is re-enacted every time a monk takes his vows. However, Buddha taught the middle path a path of moderation away from the extremes of self-indulgence and self-mortification. The middle way also marks Buddhism's confrontations with other religions and philosophies, as it appears for instance in the dialogue of a French Buddhist monk with his philosopher father (Revel and Ricard, 1999). The monk argues that there is no necessity of choosing between 'scientific pursuit' and 'spiritual quest', in the sense of renouncing one for the other, the middle way would entail making the best of both approaches: in the present case, engage in scientific pursuit without relegating the individual quest for wisdom. The middle way can also account for the blending of Buddhism with pre-existing religions in the countries to which it spread (for example, Bön religion in Tibet, Taoism in China) as well as the adoption of the vernacular, including for higher learning.

From the beginning, starting from the first council at Sarnath, where Buddha set the wheel of *Dharma* into motion, the early disciples were organized in a learning community (*Sangha*) under the guidance of 'the teacher of men and gods' (*Sattha devanussanam*, one of the names given to Siddhartha Gautama). They wandered from place to place, teaching the best part of the year, settling down during the monsoon period, which was devoted to study. One of the educational functions of the *Sangha* was also to provide basic education to the laity.

Subsidiary to education, ignorance and knowledge are central notions in Buddhism, although they are not defined in the 'western' sense. Ignorance is not lack of knowledge but an expression of the human condition. Knowledge is not synonymous to accumulation of information, but the gradual identification of the workings of the mind, in order to cut through its limitations. The teacher's task is to help advance on this path towards freeing oneself of the human condition of suffering. The teacher thus becomes a very important figure. Killing a teacher, is for instance, considered a worse crime than killing one's parents. The teacher–student relationship is well documented in Buddhist texts.

In the wake of growing interest in Buddhism in the West, researchers in education have lately found a source of inspiration in the Buddhist educational views, as a model of philosophy of education (Kojevnokova, 2004), in an intercultural perspective comparing the Buddhist principles of education (in particular, meditation) and Western educational science (Keuffer, 1991), as a way to renew and improve the student–teacher relationship (Craig, 1996; Filliot, 2004), and to provide trainee teachers with alternative lenses (Johnson, 2005). Johnson, an Indian teacher who emigrated to Australia, gives an interesting account of how the 'majority world' can contribute a novel answer to the pressure to 'internationalize the curriculum', and help develop a 'pedagogy of respect' by confronting Western and non-Western traditions of enlightenment. This 'pedagogy of respect' avoids cultural hierarchy, respects diversity, provides students with 'multi-, cross- and trans-cultural approaches to learning and teaching', promotes debate and reflectivity as well as a holistic approach of human growth (Johnson, 2005: 11).

This type of research is generally conducted by people who are able to adopt a combined 'emic' and 'etic' approach to the field of non-Western educational philosophies, either because they are practicing Buddhists in the West or because, born and raised in a Hindu or Buddhist environment, they have emigrated to the West, and sought to integrate both traditions.

Due to the strong focus of Buddhism on education, not only for monks but also for the laity, it seems that before compulsory schooling was introduced, the literacy rates were higher in Buddhist countries. However, the development of modern schooling following a Western model led to a drastic decrease of laic Buddhist schooling in the same countries. The *Sangha* has become one of the least used educational resources in Buddhist countries. Only people lacking economic opportunities, living in geographically isolated areas, or, more rarely, professing strong 'old-world' values still benefit from the educational functions of the monastery (Nithiyanandam, 2004).

In this chapter, we will try to show that Buddhism presents strong arguments for a successful blending with modern schooling, especially maybe in the light of the 'value crisis' affecting the latter. These arguments can be found in the historical development of Buddhism in India, especially the golden age of the great universities, in the reflective skills (as acquired by meditation and debate) fostered both by the Sanskrit and Buddhist traditions, but also in some specific features of Buddhist education.

The last part of the chapter will investigate the challenge to modern schooling in the case of the schooling of Buddhists in exile with the example of the Tibetan Children's Village (TCV) in Dharamsala and the spreading of Buddhism in the West. Could modern schooling, beyond the (re)introduction of 'moral' values, integrate Buddhist principles of education, as an alternative (or complementary) approach to the quest for new teaching and learning methods? In Buddhist countries, this could help reduce the distance between the population and a still very Westernized school system.

Buddhism has theorized education and developed an age long practice, why not benefit from this experience? How to do so is however not a simple question. Is it possible to go beyond just adding Buddhist studies to the curriculum? Will specific features like the teacher–student relationship or the art of debate resist the imperatives of modern life?

We have chosen to investigate these questions in the birth land of Buddhism rather than in other Buddhist countries, for different reasons: to be able to 'compare' with Sanskrit schooling and because Mahayana (great vehicle) Buddhism, which developed first in India and was then imported into Tibet, gives greater importance to the attainment of enlightenment by laymen than the Theravada (Sayings of the elders, small vehicle) tradition and has further developed debate. Sri Lanka and Thailand, where experiences of creating Buddhist lay schools have taken place (which we will briefly mention) are Theravada. In other countries to which the Mahayana tradition has spread, like China, Korea, Japan, and Taiwan, Buddhism has been transformed into a distinctly local institution, syncretic Confucian orthodoxy in China and Taiwan, a mix of Confucianism and Shintoism in Japan (Hall and Roger, 1998; Lusthaus, 2006; Maraldo, 1998). Although the teacher–student relationship is important in Chan and Zen Buddhism, which stresses the intuitive, personal, experiential, non-textual aspects rather than the more scholarly ones, it takes different forms, for instance as related in Zen tales, the sometimes violent[1] disruption of mental and emotional habits in order to eventually provoke the sudden enlightenment of the student.

DEVELOPMENT OF BUDDHIST EDUCATION IN INDIA

Some authors assert that Buddhism is a phase of Hinduism (Londhe, 2006; Mahajan, 2006). Without going so far, we have to admit that Buddhist education is deeply rooted in the pre-existing Hindu system of education. Besides, Buddha was himself the product of the then prevailing Hindu educational systems. Traditional iconography usually shows him at school, as a Brahmin teacher instructs him along with three other boys or as he practices writing or learns music (Londhe, 2006).

Buddhism developed along with Jainism, but because of the spread of its doctrine wide and far by itinerant monks, it became a very proselyte religion. The specificity of Buddhism's expansion is a different evolution and a different adaptation according to periods and locations. In India, Buddhism flourished with the development of cities, urban kingdoms and nobility. Adepts of ancient Buddhism were mainly recruited in the big families of the nobility and the rich middle class but Buddhism was never socially exclusive (Weber, 2003).

The Buddhist system of education became monastic probably not very long after the Buddha's death (Weber, 2003). Before giving birth to large-scale monastic universities, the training of monks was organized, within monastic life, like the Sanskrit schools (*Brahmacārin*) of that time: a single individual teacher with his small group of pupils. During the rainy season, the itinerant monks who needed space for meditation, study and discussion, had to take shelter in protected places. That is how, in the area of Karnataka, cave-resorts (*Guhālayas*) came into existence. They were built out of rock in order to accommodate numerous monks, students and the laity on special occasions (Kamat, 2005).The first caves were quite simple but the later ones, like Karla, Ajanta and Ellora (Maharashtra), were decorated with sculptural ornaments. The latter were also very well organized: double storeyed, prayer halls, meditation centres and hostels, all in the same structure.

Early monastic education seems to have focused on hymnology and the fundamental Buddhist doctrines, on the rules of discipline (*Vinaya*) and on the accounts of the previous lives of the Buddha (Nithiyanandam, 2004). At their ordination, the neophytes were assigned a spiritual guide (*Upajjhāya*) and a senior monk as a regular instructor (*Ācārya*). They practiced frequent recitation and, on special occasions, chanting with the whole congregation. The debates on doctrines seem to have been already quite significant in those early days. The qualified monks were free to argue, dispute and debate about the *Dharma* and the *Vinaya* and each of them was expected to think, reason and decide for himself on this matter (Nithiyanandam, 2004).

The development of Buddhism favoured the expansion of literacy and education on a large scale. Gradually, as the monastic institutions grew in size and complexity, the pattern of education expanded. Oral transmission was still encouraged but since the apparition of texts, their copy was often used to help memorization—it was also a way to constitute libraries. Children were allowed to attend temple-school at the age of seven (considered to be the best age to start schooling)—where they started their education by learning the alphabet. After mastering the alphabet, the pupils learned grammar, arithmetic, some elements of a skilled profession (painting, carpentry, weaving and sculpture) and some principles of mechanical arts, reasoning, medicine, the doctrine of karma and the degrees of religious attainment came gradually afterwards. This curriculum, designed to train Buddhist monks, became open to lay students. The impact of such an education with an emphasis on medicine and vocational skills was very important for the whole population (Kamat, 2005).

As Buddhism became more popular, the number of monasteries increased and monastic universities, like Nalanda (contemporary Bihar) or Valabi (Karnataka), arose close to big cities. These institutions were supported by royal grants or by noblemen and tradesmen. Hsuan Tsang, a Chinese pilgrim who visited India between AD 629–646, reported that Nalanda University employed about 1,500 teachers for 10,000 students. Nalanda became famous for its 'Schools of Discussion' and started to attract students not only from all over India but from the Far East and later on, from Tibet (Nithiyanandam, 2004). Buddhist scholasticism certainly began at this period when the monks and the nuns had to become more competitive in terms of pedagogy.

During the 13th century, it seems that the rise of Hinduism weakened people's interest for Buddhism. Deprived of the support of the nobility, the Buddhist monasteries became very vulnerable and when Muslim invaders destroyed the last big monasteries, the influence of Buddhism in its region of origin declined very quickly (Eckel, 2003).

Sanskrit education versus Buddhist education

Ancient Sanskrit education essentially took place in the house of the master (*Gurukul*) and admission was almost strictly reserved for Brahmins (that is, only the elite received an education). The sacred teachings were transmitted in Sanskrit, the language considered sacred for the transmission of the Brahminical scriptures and rites. The students paid *Gurudakshina*, a contribution after the completion of their studies (if not, they worked for their guru). The master taught all the subjects and there was no specialization. Finally, the countryside environment, which was one of the characteristics of these schools, did not favour the expansion of a small school under an individual teacher into a large educational institution.

With Buddhism, education shifted from the home of the master to the monastery and to universities. Monasteries and universities were built very close to towns. Buddhists never believed in caste distinctions and students from all castes were admitted to Buddhist *Sangha* and Universities. In India, even untouchables and women were allowed to join the Buddhist *Sangha* where they were given opportunities to study. Sanskrit was taught in Buddhist Universities but the language used for transmitting sacred teachings was Pali, the language of the masses. Admission was open not only to monks and nuns but also to seekers of knowledge, who did not want to become monks, it was even open to non-Buddhists and education was free of charge for all. Buddhist education offered not only personal and spiritual development but a professional training (carpenter, painter, sculptor, and so on).

ARGUMENTS FOR A SUCCESSFUL BLENDING OF BUDDHIST EDUCATION WITH MODERN SCHOOLING

Historical arguments

Buddhism has shown throughout its development its tolerance for diversity and capacity of acculturation. Its transmission has always been a pacific one, more in the nature of merging than conquest, with the adoption of the vernacular (a recommendation of Buddha himself), and the taking on of local specificities. It does not mean that war never played a role: Emperor Ashoka's conversion to Buddhism followed his realization and consecutive rejection of the atrocities of war. War in Tibet contributed to the return of Buddhism to India and to the renewed transmission in the West with the Tibetan refugees.

The bridges to and from laity are kept open. As seen above, in the 'golden age', the great Buddhist universities also became the centres for higher secular learning in India, open to lay students. Moreover, the *Sangha*'s interdependence with the laity keeps it connected to the world. The *Sangha* depends on the lay community for it's material subsistence, in exchange, monks provide basic literacy skills, medical attention, perform rituals either at the monastery or at the homes of the people. However, the conflict between the 'this-worldly' objectives of modern schooling (access to vocational training, material subsistence, social status, and so on) and the 'other-worldly' objectives of Buddhist education (transcendence, individual development) may partly explain why Buddhist countries did not take more advantage of these traditional resources when developing generalized schooling. The colonial aftermath of an education modelled after Western academics may be another explanation. The two systems exist generally in parallel. Nonetheless, in the last century Buddhist countries like Sri Lanka and Thailand have known a tentative revival of the formal educational role of the monastery, although it seems to have taken the form of a 'contamination' by the modern aspects to the detriment of the more interesting features of traditional education (Nithiyanandam, 2004). Thailand in the second half of the 20th century has for instance tried to reintroduce Buddhism in the education system: offering pre-school temple education as an alternative for poor people and introducing Buddhist ethics in general schooling to counterbalance 'western imperialism' (Sirikanchana, 1998). In Sri Lanka, Henry Olcott, co-founder of the Theosophical Society helped in promoting Buddhist native schools like Mahinda College in Galle, Ananda, and Nalanda Colleges in Colombo as early as 1924, as an alternative to missionary education under British rule.

The question of women's place was tackled early on in Buddhism. Although reluctant at first, convinced by his disciple Ananda, Buddha created a nun's order under the guidance of his aunt (see the *Therigata*, or *songs of the elder nuns*). This does not mean that nuns had equal access to higher Buddhist education, they were generally confined to practicing rituals and did not engage in the study of Buddhist texts or become teachers. This has been changing recently for Tibetan nuns, under the encouragement of the Dalai Lama (Dechen, 1999). Several nunneries have been opened, where nuns can study, up to the *Geshe* degree,[2] the highest level of religious studies, if such is their wish.

Educational arguments

A rich curriculum

The traditional framework for Buddhist education consists of the ten aspects of knowledge (*vidayas*), five minor aspects (poetry, astrology, terminology or rhetoric, performing arts, naming), and five major aspects (creative arts, healing, sound or philosophy of language, logic and metaphysics, including the practice of meditation). These fields of knowledge are all aimed at improving the human being's understanding of himself and his relationship with the environment, in order to cut through the traps of habits and eventually attain freedom from the ignorance and suffering of the human condition. For example, creative arts should help discipline the relationship and expand the communication between the inner and outer world; logic explores conceptual analysis as a remedy for confusion, and so on.

These aspects were the basis of the curriculum of Nalanda University, and can also be found in the present-day curriculum of Naropa institute, an American college in Colorado modelled consciously after the Gupta era of Nalanda University. The general goal of Naropa is to develop an intuitive relationship to knowledge, and the *vidayas* are taught with the intention to understand and apply their principles to contemporary curriculum, teaching, and learning (Naropa core program, 2005; Nithiyanandam, 2004).

Diversified teaching aids

Teachings aids are numerous. Moral education which is the first stage of Buddhist education (philosophy and religious instruction occurring only at a later stage) is carried out with the help of stories, like the *Jatakas* (stories of the Buddha's previous lives). We have seen with the *Vidayas* that metaphorical thinking and the approaches provided by poetry and theatre complete abstract reasoning. Monks have at all times produced verse and literary work. Buddhist education seems also to have been pioneering in visual aids: there is an account of the use of diagrams in Buddha's time, and the sculptures on temple walls also had this function.

As a rule, any incident or encounter is used as an opportunity to teach, which is often the case in oral transmission. However, Buddhism cannot be considered an oral tradition based on texts as Goody (1993) discusses it for the *Vedanta*. The appropriation of root texts goes further than rote learning and recitation, the texts are commented, discussed and analysis and commentary has been put into writing very early by the monks.

Diversified methods

The Buddha's teaching cannot be reduced to lecturing, he started as a principle from the known, and led the audience or student step by step to the point he wished to make, taking care to ascertain that each was understood. He used examples from everyday life. Discovery methods were also an option, as is shown in the story of the grieving mother who was sent to beg for mustard seed in a home which had not known death, discovering in the process the universality of death (Quentric-Séguy, 2003). He resorted to maieutic questioning with individuals and when talking to a group, adapted to the nature and composition of the public. The same idea will thus be found expounded in many different ways (Nithiyanandam, 2004).

In Buddhist education, individual differences are taken into account. For instance, individualized meditation courses will be developed according to each one's psychological characteristics. Collective teaching is rare, or a recent development, used rather as remediation—the learning process is personal, under the supervision of one's teacher.

The traditional pattern of one monk giving a lesson or sermon knows some variations too. Several 'two voiced' alternatives exist (*sermons from two seats*). Two monks take the floor: one will recite a sutra and the other will illustrate it with background information and supporting narratives; or they will both conduct an impromptu debate; or impersonate a dialogue between mythical or historical figures, and so on.

Teacher–student relationship

Teacher–student relationship is at the core of Buddhist pedagogy, lay or religious. It is also often what gets lost and is missed when modernization attempts are made (cf. Eckel writing about the Central Institute for Higher Tibetan studies in Sarnath [in present day Uttar Pradesh, India], in Pollak, 1983).

In monastic education, although a student may have several teachers, he will have a main teacher responsible for him. The teacher is a facilitator, a guide, which in no way means he plays a passive role. As the finality of learning is not knowledge in itself, but the practice of knowledge, he is supposed to embody wisdom and be a source of inspiration for his student. This is often what attracts foreigners to the Buddhist way, people who seem to be what they teach (Revel and Ricard, 1999). The following metaphors could apply to the dangers of modern Western education: being 'a cowherd looking after cattle for other people's benefit', that is, store knowledge without effort to practice what was learnt, and being 'a beautiful flower with no fragrance' as applied to learning without ethical sensitivity and moral principles (Nithiyanandam, 2004: 119, 136).

Texts (*Sigalovada sutta*) define the duties of pupils, which are similar to those in the *gurukul* system, but also the teachers' responsibilities. The pupil should attend to his teacher's comfort, treat him with all due respect, listen and obey instructions; the teacher should show his pupil affection, train him in good manners and virtue; instruct him, speak well of him to others and guard him from danger (Nithiyanandam, 2004: 121).

Ideally, the respect due to the teacher by the pupil does not entail unquestioned acceptance of anything on the authority of the teacher as we can see in the following text:

> Do not believe in what you have heard. Do not believe in traditions, because they have been handed down for many generations. Do not believe in anything because it is rumoured and spoken of by many. Do not believe merely because it accords with your scriptures. Do not believe in conjectures. Do not believe anything by mere inference. Do not accept anything by merely considering the reasons. Do not believe anything because it agrees with your preconceived notions. Do not believe anything because it seems acceptable. Do not believe anything on the authority of the teachers or elders thinking that they are respected. But when you know for yourself, after observation and analysis, that these things are moral, blameless, praised by the wise and, when performed and undertaken, conduce to well-being and happiness of one and all, then accept it and live up to it. (*Kamala sutta*, Nithiyanandam, 2004: 122)

The art of debate

The emphasis on debate is another important feature of Buddhist education, inherited from the Sanskrit practice of debate, and developed with some innovations by Tibetan traditions, especially the *Geluk* school. Debate is a way of learning, of appropriating commentary. In the *Geluk* school it takes up a lot of study time (ten hours a day in Tibet, five hours in exile). It is also the way learning is assessed, up to the final *Geshe* examinations. For teachers it is part of their continuing education and a lifelong learning process.

Tibetan debate is a lively (even physical) dialectical practice that provides those engaged in it with valuable intellectual resources (Dreyfus, 2003). It is one of the ways of approaching one of the *Vidayas*: logic. Logic here is not in the Western[3] sense of deductive reasoning, the goal of debate being to prove the formal validity of reasoning, but in the Indian sense of proving its soundness.

For the Tibetan tradition, debate is a dialectic of commentary (authority) and debate (room for personal inquiry and appropriation within tradition). The question follows: does debate have a critical dimension, is it really a mode of inquiry? Answers will differ according to lamas and whether they focus on helping students internalize the truth of Buddhist doctrine or on fostering the capacity of thinking on their own as in the above citation of the *Kamala sutta*.

Dreyfus (2003) in his book on the Tibetan scholastic tradition. *The Sound of Two Hands Clapping*, refers to the sound that opens and punctuates debate as compared to the mystical 'one hand clapping'. He relates his own experience:

> When I started to study the great texts, my teachers would often ask me if I had any questions. I often did, for these texts were difficult and at many points obviously needed clarification. But these immediate questions were not what my teachers had in mind. They wanted to know whether I was able to go beyond what the text was saying, whether I was able to question the concepts within the text rather than accept them as self-evident. (p. 268)

He defends the point of view that Tibetan Buddhist intellectuals are 'vigorous thinkers in their own right' (p. 9), and debate a practice of inquiry with intrinsic worth. He himself noticed the difference between his training in outspoken critical thinking and that of his fellow students when he went over to Western academics after leaving monasticism once he had completed his *Geshe* examinations. He made teachers and/or students uncomfortable when trying to engage in debate.

SCHOOLING OF BUDDHISTS IN EXILE

Culture and identity

The education of Tibetan Buddhists in exile in India (and elsewhere) faces a double responsibility: to maintain and perpetuate a cultural tradition in exile that is threatened in the country of its origin, and that goes for general as well as monastic education. There are currently eighty Tibetan schools in India, Nepal, and Bhutan which can be grouped into the following categories depending on which institution funds and administers them: the CTSA schools (Central Tibetan Schools Administration Schools), and the autonomous schools, among them the TCV (Tibetan Children's Village) (Pema, 2005).

The mission these schools have in common is to preserve, promote and renew the Tibetan cultural heritage and provide children with the best of both modern and Tibetan education. Young generations should be able to keep a strong Tibetan identity, have the capacity to integrate into modern-day India and be prepared to bring back Tibetan culture to Tibet should it one day be possible. Lately the educational policy has been to put a greater emphasis on Tibetan culture: teaching material in Tibetan is being produced, spiritual teachers recruited, and so on.

In the case of the TCV, the Tibetanization programme is on its way since 1986. The proceedings of the sixteenth TCV Education development committee meeting reveal a trend towards improving the integration of modern and Tibetan education: they stress the importance of the teacher–student interaction inside and outside the classroom, the need to strengthen value education, as well as the shift to child-centred and experiential learning approaches. These guidelines have of course implications in terms of teacher training: the TCV has created a teacher-training centre, which provides Montessori and language (Tibetan) training (TCV, 2001).

Campbell (1999), an American teacher working with the Multiple Intelligence (MI) approach, was invited to the TCV to facilitate a workshop for the teaching staff. His observations from an outsider's point of view show traditional (Western) teaching methods coexisting with a focus on Buddhist philosophy:

> The school from early childhood through Grade 12 is quite traditional. Instruction is pedantic with teachers lecturing, students taking notes, and the use of regular exams. But again, the focus in every subject is guided by the foundation of Buddhist philosophy. The literature often concerns stories of saints and avatars. The writing focuses on personal awareness and spiritual growth. Math and science are seen as bodies of knowledge to understand the world in which this incarnation is unfolding, the one where His Holiness, the fourteenth Dalai Lama has joined us, the one where the Buddha himself once walked. Even the artwork of students reflects the imagery and beauty of the spiritual world they experience. (p. 1)

The MI workshop made the teachers realize as Western teachers had, that' even in a homogeneous culture each student may think and learn in a unique way. They discovered that by providing multiple entry points into the content area, more students would be successful' (p. 1). These are precisely features of traditional Buddhist education... Maybe these Tibetan teachers could have made the same realization revisiting their own tradition?

The generation gap

About ten years earlier, Monnier (1989) observed classroom practices and interviewed students and teachers at Dharamsala during field research in the TCV. Like Campbell he reports a rather 'classical' pedagogy. He attended, for instance, a 'debate happening' in front of the whole school, where students were not called upon to practice critical thinking, but delivered a prepared speech, quite far from the traditional Buddhist debate.

One of his main findings was a generation gap: between teachers who had gone to school in Tibet and those who had not, and between young people and elders.

For older teachers educated in Tibet, the spiritual type of student–teacher relationship was missing in the TCV, teachers were no more models. They thought it explained students' bad performances and behaviour, combined with the lack of religious training and the bad influence of Hindi films. Younger teachers did not recognize themselves in the older generation; they had other aspirations. One of them reported literally not understanding one of his elders, because of his traditional metaphorical, indirect and ironical way of talking. Due to respect to elders, disagreements were however rarely publicly expressed.

One teacher educated both in Tibet and an Indian public school took another stand: for him lack of respect towards elders was not a new issue. What made the difference was the exile situation, being projected from one moment to another in an entirely new environment. This can lead to a fixation on the past, which younger teachers and students often reproached their elders with.

This tension between tradition and modernity is also felt in the monastic world (Dreyfus, 2003), all the more so with the new refugee flows from Tibet. Some encourage the process of accommodation to modernity (introducing modern subjects in the curriculum for example), like the Dalai Lama; others resist it, fearing that monks will be lured away. Younger monks find the curriculum too long, criticize the emphasis on debate because it does not have any direct application to the real world, and so on. They see their studies as an access to a monastic career, and not as a lifelong enterprise towering in the ultimate *Geshe* title.

The science programme for monks created in 1998 at the instigation of the Dalai Lama illustrates one of these attempts to bridge modernity and tradition. The now yearly workshop is intended as a dialogue between Western science and Buddhist philosophy in the tradition of philosophical enquiry as it was practiced at Nalanda (McDonald, 2003). One of the aims is to develop a scientific vocabulary in Tibetan. There also, the project has encountered resistance of more traditional monasteries.

THE SPREAD OF BUDDHISM IN THE WEST

Non-monastic Buddhist education for Westerners

Tibetan refugees among others have contributed to the spread of Buddhism in the West. Apart from the meditation and philosophy courses for adults, some centres have started offering 'Buddhist Sunday schools' for children, debate activities for adolescents and engaging in a reflection about how to provide children with a basic Buddhist education (Carey, 1991).

The Naropa institute mentioned above is an interesting experiment of blending Buddhist and modern approaches to education. It was founded thirty years ago in Boulder, Colorado, by a prominent exiled Tibetan monk (Chogyam Trungpa Rinpoche) responsible for much of the rising profile of Tibetan Buddhism in the West. Naropa began as a summer institute; then became a graduate programme in 1999. It presents itself as a secular university: Buddhist-inspired but open to all students, offering a 'contemplative education', which blends academic theory with artistic practice. Some students think Naropa does not prepare them for the outer world, others find that it provides adequate education 'If you want to be a writer, teacher, therapist, or social activist' (Hsu, 2005: 44).

Socially engaged Buddhism

A further argument for bridging Buddhist education with Western schooling could be the socially engaged nature of Buddhism, another area where the tensions between modernist and traditionalist views within Buddhism can be observed. Henry (2006) addresses the question of socially engaged Buddhism by investigating Western Buddhism as 'religious identities in transition' (p. 2) beyond the dichotomy between immigrant (more traditional, devotional, and ritualistic) and convert (more meditative, rational, and scholarly) congregations. The 'otherworldly' view of Buddhism as presented by Weber (1958) seems contradicted by forerunners of an engaged Buddhist ethic like Olcott, who founded the Buddhist Theosophical Society in British Ceylon in the 1920s and thus actively participated in the resistance against the colonial christianization of the population, or Ambedkar's Marxist inspired neo-Buddhist revival in India in the 1950s (Omvedt, 2003), as well as by the Buddhist support in the United Kingdom for the 'stop the war campaign' over the Iraq war (Henry, 2006).

However, within the area of socially engaged Buddhism itself, one can distinguish various practices on a continuum between tradition and modernity. The traditionalist view holds that modern forms of Buddhism are essentially continuous with traditional forms and that the spiritual life of a Buddhist has always included social engagement; what changes, is the levels of articulation. The Dalai Lama's actions toward bridging the Buddhist way of life and the demands and developments of modern life represents such a 'continuity within tradition'. On the other hand, the modernist view considers the need to reform Buddhism, either by recovering '"pure" Buddhism from its superstitious village forms' (King, 2004, in Henry, 2006), or by improving it under the influence of Western thought. Ambedkar, the Indian Dalit leader, who considered Buddhism a challenge to Brahminism, as a world-transforming religion and a fundamental alternative to Marxism (Omvedt, 2003) would be a representative of the reformist trend. For him the *Sangha* was the ideal of a communist society and he reinterpreted Buddhism to the extent that he rewrote parts of the Pali canon and added new ones.

CONCLUSION

Is a 'real' blending of traditional Buddhist approaches and modern education possible? And what would that imply in terms of curriculum and teacher training? In monasteries, the introduction of modern subjects gives way to a curriculum in two separate parts, as has been the case in other religious traditions. When attempts towards integration occur in a lay setting, the tendency is to add specific content: philosophy and spirituality and not necessarily to adopt the Buddhist teaching and learning methods. We have seen that even in monastic education some young monks resent the time cost and lack of connection with the outer world of a learning method like debate.

However, one fact appears clearly, the world of Buddhist education, both in the East and the West is certainly not static. Experiments and evolution are taking place and involve a South–North dimension. The fact that Buddhism is first of all an education, open to other faiths, certainly participates in this evolution.

If we return to the example of the Tibetan Children's Village, it appears there is a movement towards integrating traditional and modern approaches in a Buddhist environment. It would be interesting to investigate the effects of the new educational guidelines in terms of identity issues, teacher training and metacognition, allowing thus for a comparison with research on Sanskrit schools. A comparison with the effects of Buddhist education (for example debate) on young Westerners, in a non-Buddhist society could as well be of interest.

NOTES

1. Blows, shouts or paradoxical statements such as 'if you meet the Buddha on the road, kill him!' (Lusthaus, 2006).
2. *Geshe* is an academic degree for scholars in the *Sakya* and *Geluk* schools of Tibetan Buddhism, a title, which means 'scholarly spiritual friend'. The curriculum consists of six subjects and takes between fifteen to twenty years to complete. The examination is based upon one's proficiency in dialectical debate on these areas—the core texts and commentaries are memorized by the applicant, in order to be able to refer to them as necessary. There are four *Geshe* degrees, the titles are ranked according to the kind of examination that candidates undergo (Dreyfus, 2003).

3. Debate is a feature of most scholastic traditions. It was, for example, a central element of the Western scholastic culture in the Middle Ages.

REFERENCES

Campbell, B. 1999. 'Multiple Intelligences Reaches the Tibetan Children's Village', *New Horizons for Learning*. Available online at http://www.newhorizons.org/trans/international/campbell2.htm (downloaded in February 2007).

Carey, P. 1991. 'UK Buddhist Education: A Dhammic Perspective', a report on a weekend conference held at Sharpham House, Devon, 6–9 June. *Forest Sangha Newsletter*, October 91, 2534, 18. Available online at http://www.fsnewsletter.org/(downloaded on 15 July 2008).

Craig, R. P. 1996. 'Student-Teacher Relationship: A Buddhist Perspective', *Clearing House*, 69(5), 285–86.

Dechen, L. 1999. Systematic Education in Dolma Ling Leading to Gender Equality. *Journal of Religious Culture*, 27–07: 1–5. Frankfurt am Main: Institut für Wissenschaftliche Irenik, Johann Wolfgang Goethe-Universität.

Dreyfus, G. B. J. 2003. *The Sounds of Two Hands Clapping. The Education of a Tibetan Buddhist Monk*. Berkeley, CA: University of California Press.

Eckel, M. D. 2003. *Bouddhisme: origines, croyances, rituels, textes sacrés*. Paris: Gründ.

Filliot, P. 2004. 'L'éducation spirituelle: ou l'autre de la pédagogie. Approche transversale de la relation Maître-Elève dans quatre traditions occidentales et orientale: Boudhisme Zen, Yoga, Christianisme, spiritualité philosophique'. Available online at http://www.barbier-rd.nom.fr/journal/article.php3 ?id_article=337 (downloaded on 20 May 2008).

Goody, J. 1993. *The Interface between the Written and the Oral*. Cambridge: Cambride University Press.

Hall, D. L. and Roger T. Ames. 1998. 'Chinese Philosophy', in E. Craig (ed.), *Routledge Encyclopedia of Philosophy*. London: Routledge. Available online at http://www.rep.routledge.com/article/G001SECT10 (downloaded on 11 November 2006).

Henry, P. 2006. 'The Sociological Implications for Contemporary Buddhism in the United Kingdom: Socially Engaged Buddhism, a Case Study', *Journal of Buddhist Ethics*, 13: 1–23. Available online at http://www.buddhistethics.org/13/henry-article.html (downloaded on 30 May 2008).

Hsu, C. 2005. 'To Learn in the Moment: Naropa University', in *Choosing a School: America's Best Colleges*. Available online at http://www.naropa.edu/news/articles/usnewsreportarticle.pdf (downloaded on 20 May 2008).

Johnson, R. 2005. 'Locating non-western enlightenment texts for a global curriculum', *Intercultural Education*, 17(1): 21–32. Available online at: http://www.ingentaconnect.com/content/routledg/ceji/2006/00000017/00000001/art00002 (downloaded on 20 May 2008).

Kamat, J. 2005. 'Education in Karnataka Trough the Ages. Buddhist System of Education', *Kamat Research Base*, pp. 1–8. Available online at http://www.kamat.com/database/books/kareducation/buddhist_education (downloaded on 20 May 2008).

Keuffer, J. 1991. *Buddhismus und Erziehung*. Münster: Waxmann.

King, R. 2004. 'Cartographies of the Imagination, Legacies of Colonialism: the Discourse of Religion and the Mapping of Indic Traditions', *Evam: Forum on Indian Representations*, 3(1–2): 272–89. Available online at at http://www.samvadindia.com/evam/ (downloaded on 20 May 2008).

Kojevnokova, M. 2004. 'Perspectives on the Interpretation of Buddhism as a Model of Philosophy of Education: Setting the Problem', paper presented at Philosophy of Education Society of Great-Britain, 2004 conference, The Institute of Education, University of London, London, April 2–4. Available online at: http://www.ioe.ac.uk/pesgb/z/Kojevnikova.pdf (downloaded on 20 May 2008).

Londhe, S. 2006. Education in Ancient India. *Hindu Wisdom*. Available online at http://www.hinduwisdom.info/index_news.htm (downloaded on 20 May 2008).

Lusthaus, D. 2006. 'Buddhist Philosophy, Chinese', in E. Craig (ed.), *Routledge Encyclopedia of Philosophy*. London: Routledge. Available online at http://www.rep.routledge.com/article/G002SECT9 (downloaded on 11 November 2006).

Mahajan, V.D. 2006. *Ancient India*. Delhi: S. Chand.

McDonald, A. 2003. 'Standing at the Blackboard', *Science Education Project, Science for Monks*, pp. 1–3. Dharamsala: Library of Tibetan Works and Archives. Avaiblable online at http://www.scienceformonks.org/blackboard (downloaded on 20 May 2008).

Maraldo, J. C. 1998. 'Buddhist Philosophy, Japanese', in E. Craig (ed.), *Routledge Encyclopedia of Philosophy*. London: Routledge. Available online at http://www.rep.routledge.com/article/G101SECT3 (downloaded on 11 November 2006).

Monnier, M.A. 1989. 'Les rites dans une école de réfugiés tibétains en Inde', *Mémoire de diplôme de recherche*, No. 46. Genève: IUED.

Naropa core program. Available online at http://www.naropa.edu/about/index.cfm (downloaded on 20 May 2008).

Nithiyanandam, V. 2004. *Buddhist System of Education*. Delhi: Global Vision.

Omvedt, G. 2003. *Buddhism in India. Challenging Brahmanism and Caste*. New Delhi: Sage Publications.

Pema, J. 2005. 'The Tibetan Children's Village', Paper presented at the 25th International Montessori Congress, Sydney, July 14–17. Available online at http://www.montessori-ami.org/congress/2005sydney/CongressPapersJP. pdf (downloaded on 20 May 2008).

Pollak, S. 1983. 'Ancient Buddhist Education', paper from the Project on Human Potential. Cambridge, MA: Harvard University, Graduate School of Education.

Quentric-Séguy, M. 2003. *Contes des sages de l'Inde*. Paris: Seuil.

Revel, J.-F. and M. Ricard. 1999. *Le Moine et le philosophe*. Paris: Pocket.

Sirikanchana, P. 1998. 'Buddhism and Education: The Thai Experience', in B. Saraswati (ed.), *The Cultural Dimension of Education*. New Delhi: Indira Gandhi National Centre for the Arts. Available online at: http://ignca. nic.in/cd_06017.htm (downloaded on 20 May 2008).

TCV. 2001. Available online at http://www.tcv.org.in/ (downloaded on 20 May 2008).

Weber, M. 1958. *The Religion of India*. Glencoe, IL: The Free Press.

———. 2003. *Hindouisme et Bouddhisme*. Paris: Flammarion.

13
EDUCATION IN VOODOO CONVENTS IN BENIN

ADJIGNON DÉBORA GLADYS HOUNKPE

INTRODUCTION

This chapter deals with one particular educational issue in Benin: the religious and traditional education provided in voodoo 'convents' as well as the modern education received at school. This analysis underscores the cultural maladjustment of school and the secret nature that socialization takes on in such convents. Though each of these two educational systems has its own weaknesses, the Beninese society promotes school, without however totally giving up the education and practices typical of voodoo convents.

In the Beninese traditional culture there are some compounds, the *Hounkpamin*,[1] where voodoo[2] followers are trained. They belong to secret societies whose members share the belief in divinities. Such boarding schools are known as voodoo 'convents', kinds of temples where future voodoo priests live and are initiated.

This study on education in voodoo convents concentrates on the Southern part of Benin in West Africa. The chapter is organized into four parts:

1. Definition of the voodoo convent.
2. Pedagogy and curriculum of voodoo convents.

3. Social functions of voodoo convent followers.
4. What are the relationships between voodoo convents and modern school?

This review is based on the following questions: Could education in voodoo 'convents', where the esoteric and solemn sacred knowledge is transmitted, provide a suitable education for children in the Beninese context? What are the educational functions of voodoo 'convents'? What are their main features? Why do they still exist? Can the education promoted by voodoo convents be reduced to a mystical approach? Is it possible to find a suitable way that would enable to introduce part of convents' education in school curricula at all levels in Benin? This would include a pharmacopoeia and original names of things, which are teachings that were given to initiates in the days of traditional education. What sets voodoo 'convents' apart from the educational system established by the various Benin governments? Can both education systems complement each other? Could these places be considered as teaching places for a science and a religion that are at the service of the society's development? What should the process be for a scientific study in such closed and sacred places?

A study on education in voodoo 'convents' could enable educational research in Benin to think of a type of education that better fits the context of the Beninese child. Thus, voodoo 'convents' could reveal an education and a philosophy typical of Benin's culture.

DEFINITION OF THE VOODOO CONVENT

The voodoo convent is a structure or an environment where voodoo religious followers are trained. In this respect, Augé (1983) points to the existence of lineage convents, that is, convents where the voodoos are linked to families. In such convents, voodoo 'priests' use 'spiritual' diagnostic methods,[3] as well as various sorts of treatments requiring the healing force of plants (Reynier, 1999). To each voodoo are associated some plants, mineral and organic substances. Only the convent's priests and initiates know of such compositions, which they keep secret. Rituals and libations come in support to the treatment.

Voodoo entails the materialization of spirits in the world of mere mortals, humans, and much symbolism. Such know-how is passed down from generation to generation, originally by the way of oral tradition and experience. It is the heritage from the past which is tied to a whole family, a community and a people.

Definitions of the voodoo

In the *Fon* language, voodoo means–*what cannot be cleared up, the effective power*. It can also mean a god, or a spirit. It is the set of divinities or *orisha* that are worshipped in most of Adja Tado (South of Benin) and Yoruba regions (Merlo, 1940; Chesi, 1982).

According to Adandé (2003), voodoo is animism with a polytheist face insofar as the followers recognize gods that they worship among a multitude of divinities. Voodoo can also be seen as a monotheist religion with one unique unapproachable God, whose various facets are manifested by cosmo-telluric actions such as lightning or eruptive diseases like smallpox (still feared in Africa, despite the progress achieved by medicine). According to initiates, in the full meaning of the word, voodoo, is at first an immaterial entity that surpasses man. Voodoo is a power, an energy which can reveal itself through many ways. Adandé thinks that it is difficult to define voodoo and to describe the pantheons' components. In the Fon ethnic group in the South of Benin, ethnologists agree to classify voodoos in two main groups: *to vodou* or collective veneration voodoos and *hennu vodou* or family voodoos.

Various types of voodoos

According to voodoo followers, the creators are *Mawu* and *Lissa*, incarnation of the male and female principles. They have given birth to fourteen children endowed with supernatural powers. Among the descendants are *Chango*, or *Gou*, the thunder god, and *Sakpata*, the earth god or smallpox god. To these two main gods, who are the basis of the voodoo, are added other inferior gods the number of which Beninese researchers estimate at 260. Bogniaho (2001) made an onomastic list in South Benin convents, especially those of the Oueme valley. He gives every initiate's name according to his spiritual function in the convent. This name is very significant and characterizes him.

We can list the following examples:

1. *Achina,* is a 'ta voodoo', a voodoo carried on the head or on the shoulders. Its carrier has a specific name depending on his function in the convent that he keeps till his dying day.
2. *Hêviosso,* thunder and lightning voodoo; its believers carry a two-bladed hatchet (Agboton, 1997: 64).
3. *Legba,* a voodoo both generous and terrific.
4. *Ninssouhoué,* representative of ancestors, they deserve veneration. (Agboton, 1997: 65).
5. *Tohossou,* is a god who incarnates in the women known as *innocent,* whose children are dwarfs. They are very gifted, respected and provide material wealth to their family. When they die (they generally die very early), after some ritual ceremonies they are thrown into the sea, and are thus believed to return to their vital space.
6. *Mamiwater* is the sea goddess. She is fond of luxury and her followers are adorned with jewels, most beautiful and perfumed. They are always dressed in white. They receive their training in special convents and are called *mamissi.*
7. *Abikou,* subnormal children's benefactor god. His favourite place is the forest (Quenum, 1998: 50). He protects automatically all children born after repeated miscarriages or after their elders' death. He *ties* them to life by keeping their dead elder brothers and sisters in their world, on the other side of the mirror.
8. *Hovi,* highly venerated divinities who are in fact twins. The mothers of twins are highly respected (Quenum, 1998: 65). The town of Ouidah is called the city of twins (Merlo, 1940). Once a year all the twins of South Benin gather in the town in a big festival under the aegis of voodoos.
9. *Kocou* is a very violent and bellicose voodoo. He likes making an exhibition of himself, but in the end always goes wrong. Many families don't approve of his followers. Once they are in trance, they wound themselves with knives, fragments of broken bottles or any other sharp object. Women in trance are able to cut the throat of a sheep with their teeth or to eat a living chicken with its blood and feathers.
10. *Koutito* or *egoun goun,* 'spirits of the dead, ghosts'.
11. *Zangbéto,* 'night protector'.
12. *Dangbé,* the sacred python.
13. *Dan Aïdowèdo,* the rainbow; he represents fertility and wealth.
14. *Oro* is a terror sowing voodoo, his punishment is intransigent. He will not tolerate non-initiates on his way. He comes out mainly in the Nago area. He makes disappear all curious women, who dare hide with the intention of watching him. Quenum (1998: 39–44)

shows to which extent this voodoo sows terror and obliges women to display a good behaviour in their households. He wrote:

15. 'In the traditional environment, *Oro* is taboo. Nobody has the right to talk about *Oro* apart from initiates among themselves, in the initiates' circle. *Oro's* world is first of all nocturnal. This world of secret societies is supposed to be one of terror from where adult men draw their power. As a general rule, it is forbidden to leave one's house. Should it happen that somebody goes out, he would never see his people again. He will be said to have disappeared forever, *lo gbé è*'. (Quenum, 1998: 39–41)

I remember having experienced *Oro's* horrors when I was 14 years old. I was spending my holidays in Sakété, an area in the Plateau region in Benin, near the border with Nigeria, *Oro's* region par excellence. It was in July and the voodoo's ceremonies were taking place. For three days and three nights, nobody had the right to see daylight or the stars by night. Only initiates could leave their house and run errands. This voodoo is very sexist and misogynous. No woman is accepted in his convent. Women are responsible for all faults. Oro blames women for all of society's faults. My aunt, respected main midwife of the area, was the only person authorized to negotiate so that women in childbirth were allowed to go to her house, wearing a veil, to give birth. My aunt used to discuss with one of the priests, her back turned to the locked door.

Links between convents and voodoos

In Benin, *hounkapmin* are places where future voodoo priests and priestesses are trained. According to Augé's (1983) research, each convent celebrates the cult of a number of voodoos (Reynier, 1999). The priest, *hounnon* is in charge of the cult. Most often it is a man. Convent boarders are called *vodounsi* or *hounsi*. This Fon word means spouse of the voodoo—it applies to both male or female initiates. It is worth mentioning that convents are not mixed. Besides, admission in a convent is different from enrolment in modern school, since it requires that one hear the call of the voodoo. According to Augé, the signs for such calls are diseases. After consulting the *fâ* oracle, the *bokonon* or soothsayer reveals its cause and directs the patient to his voodoo convent. Moreover, certain people are drawn to the convent by an indescribable force. But, because voodoo has been forbidden and because fewer and fewer families submit to voodoo calls, convent priests organize the abduction of children and mainly young girls. In reaction to such practices, some women lawyers denounce the obscurantism that characterizes such an education and its consequences. Quenum (1998: 62–63) notes that:

'Admission in convents is strictly selective. Recruitment is made:

1. On the obligation made to the convent head to give one of his own people.[4]
2. The obligation made to the woman who has resorted to the voodoo's help to conceive a child to give the said child to the voodoo. But there are also some spontaneous recruitments: the new recruit is driven by a force, in a state of trance, to the convent.'

ABOUT CULTURE AND CULTURAL MALADJUSTMENT OF SCHOOL

The issue of culture is unavoidable in a debate that includes school and a mode of religious education.

For Tevoedjre (quoted by Agboton, 1997: 15–16), if there is an issue that every African should dread, wherever he is on the continent, if there is an issue that will leave unconcerned none of those who admit to come from our particular universe of people scattered throughout the world, it is indeed the issue of culture. Culture prescribes us to search and resort to our origins, to our history. Culture enjoins us to define, describe, and appreciate the biological, physical and human environment in which we have known mother, family, society. If there is a vision of man and destiny that constantly goes to our hearts, it is indeed the one we are taught by culture.

Actually, culture provides man with the capacity to reflect on himself. It makes us specifically human, rational, critical, and ethically committed beings. It is through culture that man expresses himself, is conscious of himself, recognizes himself as an incomplete project, questions his own achievements, tirelessly seeks new meanings and undertakes works that transcend him (Agboton, 1997).

If culture defines to such an extent the individual, how can we understand the incapacity of the modern educational system to adapt itself to Beninese culture? Can education stakeholders find at the very heart of Benin culture some solutions to the weaknesses of the modern school? If school keeps on inculcating to the youth foreign notions borrowed from the European civilization, isn't there a huge risk for Benin's culture and development in the years to come? It is obvious that modern school produces hybrids, persons who have difficulties to integrate themselves in the society (Freire, 1977).

Durkheim (1938), in *L'évolution pédagogique en France* (The evolution of education methods in France) urges us to think of the revolution that occurs in the child at his first time at school. He changes his way of being and almost his nature. From that moment, there is inside him a real duality. When he comes back home his parents have the feeling that he less and less belongs to them. The generation gap starts right there. Submitted to the school's discipline, the child, the teenager gradually discovers a social world external to the family, where he will make his own place only if he submits to it, if he incorporates himself to it. The family itself is thus gradually modified.

Africans continue to experience the discomfort related to school as a very disrupting structure that displays little respect for cultural identity. There is an omnipresent conflict between modern school, family and traditional education. Cheick Hamidou Kane (1961) has made of this issue the central theme of his novel *L'Aventure ambiguë*. He wrote:

> I have come to tell you this: I, Grande Royale, I don't like the foreign school. I hate it. Yet, my opinion is that we should send our children (...) The school to which I'm pushing our children will kill in them, what we love today and rightly keep with care. Perhaps, even our memory will die in them. When they will come back to us from school some among them will not recognize us. What I am suggesting is that we accept to die in our children and that the foreigners who have defeated us take in them all the place that we would have left free. (quoted by Brahimi and Trevarthen, 1998: 41–42)

Aminata Traoré (2002), in her book *Le viol de l'imaginaire* (The Rape of Imagination) fully agrees with the aforementioned authors, as she recalls the memories of her school days in Africa, Mali, in the 1950's, but mainly the fear of her mother, a traditional woman who saw her daughter attend a structure which she didn't trust at all:

> My father (...) of course was sceptical but not opposed at all to the schooling of his daughters. My mother, as for her, was afraid of exposing them to multiple dangers of an external world engaged in the process of westernisation; she dreaded especially early sexual experiences,

precocious maternity, and delay of marriage. I was not for all that excused from little household works usually assigned to children of my age. (...) My insertion, through such ways, in the world of women of my home environment was for my parents a manner not to rely only on school, from which one came out, according to them, *half-fawn, half-bird* in case of failure. (Traoré, 2002: 27–28)

Ideas conveyed through these quotations highlight certain phenomena such as the fear of the modern school system and its effects on the youth, but also the fear of seeing some traditions disappear. But, there are some structures which, if improved, could be an asset in the process of resisting the uprooting: namely the voodoo convents.

But, to what extent should the training and pedagogy in such traditional religious structures be improved, so as to make them less esoteric and more beneficial to the whole nation? How can we explain the fact that education stakeholders remain reluctant to seek solutions at the very heart of Beninese culture?

The choice of this topic is both complex and relevant because voodoo convents remain a very present phenomenon in the Beninese society. Yet, it is difficult to comprehend thoroughly their operating mode, their limits and their potentials for the development of human beings in symbiosis with their environment.

The presence of catholic missionaries who came from Lyon in the 19th century with a view to christianize the Beninese, entailed consequences for the organization of voodoo convents and their impact in the society. Actually, they were at the same time feared, rejected and venerated as well.

During the 1972–90 period, the Marxist-Leninist government led by Mathieu Kerekou implemented a repression policy against voodoo convents and they again fell into anonymity. All such pressures contributed to stigmatize them, but did not succeed in making them disappear. In this respect, Adandé thinks that some photographs by Verger (1954) relate the history of certain initiation convents, most of which reduced their activities under the threat of the Marxist-Leninist ideology, in the framework of which was started in the mid-70's 'the fight against obscurantism and backward practices'. Convents that succeeded in maintaining themselves, could do so only thanks to their remoteness and the submission to an autarchy from which they had just begun to recover.

Problem statement

The purpose of this chapter is to highlight the social and educational functions of voodoo convents. The approach consists of presenting them as a socialization structure in the Beninese context and, on the other hand, seeing to which extent they are a traditional, religious and vocational training place, building psychological stability for a harmonious life for the child within his biotope. Dasen and Akkari (introduction to this volume) recognize the 'cultural imperialism' by which the West appropriates the cultural heritage of the South by looting the knowledge, medicinal knowledge for instance, of indigenous people. The same applies to this aspect of the Beninese culture: considered at first as paganism, it is now looked at as folklore. Most of Beninese intellectuals and political leaders display very little concern for these cultural realities that have become restricted to villagers. A political will is indispensable to reform convents, reorganize their structure, and make their psychological and medicinal knowledge known to children of schooling age. I remain nevertheless doubtful of these prospects, considering the too markedly sacred and hermetic nature of such places of cult and traditional science. Priests can be conceded the safeguarding of certain mysterious aspects but there is some underlying natural knowledge to be drawn from these training places, relegated to obscurantism.

Both the modern school, vector of another civilization, and the voodoo convent are interested in the human being. Yet, some issues of concern remain:

1. Must one or the other be relinquished?
2. Isn't it possible to find a link between these two diametrically opposed types of socialization?
3. Isn't it possible to reform voodoo convents, grant them a more prestigious status, grant them a scientific recognition, and thus enable them to be vocational training schools?

One can no longer live focused on the traditional culture, which may maintain us, in some respects, in a kind of archaism. It would be more adequate to work on a symbiosis between modernity and tradition.

In Benin, traditional religions hold a major place. The voodoo, whose followers are animists and represent 62 per cent of the population (Pliya, 1993: 106). Generally speaking, voodoo gods are very present in daily life. Agboton (1997) thinks that the Benin population as a whole is rooted deep in that sacred atmosphere, from old aunts, custodians of tradition and customs, to the highest personalities of the State.

The author suggests three postulates to facilitate the understanding of such a culture. According to him, these three postulates are the main pillars of the philosophical and cosmogonic understanding of the Beninese.

1. In his body, in his double male and female identity, in his *Se* (spiritual principle), in his relations with the *Weke* (the visible and invisible universe, all things created whether living, breathing or not) and also as a community member, Man is the centre of Life, *Gbè*, which proceeds from *Mawu*: supreme power, creating God, progenitor and absolute master of breath-life and as a result, of death.

2. All 'created things' are a set of systems without watertight limits, and a fabric of vital energies: set and fabric in which circulate, like a fluid, 'vitalistic forces'.

3. The cosmos is a jungle, an always virgin forest of vital forces and momentum, which man can appeal to, capture, exploit, lead, or neutralize, not through technology and exact sciences, but through 'religious participation' (religion considered under its etymological meaning, *relegere* to gather, bring together). (Agboton, 1997: 61–62)

Animism recognizes the existence of a supreme God, called *Mahou* in Fon communities. *Mahou* is the Creator of the visible and invisible universe. It is the entity that is beyond everything.

The Vodou represents the intermediary between human beings and God. There are some myths that explain God's remoteness. The most widespread asserts that God used to live among human beings and the Creation. But because of the woman, who pounded her maize too noisily, and threw waste water on the canopy of heaven, God withdrew in order to have peace and quiet, and more respect: henceforth, human beings could reach him only through the vodou.

Inspite of the presence of Christianity and Islam as monotheist religions, the Beninese remain, in the largest majority of the population, faithful to traditional cults, from which follows the current syncretism (Pliya, 1993: 106). Benin is recognized as the cradle of the voodoo because this practice has stood the test of time and oppression. This practice which is found in Brazil and the West

Indies, notably Cuba and Haïti, originated in Dahomey (current Benin) and reached such areas as a result of the slave trade.

PEDAGOGY AND CURRICULUM IN VOODOO CONVENTS

The voodoo convent follower is by definition the disciple of the representative of a certain god supposed to be *dancing on his head*, which means that the follower is under the thumb of the said god. So shall he remain for a while, and training is indispensable for him during that period which generally lasts for seven years (Quenum, 1998: p. 63). Nevertheless, specific research on educational and functional aspects of voodoo convents is lacking. Those who examined the issue did so very superficially. This approach deserves being more thoroughly examined, even if convents remain sacred places where secrecy is a rule. Some researchers have lived in such structures, but no detailed description is provided by their writings, which remain vague as regards certain relevant issues. This aspect sometimes explains the criticism on voodoo convents seen as obscurantist places. If priests in charge of the training accepted that those who have sojourned with them, with a view to better understanding their training methods, publish their theses, some positive aspects would be retained, and certain potentials in the field of education and life philosophy would be better exploited. The socialization processes thus discovered could serve a programme more adapted to local cultural realities.

First of all, it is a pedagogy based on speech, orality, and authority where the master, here the voodoo priest, is the omniscient. The followers are deemed to have no knowledge a priori; they watch, listen and imitate. It is a process of transmitting customs and traditions, including all that is related to habits, traditional practices, collective ways of doing and thinking. Pupils are taught to forget their past, for they are born again. The loss of their name and the taking of a new name according to the oracle and the spiritual function are their new life agenda. Later on, their faith is inculcated in that remote God, whose only intermediaries are the voodoos, represented by clods of earth, wood or iron, depending on the attributes of those gods. They are taught hierarchy, prudence among *akotonons*, that is, the relatives of the larger family generally jealous of the social position. It is against them that the Beninese, initiated or not, *hounsi* or not, *armour* themselves whatever their religious faith.

A child socialized in a convent is often aware that in Benin, it is forbidden to cut down an iroko tree, he is taught to respect his environment. In animism, everything is sacred, and plants host souls and spirits Pliya (1971). The iroko tree is the first deified tree in Benin. It is the tree that protects populations against misfortunes. In his short story collection, entitled *L'arbre fétiche* (*The Fetish Tree*), Pliya (1971) the Beninese writer, geographer and historian, emphasizes the sacred nature of that tree where ceremonies and agapes of the world of spirits are carried out at strategic hours.

The road laid out by the French colonizers required the cutting down of the century-old tree. All the prisoners mobilized for the task, disobeyed inspite of punishment. They refused to touch that tree. The colonial administration doubled the price for the foolhardy. The woodcutter named Dossou, who had no family left, agreed to take the challenge. Three days of combat. Even though he was initiated, and took on his spiritual combat arsenal, the end was fatal to him. He cut the iroko tree, but in its fall the tree changed its trajectory and crushed him.

Hypotheses by French literary critics aimed at explaining the fall of the tree and Dossou's 'accident' reflected the Cartesian rationality: it was an accident, for Dossou oriented the tree's fall in the wrong way. But, for the Beninese, the hypothesis was tainted with traditional belief: The sacred tree had taken revenge on the god killer Dossou.

As regards training in convents, Quenum (1998: 63) suggests four major aspects:

1. The good command of the convent's language. The new recruits are entrusted to the specialists of a language, which generally is not that of the area where the convent is located.
2. The adequate dance to the voodoo.
3. An occupation: basketwork, sculpture, bas relief modelling.
4. Various games and physical exercises aimed at relaxing.

This list of voodoo convent curricula, drawn up by Quenum is not restrictive. Actually, many other elements could be added to it. Contrary to modern schools pedagogy, which consists of transmitting knowledge acquired from books, convent pedagogy is based on traditional education and is transmitted through speech, in the form of initiation (Pliya, 1987). The voodoo followers are known as initiates, but being an initiate does not necessarily mean that one has been in a convent. There are some initiates, who have inherited such a capacity from a parent, holder of a sublime power, who as he feels on the verge of his death, decides to leave his 'spiritual heritage' to his most virtuous child. Indeed, either inside or outside the convent, the initiation is always selective. That is what is described in a sublime way by the Beninese writer Olympe Bhêly-Quenum (1965, 1968, 1994), son of a Sakpata follower, born in a convent. In his novel L'initié (The Initiate), Bhêly-Quenum (1979) describes a terrible spiritual combat between a young doctor Kofi-Marc Tingo and a village traditional practitioner named Djessou.

Marc Tingo, returned from France where he graduated in medicine, and decided to put himself at the disposal of his people, who were being swindled and intimidated by the only, corrupted and inefficient village healer. This latter considers Marc Tingo as a rival to get rid of with no mercy. Attacked by occult forces and witchcraft, the young doctor gets very sick. His uncle Atchê, realizing the extent of the struggle, decides to pass his spiritual heritage to his virtuous young nephew. Atchê initiates Marc Tingo to the real names of everything, specificities of each day and each hour, properties of plants, sacred speech and incantations. Marc Tingo, once initiated, faces the village healer. He plays the game of 'return to sender' and the healer dies, struck by Hêviosso, the thunder god, who does not tolerate injustice, wanton maliciousness and unhealthy use of his powers.

In his novel Les tresseurs de corde (The Rope Makers), Pliya (1987) made a narrative similar to Olympe Bhêly-Quenum's, between his hero Trabi, a young agnostic agronomist and Tchakato a healer as corrupted and malicious as Djessou. Trabi has some knowledge in nutrition science and could heal with garlic, clay, lemon and a healthy and balanced diet. In Preketo tchè village where he was forced to exile for political reasons, he healed many people. Tchakato did not appreciate this, since he considered it an affront. Trabi is attacked by occult forces and witchcraft. He pulled through owing to his innocence and his kind-heartedness, but also owing to Boni, the eldest son of the host family, who is initiated in secrets of spiritual struggle against evil forces.

Pedagogy in convents may resort to modern didactic equipment such as copybook and pencil as far as learning the fa (the oracle) or the divinatory art is concerned. That is what Beninese researchers have called mathematics or algebra. It also resorts to writing for the drawing of the dou, the oracle's message construed through signs and lines. Generally, every initiated person can construe such signs.

In his novel, *Un piège sans fin* (*The Endless Trap*), Bhêly-Quenum (1960) shows through the narrative of the Bakari family, how ignorance of one's *dou* can bring about unlimited disasters in a family. Born under the sign of *fâ Aidegoun Gbégouda*, Bakari, the father of the family must not eat tubers. But, Bakari does not take seriously the injunctions of his protecting voodoo. The voodoo turns away from him, and the wealthy and prosperous farmer and stock-breeder becomes poor.

One morning, Bakari finds his cattle devastated by anthrax. Three days later, his farm is destroyed by locusts. In the same period, he, the dignitary, is summoned for hard labour by the colonial administrator. Battered and humiliated by a mere guard, then by the administrator, Bakari commits suicide by thrusting his dagger into his chest in front of his fellow villagers. His son Ahouna enjoyed a peaceful life as long as he didn't eat tubers. But, once he ate cassava, his life collapsed. He went through incessant traps until the day he was crucified and burnt alive, for having killed a widow as he was wandering. The *bokonon*, Adanfô had already predicted these occurrences by consulting the oracle.

In convents, agriculture, natural science, herbal medicine, and literature are taught through proverbs, tales, myths, legends, epic tales and riddles. Art holds an outstanding place though basketry, but also and mainly through dances, songs, and music. Every initiate must have a good knowledge of plants and their double vital and deadly functions (Quenum, 1998: 57–62).

Verger (1997) in his book *Ewe, Le verbe et le pouvoir des plantes chez les Yoroubas* (Nigeria Benin) (*Ewe, the word and the power of plants in Yoruba culture*) lists 447 medicinal and magic formulas, lexicons, names of plants and scientific classifications. Such a wealth of herbal medicinal knowledge revealed by an initiate should not be left in the hands of anyone. But, as it is said in Benin 'Westerners do not keep secrets'.

Drums, castanets, gong and flute are mastered and played with dexterity. Art, personal hygiene, and cleanliness of one's environment are the various subjects taught to the vodou follower. Adandé (2003) notices to that effect that education in these boarding places relies on a very thorough knowledge of the environment in general. There, one is taught the healing properties of plants, not disregarding of incompatibilities, and also to handle poison with extreme dexterity. They are taught how to increase or decrease the vibratory rate of the body. Above all, the voodoo is mainly based on the speech and sounds that are emitted by human voices as well as percussion instruments.

In addition to all the teaching which contributes to strengthening their knowledge and forming their behaviour with a view to their social insertion, the initiates are taught silence, or how to keep one's tongue (translated from the Fon language *hin noun*). It should also be underscored that cooking holds an important place and is included in the subjects. The *hounsi* are perfect women, who enjoy great prestige and veneration in society. In this respect, there is a saying which states: *wa man mon non mon non da hounyo* which means: the poor man cannot marry a voodoo follower. Such women socialized in convents are precious and have a lot of sacred restrictions which their husbands must abide by, otherwise they will be accountable to the electing voodoo.

It can be said that the convent forms the body, the soul and the spirit. It shapes followers of a specified voodoo, some among whom will later become priests and priestesses, taking over the initiation of future generations.

The convents' pedagogy, which is *Magister Dixit,* does not encourage the questioning of the transmitted knowledge. Neither does it allow the development of a rational and discerning spirit. Contradiction is not allowed, neither, is questioning and doubt. We are in the religious world, the world of the solemnly sacred.

Are there any possibilities for the learner to rise beyond the voodoo priest's knowledge? Quenum (1998, p. 30) thinks that it is a symbolic, magic-religious knowledge that focuses on a certain absolute, the wisdom of ancestors and the pre-eminence of the past. It is intended to make a young person 'an elder', since the privileged place in society belongs to ancestors. This belief is present in the whole of Black Africa. Birago Diop (1958) revealed it in his famous poem written in prose and entitled *Souffle (Breath)* 'In Africa, the dead are not dead, they are in the water that flows and the wind that blows'.

SOCIAL FUNCTIONS OF VOODOO CONVENT FOLLOWERS

The voodoo is preoccupied by the relations established between human beings and other spiritual levels. Convent followers stand as a link between the non-initiate and the deity. They exercise all spiritual functions related to rituals and ceremonies that a person must undergo in order to enjoy a more stable social life. I don't share entirely Jean-Claude Quenum's opinion according to which, once they leave the convent, the *hounsi* can no more be useful and must socialize again so as to adapt themselves to the society. In that respect, he wrote:

> Initiates, when they come out, are not able to implement the knowledge acquired in the convent: the language, they can only speak when they are in trance; dance, they cannot perform in public except in a ceremonial context that is appropriate to the voodoo; as for physical, chemical, and metaphysical knowledge, all that remains absolute secret'. (Quenum, 1998: 64)

I have not found any writings investigating this aspect of the issue, but I know that those persons officiate and participate actively within their cult group in all spiritual activities. For instance at given periods, followers of *Ninsouhoué*, who is a comic voodoo whose followers are very cheerful, generous and very immodest, whether they are male or female, hold a wood carved in the shape of a phallus and perform lewd dances that make the crowd laugh. They gather and go from house to house with a view to singing, dancing and purifying all the inhabitants by *warding off misfortunes*. Of course, to meet their needs, they have to carry out a vocational activity.

Nevertheless, certain convent followers may become a threat to their community when they put their secret knowledge at the service of evil. They become witches. But, the community sees to that and the trainers too. Should it happen, the priest is entitled to annihilate their power or put an end to their lives with occult processes. I have not found research on this issue, but Pliya describes a situation of the like in his short story *Le gardien de nuit* (*The Night Watchman*) published in the short stories collection *L'arbre fétiche* (Pliya, 1971).

Zannou, the night watchman is an initiate, so is his female friend Ayélé. The latter switches to the opposite side and tries to kill Zannou. She fails because Zannou is strong, loyal and respectful. Ayélé next attacks the young Cicavi, Zannou's unique motherless daughter. She succeeds in transforming Cicavi into a chicken of which she makes an appetizing meal. Zannou, aware that his daughter is on the brink of death, waits till the dead of the night to attack his opponent. For that combat, he has to appeal to the help of the *bokonon*, the soothsayer who helps him to understand the message of the spirits through the *fâ*, the oracle and to be sure that Ayélé is indeed the one responsible. Incantations, litanies, Zannou resorts to the skills learnt in his entire training to catch Ayélé who has changed into an owl, (which is seen in Benin, by the collective conscience, as the messenger of witches). Ayélé is beaten but Cicavi has not been saved. This short story also raises the issue of witchcraft, which has a strong presence in Benin.

What are the relationships between voodoo convents and modern schools?

Modern school refers to the institution that is a reformed heritage of colonialism. According to Quenum (1998), the education that is the most valued in Benin is the one that takes place through school, as the structure that develops rationality of the human being, and which hides another education, the socialization by the traditional education system. The issue breaks up into two levels: the social image and the economic effects. The point is not to give up the socialization of Africans by the system of the 'rational' school, vector of foreign civilizations and modernity, but instead to take cultural values into consideration and adapt them to the current context in such a way as to end in a *mixing*. That is why we should endeavour to achieve *cultural syncretism*.

CONCLUSION

Through this study, I have intended to show that voodoo convents exist and are structures of traditional and religions education and vocational training. However, they vegetate in oblivion because they include some secret structures. In that respect, it is to the credit of Alexandre (1981) to have revealed the sacred and esoteric nature of religious groups and practices in Africa. This fact makes every scientific research almost unachievable. In Benin, it is difficult or even impossible for a researcher to divulge information collected during a participatory research in voodoo convents.

Traditional religious priests, the only custodians of the tradition, must however understand that for a culture to live, it needs to be transmitted. Moreover, in the competition with modern school, which seems to be prevailing, it will be necessary to open themselves to other references. The economic issue, difficulties in the employment market, the bureaucratic nature of the Beninese society, the hope to access a better life standard, to a rise in social status, and a blooming life, widely opened to the West, all promote modern school, which symbolizes hope for a better life, contrary to voodoo convents that remain firmly turned toward the past and rooted in the sacred.

Despite such a typical pattern, families, whether in rural or urban areas, are most concerned that their *Akowé* should be conscious of their origins, their roots (*Akowé* is a Yoruba term widely used in Benin to refer to educated children). At the same time, it implies a very hopeful programme for the whole family. Indeed, the social achievement of this child sent to school is to the advantage of the whole lineage. But, if the child is left in the village in the hands of the voodoo priest, the family has no hope to see him grow up to become a minister, parliament member or even an ambassador of his country, as it happens in white men's country (*yovotome*), the longed for *El Dorado*. Yet, before sending the child to school, parents place him under the protection of the family's deity. They consult the *fâ* to obtain some information on the course of his existence. Generally, when an obstacle occurs, the individual appeals to the voodoo priest, or the *bokonon*.

Modern school does not provide Beninese with the means to be perfectly rooted in their culture. Unlike voodoo convent followers, elites of modern school (apart from a few exceptions) do not have the knowledge of plants, their healing properties or incantations to be used with them. There is no choice but to accept that there is a clear difference between the two modes of socialization, even if the centre of the interest remains the human being. As regards the socialization process, their approaches are quite different in terms of content and targetted goals. Nevertheless, as is suggested by this analysis, an additional approach can be envisaged with a view to benefitting from pedagogical advantages offered by both educational systems. Thus, a future-oriented solution would be the opening up of modern school to traditional teaching so as to enable voodoo convents' priests to deliver some lessons. Such a solution can also be applied to voodoo convents with a view to opening them up toward the formal educational system.

NOTES

1. In the *Fon* language, this word literally means 'the voodoo's enclosure'.
2. You may notice several spellings of 'voodoo', all of them are admitted.
3. That has mainly to do with the consultation of the oracle, to determine the cause and nature of a disease.
4. Every voodoo priest must prepare someone to take over from him; to that purpose, he initiates a child among his descent.

REFERENCES

Adandé, J. 2003. 'Animism in Benin: Introductory Text on Vodoun', Available online at http://www.bj.refer.org/benin_ct/tur/vodoun/present. htm (downloaded on 20 May 2008).

Agboton, G. 1997. *Culture des peuples du Bénin.*. Paris: Présence Africaine.

Alexandre, P. 1981. *Les Africains: Initiation à une longue histoire et à de vielles civilisations de l'aube de l'humanité au début de la colonisation.* Paris: Lidis.

Augé, M. (ed.) 1983. *Le sens du mal. Anthropologie, histoire, sociologie de la maladie.* Paris: Editions des Archives Contemporaines.

Bhêly-Quenum, O. 1960. *Un piège sans fin.* Paris: Stock.

———. 1965. *Le chant du lac.* Paris: Présence Africaine.

———. 1968. *Liaison d'un été.* Paris: Sagerep.

———. 1979. *L'initié.* Paris: Présence Africaine.

———. 1994. *Les appels du vodou.* Paris: L'Harmattan.

———. 1998. *La naissance d'Abikou.* Cotonou: Phoenix.

Bogniaho, A. 2001. 'People, Convent and Confession' inaugural lecture delivered at the Faculty of Arts and Human Sciences of the National University of Benin, Benin, February 12. Abomey-Calavi: UNB/Flash, Intergraphic Printing-House.

Brahimi, D. and A. Trevarthen, 1998. *Les femmes dans la littérature africaine.* Paris: Karthala.

Chesi, G. 1982. *Vaudou.* Paris: Fournier.

Diop, B. 1958. *Nouveaux contes d'Amadou Koumba.* Paris: Présence Africaine.

Durkheim, É. 1938. *L'évolution pédagogique en France.* Paris: Félix Alcan.

Freire, P. 1977. *Pedagogia do oprimido. Rio de Janeiro.* Rio de Janeiro: Paz e Terra.

Kane, Ch. H. 1961. *L'aventure ambiguë. Ambiguous adventure.* Paris: Julliard.

Merlo, C. 1940. 'Hiérarchie fétichiste de Ouidah', Bifan II, no 12. Dakar: Institut français d'Afrique noire (IFAN).

Pliya, J. 1971. *L'arbre fétiche*. The fetish tree. Yaoundé: Clé.

———. 1987. *Les tresseurs de corde*. Paris: Hatier.

———. 1993. *L'histoire de mon pays, le Bénin*. Porto Novo: Centre National de Production de Manuels Scolaires.

Quenum, J.C. 1998. *Interactions des systèmes éducatifs traditionnels et modernes en Afrique*. Paris: L'Harmattan.

Reynier, M. 1999. *Les dimensions sociales de la maladie*. Available online at http://www.reynier.com/anthro/ethnomedecine/dimensions.html (downloaded on 20 May 2008).

Traoré, A. 2002. *Le viol de l'imaginaire*. Paris: Fayard.

Verger, P.F. 1954. *Dieux d'Afrique*. Paris: L'Harmattan.

———. 1997. *Ewe, le verbe et le pouvoir des plantes chez les Yoroubas (Nigeria Bénin)*. Paris: Maisonneuve Larose.

Websites

http://perso.wanadoo.fr/jacquver/texte/vaudouafr.htm
http://www.dhdi.free.fr/recherches/bulletins/bull25.htm
http://www.profildubenin.com/le_benin/population/les_religions.htm

Section IV   Global Political Issues

14
PAULO FREIRE: BUILDING A MULTICULTURAL PEDAGOGY FOR SILENCED VOICES

ABDELJALIL AKKARI AND PERI MESQUIDA

For almost five centuries, the majority of scientific and technological discoveries have been made in European countries or countries under European control. This supremacy, which has been of short duration on the scale of human history, was developed at the same time as a colonial and dominant relationship between Europe and the rest of the world. European supremacy in the production of knowledge has been weakened by decolonization and the unfinished battle of cultural minorities for equality. In education and pedagogy, the contribution of Paulo Freire is fundamental. A book on the pedagogies of the 'Majority World' has to include a text on his work.

Writing about Paulo Freire is a difficult challenge. Both the author and his theory have been at the centre of many pedagogical discussions around the world. Interpretation of his legacy varies according to the context in which it takes place. In Europe, Freire is better known for his method of literacy training used in adult education. In the US, critical theorists have used several Freirian concepts to address educational inequalities (Apple, 1996; Giroux, 1997; McLaren, 1997a, 1997b). In Latin America and other Third World countries, the main point of interest centres around the socio-political value of Freire's pedagogy (Loiola and Borges, 1996; Nóvoa, 1996).

The goals of this chapter are to explore four areas of Freire's theory that might inform educational reforms in the Majority World. First, we argue that scholars of comparative education may turn to Freire's theory in order to differentiate between schooling and education. In the second section, we look at Freire's ideas in practice. We examine the power of Freire's approach to literacy in the third section. In the fourth section, we conclude by suggesting some propositions to build a critical education based on Freire's pedagogical heritage.

EDUCATION RATHER THAN SCHOOLING

In order to work with oppressed people, it is necessary to situate schools within the broader socio-cultural context. However, as suggested by Dardar (1991), the traditional uncritical acceptance of the existing relationships between schools and the larger society has supported inequity in the educational system. Schools are viewed as neutral and non-political institutions whose sole purpose is to instruct students with the necessary knowledge and skills to render them functional in society. Freire viewed education in a very different and more radical way than the mainstream thinking about schooling. He considered the relationship between education and liberation to be both complex and dialectical. Additionally, he believed that rather than the educational system being necessarily qualified to shape society's structure, it is actually society that models education according to the interests of those who have power. According to Freire (1976), no society is actually based upon its educational system. In other words, mainstream formal schooling cannot be expected to be accountable for positive social change. It mostly acts as an instrument that reinforces and reproduces the capitalist class-structure.

In order to forgo this contradictory position of a need for liberatory education in a non-egalitarian society, Freire promoted a philosophy of education based on an eclectic synthesis of Marxist theory, with a particular emphasis on Gramsci, and Christian philosophy, with a special focus on Mounier (Freire, 1967). In the early 1960s, the Brazilian *Ação Popular Movement* greatly influenced Freire by suggesting that consciousness is raised when individuals critically examine the world in order to produce social and political change.

As such, Freire's stance subsequently led to a malleable and heteroclite educational theory that was continually evolving. Escape from alienation is reached more through spiritual and social *conscientização* (consciousness-raising) than radical revolution:

> In order to achieve humanization, which presupposes the elimination of dehumanizing oppression, it is absolutely necessary to limit situations in which people are reduced to things. Problem posing education affirms men and women as being in the process of becoming as an unfinished, uncompleted being in and with a likewise unfinished reality. (Freire, 1993: 65)

Freire has examined the contradictions regarding the relations between educators and students, mentors, and protégés. Formal schooling, in the simplest terms, operates from the position that the teacher, as knowledge expert, is presumed to know, and the learner to not know. The teacher must transfer or export knowledge to the learner, who 'receives' that knowledge in a manner that denies the validity of ontological and epistemological productions by the learner and the learner's community. This is an authoritarian and manipulative 'banking' pedagogy, which negates the learners who are silenced and denied the opportunity to be authors of their 'own histories' (Freire et al., 1997).

Freire's philosophy of education is opposed to this banking education, to this traditional formal schooling in which students are supposed to digest useful knowledge and information with little reference to their surrounding socio-political context. One of his most interesting tenets is that education is primarily political. Learning to take control and obtain power are not individual objectives, but rather acts of collective empowerment. Community power is shared; it is not the power of a few dominant individuals who improve themselves at the expense of others, but the power of a group that finds strength and purpose in a common vision. Rather than unconnected individuals receiving knowledge in a vacuum, Freire suggests collective learning activities within the community context.

O'Cadiz et al. (1998), rightly pointed out that despite his fame and the global dissemination of his revolutionary philosophy of education, until 1989, Freire had not yet had the opportunity to extensively implement his ideas in a formal public school setting in his country of origin, Brazil. Freire's late interest in formal education limited his influence in educational reform movements in Brazil, which are mainly concerned with Piaget and Vygotsky.

Although Freire advanced the notion of popular public school (*escola publica popular*), he never conceptually addressed it. He stayed vague and rather general as shown in the following two examples in which Freire explains his work as the head of the Municipal Administration of Education in Sao Paulo:

> The quality of universal public school is not measured solely by the quantity of transmitted knowledge, but also by the class solidarity which needs to be built and by the opportunities that each of the school's partners, including parents and the community, have to use the school as a space for the expression of their culture. (Freire, 1991: 15–16)

> We hope to change the face of our school. We do not think that we are the only ones, or even the most competent, but we believe that we are capable and that we have the political resolve to do it. We dream of a public school which is built progressively in an arena of creativity. A democratic school where problem-posing pedagogy is practiced and where one learns in a serious way without the process turning into dogmatic instruction. A school that teaches content, but also a way of thinking. (Freire, 1991: 24)

Freire (1967, 1973, 1993) considers that mainstream schooling, as a preparation to enter the job market, has nothing to do with education. Can schooling ever be more than institutional indoctrination into a social system and a dominant culture that reproduces, reinforces and fortifies the devaluation of silenced voices? Schooling functions as an instrument that is used to facilitate the integration of the younger generation into the logic of the present system and to bring about conformity. However, to truly educate young people and adults, one needs a political engagement in order to improve community life and to change social and political structures. Education then becomes the practice of freedom, the means by which men and women deal critically and creatively with reality and discover how to participate in the transformation of their world. Put another way, education is a political and creative action as well as the production of local and appropriate knowledge.

Freire emphasized a dialogical relationship between the teacher and students, where both were learners, as opposed to the banking concept of education (with students as depositories of learning).

Table 14.1 provides an attempt to summarize the singularity of Freire's pedagogy compared with mainstream schooling. With problem-posing education, on the other hand, the educator not only teaches, but also engages in dialogue with the student, in order to change society.

Table 14.1 Contrasting mainstream schooling with Freire's pedagogy

	Mainstream schooling	Freire's pedagogy
Pedagogical approach	-'Banking' schooling -Approach to learning centred on technical (instrumental) transmission.	-Adult literacy and popular education [educação popular] as problem-posing. -Approach to learning centred on discovery and social responsibility.
Learning process	-Curriculum and textbook-centred. -Out-of-context teaching. -Conviction that the student is a passive recipient.	-Participants seen in-context as socially and politically engaged. -Respecting the freedom of the learner.
Thinking	-Transferring of information. -Priority to the individualization process. -Teacher shapes the student's cognition.	-Critical consciousness. -Priority to the conscientização/ liberation process. -Educator as facilitator (spit it out/walking together).
Learner's mind	-Metaphor of learner's mind as clay to be externally transformed (knowledge is located in the teacher's mind and in textbooks).	-Metaphor of reminiscence (knowledge is located in the learner's mind).
Power of languages and literacy	-Monolingual and monocultural.	-Reading words and the world.

FREIRE'S PEDAGOGY IN PRACTICE

Freire's work has been cited by educators throughout the world and constitutes an important contribution to critical pedagogy not simply because of its theoretical sophistication, but because of Freire's success at putting theory into practice. The work of Freire, where theory and practice are closely connected and overlapping, might then be extremely useful. One particularly important application of Freire's ideas is the adoption of his conception of curriculum. Freire viewed curriculum as a strategy by which educators and learners achieve more 'social centred goals'.

When Freire (1976) discusses liberation, oppression, violence, and freedom, they are not hypothetical categories but historical ones. The Freirian curriculum is a 'socially-centred curriculum' based on the real life of people.

Freire's message has spread to educators worldwide not only through his various published works but also through practical situations in which he attempted to put his ideas and theory into practice, beginning with his early work in Recife. One interesting pedagogical experience of Freire's was the work he conducted in various Third World regions. By developing literacy among the oppressed, for example with landless farmers in Guinea-Bissau, he contributed to the transformation of an oppressive, colonial educational system into an instrument for political and cultural liberation. According to Escobar and Escobar (1981), Freire's contributions included a national reconstruction of history and thinking. From the colonial Portuguese perspective, only the colonizers have a history, beginning with their 'civilizing' arrival and presence. Only the colonizers have a culture, an art or a language, and are civilized citizens of the 'saviour world'. The oppressed are said to have had no history before the merciful effort made by the colonizers; they are seen as illiterate, barbarian natives. Freire's work in Guinea-Bissau aimed to destabilize the colonial fossilization of minds.

On the results on his literacy method, one needs to acknowledge that some scholars have raised concerns about the real efficiency of the projects launched by Paulo Freire in Brazil, Chile and Guinea-Bissau. One of the most valid criticisms is that Freire's experiments were mostly all on a small scale (Harasim, 1983).

Another interesting situation in which Freire tried to implement educational reform took place during his participation on the municipal board of education in Sao Paulo. In 1988, the Workers' Party, which Freire had helped found, won the Municipal elections in Sao Paulo, Brazil's largest and richest city. Freire was invited to take over the position of Municipal Secretary of Education in the administration for 2 years (1989–91). Many ambitious objectives originated under his leadership: (*a*) increased access to schooling, (*b*) democratization of school administration, (*c*) improved instructional quality, (*d*) expanded educational opportunities for working youth and adults, and (*e*) preparation of critical and responsible citizens (Lindquist Wong, 1995). Moving from educational theory to educational planning allowed Freire to measure the long road to go before building public schools in Brazil (Freire, 1991). In 1989, Freire implemented the Movimento de Alfabetisação da Cidade de São Paulo (MOVA-SP, literacy movement of the city of Sao Paulo) where the grassroots and the social movements dealing with literacy and post-literacy worked together with the Municipal Board of Education.

According to Saul (1996), Freire's experience with the Sao Paulo municipality brought about a shift in the traditional conception of educational curriculums in Brazil. From a static transmission position, the curriculum became a problematization of learners' and educators' contexts. In order to substitute the traditional terminology associated with adult education by more appropriate concepts, Freire replaced 'literacy classes' by 'cultural circles', where educators are called 'cultural facilitators'. Instead of 'illiterates', Freire used the term 'mutual learners'. Rather than focusing on some particular lesson or moral to be learned, people from the community discussed issues and concerns in their own terms (Freire, 1988). However, others articles on Freire's experience as educational policy maker in Sao Paulo are more reserved than Saul (Torres, 1994; O'Cadiz et al., 1998). Freire's success was partial at best. The biggest challenge Freire faced during this experience was the hostility of federal and state governments, which were under the control of other political parties that were hostile to the political and social goals of Freire and of the Workers Party.

In spite of the partial achievement in the implementation of his adult literacy method and the mitigated results concerning the generalization of his approach in the school system, we advocate that Freire greatly contributed to the reorientation of educational thought in the second half of the 20th century—from a focus on the psychology of education to a more socially and politically oriented pedagogy. In the Freirian approach, learning is exercised by a collective control over the curriculum, its methods and contents, and not exclusively governed by cognitive growth brought exclusively by an instructor. Clearly, Freire pushed for a radical shift in pedagogy. From instruction by docile listening, learning became a deconstruction–reconstruction of social contexts. Freire pointed out that learners are not passive receivers of knowledge. They are not blank slates on which knowledge is inscribed independent of its context of use.

In a book of interviews, Freire used an analysis developed by the African revolutionary leader Amilcar Cabral. The distance between the general masses and the tiny, dominant elite in a decolonized country becomes larger and larger all the time. From this comes the need for the 'class suicide' of the dominant elite. In order to not betray the objectives of liberation, the petit bourgeois has only one path: to reinforce the revolutionary conscience, to fight against the natural inclination of its class mentality (Freire and Faundez, 1985).

A critical awareness in the mind of the oppressed inevitably implies the existence of an awareness of themselves as an oppressed social class. Consequently, the cultural facilitator has two options: either to contribute directly to the strategy of the oppressor, or to commit suicide as a petit bourgeois in order to be reborn as a cultural facilitator with and for a multi-cultural society in which silence no longer exists (Freire et al., 1997).

It seems that Freire's principal contribution is to be found in the operationalization of the connections between theory and practice in community education in Third World countries. This operationalization, in the final analysis, can only be of a political nature as illustrated by the following discussion by Freire (1992) of community education:

> In countries where authoritarian regimes block the redistribution of social resources, community education takes another form. It exists not for its own sake, but is instead part of the grassroots and liberation movements. It is never merely passively concerned with education movements; representatives of women's organizations in the Third World, for example, are lay people, but nevertheless experts: in self-help education for young children, in the creation of neighbourhood schools, in the training of women workers. In these countries community education has developed as popular education—utilizing concepts that deliberately stand apart from the conservative values. . . (p. VII–VIII)

According to Freire (1991), community education is a resistance movement against false ideas of learning, against the preoccupation of schools with the myths of the ruling classes, oligarchies, one-party states and the military. Community education stands for the organization of learning from below, for the connection between learning and the socio-political organization of the poor. Learning in the community, with it and for it, means dealing with the history of one's own area outward from the culture of silence.

We conclude this section by pointing out a key limitation in Freire's pedagogical thought. Freire sees education as having two possible outcomes, either 'emancipation-truth' or 'alienation'. However, we suggest that learning may include both a risk of socio-cultural reproduction of inequality and the possibility of change-liberation. The importance of language in Freire's thought relates to his concept of truth, and the importance of a class struggle that will allow the marginalized and repressed an authentic voice. It is as if the self-evident knowledge of the oppressed is less false than that which their oppressors hold as valid. With no importance given to the language of the oppressors there is a danger that the oppressed will remain closed off from the rest of the world. In addition, Freire advocates that the interests of all oppressed people are the same, and that one general theory exists for deciphering repressive reality and for developing the potentiality present in their collective memory (Gur-Ze'ev, 2005).

FREIRE'S LITERACY APPROACH

Freire advocated literacy education based on the concerns of the students, which were in discussions based around themes that were generated by the participants' concerns. According to his view of literacy, reading a text is also a reading of the social context (the world), to which it is related.

In Freire's point of view, there is no separation between 'thought-language' and 'reality'. In other words, to read a text requires reading its social context. It is not sufficient to mechanically reproduce the right sounds; it is necessary to understand the social context behind each reading activity. Understanding 'words' requires understanding the 'world' (Freire and Macedo, 1987; Gibson, 1994).

Freire initially developed the concept 'generative theme' in his early work in Recife. A generative theme is chosen on the basis of its richness, which is as much sociological and political as it is phonetic.

A generative theme must constitute a key word in a person's vocabulary, and it should always be related to very concrete problems of society (inequality, justice, hunger, land...). The generative theme represents one path towards getting to know, understand and intervene critically in a particular studied reality' (Escobar and Escobar, 1981). A generative theme is one that emerges from the lives of learners as they engage in a course of study. It presents a point of entry for learning that has meaning and relevance to a particular group of learners at a particular time in one specific context.

From Freire's perspective, *codification* is the presentation of an existential situation that is related to the generative word. It is the presentation of certain aspects of the reality that we would like to study. Codification also expresses moments in the concrete context, and it should be seen as an object of recognition, or as the symbol of the topic that is to be discussed. In other words, codification is the creation of a representation of reality for the purpose of analysis (or representation of the existential situations of the learners). Freire pointed out that codification allowed learners to gain a distance from their everyday lives so that they could see their situation in a new way.

The process of analyzing a codification is called *decodification* and involves dialogue. Decodification dissolves a codification into its constituent elements and is the operation by which learners begin to perceive relationships between elements of the codification and other experiences in their day-to-day lives and among the elements themselves. Thus, decodification is analysis that takes place through dialogue, revealing the previously unperceived meanings of the reality represented by that codification. Decodification is the principal work of a *circulo de cultura* (culture circle). Decodification is one of the most important elements in the process of learning. In order to conduct an efficient analysis of the learning process, Freire discusses the role of cultural facilitators, and defines terms such as *cultural circle, liberation, domestication of literacy*, and *dialogue*.

The methodology developed around this concept of generative themes includes notions such as individual growth through collective work, discussion, problematization, questioning, conflict, and participation (Lindquist Wong, 1995). According to Freire, knowledge is embedded in social reality and we need to be able to apply such knowledge. In others words, in addition to Dewey's well-known statement of *learning by doing*, the gaining of knowledge involves learning by *critical social acting*. Freire's framework of learning could be called socio-political literacy:

> The generative themes, based on the real life situations, problems and concerns of the learners, are used as building blocks in the construction of locally relevant curriculum which at the same time relates that local reality to a broad range of individual, community and societal problems, e.g., peer group relations in the school, public transportation, violence and public safety, and air and water contamination in an industrial city like Sao Paulo. (O'Cadiz et al., p. 11)

Although Freire extensively used the generative theme method in his work, he balanced a centred position between an underestimation of pedagogical methods and an overestimation of their powers. He stated that methods are constructed and deconstructed in the praxis. Freire believed there is a need for clarity regarding the political options of the educator, particularly the values and principles he supports and the possible dreams to be concretized.

Freire extensively presented his method of literacy in his book 'Education for critical consciousness' (Freire, 1973). His method involves five phases: (*a*) research into the spoken language of the subjects with an emphasis on the finding of words which are culturally, politically, and phonetically familiar, yet useful as a base for phonetic development and political discussion, (*b*) selection of generative words which will syntactically and politically make reading instruction possible, that is, words which can be manipulated to create other words and expand meanings constructed by participants, (*c*) the selection of codifications which already contain the generative words (representations of typical existential situations of the group which open perspectives for the analysis of local and national problems), (*d*) the elaboration of a programme of learning sufficiently flexible to meet the needs of the community, and finally (*e*) the preparation of cards with phonemic families which correspond to the generative words.

As suggested by McLaren (1997b), few educators have helped us as much as Paulo Freire to recognize the political effects of language practices. Clearly, Freire does not proclaim that individuals and groups are to be *agentless* beings invariably trapped and immobilized by the effects of language. Rather, human beings are politically accountable for their language. Freire's position reflects Gramsci's notion that the *structural intentionality* of human beings needs to be critically examined through a process of consciousness-raising. Freire rejects the myth of the political neutrality of literacy. Critical educators have to respect the level of understanding that those becoming educated have of their own social reality (Freire and Macedo, 1987). Even if Freire's literacy method seems a simplistic approach to a complex problem (literacy), it constitutes one of the pillars of his pedagogical thought. His method is easily embraced by practicing educators (Gur-Ze'ev, 2005).

TOWARD A CRITICAL EDUCATION

Freire makes a strong contribution to critical and alternative pedagogies that are intended to be resolutely anti-hegemonic. These pedagogies have been developed in order to reduce the effects of hierarchies in the production of knowledge and to resist the culturally reproductive work of institutionalized education. In critical pedagogies, different ways of learning and knowing emerge from cultural, class, racial, sexual, and gender differences.

Freire's philosophy grew out of his direct involvement with the education of 'silenced voices'. He considers education as a tool for change in their reality. Freire's emphasis is on collective knowledge and an 'other-education', which aims to challenge the silencing hegemonic education. The aim of Freire's critical pedagogy is to give marginalized groups back their stolen 'voices', to enable them to recognize, identify, and name the things of the world.

As a result of Freire's work, educators may find inspiration, useful methodology and hope for an optimistic outlook regarding changes in the structure of non-egalitarian societies. Freire's work draws on the philosophical, anthropological, and religious considerations about what it means to be human, and about the socio-political dimension of learning:

> Education of a liberating character is a process by which the educator invites learners to recognize and unveil reality critically. The domestication practice tries to impart a false consciousness to learners, resulting in a facile adaptation to their reality; whereas the liberating practice cannot be reduced to an attempt on the part of the educator to impose freedom on learners. (Freire, 1985: 102)

Freire distinguished between work that focuses on education striving to be liberatory in a Third World society, where inequalities and contradictions are obvious and the violence experienced by dominated classes are immediately observed, and work that emphasizes a liberatory education in a modernized capitalist society where contradictions are more veiled and where the manipulation of conscientiousness is very sophisticated. With regard to the second case, the educational system serves as a powerful instrument of social control (Freire, 1976).

When Facundo (1984) stated that Freire's theory was not transferable from the context of Northeast Brazil to the 'inner Third World' of the United States, she was both indicating the limitations of Freire's pedagogy as well as illustrating one example of its misuse. On the one hand, Freire unfortunately never addressed ethnic issues either in Brazil, the US or in Africa. It is a major limitation of his work for critical education. As a member of the Brazilian intellectual middle class, Freire's pedagogical framework avoided race and ethnicity as factors of oppression. In Brazil, he never analyzed the fact that the majority of street and criminalized children are among the descendants of the country's massive former slave population.

On the other hand, Freire never claimed to provide worldwide educators with a universal pedagogical kit, ready to use in every context. His main legacy includes general tools to be employed according to the necessity of, and relevance to, each particular context. Freire provided a transformative agenda intended to both challenge and to undo one's social oppression. For Freire, basic problems of pedagogy are not strictly pedagogical but principally political and ideological. Freire found inspiration in Gramsci's analysis of contemporary societies, effectively divided into those who lead and those who passively follow. The leaders are the bourgeoisie, the followers are the subaltern classes. Formal education and cultural hegemony allowed the dominant group to maintain their power although they are numerically inferior to the oppressed. Crudely put, hegemony lead the oppressed to collaborate in their own oppression and domination.

Freire worked for a shared deconstruction of banking education. Indeed, each learner has a legitimate knowledge that may be shared. Being in a position in which one is able to share and exchange knowledge is something that must be valued. Exchanging knowledge supercedes superficial relations. Learners need to know, understand, listen to, and respect each other.

In this respect, Freire (1997) insists on the fact that the quality of a teacher comes from his/her ability to listen to the learner, 'He or she who listens to the learner attentively and in a critical manner is able to speak *with* the learner, even if occasionally he/she needs to speak *at* the learner' (pp. 127–28).

To successfully shift from a well-designed theory to everyday practice, contemporary education needs to go beyond decontextualized curriculum to a deep and critical reading of common sense reality. In other words, it needs to build socio-cultural *conscientization*. Conscientization is a process of the dynamization of minds—a critical conscience-building process. It not only requires a change in the content of conscience, but also a change in our mental structures and behaviours. In Freire's words, the rigid and dogmatic conscience becomes dynamic, flexible and dialectical, making changes in reality possible. Conscientization is considered to be partly a utopian concept because it represents a process that will never be fully realizable for either the educator or the learner (Freire, 1997).

Narayan (2000) pointed out that Gandhi and Freire held four core values which determined all of their interventions and strategies, whether in the political arena or in educational reforms: (*a*) People-centred values, (*b*) Injustice, (*c*) Faith in people, and (*d*) Value base for social work.

CONCLUSION

Freire's work contains remarkably eclectic thinking, with inputs from Christianity, Hegel, Marx, and Gramsci. As Freire experienced relations of power and domination in Latin America and other places in the world, he developed and practiced a radical approach to education, that when linked to a social movement, made social and political change possible. For Freire, dialogue in education is the practice of freedom. Naming one's experience and placing that voiced experience in context is the essence of dialogue (Freire, 1993). Different than discussion, dialogue is characterized as a kind of speech that is humble, open, and focused on collaborative learning. It is communication that can awaken consciousness and prepare people for collective action.

Although European influences are numerous in his work, Freire is different from usual Western educators in several ways. Freire's pedagogy decolonizes contemporary educational thought. First of all, he moves pedagogy away from the technical drifts that emerged throughout the 20th century. While insisting on the political value of education, Freire elaborates a critical pedagogy adapted to the context of the Majority World where inequalities are deeper and the welfare state absent. Subsequently, in Freire's work it is difficult to distinguish the phases where he is a researcher, an analyst, an educator, a social worker, or a citizen. All of these identities are working at the same time. And on this point, he joined the pedagogues and pedagogies of the Majority World. Even his style of writing is particular. Indeed, Freire writes as he speaks and speaks as he writes. The prevalence of oral thought in his books makes Freire available to the greatest number of teachers around the world. He will remain a bridge between pedagogies in developed countries and in the Majority World for decades to come.

REFERENCES

Apple, M. 1996. *Cultural Politics and Education.* New York: Teachers College Press.

Dardar, A. 1991. *Culture and Power in the Classroom: A Critical Foundation for Bicultural Education.* New York: Bergin & Garvey.

Escobar, H. and M. Escobar. 1981. *Dialogue in the Pedagogical Praxis of Paulo Freire.* Geneva: Graduate Institute of Development Studies.

Facundo, B. 1984. *Freire Inspired Programs in the United States and Puerto Rico: A Critical Evaluation.* Washington DC: Latino Institute. Available online at http://nlu.nl.edu/ace/resources/Documents/Facundo. html (downloaded on 20 May 2008).

Freire, P. 1967. *Educação como pratica da libertade.* Rio de Janeiro: Paz e Terra.

———. 1973. *Education for Critical Consciousness.* New York: The Seabury Press.

———. 1976. 'L'alphabétisation et le "rêve possible"'. *Perspectives,* VI(1): 70–73.

———. 1985. *The Politics of Education: Culture, Power and Liberation.* Boston: Bergin & Garvey.

———. 1988. 'Lettre aux agents d'éducation pour adultes', *Revue allemande d'éducation des adultes,* 31: 95–100.

Freire, P. 1991. *A educação na cidade*. Sao Paulo: Cortez Editora.

———. 1992. 'Forword', in C. Poster and J. Zimmer (eds), *Community Education in the Third World*, pp. VII–VIII. London and New York: Routledge.

———. 1993. *Pedagogy of the Oppressed*. New York: Continuum. ———.

1996. *Pedagogia da autonomia. Sabers necessarios à pratica educativa.* Sao Paulo: Paz e Terra.

———. 1997. 'A Response', in P. Freire, J. W. Frazer, D. Macedo, T. McKinnon and W. T. Stokes (eds), *Mentoring the Mentor: A Critical Dialogue with Paulo Freire*, pp. 175–99. New York: Peter Lang.

Freire, P. and A. Faundez. 1985. *Por uma pedagogia da pergunta*. Rio de Janeiro: Paz e Terra.

Freire, P. and D. Macedo. 1987. *Literacy: Reading the Word and the World.* London: Routledge and Kegan Paul.

Freire, P., J. W. Frazer, D. Macedo, T. McKinnon and W.T. Stokes (eds), 1997. *Mentoring the Mentor: A Critical Dialogue with Paulo Freire.* New York: Peter Lang.

Gibson, R. 1994. *The Promethean Literacy: Paulo Freire's Pedagogy of Reading, Praxis and Liberation*. Unpublished doctoral dissertation. Pennsylvania: The Pennsylvania State University.

Giroux, H. 1997. *Pedagogy and the Politics of Hope: Theory, Culture and Schooling*. Boulder, CO: Westview Press.

Gur-Ze'ev, I. 2005. 'Critical Theory, Critical Pedagogy and Diaspora Today – Toward a New Critical Language in Education', in I. Gur-Ze'ev (ed.), *Critical Theory and Critical Pedagogy Today – Toward a New Critical Language in Education*, pp. 7–34. Haifa: Faculty of Education, University of Haifa.

Harasim, L. M. 1983. *Literacy and National Reconstruction in Guinea-Bissau. A Critique of the Freirian Literacy Campaign*. Unpublished doctoral dissertation. Toronto: University of Toronto.

Lindquist Wong, P. 1995. 'Constructing a Public Popular Education in Sao Paulo, Brazil', *Comparative Education Review*, 39(1): 120–41.

Loiola, F. and C. Borges. 1996. 'La pédagogie de Paulo Freire ou quand l'éducation devient un acte politique', in M. Tardif and C. Gauthier (eds), *La pédagogie. Théories et pratiques de l'antiquité à nos jours*, pp. 237–54. Montréal: Gaëtan Morin.

McLaren, P. 1994. 'White Terror and Oppositional Agency: Toward a Critical Multiculturalism', in D.T. Goldenberd (ed.), *Multiculturalism: A Critical Reader*, pp. 45–74. Oxford: Blackwell.

———. 1997a. 'Freirian Pedagogy: the Challenge of Postmodernism and the Politics of Race', in P. Freire, J. W. Frazer, D. Macedo, T. McKinnon and W. T. Stokes (eds), *Mentoring the Mentor: A Critical Dialogue with Paulo Freire*, pp. 90–99. New York: Peter Lang.

———. 1997b. *Revolutionary Multiculturalism*. Boulder, CO: Westview Press.

Mesquida, P. 2004. 'Les influences européennes sur la pensée et la pratique éducative de Paulo Freire', in A. Akkari and P. Dasen (eds), *Pédagogies et pédagogues du Sud*, pp. 275–94. Paris: L'Harmattan.

Narayan, L. 2000. 'Freire and Gandhi. Their relevance for social work education', *International Social Work*, 43(2): 193–204.

Nóvoa, A. 1996. 'Paulo Freire', in J. Houssaye (ed.), *Pédagogues contemporains*, pp. 45–74. Paris: Armand Colin.

O'Cadiz, M., P. Lindquist Wong and C.A. Torres. 1998. *Education and Democracy. Paulo Freire, Social Movements and Educational Reform in Sao Paulo*. Boulder: Westview Press.

Saul, A. M. 1996. 'Curriculo en proceso. Una experiencia en la ciudad de San Pablo-Brasil, en la gestion de Paulo Freire (1989–1992)', *Revista Latinoamericana de Innovaciones Educativas*, VIII (24). Available online at http://www.mcye.gov.ar/zonaedu/OEA/INNEDU/28 (downloaded on 20 May 2008).

Torres, C.A. 1994. 'Paulo Freire as Secretary of Education in the Municipality of Sao Paulo', *Comparative Education Review*, 38(2): 181–214.

15
GLOBALIZATION, EDUCATION, AND CULTURAL DIVERSITY
JOSÉ MARÍN

INTRODUCTION

The Westernization of the world began with the Crusades and continued through the first 'discoveries' of other continents by Portuguese, Spanish and other European expeditions during the late 15th century. The evangelization of the 'pagans', the civilization of the 'savages', the myth of 'development', and the current economic and cultural globalization are periods of the same historical process of economic, political, and cultural domination through the imposition of Western ethnocentrism in the world. In every period, cultural domination, although in different ways, has been accompanied by political and economic domination.

Currently, globalization is part of the historical process of economic domination under the worldwide expansion of capitalism. It has been consolidated after the fall of the Berlin Wall in 1989, and the disappearance of the Soviet Union (USSR) in 1991. These events symbolize the demise of the bipolar world and the beginning of the imposition of the economic capitalist model on a planetary scale. This process is led mainly by big multinational corporations and it implicates the imposition of a *cultural standardization*, which is called by some experts *cultural Mcdonaldization* (Adda, 1998; Cassen,

2000; Lempen, 1999; Ramonet, 1996, 2000, 2001; Schiller, 2000). This last period has still not been fully analyzed in its socio-cultural aspects. It is true that the origin of the current great changes and mutations is to be found in the economic sphere, but economic factors are not enough to explain the historical process fully. It is in the technical revolution, itself resulting from a larger evolution of ideas, which created the greatest revolution of information and communication technology affecting the cultural domain.

In this chapter, we mainly approach European ethnocentric history through colonial and post-colonial domination, which imposed the Westernization of the world that preceded contemporary globalization. We deal equally with the importance of preserving cultural diversity, which is as necessary as biological diversity as a heritage of humanity, and which the globalization process as it is now developing, tends to depredate and *uniformize*.

We start with 'education as' the base of our reflection for our intercultural perspective. Education could be a means to preserve cultural diversity and could create a democratic space that makes the encounter and dialogue among cultures possible. Actually, this reflection is fundamental in order to imagine how to live in the multi-culturality that characterizes contemporary societies.

The intercultural perspective as applied to education and other areas of the social sciences refers to the exchanges, interactions, reciprocity, and interdependence that exist in the relations between cultures for understanding of the world. Education from this perspective is the transmitter of fundamental values that constitute the essential base from which to imagine projects of a viable society that guarantees our needed dignity. Our chapter has an introductory nature and suffers from many limitations; we are aware that the current conundrum is large and complex, and for this reason we will provide more questions than answers.

THE WESTERNIZATION OF THE WORLD

It is the West that has invented progress, growth, and development, lives in the deep-rooted belief that its project will continue indefinitely and that its objectives constitute something positive in itself; as a consequence, it has also invented its downfall, its decadence and chaos.

Serge Latouche, *L'Occidentalisation du monde* (1989: 129).

The historical roots of the contemporary economic and cultural globalization are found in the imposition of Western ethnocentrism. The vision of the world, and the prototype of society, as a universal model to be imitated everywhere, was already present within the context of the colonial and postcolonial domination (Latouche, 1989; Marín, 1994a/b, 2001). First of all, the Spanish, Portuguese and European colonialism generally, found it necessary to legitimize the imposition of its systems over the indigenous peoples of America, Asia, and Africa. This process required the ideological construction that would permit the gradual 'fabrication' of the *inferiority of its victims*, an ideological mechanism that served to justify all kinds of unfairness. The alienation of the oppressed was the fundamental rule in the scale of values of the dominant culture, structured by the imposition of the *universality* of its civilization; it considered itself as the one and only model of world vision, society, economy, politics, and culture.

In the American context, *evangelization* began in the 15th century as the first period of European imposition of its ethnocentrism, and continued until the end of the 18th century, the period of the great Amerindian rebellions, that were mostly led by literate Amerindians. The *civilizing* of the Amerindians constituted the second period of the Westernization process. In the terminology of Western domination, the Amerindians considered 'pagans' during the evangelization process were converted into 'savages' who must be *civilized*. The baptism ritual was replaced by *alphabetization* in Spanish or Portuguese, which were the dominant languages. The schools were the instrument *par excellence* of colonial domination because such institutions permit *the imposition of the cultures and official languages.*

Schools played a fundamental role in the negation of cultural identities. The only possible 'integration' offered to the Amerindian cultures through schooling was the acceptance of the dominant official language and culture to the detriment of their real cultural and linguistic diversity. This provided the historical roots of the divorce between the official State and real society, a cleavage that prevails until today.

The third period of Westernization occurred in the name of 'development' of the 'underdeveloped', which is the period linked to the myth of modernity (freedom, justice, and a secular vision of the world). As Touraine (1993) asserts, the West has believed for a long time that *modernity* meant the triumph of reason, the destruction of traditions, identities and creeds, and the replacement of experience by calculation. Modernity impregnated European history during the industrial revolution and during the 20th century, with the creation of the nation-state as the unique political model, inspired by the creation of Spain and France. This conception of the State imposes the defence of a mythical Nation, which supposes a people with a single history, a single language and a homogeneous culture. In reality, the nation-state as a political model denies the cultural and linguistic diversity that characterizes the different peoples that inhabit the territories proclaimed by the new state. This political model is at the origin of many conflicts among contemporary nations. It is the pretence of the nation-state to homogenize different peoples in an authoritarian way that is found at the root of contemporary problems and unresolved ethnic and religious conflicts that bleed Africa, Latin America, Asia, and Europe today.

The European view of *modernity* has been regarded as the way to attain liberty, justice and the right to a more democratic society. Within the context of Latin America, and above all, the African and Asian nations, which emerged from colonial domination, *modernity* became an unfulfilled utopia. In those regions, modernity is limited to an ideological proposal, *modernization* is nothing more than an empty political declaration, to legitimize the expansion of capitalism as the realization of the *myth of progress* (Marín, 1994a/b). This myth creates the false opposition between what is modern and the knowledge of traditional cultures, between the written and oral cultures, and results in the destruction of an important collective heritage. Its negative consequences have not even shunned the industrial countries, which ironically gave birth to the myth (Amin and Houtart, 2000; Lempen, 1999; Marín, 1996; Montoya, 1992; Quijano, 1988; Touraine, 1993).

Today, the myth of progress, of development, of infinite economic growth, and globalization of the 'new economy', are confronted with the challenges proposed by ethics, human dignity, and the conundrum of ecology. In the Western conception, the ecological dimension has been absent, which explains the cleavage that we confront today, originating in the divorce between nature and economics. We should now take ecological aspects into account in all areas of human thought and activity (Costa, 2000; Ki-Zerbo, 1992; Marín, 2000; Narby, 1995). The Western perception of the world is mainly based on a rational conception of time, hence the importance of productivity and profitability, without taking into consideration the environment (space, territory and 'nature') that is so fundamental in the world views and ways of living of traditional cultures.

The Western model of school has carried with it the imposition of all these Western conceptions, which praise the written to the disadvantage of the oral culture and traditional knowledge. It carries a preferred type of intelligence and a preconceived manner of constructing knowledge. This is a process of exclusion that has resulted in the destruction of a huge collective cultural legacy. The knowledge officially instituted by the dominant culture includes only a small part of real human knowledge. The wealth of knowledge derived from daily life that is part of traditional education, for example, has been excluded by the schools imposed by the West.

Modernization in the past, and globalization today, impose a single model of culture, on which all the world's people are supposed to align themselves, irrespective of cultural diversity. From this perspective, indigenous people and other cultures are considered as retarded, and constitute an obstacle for globalized capitalism.

Ethnocentrism is not specific to Europe, but is universal. Every society centres itself on its own culture in order to reconfirm its identity (Camilleri, 1993). The problem starts when a culture imposes itself over another culture. The history of European ethnocentrism is a particular case, because of its pretence to the *universality of Western culture*.

From this cultural assumption comes the tendency to declare as inferior, the knowledge, world visions, conceptions, and ways of living of other cultures. The pretended universality of Western culture carries with it some 'truths' conceived on the basis of one and only model of society, thus implying that it is up to the other cultures to 'catch up' with Western society. This conception belongs to the cultural determinism that makes out of culture an entity resistant to change. This proposition is illustrated by the political scientist Samuel Huntington (1996), who attributes to Christian culture, the disposition for democracy, making it incompatible with other civilizations (especially Muslims) (Journet, 2000). This thesis, which is not really new, takes on special importance because it opposes the predictions about the modernization of the world.

The world is made of complexity, and its ecological and cultural diversity largely surpasses any reductionist theory, which tries to impose universal truths. We have to imagine a plural and multi-cultural society that is able to handle equality and justice within cultural diversity, an open and a tolerant society, which goes beyond 'cultural boundaries' and ancient social limits. We must become aware of the migrations as a central part of human history, from the beginning of humankind to the present day.

One of the greatest contemporary challenges is how to live together within a framework of respect between 'us' and the 'others', within the framework of multicultural societies. This is the question that must be solved by education. We must learn to find in the intercultural exchange and dialogue, the answers to contemporary challenges, learning to live with modesty and dignity and away from reduction-ist propositions and simple solutions.

The imposition of the assumptions associated with Western civili-zation's pretended 'universality', articulated by churches, schools, mass media, and other institutions of dominant culture, are char-acteristic of *the logic of excluding cultural diversity*. This exclusion is conceived as an instrument of homogenization and cultural standardization, thus attempting to impose a unique model of society, which is portrayed in the different economic and cultural facets of capitalist globalization. These are the features that characterize the contemporary planetary situation. Nowadays, this process of eco-nomic expansion is stagnant and is unable to answer the ethical and ecological challenges, and the demand for real human dignity. Those are challenges that capitalist globalization—which is missing a project for a sustainable society—cannot solve.

NEOLIBERALISM AND GLOBALIZATION

There was a time in which the economic decisions corresponded to the needs of the concerned social groups. This happened when communities showing solidarity were the rule instead of the excep-tion. This decision process, founded on the imperative of social needs, has been progressively replaced by a cold and blind efficiency guided by an economic system in which the essential value is financial benefit.

Introduction to *L'autre Davos* by F. Houtart and F. Polet (1999: 5)

Neoliberalism as the ideological base of globalization was born after World War II in Western Europe and the United States. This ideology sanctions a theoretical and political reaction against State inter-ventionism and the social state. In 1944, Friedrich August von Hayek published *The Road to Serfdom*. To some extent, this work constitutes the founding charter of neoliberalism. It is a passionate attack against any attempt by the state to impose limitations on the functioning of the free market. These obstacles are denounced be-cause they constitute, in his opinion, a mortal threat against economic and political freedom. This book emerged in the British historical and political context and the immediate target was the Labour Party during the elections of 1945 (Houtart and Poulet, 1999).

In 1947, at the moment when the basis for the Social State of the post World War II Europe were being realized, Hayek invited those who shared his ideological orientation to Mont Pélerin, near Vevey (Switzerland). Among the famous participants of the encounter are found not only the determined adversaries of the social state in Europe, but also declared enemies of the American New Deal. At the conclusion of this meeting, the Mont Pélerin Society was founded, a sort of neoliberal[1] *fraternity*, well-organized and consecrated to the propagation of its theories through periodic international meetings. It had a dual objective: First, to combat the social solidarity policies that prevailed after the Second World War, and second, to prepare for the future with the theoretical grounds for another type of capitalism, strong and free from regulations.

In 1974, the industrial capitalist countries entered into a deep recession process. Due to this reality, the neoliberal ideas began to gain attention. F. A. von Hayek and his disciples asserted that the root of the crisis was to be found in the excessive power of labour unions and generally in the labour movement. According to them, the labour unions had sabotaged the basis for accumulation and investment because of salary increases and pressure on the State to increase constantly its parasitic social expenses. Monetary stability must constitute the supreme objective of all the governments. For this reason, it was necessary to introduce budget discipline alongside restrictions of social expenditures and the restoration of a so-called 'natural' percentage of unemployment, that is, the creation of a 'labour reserve' in order to weaken labour unions. Among other policies, they recommend tax reductions on higher incomes and the earnings of corporations (Houtart and Polet, 1999). According to these neoliberal theories, growth would return naturally when monetary stability would be attained and when their main policies were re-activated (de-fiscalization, limits to social costs, de-regulation, and so on).

This programme was implemented gradually, over a decade. In 1979, a new political situation emerged. In that year, the government of Margaret Thatcher began in England. This was the first government in an industrial capitalist country that openly promised to put in practice the neoliberal programme with all the disastrous consequences for social welfare, health and public education, that we now know of. Ronald Reagan was elected President of the United States in 1980; thus neoliberalism came into power, with the planetary consequences that are so well known today. In 1982, it was the turn for Germany, and from 1982 to 1984 for Denmark, a symbol of the Scandinavian welfare State.

Thus, the hegemony of the New Conservatives in Europe and North America was consolidated. It is in the 1980s that the world witnessed the undisputed victory of the neoliberal ideology in the industrial nations. The social consequences were high unemployment rates, repression of strikes, the beginning of anti-labour legislation and the drastic reduction or elimination of important social expenditures. Another important characteristic has been the privatization of numerous economic sectors which previously belonged to the State. In the United States, where there was no Social State comparable to the European ones, the government gave preference to military expenditures and reduced the taxes on the rich. Public health services, social welfare and education were the least favoured sectors. The Social Democratic governments of Europe have also applied the neoliberal principles that are contrary to their own original political theories. On the other side of the world, in Australia and New Zealand, the neoliberal model was imposed with brutality. Undoubtedly, New Zealand represents the most extreme case; the Social State was disarticulated in a more radical manner than in Britain.

The Chilean neoliberal experience is linked to the American influence and had as its mentor Milton Friedman, Professor at the University of Chicago. The Chilean experience required the abolition of democracy and the establishment of one of the cruellest dictatorships after the Second World War. While Chile spearheaded the bitter experience of neoliberalism in the region, Latin America has also served as a site for experimental implementation of the programmes, as was the case with Bolivia after 1985. These programmes were later applied in Eastern Europe; Poland and Russia suffered the imposition of structural re-adjustment. The turn towards neoliberalism appeared throughout Latin America, in Mexico,

Argentina and Venezuela in 1988, and finally in 1990 with the election of Alberto Fujimori in Peru. None of these governments informed the voters about the content of the economic policies that they intended to enforce. Carlos Mennem in Argentina, Carlos Andrés Pérez in Venezuela and Fujimori in Peru, promised exactly the opposite of the anti-popular measures that they enforced in the succeeding years. The authoritarian tradition of Mexico's Institutional Revolutionary Party (PRI) is well known.

Of the Latin American neoliberal experiences, some experienced an immediate success against inflation, as in Mexico, Argentina and Peru, but failure in others like Venezuela. The enforcement of economic measures such as brutal de-regulation, and privatization have promoted unemployment and social inequality and injustice within the context of authoritarian and corrupt politics.

It would be a mistake to conclude that in Latin America only the authoritarian regimes can impose neoliberal policies. The Bolivian, Brazilian and Ecuadorian cases show us such evidence: the huge inflation, with its perverse pauperization effect on large parts of the population, leads people to resign themselves, and to accept the brutal measures of neoliberal policies, even when they preserve incipient 'democratic' forms. This has catastrophic social results as is the case with many Asian, African, and Latin American nations.

NEOLIBERAL IDEOLOGY AND EDUCATION

> A thought does not have any value, if it does not enter the market.
>
> Milton Friedman (Cited in T. Longo, 2001: p. 74.)

Neoliberal ideology related to education is fundamentally opposed to any political philosophy that grants the State a primary role for education. The tendency is to privatize education and to reduce government expenses in the public sector. From this perspective, education becomes a merchandise that can be regulated by the market, as is the case of health care and social services. This premise has become a reality in many countries where the neoliberal ideology has been imposed.

Teresa Longo (2001) reviews the history of different philosophical conceptions of *Liberalism and Neo-liberalism* in relation to education. Condorcet, a representative of liberalism, proclaims the *right of citizens to instruction* in the project of the French Constitution that he presents in 1793. For him, equality would remain a formal declaration as long as there remained an unequal access to knowledge. Public education becomes the basis for the construction of democracy. Condorcet wrote: 'Education is a way to exercise rights and establish a real equality among citizens and to grant them true political equality. On a secular basis, ... the objective of instruction is not just to get people to admire the existing legislation, but to enable them to evaluate and correct it' (cited by Longo, 2001: 25).

The acquisition of knowledge and values is one of Condorcet's interests. As Badinter (1988) asserts: 'if Condorcet proposes the basis for social democracy, his project is nevertheless not socialist. His conception of society remains fundamentally individualist and liberal' (cited by Longo, 2001: 25). For Jules Ferry, knowledge is always subordinated to morality. Education consists in acquiring a set of disciplines that the State has considered as priorities and that have, above all, an educational value through making everyone accept the Republic's values. What interests Ferry, is the development of the nation-state, and public instruction is the designed means for its construction (Longo, 2001).

For one of neoliberalism's mentors like Karl Popper, the State must not intervene in public education, because it imposes its truth, preventing critique and reflection. At the centre of Popper's interest is the development of a critical spirit in the private sector. For Popper, the State not only must not educate citizens, but also must not concern itself with the formation of the ruling class. For Auguste Von Hayek, the State has to guarantee public order. The State has to be a guardian that supervises and guarantees the efficiency of the system without possessing political, social, and cultural purposes. The State must not intervene in education, but may help poor families so that all have access to a basic education. The State must only guarantee the financing of basic education through a system of vouchers. In this manner, parents are free to register their children in private schools of their choice. In his conception, secondary and tertiary education must be paid for, but could be obtained through credit or as an investment (Longo, 2001: 41–65).

In Latin America, the application of neoliberalism as educational philosophy has an excellent illustration in Chile. Teresa Longo (2001) has carefully researched this case.

In sum, the neoliberal ideology reduces education to being just another merchandise in the supermarket of globalization. Education becomes a way of spreading competitive values, pragmatism and utilitarian profitability, that are the basis of an individualist paradigm. The tenets of neoliberalist education can be summarized in the following statements (Marín and Dasen, 2007).

1. Neoliberalism rejects the possibility of attributing to cultural diversity a role in social construction.
2. Knowledge and know-how become goods that are bought and sold.
3. Rejection of the idea of a society where knowledge is shared, and political decisions are derived from consensus.
4. Education in the full extent, and instruction as one of its forms, does not constitute one of citizens' rights. Beyond a 'minimal education' guaranteed by the State, secondary and tertiary education become family investment. The privatization of education forms part of this ideology's convictions.
5. Neoliberalism is a modern ideological political form, which conceives a society where all reasons for dialogue, agreements and conventions among citizens are suppressed. In case of Chile and other Latin American and European countries where this ideology has been applied, we can assert that public education is no longer a means for social emancipation.
6. Inequality in the access to knowledge creates great social differences and mutations, and results in a growing exclusion of parts of the population.
7. The degradation of public education and the impoverishment of underpaid teachers have negative consequences in the academic quality of public education.
8. This impoverishment provokes a strong erosion of social identity and it is the reason why teachers are underestimated in their social function as agents of cultural transmission.
9. Likewise, we are witnessing a de-politicization that eliminates the political dimension from education; as well as the loss of a historical conscience.
10. There is a perverse transformation of a school that pretended to bring about equality into a mercantilized school, which is managed by the blindness of the market, with all the historical weight of social exclusion and fragmentation that this means.

This analysis leaves us with the following questions:

What type of education do we need today to understand the links between the local and global levels? How can we associate a local (regional, national) education with the realities imposed by globalization? Which type of education can answer the ethical and ecological challenges we are facing? How can we understand social change and the socio-economic and cultural conflicts and prevent them? What kind of education is needed to participate fully in the worldwide multicultural society? What is the role of an intercultural perspective in an appropriate educational project in the context of globalization?

GLOBALIZATION AND CULTURAL DIVERSITY

The industrialization of culture

The industrialization of culture is associated with economic development and market expansion. This process had its origin in the 1950s (Warnier, 1999). It concerns the sectors that conjugate the creation, production, and commercialization of goods and services, the particularity of which resides in the intangibility of its contents with a cultural character, and that are generally protected by *copyrights*. The cultural industries include the printed press and multimedia, cinematographic, audio-visual and phonographic production, as well as graphics and art. Some countries extend this concept to architecture, plastic arts and acting, sport industries, construction of musical instruments, publicity, and cultural tourism. Reference is made, above all, to the *creative industries* (UNESCO, 2000).

The creative industries add to cultural activities an economic value, which generates new types of values for individuals and for society. The cultural and economic duality of these industries constitutes their main characteristic. What is the main role of the industrialization of culture in the preservation and promotion of cultural diversity, as well as in the democratization and the access to culture? This is the first question. The second question is: Who controls the economic development and expansion of this industry within the context of the economic and cultural globalization?

In the last two decades, the trade in cultural goods has quadrupled. Moreover, most of this trade has taken place among a small number of nations. For example, in 1990, Japan, the United States, Germany and Great Britain accounted for 55.4 per cent of the exportation of all cultural goods in the world and 47 per cent of the imports were made by the United States, Germany, and France. In 1998, China became the third biggest exporter of the world. Through the 1990s, the growth in cultural industries in terms of production and distribution has been exponential (UNESCO, 2000).

The case of Walt Disney is a very good illustration of this expansion. Who controls these ideological messages and what are the economic and political interests behind this globalization or 'Disneyization' of culture? What becomes of the 'copyrights' of traditional knowledge within the context of industrialization and the planetary expansion of markets? It is a question that needs to be put to the multinational corporations. It is well known that in the pharmacological industry, indigenous knowledge about medicinal plants is being pirated by some companies, which have secured patents. The World Health Organization has organized several conferences about this problem (Brush and Stabinsky, 1996; WHO, 2001).

Traditional knowledge, defined as the innovations and creativity based on tradition, including folklore, is more and more of interest to the decision makers in diverse sectors such as food and agriculture, trade and economic development, the environment, health, human rights, and cultural policies. The protection of traditional knowledge has been the theme of a conference by the World Intellectual Property Organization in Geneva in 1999 (WIPO, 2001).

Cultural diversity

The planet where we live is characterized by its bio-diversity that constitutes an immense variety of life forms developed over millions of years. The defence of this bio-diversity seems unavoidable for the survival of the natural ecological systems that are the basis of the 'cultural eco-systems', composed of a complex variety of cultures, that also need diversity to preserve the cultural heritage for future generations. This interaction between nature and culture is fundamental for our survival. It is in this diversity that the richness of our humanity is found. Bio-genetically, human 'races' do not exist; we all belong to the same species. We are all related and yet are all different (Langaney et al., 1992).

In 1992, UNESCO insisted on the need to make efforts to assume the challenges of development and to promote cultural diversity.

This proposal was taken up by the Inter-Government Conference on Cultural Policies for Development in Stockholm in 1992 (Hallak, 1998). In preparation for the meeting of the World Trade Organization (WTO) in Seattle, the notion of *cultural diversity* was again proclaimed in relation to cultural goods and services. In this meeting, it has been stated that only appropriate cultural policies can guarantee the preservation of creative diversity against the risk of a uniform culture, just as only preservation policies for bio-diversity can guarantee the protection of natural ecological systems, and thus guarantee the diversity of species.

Cultural diversity thus emerges as the positive expression of a general objective that seeks to value and protect the world's cultures against the danger of *uniformization*. In this perspective, the policy of 'cultural exception' represents therefore one of the means that may lead to the recognition and protection of *cultural diversity*. A key element of this reasoning is the affirmation that cultural goods and services (books, records, games, multimedia, films, and audio-visual material) are not comparable to other merchandize and services. It is for this reason that they deserve a different treatment or exemption in order to protect them from *commercial standardization*, which goes alongside mass consumption linked to the cultural industries (Adorno and Horkheimer, 1974).

Nevertheless, today, mass culture triumphs, especially the one imposed by the huge means of mass communication like television and publicity. This reinforces the planet's homogenization, and destroys national uniqueness for the benefit of the American model (Ramonet, 1997; Schiller, 2000). Cultural standardization reflects the American way of life, with its particular way of producing, consuming, dressing, eating, and even wasting. Today's generation is a part of yet another chapter in the historical process of Westernization that began with European expansion in the 15th century. Nowadays, Americanization is the most conspicuous aspect of the process of capitalist expansion, which transforms everything that it touches into merchandize. It reflects the transition from industrial development to *cultural industrialization*, which 'standardizes' everything that it assimilates. It is very similar to techno-bureaucratic development that makes everything anonymous, and to the mega urbanization that disintegrates traditional communities and atomizes people, depersonalizing their existence in the midst of the 'solitary crowd' as Edgar Morin asserts in his book, *Terre Patrie* (Morin, 1993; Ramonet, 1997).

The Westernization of the world, that resulted in the cultural destruction of large geographical areas as the consequence of cultural domination, colonialism and post-colonialism, now affects contemporary Europe. It is a paradoxical symbolic return to the roots of the historical imposition of supposed universal values, that originated in Europe itself. The process of imposition of European ethnocentrism that corrupted and ruined so many cultures in the world is currently attacking Europe in the disguise of *Americanization*.

Contemporary Europe is confronted by an identity crisis and its citizens are deprived of their traditional cultural references. They confront the present crisis within the context of the mutations and technological innovations to which they must adapt. The economic and cultural globalization, with the development of new technologies such as digital television, video games and internet, de-stabilizes all the economic and cultural activities, and challenges the norms and values of traditional societies (Ramonet, 1997).

How can we protect the values of cultural diversity from the compressing road-crusher of *cultural standardization*? History reminds us that these cultural conflicts are not new. The Renaissance witnesses the confrontation between faith and reason in which dogmatic truth is opposed to deductive logical truth. The emergence of rational thought influences the distinction between philosophy and religion. However, both humanism and Christianity (as well as Judaism and Islam) place man as the central figure in the universe creating the anthropocentric conception, typical of the Western vision of the world, thus separating man from nature. The creation of arbitrary limits between humanity and animality established the historical roots for the divorce between nature and culture, which is the basis of the contemporary ecological challenge. In the anthropocentric view, man has the vocation to subdue and dominate nature with the catastrophic results that we all know. It is under these premises that science and technology lead humanity to Nagasaki, Hiroshima, and Chernobyl. With the current bio-genetic modifications, we are promised the perversion of the weak equilibriums of the ecological systems that are necessary for the survival of our survival.

On the other hand, Western rationalism reached political maturity with the Declaration of Human Rights, which during the late 18th century led to the American and French revolutions. However, the tyranny of reason also produces its own monsters. Terror during the French Revolution, emerges as an expression of rational intolerance just like all the Holy Inquisition did in the name of faith (Ramonet, 1997). The triumph of European rationalism is going to bring to the other peoples of the world a cultural catastrophe with the devaluation of their languages and cultures. From the evangelization of the 15th century to our days, the pretension of universality of the Western cultural value-system has brought about the denial and destruction of other cultures. In the European continent, the scientific-technical rationality and bizarre political rationalizations have led to abominable massacres in the two world wars. The worst regression in the human spirit can be seen in the Jewish Holocaust, the Russian Gulag, apartheid in South Africa, and in the ethnic cleansing and massacre of Kurds. These tragedies were silenced in their own time with support of Western Europe and American complicity. All these historical dramas were produced in the name of reason and science and, to protect geo-political interests.

In the last decades, the economic rise of more affluent industrial societies has allowed them to pass from post-war poverty to the abundance of today. This affluence has pushed these societies into a consumerism that is encouraged by the mass media, above all by television, which has spread throughout the world one particular way of daily living. Between 'to be' and 'to have and own', the choice is *to consume and then exist*; it is the dominant mentality. In this context we also witness the erosion and destruction of family links. The family is confronted by the evolution of customs, sexual freedoms, and the erosion of value-systems in traditional societies. Likewise, there is a growing *individualism* that generates behaviour linked to competition, pragmatism, utilitarianism and the calculation of inter-personal relations, thus destroying solidarity.

In this context, individualism imposes itself as a paradigm and degrades collective life, which leads to the rise of other miseries like reinforcing spiritual misery through solitude. We face new types of *stress* and a weakening of affective links. Devaluations are not just economic devaluations, they can be worse if they are moral and spiritual devaluations. Progress and glorification of the economy, which globalization preaches, has become some sort of a new religion. Ramonet (1997) asserts that we are confronted by three serious crises: economic, demographic, and the cultural.

CONCLUSION

After World War II, culture has been colonized by trade as the consequence of cultural industrialization (Adorno and Horkheimer, 1974). Nowadays, 'we move towards a globalization where the economy deconstructs culture, just like it has deconstructed governments: 'cyberspace' replaces the territory and the market, and destroys the fundaments of the Nation State' (Ramonet, 2001: 6). When content industries transform culture into merchandise, thousands of years of cultural diversity disappear in the jungle of the supermarkets. Multinational corporations sell 'culture' in entertainment and recreation parks like those developed by Walt Disney. Likewise, tourism and travel seek to become big 'cultural' industries. Regardless of all the economic benefits that these activities can produce they are not without negative consequences for the cultural area and the environment.

In fact, we should not talk about a *globalization of culture*. As Jean Pierre Warnier (1999) perceptively asserted, we should not confuse the cultural industry with culture; it would be like taking a part for the whole. It would be like believing that the technological revolution is a global reality without considering that a large part of the population still lacks basic amenities and remains untouched by the technological revolution. A large number of people represent cultures in which life, from birth to death, has other references and are not linked to the Cathodic screen of television or computers. To believe that Westernization has become a universal historical phenomenon is to confirm the existence of a primitive ethnocentrism.

Nowadays, there is an important debate of two kinds: the first argues that we are witnessing the cultural erosion of unique cultures and the other asserts that Americanization characterizes *cultural homogenization* as a result of economic globalization. Now as in other epochs, humanity remains a machine that 'manufactures' cultural differences, that separates and produces mixtures. Cultures are in constant adaptation as they re-invent and re-create themselves. Humanity continues to re-structure societies as it elaborates the geo-politics of regions and markets. These separations and mixtures maintain existing cultures that are transmitted by tradition; they are localized, socialized and verbalized, thus creating identities. These cultures provide the references with which individuals and communities identify.

Cultures are living historical processes that are dynamic and are constantly transforming themselves between the local and the global dimensions. Westernization has always been confronted by cultural resistance, thus creating new faces and mixtures. Since economic globalization weakens the national state, it provokes the rise and recovery of different cultural identities. Despite its powerful technological machinery, the cultural industry has difficulties in standardizing other cultures and making them uniform. One of the obstacles that blocks the expansion in cultural commerce is that a large part of humanity lives in such precarious conditions, that it cannot be integrated into the big supermarkets of economic globalization.

In recent times while we have borne witness to some resistance against globalization by many sectors among the civil society, there have also been instances of erosion and destruction of some cultures. In this same process, societies develop an enormous cultural diversification and re-invention of traditions that seek new references in order to endure and survive the deep mutations and injustice in which they live. The nation-states are overpowered by the financial power of multinational corporations and are unable to assume their old political role of mediation.

The idea of a *universal culture* based on common references is also blocked by the irrationality of economic benefit that the dominant economic groups seek. They are very distanced from any collective project and social interest. Discourse such as the one about the defence of human rights is, to a very large extent, limited to political declarations and away from reality.

The resistance against economic and cultural domination is part of the long history of humanity. The 18th century philosophers of the Enlightenment developed a powerful philosophical social vision which coincides with the evolution of private property and the market. Today, we must develop a vision that has the capacity to use the extraordinary technological and economic revolution to the advantage of humanity and not against it. We do not want all our existence converted into merchandise sold over electronic networks. The way in which television has been used for this purpose is nefarious. According to the American magazine *Businessweek*, a 7 year old child watches an average of 20,000 commercials each year, and by age 12, the child's name will be in the data banks of companies that sell by mail (Schiller, 2000).

The end of the 20th century and the beginning of the 21st century were noted for the emergence of two great movements: the respect for bio-diversity and the defence of cultural diversity. The Gene Modified Organisms (GMO) are likely to provoke real catastrophes. This commercial aspect of nutrition uproots food from its cultural references. The application of bio-technology and especially the manipulation of DNA, patenting life and the cloning of mammals, in short any perversion in the food chain and ecological systems, could be catastrophic to our own survival.

The capitalist globalization provokes resistance and the emergence of new social movements of protest against this domination, which is also cultural domination. One of the greatest social conflicts of the 21st century will be for the preservation of bio-diversity and cultural diversity. Inter-cultural education will play a central role in this battle.

In the contemporary world conditions and after the imperialist military aggression against the Iraqi people, the inter-cultural perspective faces an enormous challenge: the military imposition of the pre-destined American geo-politics, with its ethnocentric and authoritarian world vision, and the monoculture impregnated by religious fundamentalism. In reality, inter-cultural education could create an opening for the respect for cultural diversity, in contrast to any mono-cultural, ethnocentric and 'excluding' education. Education in this perspective could promote our dignity and the common values of respect, solidarity, justice, and tolerance with which we recognize and identify ourselves. We need to reinforce respect for us and for the others as a source of support for the dignity that we all need.

NOTE

1. The adjective 'neo-liberal' and substantive 'neoliberalism' are of common usage in French. These terms refer to the current extreme capitalism, as an outgrowth of the earlier (17th century) philosophical and political movements that insisted on individual rights and private property against the power of governments. Even though these terms are not commonly used in English, we have kept them in this translation.

REFERENCES

Adda, J. 1998. *La mondialisation de l'économie, Volume 2.* Paris: La Découverte.

Adorno, T. W. and M. Horkheimer. 1974. *La dialectique de la raison*. Paris: Gallimard.

Amin, S. and F. Houtart. 2000. *Mondialisation et alternatives*. Genève: CETIM.

Badinter, E. 1988. *Condorcet, un intellectuel en politique*. Paris: Fayard.

Brush, S. and D. Stabinsky. 1996. *Valuing Local Knowledge: Indigenous Peoples and Intellectual Property Rights*. Washington, DC: Island Press.

Cassen, B. 2000. 'La langue-dollar', in *L'Amérique dans les têtes, Manière de voir /Le Monde Diplomatique*, 53: 88–90.

Camilleri, C. 1993. 'Le relativisme: du culturel à l'interculturel', in F. Tanon and G. Vermes (eds), *L'individu et ses cultures*, pp. 34–39. Paris: L'Harmattan.

Costa, J.-P. 2000. *L'homme-nature ou l'alliance avec l'univers. Entre Indianité et modernité*. Paris: Editions Sang de la Terre. Collection La pensée écologique.

Hallak, J. 1998. *Education et globalisation*. Paris: UNESCO.

Hayek, F. A. von. 1944. *The Road to Serfdom*. London: Routledge.

Houtart, F. and F. Polet, (eds). 1999. *L'autre Davos. Mondialisation des résistances et des luttes*. Paris: L'Harmattan.

Huntington, S. P. 1996. *The Clash of Civilizations and the Remaking of World Order*. New York: Simon & Schuster.

Journet, N. 2000. 'Penser la culture', *Sciences Humaines*,110: 22–27.

Ki-Zerbo, J. (ed.). 1992. *Compagnons du soleil*. Paris: FPH /La Découverte/ UNESCO.

Langaney, A., N. Hubert Van Blijenburg and A. Sánchez-Mazas. 1992. *Tous parents, tous différents*. Paris: Chabaud.

Latouche, S. 1989. *L'occidentalisation du monde*. Paris: Galma/La Découverte.

Lempen, B. 1999. *La mondialisation sauvage. De la fin du communisme à la tragédie du Kosovo*. Lausanne: Favre.

Longo, T. 2001. *Philosophies et politiques Néo-libérales de l'éducation dans le Chili de Pinochet 1973–1983*. Paris: L'Harmattan.

Marín, J. 1994a. 'Dimension historique de l'ethnocentrisme européen dans le processus de domination coloniale et post-coloniale de l'Amérique', in J. Blomart and B. Krewer (eds), *Perspectives de l'interculturel*, pp. 123–34. Paris: L'Harmattan.

———. 1994b. 'Ethnocentrisme et racisme dans l'histoire européenne dans le cadre de la conquête de l'Amérique et perspective actuelle', in C. Allemann Ghionda (ed.), *Multikultur und Bildung in Europa*, pp. 181–96. Bern: Peter Lang.

———. 1996. 'Le développement durable et la dimension interculturelle', in A. Giordan and J. D. Lempereur (eds), *12 Questions sur l'environnement*, pp. 127–30. Nice: Z éditions.

Marín, J. 2000. 'Une éducation appropriée aux peuples autochtones d'Amérique latine', in P. R. Dasen and C. Perregaux (eds), *Pourquoi des approches interculturelles en education?* pp. 261–80. Bruxelles: DeBoeck Université.

———. 2001. 'Histoire de l'Etat-Nation: de la politique d'intégration en Amérique Latine et en Europe', in C. Perregaux, T. Ogay, Y. Leanza and P.R. Dasen (eds), *Intégration et migrations: Regards pluridisciplinaires*, pp. 141–57. Paris: L'Harmattan.

Marín, J. and P. R. Dasen. 2007. 'L'éducation face à la mondialisation, aux migrations et aux droits de l'homme', in M. C. Caloz-Tschopp and P. R. Dasen (eds), *Mondialisation, migration et droits de l'homme: vol. 1, Un nouveau paradigme pour la recherché et la citoyenneté*, pp. 285–320. Bruxelles: Bruylant.

Montoya, R. 1992. *Al borde del naufragio. Democracia, violencia y problema étnico en el Perú.* Lima: Cuadernos de SUR.

Morin, E. 1993. *Terre patrie.* Paris: Editions du Seuil.

Quijano, A. 1988. *Modernidad, identidad y utopía en América Latina.* Lima: Ediciones Sociedad y Política.

Narby, J. 1995. *Le serpent cosmique. L'ADN et les origines du savoir.* Genève: Editions Georg.

Ramonet, I. 1996. *Nouveaux pouvoirs, nouveaux maîtres du monde.* Montreal: Ed. Fides.

———. 1997. *Géopolitique du chaos.* Paris: Editions Galilée.

———. 2000. 'La culture à l'ère d'Internet', in La culture, les élites et le peuple, *Manière de voir /Le Monde Diplomatique*, 57: 6–7.

———. 2001. 'Contrôler les esprits', in L'Amérique dans les têtes, *Manière de voir /Le Monde Diplomatique*, 53: 6–7.

Schiller, H. I. 2000. 'Décervelage à l'Américaine', in La culture, les élites et le peuple, *Manière de voir /Le Monde Diplomatique*, 57: 29–32.

Touraine, A. 1993. *Critique de la modernité.* Paris: Fayard.

UNESCO. 2000. *Culture, Trade and Globalisation. Questions and Answers.* Paris: UNESCO.

Warnier, J.-P. 1999. *La mondialisation de la culture.* Paris: La Découverte. Coll. Repères.

WHO. 2001. *Report of Inter-Regional Workshop on Intellectual Property Rights in the Context of Traditional Medicine.* Bangkok, Thailand: WHO.

WIPO. 2001. *Intellectual Property Needs and Expectations of Traditional Knowledge Holders.* Report on fact-finding missions on intellectual property and traditional knowledge (1998–1999). Geneva: WIPO.

16
THE GLOBALIZATION OF SCHOOLING: MAJOR TRENDS AND ISSUES IN THE SOUTH AND THE NORTH

ABDELJALIL AKKARI AND PIERRE R. DASEN

In this text we will discuss the principle challenges facing schooling from an international perspective. In the first section we will provide certain essential benchmarks on the origins and evolution of formal schooling. In the next section we uncover what schooling in the 'North' and the 'South'[1] has in common. In the third section we will analyze the specificities of schooling in the South, how new ways of appropriating schooling are emerging throughout countries of the South and are contributing to the ongoing discussion on schooling. We continue by enumerating some consequences of globalization on educational systems, and the need to develop a new kind of education. We also draw attention to basic education as a fundamental human right, and discuss this shortly in relation to illegal migrants in Europe. We conclude with a section on intercultural education, which was first developed exclusively in the North in relation to multicultural classrooms, but would no doubt be relevant worldwide in relation to education for citizenship and for sustainable development.

SCHOOLING: FROM COLONIZATION TO GLOBALIZATION

One can partially agree with Reagan (2000: p. xiii) when he states, 'In all societies, throughout human history, people have educated their children. Indeed, one of the fundamental characteristics of human civilization is a concern for the preparation of the next generation'. This point of view is debatable however, since he fails to make the important distinction between education, schooling and enculturation. Additionally he dismisses the particularity of formal schooling. As Vincent (1994) has asserted, formal schooling indicates a process of instituting, of effecting social rules through pedagogical practice. In French we can clearly see this process as teachers are referred to as *instituteurs*.

From a pedagogical viewpoint, formal schooling has several characteristics: The teaching is simultaneous and progressive. The teacher speaks to a class group and the school is organized in different grades. The unique status of written culture, the appearance of scholastic disciplines and teacher training institutions are also specific to the pedagogical orientation of formal schooling. The existence of formal schooling points to inclusions, exclusions and new equilibriums between the 'school as an institution' and 'society', between those who have been successful in school and those who have not.

Looking in greater detail at the historical emergence of formal schooling, it should be kept in mind that educational institutions have a much longer history than that of formal educational systems which first appeared in Europe in the second half of the 19th century. In fact, the history of educational institutions practically coincides with the history of humanity or at least with the appearance of the first human civilizations. These civilizations succeeded at domesticating certain plants through intensive agriculture and created cities and educational institutions closely linked with political and religious powers and involved only a small minority of individuals.

In Europe the close connection between religion and school continued until the 18th century where one saw the progressive removal of the Church as the sole purveyor of scholastic transmission. While the moral vision of the West was founded on Christianity for several centuries, the Enlightenment philosophy, allied with the nation-state, established that reason must be considered the foundation for the action of its citizens (Ruano-Borbalan, 2002). It is this growing distance between scholastic institutions and religion which made the spreading and the hegemony of formal schooling possible. At the same time, the emergence in the 17th century of a modern conception of childhood radically altered the position of children in society. Up to this time children joined the world of adults at an early age and their cognitive specificity was not taken into account (Ariès, 1960).

The European and North American educational systems established during the second half of the 19th century represent a radical break in the history of education. The modern school institution, founded by the promulgation of compulsory schooling, is characterized by four factors. First, it is closely connected with the development of the State and of industrialization. In other words, the educational system becomes a base for the new relationship between the individual and the political or economical authority. Second, the educational system has a universal vocation. This means, on the one hand, that it is intended for all children regardless of their social background, and on the other, that it is the guarantor of a scientific knowledge with universal intentions. Third, the development of the school coincided with the emergence of childhood and adolescence as specific periods in the life of an individual. Finally, the rise of European educational systems is intimately linked with the formation of nation-states that are generally monolingual. As an institutional phenomenon, formal schooling appears in the contemporary world as the strong-arm of the nation-state (Boli et al., 1985).

Taken together these factors lead us, in short, to an ambiguous or ambivalent scholastic institution. In one way, this institution unites prospective citizens in the same space and puts them in contact with the same knowledge, at least, during primary school. It introduces them to the world outside of the family circle. At the same time, it may be oppressive to some of these same future citizens, since it is primarily at the service of one nation, one culture and mostly, one language. Thus it is not surprising that the rise of formal schooling coincided with the peak of colonization. The colonial domination was widely accompanied by the introduction of formal schooling following the European model. It should be noted, however, that the indigenous and colonized population always received schooling in small amounts and of poor quality. Nevertheless, their contact with formal schooling led them to make demands for their rights and to desire freedom from the colonial yoke. The process of decolonization, begun in Latin America, continued in Asia and finally achieved in Africa, did not give rise to a challenge to European-styled schooling. On the contrary, the countries of the South entered a global race to catch up with European norms. The economic globalization of the past years has sped up this scholastic race as the competitiveness between nations is measured, rightly or wrongly, by the effectiveness and efficiency of their educational systems.

Globalization of schooling

Since the middle of the 19th century we have seen an unprecedented development of schooling. Statistics established by international organizations show a similar progression in the North and the South, with a gap of several decades which varies according to the regions of the South. Overall we can identify four principal periods which have led to the current globalization of schooling.

The emergence of formal schooling

The first stage, which occurred between the years 1850 and 1900, saw the beginnings of unified educational systems in Europe and North America. The most rapid development of formal schooling occurred in the Protestant nations of northern Europe. The goal of this intensive schooling was double; on the one hand it was meant to bring literacy to the entire adult population and on the other it was meant to facilitate the participation of the citizens in political life. In the colonized countries in the South this period corresponds with the first contacts with formal schooling. Overall this contact was very destructive for these societies. In Asia, Africa, and the Arab world, various forms of education were well-established prior to contact with the West. As documented in several chapters of this volume, indigenous, non-Western schools (for example, Koranic, pagoda, temple and native schools) had existed for generations, albeit with enrolments usually limited to young boys. These forms of indigenous education, mostly oriented towards inculcating religious and traditional cultural knowledge and ideals, were transformed, assimilated or destroyed as they came into contact with European school models introduced by missionary groups or colonial authorities (UNESCO, 2005: 194).

As different authors have shown (for example, Marín, this volume), the leitmotif of the colonial conquest of the South was to civilize the natives, to evangelize (where possible) and to provide formal education. Schooling and colonial control are thus intimately connected. However, it should be kept in mind that formal schooling has many advantages compared to other forms of learning: it can be universalized, leads to the dissemination of the written culture and to the possible exercise of citizenship, even if the indigenous population was generally excluded from this.

The generalization of primary education in the North and the beginning of school systems in the South

The second period, which took place between 1900 and 1950, saw the generalization of primary schooling throughout Europe and North America. For the first time ever, two or three successive generations of adults had been taught to read. This produced a genuine socio-cultural revolution in the West. Schooling became a key element in social mobility and sped up the process of urbanization and the abandonment of traditional values. During this time formal schooling expanded to some degree in the South, but the attendance rates remained small and the quality remained inferior compared to schools attended by Europeans. Furthermore, the natives who would later challenge European colonial domination were in contact with this colonial schooling. One need only think of leaders like Gandhi or Nyerere.

Figure 16.1 presents regional estimates of primary enrolment rates from 1880 to 1935–40. In South and Central America, about two out of ten school-age children attended school in 1880, whereas three to four out of ten did so by 1940. Increases in enrolment rates during this period were even greater in the Caribbean (from 24 per cent to 59 per cent), especially in British colonies. In Africa, Asia and the Middle East, where colonial rule predominated, the pace of primary school expansion was slow (UNESCO, 2005).

Mass dissemination of secondary education in the North and of basic education in the South

The third period corresponds with the mass dissemination of secondary education in the North from 1950 to 2000. Fuelled by the economic growth following the Second World War, the school systems of Europe and North America made the expansion of secondary schooling the priority during this period.

In the newly independent nations in the South, this period corresponds with the mass dissemination of basic education. Nowhere was this tendency avoided. Demographic pressure clearly led to an increase in the number of students per class and to an ad hoc training of teachers, but it is also clear that basic education became a priority for governments and international organizations.

Figure 16.1 Mean unadjusted primary enrolment rates in developing regions, 1880 to 1935–40

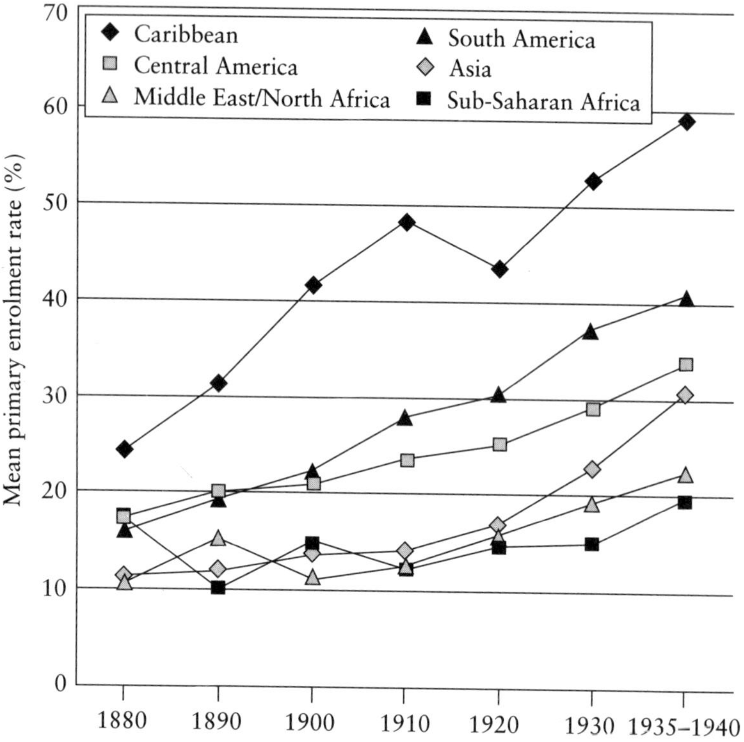

Source: Benavot and Riddle (1988).

Kim (2005) analyzed under what conditions nation-states are likely to construct modern education systems embracing educational ministries and laws over two centuries 1800–2000. He found that more than 80 per cent of contemporary nation-states have founded educational ministries and compulsory education laws over the past two centuries. Kim (2005) suggested going beyond the current explanations for the formation and expansion of national education systems focusing on functional needs of modern schooling for economic development or social progress. First, he argued, that the expanded world culture (for example, a worldwide emphasis on education) enhances the founding rates of educational ministries and laws. Second, he suggested that newly independent countries are more likely to adopt world models of educational systems. Third, he argued that nation-states that have conformed to world culture tend to incorporate world models of educational systems.

Mass dissemination of higher education in the North and of secondary education in the South

Around the year 2000 a new scholastic impulsion began taking place in the North. In many nations, between 50 and 75 per cent of all students continue their schooling beyond the secondary level (see Figures 16.2 and 16.3). The emergence of the information society has pushed many governments to facilitate university access in order to maintain economic competitiveness. In the South, particularly in South-east Asia and Latin America, a genuine mass dissemination of secondary education has been initiated. This is all the more important since a demographic transition has begun in many newly industrialized nations.

Considered across these four periods we can observe that by the beginning of the 21st century the convergence between the education system of the North and that of the South has produced a genuine globalization of schooling. The consequences of this mass schooling have been well analyzed by empirical research. As pointed out by Hannum and Buchmann (2003), substantial research attests to both the health and demographic benefits of improved educational composition. Countries with better-educated citizens tend to have healthier populations, as educated individuals make more informed health choices, live longer, and have healthier children. In addition, the populations of countries with more educated citizens tend to grow more slowly, as educated people are able to lower their fertility. According to UNESCO (2005),

> The single most significant factor influencing the spread of literacy worldwide over the past two centuries has been the expansion of formal schooling. Schools have been, and continue to be, the sites in which most people acquire their core literacy skills...There have been, however, historical exceptions to this pattern. During the seventeenth century, in certain Nordic countries, German principalities and North American colonies, the Protestant Churches supported the compulsory education (not schooling) of children to ensure the piety of families. Out of religious conviction, parents saw to it that their children learned to read and write at home (with or without a tutor) and in church. Here the historical transition to widespread literacy pre-dated the consolidation of state school systems. (p. 194)

Figure 16.2 Primary attainment, year 2000

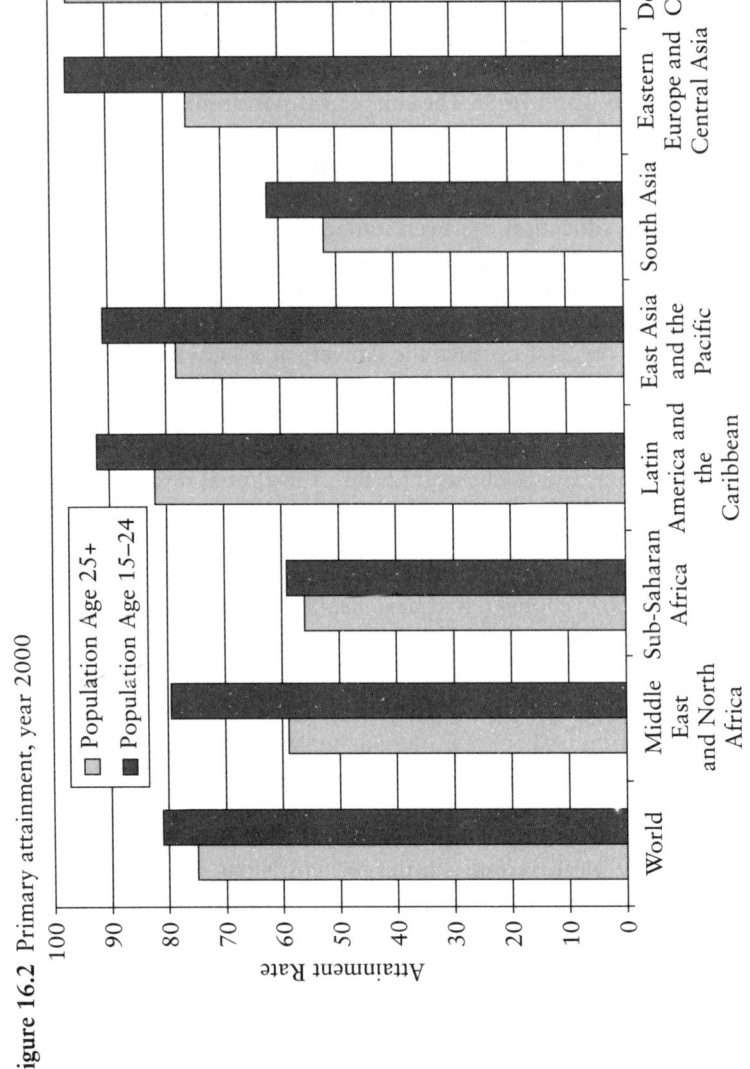

Source: Bloom, E. D. (2006).

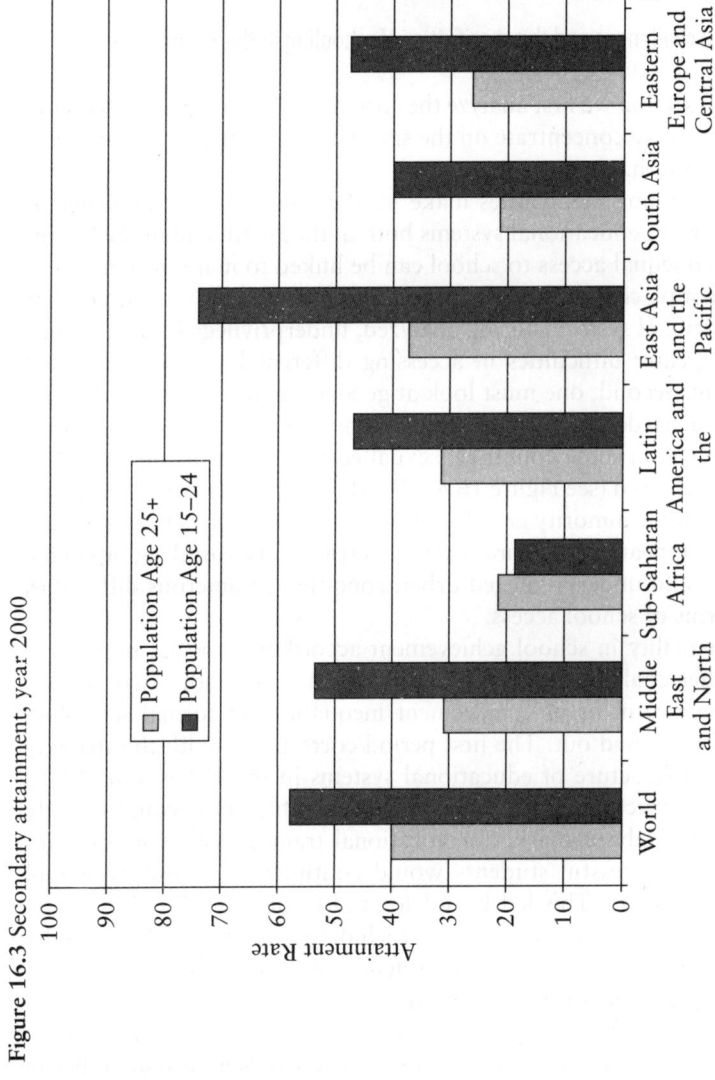

Figure 16.3 Secondary attainment, year 2000

Source: Bloom, E. D. (2006).

This quantitative and qualitative apogee of formal schooling paradoxically corresponds with its being called into question both in the
North and in the South. While we are still far from the deschooling
prophesized by Illich (1976), many voices are calling for a serious
review of the school utopia. The knowledge imparted by the school is
often the target of severe criticism.

Shared challenges and the specificities of schooling in the South

In this section we first analyze the current challenges facing schooling
and then we concentrate on the specificities of the present situation
in the South.

Continuing inequalities make up the most obvious challenge in
the current educational systems both in the North and in the South.
First, unequal access to school can be linked to many situations. In
the first place is the social category of the students. No matter what
educational system is being analyzed, underprivileged social groups
face greater difficulties in accessing different levels of the school
system. Second, one must look at gender inequalities. Overall, girls
have a harder time remaining in school, especially in the South.
However, in some countries, sexual equality in terms of access has
been achieved (see Figure 16.4). Third, being a migrant or belonging
to an ethnic minority greatly handicaps school access. Last, unequal
access appears to be connected with territoriality. Rural regions in the
South and underprivileged urban zones have numerous difficulties
in terms of school access.

Inequality in school achievement according to social position is
another challenge shared by both North and South. Two periods
in the treatment of achievement inequalities in formal schooling
can be pointed out. The first period corresponds with the strongly
divided structure of educational systems in the 1950s and 1960s.
In this structure, students experiencing difficulties would directly
enter the labour market or vocational training following primary
school. Successful students would continue to secondary school
and university. This led Beaudelot and Establet (1975: 9) to state,
'whatever takes place in school, including primary school, can fully
be explained by what occurs outside of school, that is to say by
the capitalistic division of labour'.

In the 1970s and 1980s a second period began as the question of
unequal achievement replaced unequal access. School systems began

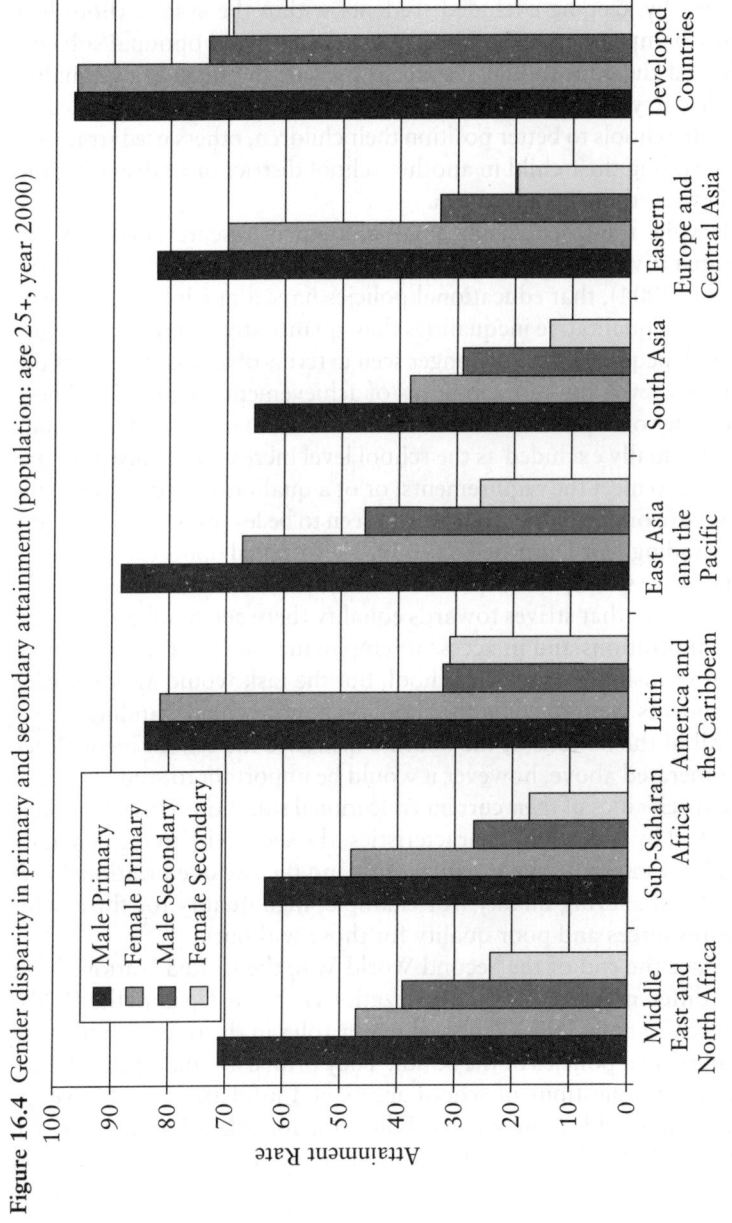

Figure 16.4 Gender disparity in primary and secondary attainment (population: age 25+, year 2000)

Source: Bloom, E. D. (2006).

to decompartmentalize the curriculum and to keep unsuccessful students within the school. Unequal achievement remained, but was hidden by keeping excluded students within the system (Bourdieu and Champagne, 1993). The increase in core and optional subjects allowed the educational system to present the illusion of equality while carrying out a subtle selection. While some parents turned to private schools to better position their children, others used strategies of enrolling their child in another school district or of disputing the policy of ethnic co-education.

Despite the fact that the small amount of research makes a full comparative analysis impossible, it would appear, according to Duru-Bellat (2004), that educational policies have a much harder time at reducing qualitative inequalities than quantitative ones. Worldwide, school inequalities are no longer seen in terms of access, at least at the primary level, but more in terms of achievement inequalities. These are either of a quantitative order: students from modest backgrounds are gradually excluded as the school level increases because they are unable to meet the requirements; or of a qualitative order: these students are oriented towards subjects seen to be less prestigious and less demanding. For Duru-Bellat (2004, 2006), equal opportunities in the school are simply one aspect of social justice. They make sense only in a society that strives towards equality (between families, between social positions and in access to employment). One cannot remove all responsibility from the school, but the task would appear easier if students were to come to school on a more equal standing.

All of the nations of the South experience the school inequalities enumerated above, however it would be important to study in detail the specificities of their current educational situation. This situation is marked by two major characteristics: the sensitivity to the demands made by international organizations and the rise of educational networks of varying quality (for example, high quality for those with the resources and poor quality for those without).

Since the end of the Second World War, the United Nations have put different international organizations in place. Up until the 1980s, UNESCO and UNICEF played major roles in the orientation of the educational policies of the South. They primarily concentrated their efforts on questions of school access and infrastructure. However, since the World Conference on Education for All, in Jomtien in 1990, the World Bank has extended an increasingly greater influence on educational policies in conceptual and financial terms. In the five years after this conference, the number of projects supporting primary education roughly doubled and commitments more than tripled. Primary education commitments rose in all regions, most noticeably in Latin America and the Caribbean, South Asia, and Sub-Saharan Africa (World Bank, 2006).

Bilateral aid by state agencies of cooperation towards basic education has practically tripled between 1998 and 2003, but this still represents less than 2 per cent of all bilateral aid. In this respect we note a strong dependence on international aid by Sub-Sahara African educational systems. Regarding World Bank policy, we remark that certain propositions appear quite adequate, such as the one that would reorient state resources earmarked for higher education towards basic education. Other propositions appear debatable, such as the greater priority given to textbooks rather than to teacher salaries. The encouragement of private education in the South has also contributed to the constitution of educational systems of varying speeds. National and international non-governmental organizations cannot replace the State in the structuring of public formal schooling.

In the North, the internationalization of educational policies has occurred through the increasing role of the Ogranization for Economic Co-operation and Development (OECD) and of the European Union. This can easily be noticed with the implementation of the Programme for International Student Assessment (PISA) survey, and also in the harmonization of European university systems following the Bologna reform. This internationalization and standardization of educational policies is extremely troubling for the South. In the North, even if the attendance rate in private schools is often high in primary and secondary education in countries like Spain, France and the United Kingdom, it cannot be said that the private network holds a monopoly on the reproduction of the elite. This would, however, seem to be the case in many regions of the South. Educating one's child in a public school means that this child will have no possibility of continuing beyond basic education. Even public school teachers place their children in private schools. Public schools generally use the national language as the medium of instruction, while private schools make exclusive use of European languages, primarily English.

Diverse ways of appropriating formal schooling in the South and the necessity of bringing schools up-to-date

The shared challenges analyzed above prompt us to describe some innovations that can be seen as alternatives to traditional schooling. We shall discuss community schools in Africa as well as the educational initiatives of landless farmers in Brazil. Even if these experiments remain marginal in terms of the numbers of children concerned, they provide an important direction for rethinking formal schooling.

In Africa, confronted by the structural weakness of the State action concerning education, local communities in many countries have come up with novel ways of schooling which lie between traditional public schooling and, for profit-based, private schooling. As a colonial legacy, formal schooling had been restricted to the use of the European model. Martin (2003) considers that the use of this model in Sub-Saharan Africa, with its functional and utilitarian mission, confined the school to defined social positions, inside of which the link between education and public administrative employment was easily maintained. The nature of this employment and the exclusive use of the colonial language in the school marked its urban orientation and thus reinforced the split with the rural world and the languages used there.

Martin (2003) uses the term 'spontaneous schools' to indicate all educational structures coming from parental, communal or associative initiatives, clearly differentiating them from other structures coming from private, for-profit initiatives. In Mali, the success of the community school formula makes them an essential element of the national educational system. They have the same six-year structure and the same pedagogical objectives as fundamental public schooling. This was not always the case, since, initially these schools were for three or four years, instruction occurred only in the local language and the objectives were often quite different. A similar growth of spontaneous schools in the educational system can also be seen in other African countries, such as Chad. This growth points to the emancipation of local communities from the State and also shows the limitations encountered when increasing and diversifying the educational field.

These spontaneous schools represent the expression of social strategies of both reproduction and innovation. Coming from different social groups, they also constitute the dynamics of a long course of social history, a reproduction of each of these groups, but not without connection with the changes in the global society and in the economic field; they appear within societal projects (Lange and Martin, 1995).

In Brazil, the Landless Workers' Movement (MST) put into place a community educational network characterized by the complete interweaving between community and school life. An indisputable reference in Brazil and throughout Latin America, the MST is one of the most dynamic social participants of the Third World. Some twenty years after its inception and despite the repression against it (assassinated and imprisoned activists, defamation in the media, persecutions of all kinds), today it represents a real force in Brazilian political life. Since the socio-political struggle for the occupation of land is at the heart of the movement, the school became a place of political socialization of the children. Over 200,000 children, whose parents are members of the MST, receive primary instruction in public schools, run by town councils or by the State, which have been opened in rural communities after obtaining land or even in temporary encampments. The MST advocates the idea of an itinerant school: as soon as an encampment materializes, a school is immediately created. If the people move on, the school follows. As soon as the MST occupies land, the school is often the first tent installed. These schools use a pedagogy nourished by the concepts of Paulo Freire, defender of a liberating popular education.

The influence of globalization on formal schooling

We have seen that historically, educational systems were conceived as an apparatus of the nation-state. The current economic globalization changes everything in that the authority of the nation-state on the economy is weakened and in that international organizations and companies exercise a growing influence of the development of educational systems. We will quickly describe a few of the principle influences of globalization on schooling (see also Marín, this volume).

First of all, globalization necessitates a redefinition of the role of the State in schooling. If international tendencies reflect a reduction in the role of the State in the financing and management of the educational system, they also show an increase in State prerogatives in terms of control, accreditation, and the evaluation of the system.

Second, globalization pushes educational systems to compare themselves both in terms of structure and of student achievement. Witness the euphoria of certain education ministers and the embarrassment of others on the day of the publication of the results of the PISA survey!

Third, globalization leads to a new debate on the content of schooling. The comparison between systems brings about changes in the school curriculum. The gap between the historical monocultural hegemony of the system and the diversity of cultural identities of the students displays an unprecedented, *de facto* multiculturality in the majority of educational systems. How should this be dealt with? The question of the language of instruction is also a key issue in educational policy. Globalization also means that public education is another market to be conquered, especially regarding information and communication technologies.

As Arnove and Torres (1999) show, globalization implies a complex set of processes. And these operate in a contradictory or oppositional fashion. Most people think of it as simply 'pulling away' power or influence from local communities and nations into the global arena. Nations do lose some of the economic power they once had. However, it also has an opposite effect. Globalization not only pulls upwards, it pushes downwards, creating new pressures for local autonomy.

One historical process that comes with globalization is the disengagement of the State in favour of the economy. This means that the most important decisions regarding the economic, social, cultural, and educational future of the planet are no longer taken by (supposedly) democratically elected governments, but are mainly in the hands of multinational corporations and international agencies such as the World Bank, the International Monetary Fund, and the World Trade Organization. The democratic sectors and civil society are being set aside (Hallak, 1998).

Even though nation-states have been weakened by neoliberalism and the ideology of privatization; they continue to impose—as Marín has shown in the previous chapter[2]—policies of assimilation or of exclusion. To take the example of Switzerland, despite its model of federalism, it is only the internal linguistic diversity (the four language regions that make up the country) that is acknowledged, and not at all the diversity brought by migrants. Hence, the study of migration policies reveals many aspects of current social policies, including those on education.

Another main issue is environment. The myth of progress, of development, of continuous economic growth, carried by Western hegemony and globalization, are in direct confrontation with ecology, made prominent by the current debate over global warming. In the Western cosmology, the ecological dimension is absent, which explains the current confrontation between the economy and the conservation of nature. We now have to take ecology into account for all spheres of human thinking and activity (Costa, 2000; Ki-Zerbo, 1992; Marín, 1996). Western cosmology is based on a rational division of time and is hence led by productivity and profit, without taking the spatial dimension—so important to traditional cultures—into account, where nature or the environment are of prime importance.

Schooling has been the vector for imposing this Western conception, favouring the written word over oral transmission, and despising traditional knowledge, which has led to sacrificing an enormous collective cultural patrimony. The official knowledge institutionalized by the dominant school culture constitutes only a small part of the world's knowledge. The wealth of daily knowledge included in traditional education has been excluded by the institutions of the dominant, official culture imposed by Western hegemony (Dasen, this volume).

One problem is that Western culture is now seen as universal. It is from this viewpoint that other ways of living and of seeing the world are considered as inferior and retarded, and hence it is up to the 'others' to catch up with the Western world. In other words, cultural evolutionism is still with us.

If education has been part of the problem, it can also be part of the solution. It is no doubt through education that we can retain some hope of finding answers to the various problems created by globalization. Therefore, education has to be seen and reaffirmed as a basic human right, not only of every child, but of every human being. Unfortunately, despite the rhetoric of international organizations, this is far from being the case today.

BASIC EDUCATION AS A FUNDAMENTAL HUMAN RIGHT

Basic education was recognized as a fundamental human right at a World Conference on Education held in Jomtien, Thailand, in 1990.

Ten years later, the World Education Forum held in Dakar (UNESCO, 2001) took stock, and had to admit that, despite some progress, the Jomtien objectives had not been met. In the year 2000, 113 million children still did not have access to primary education (60 per cent of these being girls) and 875 million adults were still illiterate (65 per cent of women), these figures pointing to a strong gender discrimination (cf. UNESCO, 2003: 25). Furthermore, it was recognized that the push towards education for all brought with it an emphasis on quantity rather than quality. Hence, in its 'Dakar framework for action' (UNESCO, 2001: 1), the Forum included the following statement:

> We re-affirm the vision of the World Declaration on Education for All (Jomtien 1990), supported by the Universal Declaration of Human Rights and the Convention on the Rights of the Child, that all children, young people and adults have the human right to benefit from an education that will meet their basic learning needs in the best and fullest sense of the term, an education that includes learning to know, to do, to live together and to be. It is an education geared to tapping each individual's talents and potential, and developing learners' personalities, so that they can improve their lives and transform their societies.

'Learning to live together' was later taken up as the main theme of the 46th International Conference on Education held at the International Bureau of Education (IBE) in Geneva in 2001. Its final report (UNESCO, 2003: 15–17) starts with an interesting list of the paradoxes brought about by globalization. For example, the fact, that the world has never produced more wealth and more scientific and technological knowledge, has never had a greater facility to exchange idea and to get to know one another, yet at the same time the gap between the rich and the poor, between those who have access to information (for example, through the internet) and those who do not is becoming wider. Also, globalization, which is in principle synonymous with open-mindedness, threatens the world with cultural uniformity, which in turn threatens cultural diversity. The people have therefore the tendency to withdraw into their identity and their nationality, which has as inevitable consequences more intolerance and the rejection of other cultures (UNESCO, 2003: 16, our translation).

In relation to these paradoxes, there is the temptation either to see education as a panacea ('Education, and education alone, could bring about the solution. A better education for all, and the world is saved!'), or to be completely discouraged: 'In this respect, education for all to learn to live together is a hypocritical pretension. How could one, for example, teach 'how to live together' to those who have much more than what they need and to those who have not even enough to survive?' (UNESCO, 2003: 17).[3] The mid-way solution is to re-think education as part of a new social order, one sustaining the values of solidarity, of living together in peace and respect individual and collective rights.

Marín and Dasen (2007: 316–18) have listed a series of conditions and suggestions for developing a new value system through education. In summary, these are the following:

1. Promote the right to an education of high quality, but refuse to set goals determined only by the economy. Education (just like health and other basic public services) should not be governed by the market and by competition. Hence, contrary to recommendations by the Bretton Woods institutions, education should not be privatized, but should remain a public good.
2. This implies that the goals of education are open to democratic debate, and are decided at the political, not the economic level.
3. Promote educational systems that are more egalitarian.
4. Promote education from an intercultural perspective, fostering the understanding of cultural diversity, of various systems of religious beliefs, and the preservation of biodiversity.
5. Promote an education that develops awareness of the socio-economic and cultural changes linked to globalization.
6. Promote an education that gives a global perspective, one which fosters the understanding of the complex relationships between the local, regional, and worldwide levels.
7. Think of education within a larger political debate, fighting neoliberal attacks against public service.
8. Think of an education producing new guidelines and values, those of solidarity, co-operation, complementarity, and the sharing of common projects.
9. Individualism as a paradigm to reach success through competition, profitability, pragmatism, and utilitarian social relationships should no longer be promoted by schooling.
10. Promote an education in which being is more important than having, for active social and political participation within the framework of a participative democracy.

11. Promote an education based on dialogue, on the recognition of diversity as well as a common belonging, on learning to listen to others as the first condition to sharing our knowledge.
12. Education should promote autonomous critical thinking as well as imagination; it should be liberating.

As an example of a similar 'world platform of struggles' emanating from the so-called civil society, Marín and Dasen (2007) quote the World Education Forum (2004), linked to the World Social Forum held in Porto Alegre in 2004, with the motto 'if another world is possible then another education is necessary'.

Education as a basic right for migrants

In the rich countries of the North, where a compulsory and free basic education is fully implemented for all citizens, there is one segment of the population for which this right is not always guaranteed: migrants, and especially 'illegal' migrants. Switzerland, for many years, had a restrictive policy for seasonal migrant workers, who were not allowed to come with their families. Of course, after some years of living nine months at a time, away from their partners and children, many of these workers brought their families along illegally. Very often, the children were not sent to school, sometimes they were even hidden away inside dwellings, without any social contact outside the family, all this leading to quite difficult developmental circumstances and often to psychological problems. In Geneva, in the 1980's, an 'illegal school' was set up, with voluntary and unpaid teachers, accepting these children for a few hours a day. The existence of this school was well known to educational authorities, who even supplied teaching materials. Many parents, however, were suspicious, fearing police intervention. This story was told in a book by Perregaux and Togni (1989), who also argued that the international convention of childrens' rights should have precedence over national laws concerning labour and migration, and they ended up winning their case. Hence, it is only since the early 1990's that schooling has become a basic right in Geneva, and subsequently in most of Switzerland.

The problem remains that the right to schooling is not extended to the right to professional training. In Switzerland, most of the professional training is carried out in a system called 'dual apprenticeship', in which the trainees spend four days a week with a master on the job, and one day in school. Apprenticeship is considered to be part of labour, and not part of education, and labour laws continue to be very restrictive. Hence illegal migrants aged 15 may continue to attend school, which is often rather inadequate to their aspirations, but are unable to enter professional training (Cattafi-Maurer et al., 1998).

We have mentioned this particular case study from our home area just to show that education (which, we think, should include professional training) as a basic human right is not such an obvious achievement, not even in one of the richest countries in the North. And it is part of the political debate, which, in the 'fortress Europe', is not taking the route of hospitality and open-mindedness (Caloz-Tschopp and Dasen, 2007). May be it is time that the North should hear of examples where countries in the South are in fact more generous despite lesser means.

INTERCULTURAL EDUCATION

It is interesting to note that 'learning to live together' is becoming a theme of discussion at the level of international organizations such as UNESCO, and in particular at the IBE international meeting of ministers of education mentioned earlier. For many years, intercultural education, as a topic of educational research, curriculum development and teacher training, has been confined to countries of the North. At the beginning, in the 1960's, it was linked, mainly in the United States, to the fight for civil rights (Akkari, 2000), and in the 1970's and 1980's to the 'problems' of dealing with immigration and classrooms that were becoming multicultural (Allemann-Ghionda, 1995, 2001). The solution was to implement compensatory measures, seeking to assimilate the newcomers as quickly as possible. For example in the German speaking part of Switzerland, this innovation was labelled 'Ausländerpädagogik', that is, pedagogy for strangers. Later, with a sort of pendulum movement away from the initial ethnocentrism, what was advocated was an intercultural education based on cultural relativism and even anti-racism, accepting and respecting cultural differences, with the inherent risk of labelling and freezing cultural identities. The advantage of this movement was that it was destined for the whole classroom: an intercultural education valuing cultural diversity could even be envisaged in a completely homogeneous school. Currently the pendulum seems to be swinging back, with a mid-line position advocating a pedagogical centring on the individual child, and new interests in broader 'citizenship education' or 'education for sustainable development' that often include elements of the previous intercultural education.

Whatever these historical fads in intercultural education may have been and still are, one thing was sure: they were of interest only in the North, a sort of luxury linked to being a rich country attracting a foreign labour force. In educational research and debate regarding the 'majority world', until very recently, cultural diversity in the classroom and school was not really dealt with, except possibly in terms of discussions around the choice of the language of instruction, or the schooling of indigenous minorities (cf. Gajardo et al., Mishra, Teasdale, in this volume). This is quite surprising, as if countries of the South were less multicultural than those of the North, as though the majority of the migrations were not taking place among 'majority world' countries themselves.

There is therefore quite an important scope for developing an appropriate intercultural education throughout the world, taking the achievements but also the mistakes made in the North into account, but searching for implementations that take the local complexities into account. Links to 'citizenship education' and 'sustainable development' are certainly vectors to be taken seriously.

CONCLUSION

This chapter shows the importance of a historic analysis of formal schooling using a North-South perspective. The impact of an ever-expanding globalization is one of the most promising challenges facing research in comparative and international education. Paradoxically, globalization has attracted many researchers to the field of comparative and international education, but at the same time has necessitated a questioning of classical analytical frameworks. Comparative education, the educational research most interested in the situation in the South, can greatly contribute to this questioning process on the condition that it remains sensitive to culture and context (Crossley, 2002).

At the heart of this debate one finds the question of the place of the nation-state in educational policy. Global forces and tendencies change the role and status of the state (World Bank and international organizations). What is interesting is to look at what the South can add to the debate. We are witnessing different effects and mechanisms of the internationalization of educational policies. The South, as shown by the example of spontaneous schools in Africa and community schools of the MST in South America, is restoring the influence of the 'local' level and is reintroducing a political dimension in pedagogy, which had been brushed aside in the North by a technical, apolitical, and instrumental impetus over fifty years ago.

As Charlot (2003) asserts, one must understand that today humanity has the following options:

1. Defend the *status quo,* where everyone organizes things for him or herself, looks after his or her own interests, without worrying much about what is going on elsewhere and where inequalities persist.

2. Accept the neoliberal globalization, which is not really global after all, and in some ways could be seen as the opposite of a true globalization. What currently exists is not a worldwide space but a collection of networks maintaining different flows (of capital, of information, of populations). Places that are unable to find a function in these articulated networks are plundered or abandoned to themselves, the symbol of this abandonment currently being the African continent. Globalization is not going global, but is constructing networks of power and abandoning parts of the world that are found useless. This globalization accentuates inequalities, especially by creating educational networks of varying qualities.

3. Mobilize in order to construct a world of solidarity, a real globalization with a new type of formal schooling where everyone has the same opportunities.

Which of these options will finally prevail? The third one may be utopian, but we remain enthusiastic optimists. In the meantime, we hope this book will have contributed to a small extent in fostering both interest and understanding of cultural diversity in educational theories and practices.

NOTES

1. As we have remarked in the introduction, in French 'South' is the current and politically correct way to speak of 'the Third World' or

of 'developing countries'. The term has a metaphorical meaning as a euphemism for poorer countries, and is sometimes applied also to underprivileged segments of the population in rich countries (the 'North').
2. The last part of the current chapter also draws heavily on a paper (in French) by Marín and Dasen (2007).
3. It is quite refreshing to find such open language and critical thinking in international documents.

REFERENCES

Akkari, 2000. 'L'éducations bilingue desminorites culturelles aux USA: enjeux et perspectives', *Educations et Sociétés plurilingues*, 8: 64–77.

Allemann-Ghionda, C. 1995. 'Managing Cultural and Linguistic Plurality in West-European Education. Obstacles, Patterns, and Innovations'. *European Journal of Intercultural Studies in Education*, 6(2): 41–51.

———. 2001. 'Sociocultural and Linguistic Diversity, Educational Theory, and the Consequences for Teacher Education: A Comparative Perspective', in C. A. Grant and J. Lei (eds), *Global Constructions of Multicultural Education: Theories and Realities*, pp. 1–26. Mahwah, NJ: Lawrence Erlbaum.

Arnove, R. F. and C. A. Torres, (eds). 1999. *Comparative Education. The Dialectic of the Global and the Local*. Lanham: Rowman and Littlefield.

Ariès, P. 1960. *L'enfant et la vie familiale sous l'ancien régime*. Paris: Plon.

———. 1973. *Centuries of Childhood*. Harmondsworth: Penguin.

Beaudelot, C. and R. Establet. 1975. *L'école primaire divise*. Maspéro, Paris.

Benavot, A. and P. Riddle. 1988. 'The Expansion of Primary Education 1870–1940', *Sociology of Education*, 61: 190–210.

Bloom, E. D. 2006. *Measuring Global Educational Progress*. Cambridge, MA: American Academy of Arts and Sciences.

Boli, J., F. Ramirez and J. Meyer. 1985. 'Explaining the Origins and Expansion of Mass Education', *Comparative Education Review*, 29(2): 145–70.

Bourdieu, P. and P. Champagne. 1993. 'Les exclus de l'intérieur', in P. Bourdieu (ed.), *La misère du monde*, pp. 597–603. Paris: Éditions du Seuil. English translation published as: Bourdieu, P. 1999. *The Weight of the World Social Suffering in Contemporary Society*. Oxford: Polity.

Caloz-Tschopp, M. C. and P. R. Dasen (eds). 2007. *Globalization, Migration and Human Rights (vol. 1): A New Paradigm for Research and Citizenship*. Brussels: Bruylant.

Cattafi-Maurer, F., G. Abriel, P. R. Dasen, C. Lack and C. Perregaux. 1998. *Vivre en précarité: L'accès à une formation professionnelle de jeunes migrants portugais à statut précaire.* Genève: Centre de Contact Suisses-Immigrés CCSI et FPSE, Université de Genève.

Charlot, B. 2003. 'Education et globalisation-éducation et *mondialisation'*, in J. Beillerot and C. Wulf (eds), *L'éducation en France et en Allemagne,* pp. 335–44. Paris: Harmattan.

Costa, J.-P. 2000. *L'homme-nature ou l'alliance avec l'univers. Entre indianité et modernité.* Paris: Editions Sang de la terre.

Crossley, M. 2002. 'Comparative and International Education: Contemporary Challenges, Reconceptualization and New Directions for the Field', *Current Issues in Comparative Education,* 4(2): 81–86.

Duru-Bellat, M. 2004. *Social Inequality at School and Educational Policies.* Paris: UNESCO.

———. 2006. *L'inflation scolaire. Les désillusions de la méritocratie.* Paris: Seuil.

Hannum, E. and C. Buchmann. 2003. *The Consequences of Global Educational Expansion.* Cambridge, MA: American Academy of Arts and Sciences.

Illich, I. 1976. *Deschooling Society.* Harmondsworth: Penguin.

Ki-Zerbo, J. (ed). 1992. *Compagnons du soleil.* Paris: Fondation pour le Progrès de l'Homme-La Découverte-UNESCO.

Kim, J. 2005. 'The Normative Construction of Modern Education Systems: Analysis of Foundings of Educational Ministries and Laws, 1800–2000', paper presented at the annual meeting of the American Sociological Association, Philadelphia, PA, August 12. Available online at http://www. allacademic.com/meta/p21343_index.html (downloaded on 05 October 2006).

Lange, M.-F. and J.-Y.Martin (eds). 1995. 'Les stratégies éducatives en Afrique subsaharienne', *Cahiers des sciences humaines,* 31(3): 563–737.

Marín, J. 1996. 'Le développement durable et la dimension interculturelle', in A. Giordan (ed.), *12 questions sur l'environnement,* pp. 127–30. Nice: Z'éditions.

Marín, J. and P. R. Dasen. 2007. 'L'éducation face à la mondialisation, aux migrations et aux droits de l'homme', in M. C. Caloz-Tschopp and P. R. Dasen (eds), *Mondialisation, migration et droits de l'homme, Volume 1: Un nouveau paradigme pour la recherche et la citoyenneté,* pp. 285–320. Brussels: Bruylant.

Martin, J.Y. 2003. 'Les écoles spontanées en Afrique subsaharienne. Champ éducatif et contre-champ scolaire', *Cahiers d'études africaines,* XLIII (1–2): 19–39, 169–70.

Perregaux, C. and F. Togni. 1989. *Enfants cherchent école.* Genève: Zoé.

Reagan, T. 2000. *Non-Western Educational Traditions: Alternatives Approaches to Educational Thought and Practice,* 2nd edition. Mahwah, NJ: Erlbaum.

Ruano-Borbalan, J-C. 2002. L'école, ça sert d'abord à faire la société. *Sciences humaines,* 36: 46–49.

UNESCO. 2001. 'World Education Forum: Dakar Framework for Action', Available online at http://www.unesco.org/education/efa/ed_for_all/dakfram_eng.shtml (downloaded on 20 May 2008).

———. 2003. 'Apprendre à vivre ensemble: avons nous échoué ?', 46ème Conférence Internationale de l'éducation de l'UNESCO, Genève, 5–8 Septembre 2001. Genève: UNESCO/BIE.

———. 2005. *Education for all 2006. Literacy for life.* Paris: UNESCO.

Vincent, G. (ed.) 1994. *L'Éducation prisonnière de la forme scolaire ? Scolarisation et socialisation dans les sociétés industrielles.* Lyon: Presses universitaires de Lyon.

World Bank. 2006. *From Schooling Access to Learning Outcomes: An Unfinished Agenda. An Evaluation of World Bank Support to Primary Education.* Washington, DC: The World Bank.

World Education Forum. 2004. *Third WEF Charter: Constructing a World Platform of Struggles.* Porto Alegre. Available online at http://www.portoalegre.rs.gov.br/fme/default.asp?mst=5 (downloaded on 20 May 2008).

ABOUT THE EDITORS AND CONTRIBUTORS

EDITORS

Abdeljalil Akkari is Professor of International Dimensions of Education at the Faculty of Psychology and Education of the University of Geneva and formerly Dean for research at the Higher Pedagogical Institute HEP-BEJUNE (Bienne, Switzerland). He received his PhD at the University of Geneva in 1992. He worked as professor of education at the universities of Geneva, Fribourg, and Baltimore. His major publications include studies on educational planning, multicultural education, teacher training, and educational inequalities. His main research interests focus now on teacher education and the reforms of educational systems in a comparative perspective. He is also consultant for the International Bureau of Education (UNESCO) and other international organizations. He is an expert on different educational projects in various countries: Switzerland, USA, Brazil, Tunisia, Algeria, Irak, and Madagascar. He is fluent in Arabic, French, English, Spanish, and Portuguese. His e-mail addresses are abdeljalil.akkari@unige.ch and djalil98@yahoo.com.

Pierre R. Dasen is Professor Emeritus of Anthropology of Education and Cross-cultural Psychology at the Faculty of Psychology and Education of the University of Geneva.

He studied developmental psychology in Geneva, was an assistant to J. Piaget, and received a PhD from the Australian National University. He studied the cognitive development of Aboriginal children in Australia, Inuit in Canada, Baoulé in Côte d'Ivoire, and Kikuyu in Kenya; he has also contributed to research in cognitive anthropology among the Yupno of Papua-New-Guinea, and in Bali. His research topics have included visual perception, the development of sensori-motor intelligence, the causes and effects of malnutrition, the development of concrete operations as a function of eco-cultural variables and daily activities, definitions of intelligence, number systems, and spatial orientation. He has also been concerned with intercultural education, and in particular with the access of illegal migrant adolescents to professional training. His main interests are in everyday cognition, informal education, and parental ethnotheories, and his current research in India, Nepal, and Indonesia is on spatial language and cognitive development.

Pierre Dasen is the co-author and co-editor of several volumes and textbooks on cross-cultural psychology and intercultural education. His e-mail address is pierre.dasen@unige.ch.

CONTRIBUTORS

Eunice W. Adzemye holds a Bachelor of Science degree in Agriculture from the Bamenda University of Science and Technology. Her research interest is in the socio-economic impact of peri-urban agriculture on poor families with special focus on children and youth. She is a Research Assistant on the Cameroon sample of a longitudinal cross-cultural research project on mother-infant interaction in collaboration with Dr Marc Bornstein at the US National Institute of Child Health and Human Development (NICHD). She is on the Board of Directors of the Human Development Resource Centre, Bamenda.

Marie Battiste is a Mi'kmaw Professor in the College of Education and Director of the Aboriginal Education Research Centre (AERC) at the University of Saskatchewan, and Co-Director of the Canadian Council on Learning's Aboriginal Learning Knowledge Centre. Her historical research of Mi'kmaw literacy and education as a graduate student at Harvard University and later at Stanford University where she received her doctorate degree in curriculum and teacher education provided the foundation for her later writings in cognitive imperialism, linguistic, and cultural integrity, and decolonization of Aboriginal education. She has co-authored *Protecting Indigenous Knowledge and Heritage: A Global Challenge* with J. Youngblood Henderson (Saskatoon: Purich Press, 2000) which received a Saskatchewan Book Award in 2000; edited *Reclaiming Indigenous Voice and Vision* (Vancouver: UBC Press, 2000); co-edited as guest editor the *Australian Journal of Indigenous Education* (May 2005), and was senior editor with Jean Barman for *First Nations Education in Canada: The Circle Unfolds* (1995, UBC Press, Vancouver). She has published widely, has an international presence, and is an active researcher and contributor to many indigenous community projects. She received the Distinguished Researcher Award from the University of Saskatchewan in 2004, and the Saskatchewan Commemorative Medal for the Centennial of Saskatchewan 2006 for significant work with the people of Saskatchewan, and Eagle feathers from Mi'kmaw Grand Council, Eskasoni First Nations community, and Stanford University Native American community. Her e-mail address is marie.battiste@usask.ca.

Marie Anne Broyon is a professor at the Teacher Training College of Valais, in Switzerland, and has been a research and teaching assistant in educational planning at the Department of Education, University of Geneva. Her PhD research is on 'Metacognition and the Development of Spatial Orientation' in Benares (India), as part of a larger project coordinated by Prof. P. Dasen, University of Geneva, and Prof. R.C. Mishra (Banaras Hindu University) on spatial language and cognition. Her current research interests are cultural differences in metacognition and reflexivity, traditional schooling, integration of migrant children into school education, intercultural pedagogy, language policy in multilingual Switzerland, and educational policies. Her e-mail address is marie-anne.broyon@hepvs.ch.

Giovanna Carrarini is an Italian anthropologist, working on a doctorate in educational sciences at the University of Geneva. The theme of her thesis is adult literacy and the construction of civil society in Bolivia from a historical perspective. She currently works for the Training Program in Intercultural and Bilingual Education for the Andean Countries at the Universidad Mayor de San Simón in Cochabamba, Bolivia. Her primary scientific interests involve the following aspects: ethnography of speaking; interculturality and bilingualism in education; oral tradition and written processes within the Andean context; promotion of cultural diversity within language and power; right to education for indigenous peoples; public policy and non-governmental actions in education (North–South, South–South). Her e-mail address is giovannacarrarini@hotmail.com.

Nilima Changkakoti studied psychology at the University of Geneva, where she also received her PhD in educational sciences. She has worked on literacy acquisition in adults and children, vocational training, and intercultural teacher training. Her current research interests are the blending of traditional andmodern schooling, migration narratives, the relationship between school and immigrant families, community interpreting, ethnopsychiatry, and trauma and migration. Her e-mail address is nilima.changkakoti@sunrise.ch.

Pascaline J. Fai holds a post-graduate Teacher Training Diploma from Yaounde University's Advanced School of Education in the English language. Her research interest is, in general, the learning of English as a second language and, in particular, the impact of ethnic languages on English language acquisition. She has received many capacity building trainings in English language teaching and life skills education and prevention of HIV/AIDS amongst adolescents. Pascaline has been an examiner for the English Language Ordinary Level of the Cameroon General Certificate of Education since 1997 and received an award as the best Form Five English Language Teacher in 2001. She is a trainer in the in-school component of the Adolescent Development and Participation Program in Cameroon and a member of the Board of Directors of the Human Development Resource Centre (HDRC), Bamenda. Her e-mail address is jivirka@yahoo.com.

Fedelis W. Forsuh is affiliated with the Human Development Resource Centre, Bamenda. He obtained his Master of Education from the Bamenda University of Science and Technology in Guidance and Counselling. His research interests are on mathematics edu-cation and understanding the challenges inherent in running a community-based counselling centre. He serves as the secretary of the Board of Directors of the Human Development Resource Centre, Bamenda.

Anahy Gajardo was born in Chile. She has studied anthropology at the University of Neuchâtel, Switzerland, and educational sciences at the University of Geneva. She is preparing a doctorate in social anthropology at the University of Fribourg on the ethnic revival of an indigenous population in Chile. She is a research and teaching assistant in the Department of Education at the University of Geneva. She has published a book on the role of ethnographic museums in the teaching of cultural diversity (*Entre école et musée: les visites scolaires. Apprendre la diversité culturelle au musée?* Université de Genève: Cahiers des sciences de l'éducation no. 108, 2005). Her e-mail address is anahy.gajardo@unige.ch.

John D. Herzog is Professor Emeritus in the Department of Education at Northeastern University in Boston, and is currently an independent researcher studying 'compagnonnage' apprenticeship in France and has delivered more than a dozen conference papers on that subject. He received his PhD in anthropology and education from Harvard University. He has had teaching and administrative assignments at Harvard, University College Nairobi, and Northeastern University. He has done fieldwork in Barbados, Kenya, the Boston area, and France. He was the president of the Council on Anthropology and Education of the American Anthropological Association, and has published in the *Harvard Educational Review* (1962), *Ethos* (1973) and *Human Organization* (1974). His e-mail address is jherzog@lynx. neu.edu.

Adjignon Débora Gladys Hounkpe has an Arts degree of the National University of Bénin and has taught French at a Catholic College and the Higher Management Institute in Cotonou. She then studied human rights in a Summer school in Geneva, and received two higher degrees from the University of Geneva, one in social sciences (gender studies) and one in educational sciences. She is interested in human rights and gender issues, particularly the right of education for all. Her current commitment is to provide literacy training for women in Bénin, particularly in poor suburbs of Cotonou. Her e-mail address is hdebbiefr@yahoo.fr.

Glory N. Lum obtained a diploma in Community Development from the National School of Community Development, Kumba (Cameroon). She is interested in community participatory learning processes. Glory is a trainer in life skills education at the Human Development Resource Centre, Bamenda, and a resource person for Cameroon's out-of-school component of the Adolescent Development and Participation Program. She serves on the Board of Directors of the Human Development Resource Centre, Bamenda.

José Marín is an anthropologist who was born and educated in Perou. He holds a PhD in anthropology from the University of Sorbonne-Nouvelle in Paris, and diplomas from the Higher Institute of Latin American Studies in Paris, and the University Institute of Development Studies and the International Environment Academy in Geneva. He has been teaching at the University of Geneva, in several higher education institutions in Fribourg, Lausanne, and Geneva (Switzerland), and throughout South America, particularly Brazil.

His main interests are in the large scale social and historical trends leading from the colonization of South America to the current imperialist globalization, and its impact on human rights and cultural diversity. He is particularly interested in indigenous populations in the Amazon basin, their cosmologies and knowledge about nature and medicine, and in the links between biological and cultural diversity. His e-mail address is p_marin@bluewin.ch.

Peri Mesquida is a professor and researcher at the Catholic University of Paraná, in Brazil. He has received his PhD in education from the University of Geneva, and has been an invited professor at the University of Fribourg, Switzerland. He is interested in the history of education in South America, particularly Brazil, and has published books on the North-American hegemony and protestant education in Brazil (*Hegemonia Norte Americana e educação protestante no Brasil*. Juiz de Fora e São Paulo: EDITEO/EDUFJF, 1994), and on Piaget and Vygotski (*Piaget e Vygotski: uma diálogo inacabado*. Curitiba, Pr: Editora Cmahpagnat, 2001). His e-mail address is mesquida.peri@pucpr.br.

Ramesh C. Mishra is Professor of Psychology at Banaras Hindu University. He obtained his doctorate from Allahabad University under the supervision of Prof. D. Sinha and has spent two years of post-doctoral studies with Prof. J. Berry at Queen's University, Kingston, Canada. He has been an invited professor at the same university, and at the University of Geneva. He is interested in all aspects of cultural influence on human behaviour, and has contributed to numerous papers and books in India and internationally on such topics as cross-cultural research on cognition, acculturation, and education. In particular, he has contributed review chapters on cognition in the *Handbook of Cross-cultural Psychology* and the *Handbook of Culture and Psychology*. He is the author (together with J.W. Berry and D. Sinha) of *Ecology, Acculturation and Psychological Adaptation: A Study of Adivasis in Bihar*, and co-editor (with J.W. Berry and R.C. Tripathi) of *Psychology in Human and Social Development: Lessons from Diverse Cultures*. His e-mail address is rcmishra_2000@yahoo.com.

Gladys N. Ngoran holds a Master of Education of the Bamenda University of Science and Technology (BUST). She is a school counsellor and a resource person and consultant for many community-based human service organizations. Her research interest is on couple relationships. She is author of *Guidance for a Successful Student Life* (2006). Gladys is the Chairperson of the Board of Directors of the Human Development Resource Centre, Bamenda.

Mairama Y. Ngeh earned the post-graduate Teacher Training Diploma from Yaounde University's Advanced School of Education in the English language. She is an English language teacher and interested in study habits and time use amongst adolescent students. She has undertaken several capacity building trainings in English language teaching and life skills education and prevention of HIV/AIDS with adolescents. Mairama is an examiner for the English Language Ordinary Level of the Cameroon General Certificate of Education. She is a resource person in the out-of-school component of the Adolescent Development and Participation Program at the Human Development Resource Centre, Bamenda, and a member of its Board of Directors.

A. Bame Nsamenang is Associate Professor of Psychology and Learning Sciences at Yaoundé University's School of Education, Cameroon, and Director of the Human Development Resource Centre in Bamenda. Prior to his current duties he held a research position as Senior Research Fellow at the defunct Cameroon's Institute of Human Sciences. He was Fellow of the Center for Advanced Study in the Behavioral Sciences (2002–2003) and the National Institutes of Health (1987–1990) as well as Nehru Chair Visiting Professor at Baroda University, India (2001).

His main research interests are on human development across the lifespan, particularly concerning early childhood care and education and adolescent/youth development in context. He is committed to the project of evolving an Africentric psychology. Despite his very low resource base, he has a lifetime commitment to developing and networking to evolve an appropriate and sensitive science of human psychology for Africa.

His publication list entails five influential books in developmental psychology and education including *Human Development in Cultural Context: A Third World Perspective* (1992). Sage Publications, Newbury Park, CA, and *Cultures of Human Development and Education: Challenge to Growing Up African* (2004). Nova Science Publishers, New York. His e-mail address is bame51@yahoo.com.

Robert Serpell is Professor of Psychology at the University of Zambia. Born and raised in England, he received his BA from Oxford (1965) and PhD from Sussex (1969). In 1978, he became a citizen of the Republic of Zambia, where he has lived and worked for most of his life at the University of Zambia, holding positions in the Human Development Research Unit, the Psychology Department, the Institute for African Studies and, most recently, as Vice-Chancellor (2003–06). Between 1989 and 2002 he was Professor and Director of Graduate Studies in Applied Developmental Psychology at the University of Maryland, Baltimore County, USA. Dr Serpell's publications have centred around the influence of socio-cultural factors on children's cognitive development, and include three books: *Culture's Influence on Behaviour* (1976), *The Significance of Schooling: Life-journeys in an African Society* (1993), and *Becoming Literate in the City: The Baltimore Early Childhood Project* (2005). In addition to basic research on children's perception, intelligence, language, literacy and socialization, he has conducted applied projects on assessment, curriculum, instruction, and program development with special attention to developmental disabilities and mental retardation in Africa. His e-mail address is serpell@umbc.edu.

George Robert Teasdale taught in the School of Education at Flinders University in Adelaide, South Australia, for 34 years. From 1997 to the end of 2003 he was Director of the Flinders University Institute of International Education. From 2004 to 2007 he was the Director of the Pacific Regional Initiatives for the Design of Basic Education (PRIDE) Project, a major EU-funded activity supporting curriculum reform in the 14 independent nations of Oceania, at the Institute of Education at the University of the South Pacific in Suva, Fiji. He is now Adjunct Professor in the David Unaipon College of Indigenous Education and Research at the University of South Australia in Adelaide.

Bob's teaching and research interests are in the fields of international, cross-cultural, and indigenous education, with a particular focus on the Australia-Pacific region. He also has worked extensively with UNESCO in the Asia-Pacific region during the past 15 years in the fields of education for cultural development and education for peace and international understanding. His e-mail address is bob.teasdale@unisa.edu.au.

Aparna Vajpayee holds an MA in Psychology from Banaras Hindu University and a PhD from Chaudhary Charan Singh University in Meerut, India. She has been a senior project fellow in an international research project directed by Prof. R.C. Mishra, Banaras Hindu University, and Prof. P.R. Dasen (University of Geneva) and a lecturer at Amity University, New Delhi.

She is interested in the psychological development of children from disadvantaged segments of the population in India, and in cognitive intervention. She has also worked on the physical and mental health of tribal women, and is interested in community development and the application of psychology to human and social development. Her e-mail address is aparnavaj@rediffmail.com.

INDEX

Aboriginal child-rearing, Australia, 41
acculturation, 35, 36, 42, 152, 292
Al-Azhar madrasa, Egypt, 228
AOCDTF *(Association ouvrière des Compagnons du Devoir du Tour de France)*, 118
apprenticeship, 18, 27–29, 34, 59, 101, 107, 112–115, 387
Association for the Development of Education in Africa (ADEA), 236
A-Zeitouna madrasa, Tunisia, 228

Benin, traditional education in. *See also* voodoo convents
Buddhism. *See also* Buddhist education, in India
  Buddha, Gautama, 286, 289, 293
    teaching methods, 293–294
    wheel of Dharma, 287
  Buddhist Theosophical Society, 301
  Dalai Lama, 293, 298, 300, 301
  education system, in Buddhist countries, 288, 293
  Geluk school, 296, 297
  Mahayana tradition, 289
  monastic education, 290, 295, 297, 302
  Naropa institute, 294, 300
  notions in Buddhism, 287
  Pali, 292
  Sangha, 287, 288, 292, 301
  spread, in West, 287
  teacher–student relationship, 287, 289, 295
  teaching methods, 293–294
  Theravada tradition, 289
  Tibetan debate, 296–297
  traditional curriculum, 293–294
Buddhist education, in India

  blending with modern schooling, arguments for, 293–297
  development of, 289–291
  Nalanda University, 291, 294
  schooling of, Buddhists in exile, 297–300
  vs. Sanskrit education, 291–292

Canada, Aboriginal education in, 169–170, 191–192
  Aboriginal Teacher Education Programs (ATEPs), 181–182
  attitude towards Aboriginal teachers, 179–180
  Council of Ministers of Education in Canada (CMEC) report, 174–175
  displacing colonial legacy, in institutions, 177–182
  educational equity programme, 180–181
  education of future teachers, need for, 177–178
  Eurocentric diffusionism and, 183–187
  First Nations children education, 170–172
  INAC education programme, report of, 170
  Indian Control of Indian Education policy, 176
  indigenous renaissance, construction of, 187–192
  need to reform, 176–177
  other educational crisis, 172
  postcolonial education, generation of, 182–187
  role of provinces, 171
  Royal Commission on Aboriginal Peoples (RCAP) report, 172–174, 190–192